HONOR AND FIDELITY

The 65th Infantry in Korea, 1950–1953

by
Gilberto N. Villahermosa

Center of Military History
United States Army
Washington, D.C., 2009

Published by Books Express Publishing
Copyright © Books Express, 2011
ISBN 978-1-780390-51-2

Books Express publications are available from all good retail and online booksellers. For publishing proposals and direct ordering please contact us at: info@books-express.com

Contents

	Page
Foreword	ix
The Author	xi
Preface	xiii

Chapter

1. Prologue: Before Korea	1
The 65th in the Period of the Two World Wars	5
Postwar Doldrums and then Renewal	10
2. From San Juan to Pusan	15
The 65th Infantry Organizes for Korea	18
The 65th Departs for Asia	24
The Borinqueneers Arrive in Korea	29
The Regiment Enters Combat	32
3. With X Corps in North Korea: November–December 1950	41
Advance into Northeastern Korea	46
X Corps in Crisis	59
Evacuation from Hungnam to Pusan	68
4. From Pusan to the Imjin: January–March 1951	77
Operations WOLFHOUND and THUNDERBOLT	80
Preparing to Liberate Seoul	91
On to Seoul and the Imjin	98
5. From the Imjin Back to Seoul: April 1951	111
The Chinese Spring Offensive of 1951	122
The Plight of the Glosters	127
Eighth Army Regroups	134

Chapter	Page
6. From Seoul to the Ch'orwon Valley: May–July 1951	139
Battle Below the Soyang	140
Toward the Iron Triangle	145
Fighting for the Sobang Mountains	153
7. Operations in the Iron Triangle: August–December 1951	163
Operation CLEANUP I and II	166
Into the Iron Triangle Once Again	173
Defending Line Jamestown	179
8. In Reserve: January–June 1952	187
Major Changes Within the 65th Infantry	191
Korea 1952: The Outpost War	199
Personnel Problems in Eighth Army	205
9. Defeat at Outpost Kelly: July–September 1952	209
The Struggle for Outpost Kelly	215
Counterattack and Defeat	222
Analyzing the Failure	231
10. Collapse at Jackson Heights: October 1952	237
Defense and Loss of Jackson Heights	245
Breakdown on Jackson Heights	252
Assessing the Failure	261
11. Courts-Martial, Reconstitution, and Redemption: November 1952–July 1953	265
A Time of Uncertainty	275
Rebuilding the Regiment	281
Vindication and Homecoming	286
Conclusion	295
Bibliographical Note	303
Abbreviations	307
Map Symbols	309
Index	311

	Page
Index of Units	323

Table

3d Infantry Division Regimental Turnover, January–June 1952	205

Maps

No.

1. The Pusan Perimeter: 15–27 September 1950	33
2. X Corps Reenters Battle: 20 October–5 November 1950	44
3. The X Corps Zone: 26 November 1950	58
4. Withdrawal from the Reservoir: 6–11 December 1950	65
5. Withdrawal from Seoul, I and IX Corps: 4–7 January 1951	79
6. Operation R<small>IPPER</small>, Western Front: 6–31 March 1951	101
7. The R<small>UGGED</small> and D<small>AUNTLESS</small> Operations, Western Front: 1–22 April 1951	113
8. The British 29th Brigade Sector: 25 April 1951	129
9. Battle Below the Soyang, 16–20 May 1951	142
10. The Iron Triangle: 1–4 July 1951	157
11. Outpost Kelly: 18–21 September 1952	220
12. Jackson Heights: 25–28 October 1952	249
13. Eighth Army Front, The West Sector: 31 March 1953	282

Illustrations

Column of American artillery in Puerto Rico	2
Maj. Gen. John R. Brooke	3
Maj. Lorenzo P. Davison	3
Soldiers of the 65th Infantry during maneuvers	7
The 65th Infantry marching onto the parade ground	9
Lt. Col. Herman W. Dammer	12
Lt. Gen. Walton H. Walker	17
Boarding the USNS *Marine Lynx* in San Juan	25
Shipboard class en route to Japan	26
Trucks carrying the 65th Infantry to the front	34
Staff of the 2d Battalion near Kumch'on	35
Col. William W. Harris, regimental commander	37
Checking the identification of Korean civilians	37
Colonel Harris with Maj. Gen. William F. Kean	39

	Page
Maj. Gen. Edward M. Almond	42
Harris with Maj. Gen. William H. Turner	50
Self-propelled 105-mm. howitzer	52
Patrol bringing in captured enemy troops near Yonghung	54
General Almond and Maj. Gen. Robert H. Soule	63
Advancing patrol from the 3d Infantry Division	63
General Almond and Brig. Gen. Armistead D. Mead	68
Equipment and vehicles being evacuated from Wonsan	71
Laying a demolition charge on a bridge near Oro-ri	71
Colonel Harris at his regimental command post	73
Generals Soule and Mead during the Wonsan evacuation	74
Lt. Gen. Matthew B. Ridgway	81
M4A3E8 medium tanks of the 65th Heavy Tank Company	83
Exploring a recaptured village during Operation EXPLOITATION	85
Light machine-gun team engaging Communist troops	88
The 15th Infantry battling Chinese troops	94
General Mead with Colonel Harris	100
Paratroopers preparing to board C–119 cargo planes	105
Lt. Cols. Edward G. Allen and Dionisio S. Ojeda	106
Infantrymen on a steep hillside trail near Uijongbu	107
Filipino troops moving to relieve elements of the 3d Battalion	109
M4A3E8 tank engaging Communist troops	114
Engineers constructing a bridge across the Hantan	115
Lt. Gen. James A. Van Fleet	116
Brig. Thomas Brodie	123
British troops before pulling back from unrelenting attacks	126
Positions of the Gloster Battalion south of the Imjin River	126
Lt. Col. Joseph P. Carne	130
M24 Chaffee tank knocked out by Chinese mortar fire	131
Members of the Gloucestershire Regiment taken prisoner	134
Elements of the 65th Infantry moving south near Uijongbu	136
Soldiers of the 3d Reconnaissance Company	140
American troops moving forward under enemy fire	144
Puerto Rican infantrymen seeking cover	147
Engineers probing for hidden mines	149
Soldiers using a captured enemy footbridge	151
Riflemen moving out to attack Hill 717	159
The effects of flash floods due to heavy torrential rains	165
Western half of Hill 487 secured by American troops	172
Col. Julian B. Lindsey	183
Col. Juan C. Cordero-Davila	190

	Page
Lt. Col. William T. Gleason	192
Lt. Cols. Charles H. Kederich and Thomas J. Gendron	197
Maj. Albert C. Davies	198
Maj. Gen. Robert L. Dulaney	198
Soldiers constructing bunkers	201
Soldiers listening to the regimental orchestra	203
Generals J. Lawton Collins and Mark W. Clark with Colonel Cordero-Davila	207
Chaplain 1st Lt. Harvey F. Kochner blessing a flag	213
Standing guard near the 65th Infantry command post	214
Aerial view of the Bubble, Little Nori, and Big Nori	217
Carrying a wounded comrade back to friendly lines	224
Firing a howitzer during the counterattack to regain Outpost Kelly	226
Lt. Col. Lloyd E. Wills	227
Exhausted men of the 65th at rest during the battle for Kelly	230
Aerial view of Jackson Heights	243
Capt. Willis D. Cronkhite Jr.	247
A 60-mm. mortar firing position near Outpost Harry	277
Sleeping bunker used by UN soldiers	285
Western portion of Outpost Harry	287
Soldier equipped for raiding and patrolling operations, early 1953	289

Illustrations courtesy of the following: cover, 2, 3, 7, 9, 12, 17, 25, 26, 34, 35, 37, 39, 42, 50, 52, 54, 63, 68, 71, 73, 74, 81, 83, 85, 88, 94, 100, 106, 107, 109, 114, 116, 123, 126 (*top*), 136, 140, 144, 147, 149, 151, 159, 165, 183, 190, 192, 197, 198, 201, 203, 207, 213, 214, 224, 226, 230, U.S. Army Signal Corps; 105, U.S. Air Force; 115, 172, 217, 243, 277, 285, 287, 289, U.S. Army; 126 (*bottom*), 130, 131, 134, Soldiers of the Gloucestershire Museum; 227, Wills Family via Cynthia Holdren; 247, Willis D. Cronkhite III.

Foreword

Originally formed at the turn of the nineteenth century to protect America's strategic interests in the Caribbean, the 65th Infantry was composed of locally recruited Puerto Rican soldiers led primarily by non-Hispanic "continental" officers. Although in existence for almost fifty years, the 65th had not experienced intense combat until it was committed to the Korean peninsula in the initial months of the war. There, despite its lack of previous wartime service, the regiment did extremely well from September 1950 to August 1951, establishing a solid reputation as a dependable infantry unit and a mainstay of the heavily embattled 3d Infantry Division. After that period, however, its performance began to suffer as experienced cadre rotated out of the regiment and were replaced by new leaders and soldiers who lacked the skills and special cohesive bonds displayed by their predecessors. The net result was a highly publicized series of incidents and disciplinary actions that have never been adequately explained or understood.

This study reviews the performance of the 65th Infantry throughout the war, providing insights not only into the regiment's unique problems but also into the status of the U.S. Army's combat forces during one of the most trying periods in its history. Its findings underscore the critical impact of personnel-rotation policies, ethnic and organizational prejudices, and the work of small-unit leaders on combat readiness and battlefield success. They also illustrate the critical role of senior leaders in analyzing problems in these areas in a timely fashion and instituting effective reforms. For the 65th, a catastrophic shortage of trained NCOs, unaddressed language problems, and inept command leadership temporarily undermined its combat effectiveness. Making matters worse, senior commanders reacted in a heavy-handed manner with little analysis of what was really going on. In the end, it was the martial traditions of the 65th's Hispanic soldiers and a host of new leaders willing to address its special problems that pulled the unit through.

The regiment's colors remained in Korea until November 1954, when the unit returned to Puerto Rico. Today, the 1st Battalion of the 65th Infantry remains as part of the Puerto Rican National Guard, a testimony to a unique combat unit that served the United States Army well for over one hundred years. Yet, what has sometimes been called the Forgotten War is still rich in lessons that the Army of today can ill afford to forget if it is to succeed on the battlefields of tomorrow.

Washington, D.C.
2 June 2009

JEFFREY J. CLARKE
Chief of Military History

THE AUTHOR

Col. Gilberto N. Villahermosa is a 1980 graduate of West Point, where he received a Bachelor of Science in Engineering. Commissioned an Armor officer, he has served with troops in Germany and the United States, including several tours with the XVIII Airborne Corps and the 82d Airborne Division at Fort Bragg, North Carolina. His staff experience includes assignments with the Joint Staff; Supreme Headquarters Allied Powers Europe; International Security Assistance Force, Afghanistan; and Combined Joint Task Force, Allied Force North, Netherlands. Colonel Villahermosa has earned a Master in International Affairs, Master in Philosophy of Political Science, and Certificate in Advanced Soviet Studies from the Harriman Institute, all at Columbia University. Born in San Juan, Puerto Rico, he is fluent in Spanish and Russian. He is currently assigned as the chief, Office of Defense Cooperation, U.S. Embassy, Sana'a, Yemen.

PREFACE

In 1999, at the urging of Puerto Rican veterans who felt that official recognition was overdue, Secretary of the Army Louis E. Caldera asked the U.S. Army Center of Military History to conduct a full and impartial examination of the 65th Infantry's performance in the Korean War. The first study I prepared looked at the regiment's controversial actions at Outpost Kelly and Jackson Heights in 1952. Later, the chief of military history, Brig. Gen. John S. Brown, taking advantage of rich source material, decided to expand the account into a full-length treatment of the Puerto Rican unit's combat experiences across the entire three-year span of a deadly war. This book is the result.

The 65th left San Juan, Puerto Rico, in much better shape than most U.S. infantry regiments headed for Korea. Its ranks were filled with experienced regulars and enthusiastic prior-service volunteers. During the first year of the war, the 65th experienced many triumphs and few setbacks. This situation began to change as personnel-rotation policies led to the departure of combat-proven veterans who were replaced by mobilized Puerto Rican National Guard soldiers beginning in the summer of 1951. When the bulk of the National Guardsmen left a year later, they were replaced with draftees who lacked English-language skills. The story of the regiment, which labored under mounting difficulties, makes for a compelling study of stresses placed upon infantry units in combat.

During the course of my research and writing, I have received support and encouragement from many individuals. First and foremost, I remain deeply indebted to successive chiefs of military history, Brig. Gen. John S. Brown and Dr. Jeffrey J. Clarke, for recognizing the value of this work and helping to see it through to completion. The leadership of Histories Division, notably Drs. Richard W. Stewart and Joel D. Meyerson, also contributed importantly to this volume, as did several of my colleagues in the division: Dr. William M. Donnelly, Dr. William M. Hammond, Jon T. Hoffman, and Dr. Erik B. Villard. Special thanks go to my friend, Lt. Col. (Ret.) Mark J. Reardon, also of Histories Division, who juggled many priorities to remain involved with every aspect of the book's development after my departure from the Center for another assignment. The narrative is a better one for his generosity.

Others at the Center of Military History also deserve mention. In Publishing Division, Diane M. Donovan edited the text with painstaking dedication and attention to detail; Sherry L. Dowdy updated existing maps and created new ones to accompany the text and photographs; Beth F. Mackenzie, chief of Production Branch, helped in the development of the map plan and in the selection and procurement of photographs. Frank R. Shirer and James B. Knight of Field Programs and Historical Services Division located key documents and books relating to the Military Department of Puerto Rico and the 65th Infantry.

Useful comments came from the review panel chaired by Dr. Richard W. Stewart, now the Center's chief historian. For the panel's diligence and observations, I wish to acknowledge the efforts of its members: Dr. Allan R. Millett, Cols. (Ret.) Kenneth E. Hamburger and William T. Bowers, and Dr. William M. Donnelly.

A number of people outside the Center provided valuable advice and assistance, including Dr. Richard J. Sommers and David A. Keogh, who provided access to the James Van Fleet Papers, the Clay Blair Collection, and the Korean Veterans Questionnaires maintained by the U.S. Army Military History Institute, Carlisle Barracks, Pennsylvania; the staff of the General Archives of Puerto Rico in San Juan, Puerto Rico; and George Streatfeild, curator of the Soldiers of Gloucestershire Military Museum, Gloucester, England, and Graham Gordon, a museum staff member, who provided photographs and accounts of the "Glosters" in Korea. Willis D. Cronkhite Jr. provided an interview conducted with his father, Capt. Willis D. Cronkhite, commander of Company F at Jackson Heights. I also owe a debt of gratitude to Cynthia Holdren, daughter of Lt. Col. Lloyd E. Wills, who donated photographs of her father as a battalion commander with the 65th Infantry in 1952.

Many 65th Infantry combat veterans assisted me with their knowledge of events and personalities. Col. (Ret.) George D. Jackson explained in detail the fighting on Jackson Heights during October 1952. Col. (Ret.) William F. Friedman recounted the 65th Infantry's deployment to Korea and its combat performance from September 1950 through April 1951. I benefited from Lt. Col. Carlos Betances-Ramirez's willingness to share his experiences as the 2d Battalion's commanding officer during the autumn of 1952. Colonel Betances-Ramirez opened his home to me for a lengthy session on Outpost Kelly and Jackson Heights. Other veterans who contributed include Charles E. Boyle, Walter B. Clark, Winfred G. Skelton Jr., and Duquesne A. Wolf.

Finally, I would like to thank my wife Natalie and my sons Alexander, Nicholas, and Michael for their support, understanding, and assistance during the time spent creating this volume. My father, Jesus Villahermosa, whose service as a young infantryman in the 65th Infantry during the Korean War inspired me to begin this project, also assisted in ways too numerous to mention.

It remains only to note that the conclusions and interpretations expressed in this book are mine alone and that I am solely responsible for any errors. The views expressed herein do not necessarily reflect the official policy or position of the Departments of the Army and Defense or the U.S. government.

Sana'a, Yemen
2 June 2009

GILBERTO N. VILLAHERMOSA
Colonel, U.S. Army

Honor and Fidelity

The 65th Infantry in Korea, 1950–1953

Chapter 1

Prologue: Before Korea

On 18 October 1898, following the end of the Spanish-American War, the U.S. War Department established the Department of Puerto Rico, with headquarters in San Juan, to administer the island. The department was responsible for all insular military affairs on Puerto Rico as well as the islands and keys adjacent and belonging to it.[1] Maj. Gen. John R. Brooke was appointed the first commander of the department and the military governor of the island. The withdrawal of Spanish troops and police after the signing of the peace protocol was followed by what General Brooke described as "a Saturnalia of crime," including "forced contributions, out-and-out robbery, burning, assassinations," and "violence to women."[2] The U.S. Army encountered great difficulty in stopping this crime wave. Furthermore, it had to do so with a diminishing number of troops as President William McKinley had ordered one hundred thousand U.S. Volunteers mustered out of service and returned to the United States as quickly as possible. The burden of administering the island thus quickly passed to the Regular Army.

Maj. Gen. Guy V. Henry, U.S. Volunteers, replaced Brooke as the department commander on 9 December 1898. When Henry took command, the Department of Puerto Rico had only 176 officers and about 3,000 enlisted men.[3] This was about one-third of the troops previously employed by the Spanish to administer the island.[4] To offset troop shortages, General Henry initially retained many of the police and firefighting organizations the Spanish had established. A new insular police force of 313 members, charged with the "prosecution of evil-doers, the capture of fugitives, and

---

[1] *Annual Reports of the War Department for the Fiscal Year Ended June 30, 1899*, 1899, vol. 1, pt. 3, pp. 319, 376 (hereafter cited as *WD Annual Reports, 1899*).

[2] *Annual Reports of the War Department for the Fiscal Year Ended June 30, 1900*, 1902, vol. 1, pt. 6, p. 97 (hereafter cited as *WD Annual Reports, 1900*).

[3] "General Return of Exhibit Showing the Actual Strength of the Army of the United States According to the Latest Returns Received at the Adjutant General's Office," in *WD Annual Reports, 1899*, vol. 1, pt. 3, p. 382.

[4] *WD Annual Reports, 1900*, vol. 1, pt. 13, p. 17.

Column of American artillery entering Ponce, Puerto Rico, in August 1898

the preservation of public order," was formed between 25 and 27 January 1899.[5]

While the insular police force was well suited to deter minor criminal activity, it was poorly prepared and equipped to confront organized gangs, armed insurrection, or external aggression. American officials determined that a standing military force would be needed to accomplish those tasks. Rather than permanently stationing large numbers of American troops in Puerto Rico, the War Department cabled General Henry in February 1899 to ask for his views as to the advisability of recruiting a battalion of infantry from the island's population.[6] Henry responded that military employment of the island's native population "may prove to have an excellent effect upon the people of Porto Rico" and advised that the island possessed "an abundance of fine material" from which soldiers could be selected.[7] In response, the War Department ordered Henry to form four companies of one hundred men each "from among the natives of the islands for such military service as he may deem it desirable."[8] On 2 March 1899, Congress formally authorized the formation of the Puerto Rican Battalion of Volunteer Infantry.

Maj. Lorenzo P. Davison became the first commander of the Puerto Rico Battalion. An experienced officer, Davison was an 1885 graduate of West Point. He had previously served on frontier duty as a lieutenant with the U.S. 7th Cavalry and 11th Infantry. During the Spanish-American War, he had fought with the 5th Infantry. Shortly after Congress authorized the

---

[5] Ibid., p. 50.
[6] *Army and Navy Journal* (18 March 1899): 670.
[7] Ibid.
[8] Ibid.

Prologue: Before Korea

General Brooke   *Major Davison*

formation of the Puerto Rico Battalion, Davison received orders from the War Department to take command of the newly raised unit. Along with the assignment came a promotion to major in the U.S. Volunteers.[9]

By the end of the first year of existence, the Puerto Rico Battalion had proven so effective that the Army decided to expand the unit. The Army also decided to mount the unit on horseback to give it the capability to move quickly to any threatened point on the island. On 12 February 1900, Secretary of War Elihu Root issued instructions to organize a mounted battalion of Puerto Ricans. Department of Puerto Rico General Order no. 34 directed that this battalion would consist of four companies (E, F, G, and H) and be designated the Mounted Battalion of the Puerto Rico Regiment. It was to be equipped with Springfield carbines; Colt pistols; and U.S. Army saddles, bridles, and saddle blankets.[10]

On 20 February, Headquarters, Department of Puerto Rico, issued General Order no. 38, formally designating both battalions as the Puerto

---

[9] The U.S. 5th Infantry would provide three commanding officers to the Puerto Rico Battalion and later the Puerto Rico Regiment. *Official Army Register for 1901* (Washington, D.C.: Adjutant General's Office, 1900), p. 142; *Register of Graduates and Former Cadets, 1802–1980* (West Point, N.Y.: U.S. Military Academy, Association of Graduates, 1980), p. 272.

[10] *WD Annual Reports, 1900*, vol. 1, pt. 13, p. 106.

Rico Regiment, U.S. Volunteers. This made it the last of the U.S. Volunteer regiments to be formed in the wake of the Spanish-American War. The order directed that the second battalion be stationed at Camp Henry in the mountainous Cayey region of southeastern Puerto Rico.

On 1 May 1900, the military governor of Puerto Rico transferred control of all civil affairs to a new civilian governor. Two weeks later, the Department of Puerto Rico was absorbed by the Department of the East.[11] At that time, the island's garrison numbered 1,635 officers and men, including the 900 officers and men of the Puerto Rico Regiment and 475 police. Natives thus made up the overwhelming percentage of military forces stationed there.[12] By early the following year, most of the American military personnel still in Puerto Rico were redeployed back to the mainland United States.

On 20 May 1901, the War Department directed that the existing regiment be replaced by a new formation, designated as the Puerto Rico Provisional Regiment of Infantry. The new organization would consist of two battalions of four companies each and a band. With these modifications, the Puerto Rico Provisional Regiment of Infantry came closer to mirroring the organization of Regular U.S. Army formations. Although each infantry company was authorized 104 officers and enlisted men, the unit's ranks would not be at full strength because of a presidential order imposing on the regiment a ceiling of 554 active-duty personnel.[13] This was not an uncommon situation in U.S. Army units of the period. In order to meet peacetime fiscal constraints, most regiments consisted of cadre units that could be augmented with volunteers in the event of hostilities.

On 30 June 1908, the Puerto Rico Provisional Regiment of Infantry became part of the Regular Army as directed by an act of Congress and General Order no. 100 of the War Department dated 27 May 1908.[14] The unit was renamed the Puerto Rico Regiment of Infantry, United States Army. "The company officers of the regiment are now entitled to practically all of the rights and privileges enjoyed by other officers of corresponding grade in the army," reported Secretary of the Army Luke E. Wright to Congress and the president:

> It has heretofore been impossible to keep the lowest grades filled while restricting appointments to these grades to natives of Porto Rico. It is

---

[11] The U.S. Army consisted of a number of subordinate administrative headquarters, to include the Department of the East. Responsible for various posts, commands, and installations located along the Atlantic seaboard of the United States, it had been established initially as the Eastern Department in 1821 and was redesignated as the Department of the East in 1837.

[12] *WD Annual Reports, 1900*, vol. 1, pt. 13, p. 106.

[13] Ibid.

[14] *Annual Report of the Secretary of War for the Year 1908*, 1908, p. 5.

now hoped, since the regiment has been placed on a permanent basis, that sufficient properly qualified citizens of the island will apply for appointment as second lieutenants to fill the existing vacancies.[15]

The inclusion of the regiment in the Regular Army was indicative of its growing importance. The unit had evolved from a constabulary detachment into a regular formation responsible for the defense of Puerto Rico, which, along with Cuba, guarded the nation's key Atlantic approaches. The authorized active-duty strength of the regiment was also increased from 554 personnel to 611, of which 28 were officers and 583 were enlisted men.[16]

Changes in composition accompanied the reorganization. For the first time since the regiment's formation, Puerto Ricans began advancing steadily in rank. On 14 May 1909, Father John Rivera became the first Puerto Rican to be accepted as an Army chaplain. Commissioned a first lieutenant the same day, Rivera received his assignment with the regiment on 23 June.[17]

On 9 November, the War Department detailed 1st Lt. Pedro J. Parra as military aide to the governor of Puerto Rico. The first native officer to be so designated, Parra had served as an enlisted man in the regiment since 1906.[18] Rivera and Parra were part of a growing contingent of Puerto Rican officers in the regiment that by 1909 included eight first lieutenants and three second lieutenants.[19] Four years later, there were twenty-one Puerto Rican officers serving in the unit, including a captain (the chaplain), ten first lieutenants, and ten second lieutenants.[20]

The 65th in the Period of the Two World Wars

On the eve of the United States' entry into World War I, the War Department began taking steps to increase national military readiness. These steps would have an impact on the Puerto Rico Regiment. On 1 July 1916, the War Department authorized a 3d Battalion, a machine-gun company (with a peacetime establishment of fifty-three that would expand to seventy-four in time of war), and a regimental supply company of thirty-seven men. In addition, the number of enlisted men in the infantry

---

[15] Ibid., p. 20.

[16] Ibid., p. 5.

[17] *Official Army Register for 1910* (Washington, D.C.: The Adjutant General's Office, 1909), p. 105.

[18] Jose A. Muratti, *History of the 65th Infantry, 1899–1946* (San Juan, Puerto Rico: n.p., 1946), p. 7; *Official Army Register for 1909* (Washington, D.C.: The Adjutant General's Office, 1908), p. 383.

[19] *Army Register for 1909*, pp. 381–83.

[20] Ibid., pp. 421–22.

companies increased from one hundred to one hundred fifty.[21] As a result of these changes, the regiment grew to more than fifteen hundred officers and men.[22]

Although the United States raised large numbers of Puerto Rican troops during World War I, their battle casualties came to only one killed and five wounded.[23] These numbers reflected U.S. Army policies that restricted most predominately nonwhite units to noncombat roles. Nonetheless, Puerto Rico contributed more than an infantry division's worth of combat troops to America's homeland defense during the war. Puerto Ricans guarded installations throughout the Caribbean and freed an equivalent number of American soldiers for overseas duty, a process that would be repeated during World War II.

During the interwar period, the regiment found itself subject to the same money-saving efforts as the rest of the Army. Its authorized strength decreased in light of congressional efforts to limit defense spending. On a more positive note, the regiment took another step toward integration into the U.S. military establishment when it was redesignated as the 65th Infantry.[24]

During the two decades between World Wars I and II, the 65th trained as much as the miniscule War Department budget permitted. Inspections, marches, weapons firing, proficiency tests, and tactical field problems were the order of the day. The unit's home station, however, afforded it unique opportunities not available to stateside infantry regiments. In February 1938, for example, the regiment's 1st Battalion participated in the U.S. Navy's Fleet Landing Exercise no. 4 at Culebra, Puerto Rico, as part of a provisional Army expeditionary brigade that included several Marine units. Beginning on 13 January and ending on 15 March, the exercise was the most comprehensive and instructive landing operation held by the U.S. Navy and Marine Corps to date.[25]

In a fashion similar to preparations for World War I, the conflict that began during September 1939 in Europe prompted the Army to increase

---

[21] Muratti, *History of the 65th Infantry*, p. 8; "Participation of Puerto Ricans in the Armed Services with Emphasis on World War I, World War II, and the Korean War," 13 Aug 65, GEOG G 314.7, sec. 1, p. 2, U.S. Army Center of Military History (CMH), Washington, D.C.

[22] Muratti, *History of the 65th Infantry*, p. 8

[23] *Annual Report of the Secretary of War for the Year 1926*, p. 221.

[24] General Orders (GO) no. 67, 11 Nov 20, *General Orders and Bulletins, War Department, 1920* (Washington, D.C.: Government Printing Office, 1921).

[25] Albert N. Garland, *Study No. 6: Amphibious Doctrine and Training* (Washington, D.C.: Historical Section, Army Ground Forces, 1949), p. 11; William M. Miler, *A Chronology of the United States Marine Corps 1935–1946*, 26 vols. (Washington, D.C.: Historical Branch, Headquarters, U.S. Marine Corps, 1965), 2: 1–3.

Prologue: Before Korea

Soldiers of the 65th Infantry form up for their evening meal during maneuvers held in August 1941.

the regiment's combat readiness. By late 1940, President Franklin D. Roosevelt had called a number of National Guard divisions into federal service while Regular Army units received additional officers and men to bring them to wartime authorized strength. By January 1941, the 65th numbered 125 officers and 2,945 enlisted men.[26]

The regiment used the infusion of additional manpower to plan and execute a series of full-scale field exercises. In February 1941, the 65th conducted nighttime tactical problems in the Salinas maneuver area for the first time as a complete regiment. In August and September, it had another opportunity to conduct large-scale training under field conditions during the Puerto Rico Department maneuvers.

On 7 December, word of the Japanese attack at Pearl Harbor reached Puerto Rico. Uncertain where the enemy might strike next, the Puerto Rico Department ordered the 65th Infantry to send a rifle company to secure the Roosevelt Roads Naval Radio Station and Dry Dock. When the enemy

---

[26] "Regimental History of the Sixty-fifth Infantry, 1941," Entry 427, Rcds of the Adjutant General's Office (AGO), Record Group (RG) 407, National Archives II, College Park, Maryland (NACP).

did not attack Puerto Rico, the 65th resumed its rigorous program of tactical training, now interspersed with alerts, readiness inspections, and false rumors of pending transfers.

Thirteen months after Pearl Harbor, the 65th Infantry departed Puerto Rico, arriving in the Panama Canal Zone in early January 1943.[27] The unit had been transferred to Panama to become part of the Canal Department's mobile force. Its mission there included protecting vital installations in the Canal Zone and manning observation posts on both the Atlantic and Pacific coasts. But the 65th's defense responsibilities were not limited to American possessions. On 19 August 1943, Companies E and F and the Anti-Tank Company departed the Canal Zone for the Galapagos Islands, arriving three days later. A portion of the force relieved elements of the 150th Infantry while Company E proceeded to Salinas, Ecuador, to assume responsibility for securing critical harbor installations.

The 65th also participated in several other homeland defense missions. On 24 October 1943, one officer and nine enlisted men from the regimental reconnaissance platoon departed Panama for two-week deployment to the Cocos Islands in the middle of the Indian Ocean. Selected rifle companies from the 65th also rotated through the U.S. Army Jungle Training School in Panama, where they performed as demonstration troops for student officers from neighboring Latin American countries. As a result, the regiment attained a high degree of proficiency in jungle operations and received praise from the commanding general of the Panama Canal Department's mobile force.[28]

On 25 November 1943, Col. Antulio Segarra assumed command of the 65th Infantry. A 1927 West Point graduate and a 1942 Command and General Staff School graduate, the 37-year-old Segarra had led the Puerto Rican National Guard (PRNG) 296th Infantry prior to taking command of the 65th Infantry.[29] Segarra was the first Puerto Rican Regular Army officer to command a Regular Army regiment.

With casualties rising in Italy and preparations for an invasion of northwest Europe well underway, in early 1944, the U.S. Army made ready to send Puerto Rican troops overseas. First, the 65th departed Panama for Fort Eustis, Virginia, where the men drew new uniforms and equipment and had training. Then, an advance party departed for French Morocco, arriving at Casablanca on 16 March. The remainder of the regiment followed on 5 April.[30]

---

[27] Rpt, HQ, 65th Inf, 28 Feb 44, sub: Regimental History of the 65th Infantry for the Year 1943, p. 1, RG 407, NACP.

[28] Ibid., pp. 2–4.

[29] *Official Army Register, January 1, 1943* (Washington, D.C.: Government Printing Office, 1943), p. 795; *Register of Graduates and Former Cadets, 1802–1980*, p. 359.

[30] HQ, 65th Inf, Rpt, 20 Jan 45, sub: Regimental History of the Sixty-Fifth Infantry for the Calendar Year 1944, pp. 2–3, Entry 427, RG 407, NACP.

Prologue: Before Korea

Troops of the 65th Infantry march onto the Fort Buchanan parade ground to set up tents and field equipment for a formal inspection by the Puerto Rican Department staff, 5 February 1942.

Once deployed overseas, the unit served mostly in security missions. Its 3d Battalion, for example, was assigned to guard Twelfth Air Force installations on Corsica.[31] The remainder of the regiment conducted amphibious training in North Africa while also performing a variety of security missions, which included protecting roads, railheads, supply depots, and airfields from attack by enemy saboteurs and commandos.[32]

On 22 September, the main body of the 65th departed North Africa for an assignment with the Seventh Army in France, arriving in Toulon on 1 October. Within weeks, the 1st Battalion found itself securing the Sixth Army Group and Seventh Army command posts as well as several fuel depots and railheads.[33] The 2d Battalion, meanwhile, protected trains moving war supplies from Marseille to northern France.[34]

---

[31] Muratti, *History of the 65th Infantry*, p. 11.

[32] "Participation of Puerto Ricans in the Armed Services," sec. 2, pp. 2–3.

[33] Muratti, *History of the 65th Infantry*, p. 12; Rpt, HQ, 65th Inf, 20 Jan 45, pp. 3–4.

[34] William F. Ross and Charles F. Romanus, *The Quartermaster Corps: Operations in the War Against Germany*, U.S. Army in World War II (Washington, D.C.: U.S. Army Center of Military History, 1965), p. 126.

The remainder of the regiment, which included the 3d Battalion, the regimental headquarters, the Cannon Company, the Anti-Tank Company, and the Service Company, was attached to the 44th Anti-Aircraft Artillery Brigade guarding a portion of the Franco-Italian border along the Maritime Alps. There, the regiment held a sector extending from Roquebillière to Monte Grosso, protecting the Sixth Army Group's far right flank. The 65th's mission was to provide early warning should the German Army in Italy attempt to attack into southern France.[35]

The 442d Regimental Combat Team (RCT) was on the 65th Infantry's right, while the 899th Anti-Aircraft Artillery Battalion, fighting as infantry, was on the left. Facing the regiment was the German *34th Infantry Division*'s *107th Grenadier Regiment*. On the night of 15 December 1944, during a German raid on Company L, Pvt. Sergio Sanchez-Sanchez and Sgt. Angel G. Martinez became the first of the 65th Infantry's men to fall in combat. In all, seven men of the regiment were killed in action during December, including two officers and a noncommissioned officer (NCO). Another ten were wounded, including two officers and three NCOs.[36]

With the threat of a German assault into France from Italy evaporating, the Sixth Army Group began making plans to relieve the 65th Infantry from its assignment with the 44th Anti-Aircraft Artillery Brigade. The first element to depart was the 3d Battalion, which was relieved from duty in the Maritime Alps on 26 February 1945. The rest of the unit followed shortly afterward. The regiment reassembled in Lorraine, France, in anticipation of further combat in southwest Germany. The 65th crossed the Rhine in March 1945, remaining in Germany as part of the Army of Occupation until October 1945, when it was ordered to Calais, France, in preparation for the return home. The regiment arrived in Puerto Rico on 9 November 1945.[37] While on the front lines, its soldiers collectively had won a Distinguished Service Cross, two Silver Stars, and ninety Purple Hearts.[38] The unit received battle participation credits for the Naples-Foggia, Rome-Arno, Central Europe, and Rhineland campaigns.

Postwar Doldrums and then Renewal

Upon its return from Europe, the 65th Infantry took up a variety of assignments in Puerto Rico and elsewhere. The regiment was temporar-

---

[35] Rpt, HQ, 65th Inf, 1944, pp. 3–4.
[36] Ibid.
[37] "Participation of Puerto Ricans in the Armed Services," sec. 1, p. 4.
[38] Jose A. Norat Martinez, *Historia del Regimento 65 de Infanteria* (San Juan, P.R.: n.p., 1992), p. 55.

ily stationed at Camp Losey on the south-central coast of the island east of Ponce. Then the 1st Battalion was moved to Fort Buchanan, just south of San Juan, and the 2d Battalion went to Camp O'Reilly and later to Henry Barracks at Cayey, sixty miles to the southwest. After a brief stay in Puerto Rico, the 3d Battalion deployed to the Island of Trinidad, British West Indies, where it provided security for Fort Read and Waller Field. While on Trinidad, a reinforced platoon from Company I departed for French Guyana to protect the U.S. Air Force Base at Rochambeau during a local rebellion. In September 1947, the 3d Battalion was airlifted back to Puerto Rico, where it took up residence at Fort Buchanan prior to being inactivated.

During the following months in Puerto Rico, the 65th Regimental Combat Team, which included the two remaining infantry battalions, the 504th Field Artillery Battalion, the 531st Engineer Company, and a tank company from the 18th Mechanized Cavalry Squadron, trained at the Salinas maneuver area. The 65th RCT also regularly supported joint Army-Navy exercises, which afforded it training opportunities enjoyed by few other U.S. Army infantry regiments during this period.

On 26 July 1949, Col. William W. Harris assumed command of the 65th Infantry. While the 42-year-old Harris had accrued much staff experience, this was his first assignment with troops in many years. A 1930 West Point graduate who had attended both the Infantry School and the U.S. Army Command and General Staff School, Harris had served with the U.S. Army Ground Forces headquarters in Washington, D.C., and the Operations Division of Allied Forces Headquarters in the Mediterranean Theater during World War II.[39]

Although Harris' selection to command the 65th Infantry may have been a reward for years of faithful service, he was not happy with his new assignment. "I was outraged," he remembered, "at what I considered being sent to pasture for two years to command what the Pentagon brass referred to as a 'rum and Coca Cola' outfit. Like any other eagle colonel in the regular army, aged forty-two, I was ambitious. Going to the West Indies to command the Puerto Rican Regiment was not my idea of either where or how to prove my command ability."[40]

Harris was dismayed with conditions when he arrived in Puerto Rico. The regiment had only two rifle battalions and lacked a heavy mortar company. Worse, the rifle battalions were located sixty miles apart, making it difficult for him to visit them on a regular basis. The 65th was also

---

[39] "Brigadier General William Warner Harris," Gen Ofcr Bio files, CMH.
[40] William W. Harris, *Puerto Rico's Fighting 65th U.S. Infantry: From San Juan to Chorwan* (San Rafael, Calif.: Presidio Press, 1980), p. 1.

Colonel Dammer

short essential equipment, including vehicles. "These were all major deficiencies," observed Harris:

> I estimated that they would reduce our combat capability by at least 40 or 50 percent. Not that the 65th was going off to war or anywhere, but a commander must evaluate his command somehow, and combat capability is the best gauge to use because it has the lowest common denominator—estimated combat effectiveness.[41]

On the plus side, the regiment received training opportunities denied to many stateside infantry units. It also had an extremely competent group of field-grade officers. The 39-year-old regimental executive officer, Lt. Col. George W. Childs, was a 1936 West Point graduate and World War II veteran who had been decorated with a Silver Star, a Bronze Star, and a Purple Heart.[42] The 1st Battalion commander, 33-year-old Lt. Col. Howard B. St. Clair, graduated West Point in 1939 and had served on the staff of the 99th Infantry Division during the war.[43] The 2d Battalion commander, 39-year-old Lt. Col. Herman W. Dammer, had led the 1st Ranger Battalion at Anzio, earning a Silver Star and a Purple Heart. He was a graduate of both the Command and General Staff College and the Armed Forces Staff College.[44]

Harris moved quickly to win the confidence of his officers and men. One of his first actions was to rescind an order, issued by his predecessor, which forbade the men of the regiment to speak Spanish under penalty of court-martial. "I did, however, remind everyone that English is . . . the official language of the United States Army, and that any written communications directed to the headquarters would be in English," wrote Harris.[45]

---

[41] Ibid., p. 6.

[42] *Register of Graduates and Former Cadets, 1802–1980*, p. 403; Harris, *Puerto Rico's Fighting 65th*, p. 4.

[43] *Register of Graduates and Former Cadets, 1802–1980*, p. 422.

[44] *Official Army Register: Volume I, United States Army Active and Retired Lists, 1 January 1950* (Washington, D.C.: Government Printing Office, 1950), p. 133.

[45] Harris, *Puerto Rico's Fighting 65th*, p. 9.

This small concession by Harris made a very positive impression on his troops.

Harris' negative feelings toward his new assignment faded as he realized the benefit his unit would reap by virtue of its location near a training area used for large-scale joint exercises. The U.S. Atlantic Fleet exercises of 1948 and 1949 had provided the 65th Infantry with a solid foundation in combined-arms training prior to Harris' arrival. He was able to gain additional insight into the regiment's proficiency while exercising his own skills as a troop leader during the 1950 Puerto Rico Exercise (PORTREX). After taking manpower and equipment shortfalls into account, Harris believed the exercises helped the 65th Infantry to reach a level of combat effectiveness superior to most U.S. Army infantry regiments when the Korean War broke out.

Chapter 2

From San Juan to Pusan

While many of the soldiers with the 65th hailed from mountainous regions on their home island, they would find little similarity between those lushly vegetated ridges and the jagged rocky peaks that dominated the harsh topography of the Korean peninsula. Jutting from central Asian mainland with a conformation that somewhat resembles the state of Florida, Korea boasts more than five thousand four hundred miles of coastline. The Yalu and Tumen Rivers mark its upper limits. China lies above the two rivers for five hundred miles of Korea's northern boundary; the Soviet Union occupied some eleven miles of the border along the lower Tumen River. The rest of Korea's borders are defined by three major bodies of water: the Sea of Japan to the east, the Korea Strait to the south, and the Yellow Sea to the west.

The country varies in width between ninety and two hundred miles and in length from five hundred twenty-five to six hundred miles. High mountains drop down abruptly to deep water on the east; but on the south and west, a heavily indented shoreline provides many harbors. Summers are hot and humid, with a monsoon season that lasts from June to September; in the winter, cold winds roar down from the Asian interior. Korea's rugged landscape, lack of well-developed roads and rail lines, and climatic extremes made it difficult for large-scale military operations to be conducted.

Korea's population totaled approximately 30 million. Twenty-one million lived below the 38th Parallel that divided the peninsula with Kim Il-Sung's authoritarian Communist regime in the North and a democratically elected government headed by Syngman Rhee to the South. The Soviets and American devised this artificial political demarcation at the end of World War II. This arrangement, however, left most of the heavy industry in the north separated from the bulk of the population and agriculture remaining in the south. Both Rhee and his Communist opponent had publicly stated their desire to reunite the Korean people under a single flag, using armed force if necessary.

On Sunday, 25 June 1950, seven infantry divisions from the North Korean People's Army swept south across the Republic of Korea's border from coast to coast. Consisting of ninety thousand men along with one hundred fifty Soviet-made T–34 tanks and one hundred eighty Soviet-made aircraft, the onslaught, heavily supported by artillery, slammed into the surprised and unprepared Republic of Korea (ROK) Army.

Although the 38th Parallel was defended by four South Korean divisions and one separate infantry regiment, only one regiment from each division and one battalion of the separate regiment were occupying defensive positions when the attack began. Nor were the South Koreans well armed. They had U.S.-made M1 rifles, .30-caliber carbines, 60-mm. and 81-mm. mortars, obsolescent 2.36-inch rocket launchers, and a few 105-mm. M3 howitzers. They lacked tanks, medium artillery, heavy mortars, recoilless rifles, and close air support. Furthermore, they did not have enough artillery and mortar ammunition to sustain their forces for any length of time.[1]

By 28 June, the North Koreans had captured Seoul, the South Korean capital. On 5 July, Task Force SMITH, a force of five hundred U.S. soldiers from the 24th Infantry Division, was defeated near Osan, thirty miles south of Seoul, by two regiments of the North Korean *4th Division* supported by thirty-three T–34 tanks. Badly outnumbered and lacking effective anti-tank weapons, the American task force succeeded in delaying the enemy advance for several hours before suffering 50 percent casualties by the time it finally withdrew.[2]

Maj. Gen. William F. Dean, the commander of the 24th Infantry Division, committed the newly arrived 21st and 34th Infantry regiments to slow the enemy advance and gain time for a reorganization of the South Korean Army and the arrival of additional U.S. troops. Rushed to the war from Japan, where it had been performing occupation duties at reduced strengths, the division had significant training and equipment shortages and inexperienced unit commanders unfamiliar with their men. By 20 July, the 24th Division had been badly mauled, suffering 30 percent casualties and the loss of much of its equipment.[3]

The reorganization of the South Korean Army into two corps and five divisions and the arrival in Korea of the U.S. 1st Cavalry and 25th Infantry Divisions, helped to slow but not halt the enemy onslaught. These units fell under command of the U.S. Eighth Army, which redeployed most of its headquarters elements from Japan to Korea. On 29 July, Lt. Gen. Walton H. Walker, the Eighth Army commander, issued a stand-or-die order to his

---

[1] Roy E. Appleman, *South to the Naktong, North to the Yalu*, U.S. Army in the Korean War (Washington, D.C.: Office of the Chief of Military History, 1961), pp. 8–17.

[2] Ibid., pp. 75–76.

[3] Ibid., p. 213.

troops, saying that the retreat must stop.⁴

Three days later, the North Koreans bypassed the Eighth Army's westernmost units. Walker was left with no alternative but to order his troops to withdraw, this time behind the Naktong River. It was along that watercourse, and what became known as the Pusan Perimeter, that Eighth Army finally held.

The Pusan Perimeter encompassed a rectangular area about one hundred miles from north to south and fifty miles from east to west. The Naktong River formed the line's western boundary except for the southernmost fifteen miles, where the river turned eastward. The Sea of Japan formed the perimeter's eastern and southern boundaries. Its northern boundary was an irregular line that ran from Waegwan, a town seventy miles northwest of Pusan, to Hunghae on the coast. From the southwest to the northeast, the remnants of five South Korean and three understrength U.S. divisions manned the line. Facing them were two North Korean corps composed of nine infantry divisions, one armored division, and an independent infantry regiment.⁵

General Walker

With U.S. forces under heavy pressure, General of the Army Douglas MacArthur requested immediate reinforcements from the United States. President Harry S. Truman agreed, and the Army dispatched the 2d Infantry Division as well as a regimental combat team built around the 11th Airborne Division's 187th Airborne Infantry. Although the Army had to strip many units in the United States to fill out the 2d Division before it deployed, lead elements of that unit began arriving on 31 July. By 20 August, the entire division was in Korea. Its arrival, along with the 5th Regimental Combat Team from Hawaii and 1st Provisional Marine Brigade, provided General Walker with the additional men and equipment he needed to stabilize the Pusan Perimeter.⁶

---

⁴ Ibid., pp. 207–08.

⁵ Ibid., pp. 252–55.

⁶ James F. Schnabel, *Policy and Direction: The First Year*, U.S. Army in the Korean War (Washington, D.C.: Office of the Chief of Military History, 1972), p. 127.

Not content to maintain a defensive posture for long, General MacArthur began planning for an amphibious assault that would outflank the main body of the North Korean Army pressing in against the Pusan Perimeter. The assault would take place at Inch'on, a small harbor town located on the west coast of Korea just to the west of Seoul. Because MacArthur intended to use his theater reserve, the U.S. 7th Infantry Division, as part of the assault, he requested deployment of the 3d Infantry Division, the last infantry division remaining in the United States.

The 3d Division had been one of the units the Army had stripped to flesh out the 2d Division. After much debate, President Truman and the Joint Chiefs of Staff authorized the unit's deployment on condition that it would serve for the time being in Japan as a theater reserve. They assumed that because of the division's relatively low combat effectiveness, MacArthur would permit it sufficient time to reach a minimum acceptable level of training before committing it to battle.[7]

When the 3d Division received word that it was going to the Far East, it had fewer than five thousand of its authorized eighteen thousand men and little of its equipment.[8] In an initial attempt to rectify the personnel problem, the division commander, Maj. Gen. Robert H. Soule, reduced his 30th Infantry to cadre strength, dividing its officers and men between the 7th and 15th Infantries.[9] Even so, it was clear that the 3d Division would need additional units if it was expected to enter combat any time soon.

The 65th Infantry Organizes for Korea

A solution to the manning challenges facing the 3d Infantry Division surfaced on 22 July, when Maj. Gen. Charles L. Bolte, the Army assistant chief of staff, G–3, Operations, expressed concern that the Army Staff was doing too little to help General MacArthur. During a meeting chaired by the Army's deputy chief of staff, Lt. Gen. Matthew B. Ridgway, to identify ways to increase the amount and tempo of assistance to the Far East Command, the deployment of units from Puerto Rico and Panama was discussed. Ridgway directed Bolte to submit recommendations on using such units.

After studying the issue for a few days, Bolte's staff recommended that the 65th Infantry become the 3d Division's third maneuver regiment. Within three weeks, Governor Luis Muñoz Marin of Puerto Rico received

---

[7] Ibid., p. 134.

[8] John B. Wilson, *Maneuver and Firepower: The Evolution of Divisions and Separate Brigades* (Washington, D.C.: U.S. Army Center of Military History, 1998), pp. 241–42.

[9] Monthly Cmd Rpt, 30th Inf Rgt, 5 Apr 51. Unless otherwise noted, all Cmd Rpts and War Diaries are in Entry 429, Rcds of the AGO, RG 407, NACP.

formal notice that the 65th was being alerted for movement overseas.[10] The division would also receive the 2d Armored Division's 58th Armored Field Artillery (AFA) and the 64th Heavy Tank Battalions, as well as Third Army's 999th AFA Battalion.[11] All three battalions were composed of black troops led mostly by white officers.

The addition of African American and Puerto Rican units made the 3d Infantry Division one of the most racially diverse in the Army. The 15th Infantry's 3d Battalion, commanded by Lt. Col. Milburn N. Huston, was also composed of black troops with predominantly white officers, although Company I was commanded entirely by blacks. Thus configured, the division would enter combat in Korea with 7 white battalions (5 infantry and 2 artillery); 4 black battalions (2 artillery, 1 infantry, and 1 armor); and 3 Puerto Rican battalions (all infantry).[12]

General Soule took command of the 3d Division soon afterward. The division was fortunate to gain a commanding general with Asian experience. At the end of World War I, Soule had served briefly in Siberia before accompanying the 31st Infantry regiment to the Philippines in April 1920. He had studied Mandarin Chinese in Beijing prior to being assigned to the 15th Infantry at Tianjin, China, and returned to the United States in the summer of 1938. During World War II, he commanded the 188th Glider Infantry, which he led into combat in Leyte and Luzon. Promoted to brigadier general in 1945, Soule became the assistant division commander of the 11th Airborne Division and then the 38th Infantry Division. From 1947 to 1950, he was the military attaché to China, where he observed firsthand the Chinese Civil War and the Communist defeat of the Nationalist Chinese.[13]

The decision to send the 65th Infantry to Korea and attach it to the 3d Division represented a milestone in the Army's racial policies. In the past, Puerto Ricans had been assigned exclusively to segregated units in Puerto Rico and the Panama Canal Zone. Even so, the 65th's deployment to Korea was hardly a move toward permanent change. It was driven more by the severity of the crisis in the Far East and the immediate need for infantry units than by confidence in the Puerto Rican regiment.

Late in August 1950, after a series of inspections, General Mark W. Clark, the chief of Army Field Forces, reported that due to personnel

---

[10] MFR, Lt Gen Matthew B. Ridgway, 11 Aug 50, Hist Rcds, Aug–Oct 50, Matthew B. Ridgway Papers, U.S. Army Military History Institute (MHI), Carlisle Barracks, Pa.

[11] Capt Max W. Dolcater, ed., *3d Infantry Division in Korea* (Tokyo: Toppan Publishing, 1953), p. 58; Wilson, *Maneuver and Firepower*, pp. 241–42.

[12] Clay Blair, *The Forgotten War: America in Korea, 1950–1953* (New York: Times Books, 1987), pp. 410–11.

[13] "Maj Gen Robert Homer Soule, USA," Press Br, Ofc of Public Information, Department of Defense (DoD), Gen Ofcr Bio files, CMH.

shortages the 3d Division was only 40 percent combat ready. There were no major equipment shortages, however, and the unit was thought to be structurally sound. Clark felt that it could be brought to a high state of combat readiness in another two-and-a-half months.[14] On 30 August, minus the 65th Infantry, the 3d Infantry Division sailed from San Francisco for Japan.

When the 65th received the alert for overseas movement on 11 August, its elements were still scattered across Puerto Rico. Colonel St. Clair's 1st Battalion was located at Camp Losey, while Colonel Dammer's 2d Battalion was stationed at Henry Barracks in the mountains, some sixty miles away. Although authorized almost 4,000 troops, the regiment had only 92 officers and 1,895 enlisted men on hand.[15] It consisted of two rather than three infantry battalions, a headquarters company, a service company, a recently activated heavy mortar company, and a medical company. The unit also lacked heavy fire support. Although most regiments of its size had a tank company, its own was missing; moreover, its newly formed mortar company lacked 4.2-inch mortars, firing tables, and ammunition.[16]

All components of the 65th Infantry were short of officers, NCOs, and enlisted personnel. For example, the rifle companies were authorized 211 officers, warrant officers, and enlisted men and the weapons company 165; but the four companies of the 1st Battalion had an average assigned strength of about 150 and a present-for-duty strength of only 105. Capt. Dominick J. Lostumbo's Company C was the strongest, with 172 soldiers present for duty. First Lt. Eladio Burgos' Company D, the heavy-weapons company, was the weakest with only 99. Capt. George F. Ammon's Company A had 114 present for duty, while 1st Lt. Joseph W. St. John's Company B had 137. The four rifle companies averaged only 4 officers and 30 NCOs apiece.[17]

About 60 percent of the 65th Infantry's officers were from the continental United States. In the 2d Battalion, for example, the battalion commander, Colonel Dammer, was continental, while his executive officer, Maj. Maximiliano Figueroa, was Puerto Rican. Two company commanders, Capts. Floyd Frederick and Patrick J. McDonnell, were continental, while the other two, Capts. Jose M. Martinez and Marcial Yunque, were Puerto Rican. Twelve of the battalion's nineteen lieutenants were continental, seven Puerto Rican. The battalion also had

---

[14] Schnabel, *Policy and Direction*, p. 134.

[15] Col William W. Culp, *Training and Future Utilization of Insular Puerto Rican Military Manpower in the United States Army* (Carlisle, Pa.: U.S. Army War College, 1953), p. 8.

[16] Ibid.

[17] Co Morning Rpts, 1 Aug 50, 1st Bn, 65th Inf, Mil Rcds Br, National Personnel Records Center (NPRC), St. Louis, Mo.

one Puerto Rican warrant officer, WO2 Sady Garcia.[18] The lower ranks were composed entirely of Puerto Rican NCOs and enlisted personnel, the majority World War II veterans with many years of service in the regiment.[19]

The Army chose the 3d Battalion, 33d Infantry, stationed at Fort Kobbe in the Panama Canal Zone, to provide the nucleus for the 65th Infantry's newly formed third battalion. A better cultural match could not have been found. Although the 33d Infantry had been reactivated only in January 1950 (sixteen months after it was inactivated), it was one of the oldest Army units ever to serve in the Caribbean and it contained a large number of Puerto Rican soldiers. It had also trained with the 65th before and during PORTREX earlier in the year. Lt. Col. John A. Gavin, a 1932 West Point graduate, commanded the battalion and would be the one to take over the new unit. The 40-year-old infantry officer had served with Headquarters, Army Ground Forces, and the U.S. Fifteenth Army in Europe during World War II.[20]

Creating a new third battalion for the 65th entailed stripping Gavin's unit of all but a handful of officers, NCOs, and enlisted men. However, this course of action still would not produce a completely manned and equipped rifle battalion, since the strength of the 33d Infantry was even lower than that of the 65th, averaging fewer than one hundred officers and men per company.[21] To remedy the shortfall, additional soldiers had to be transferred from the 33d Infantry's 1st and 2d Battalions to serve as individual fillers in the newly created unit.

If innovative measures had solved many of the personnel challenges the regimental commander, Colonel Harris, faced prior to the 65th's deployment to Korea, he was also planning for future eventualities. Anticipating that the regiment would probably find it difficult to obtain replacements from Puerto Rico after it entered combat, he requested permission to deploy overseas with a 10 percent overage in company-grade officers and enlisted personnel, a luxury few other infantry regiments could afford. Aimed at ensuring the 65th would be able to maintain its combat readiness even after suffering numerous casualties, his request was approved.[22]

---

[18] GO no. 55, HQ, Henry Barracks, P.R., 17 Aug 50, sub: 2d Battalion Officers and Non-Commissioned Officers, Historians files, CMH.

[19] Ibid.

[20] *Register of Graduates and Former Cadets 1802–1980*, p. 381; *Official Army Register: Volume I, United States Army Active and Retired Lists, 1 January 1950* (Washington, D.C.: Government Printing Office, 1950), p. 203.

[21] Co Morning Rpts, 1 Aug 50, 3d Bn, 33d Inf, Mil Rcds Br, NPRC.

[22] Interv, Clay Blair with Brig Gen William W. Harris, n.d., Clay and Joan Blair Collection, MHI.

In an effort to recruit additional men with prior service to fill out the ranks of the regiment before it departed Puerto Rico, Harris enlisted the assistance of radio stations and newspaper publishers. On 14 August, *El Imparcial*, one of Puerto Rico's leading newspapers, announced that the Department of the Army had requested two thousand Puerto Rican volunteers to fight in Korea. The announcement noted that prospective candidates could be single or married, should be less than thirty years old, and must have served honorably during World War II.[23]

Puerto Rico's other leading newspaper, *El Mundo*, reported shortly thereafter that the Army was seeking some sixteen hundred men for the 65th Infantry and that the term of service was twenty-one months.[24] By the next day, 18 August, more than seven hundred veterans had responded to the call.[25] By the deadline for filling the regiment up to wartime strength, 22 August, the Department of the Army had also recalled another 1,200 members of the enlisted reserve corps.[26] When the 65th sailed for Korea, its ranks had ballooned to 3,880 officers, NCOs, and enlisted men. Sixty-four of the 206 officers were Puerto Rican.[27]

While the bulk of the men were volunteers, not all of the Puerto Ricans went to Korea voluntarily. Writing on behalf of 172 soldiers who had enlisted in the Army at Fort Buchanan on 18 May 1950, Pfc. Rafael A. Zapata of the 3d Battalion's Company K later complained to the inspector general of U.S. Army Forces, Antilles, in Puerto Rico: "We signed papers stating: 'I enlisted for service in the Department of Panama Canal Zone Units.' How is it that we have been sent over to the Far East Command? Request that for the benefit of future enlistees in the territory of Puerto Rico, appropriate action be taken to correct this situation."[28]

The bulk of the 65th's soldiers went to war willingly. World War II veterans made up the vast majority of those who joined up. Most spoke English as well as Spanish, although the degree of fluency in the former varied. "Over the years those who served in the Regiment were in a status of life above that of most of the people on the island," remembered the reg-

---

[23] "Ejercito Pide 2 Mil Boricuas" and "Queremos Pelear En Seguida," *El Imparcial*, 14 August 1950, copy in Historians files.

[24] "Deben Servir Por Periodo De 21 Meses," *El Mundo*, 17 August 1950, copy in Historians files.

[25] "700 Veteranos Acuden A Llamada A Las Armas," *El Imparcial*, 15 August 1950, copy in Historians files.

[26] "Regimiento 65 Ha Alistado Ya Total de 1,474," *El Mundo*, 22 August 1950, copy in Historians files.

[27] Co Morning Rpts, 1 Sep 50, 65th Inf, Mil Rcds Br, NPRC; Monthly Cmd Rpt, 3d Inf Div, Nov 50.

[28] Shelby L. Stanton, *America's Tenth Legion: X Corps in Korea, 1950* (Novato, Calif.: Presidio Press, 1996), p. 170.

iment's assistant intelligence officer, Capt. Carl H. Griffin. "Throughout their history the Regiment has always been proud of their achievements and hoped to be given the opportunity to prove itself."[29]

Governor Muñoz Marin also offered to form an all–Puerto Rican division of eighteen thousand men for the U.S. Army to send to Korea. The division would have consisted of the 65th, 295th, and 296th Infantries, the latter two National Guard units.[30] While the Puerto Rican National Guard's 295th Infantry was federalized on 14 August, however, the 296th was not, ending any chance that an all–Puerto Rican division would be available for overseas service.

More important, just before the regiment departed, Brig. Gen. Edwin L. Sibert, the commanding general of the Antilles Command, authorized the creation of a personnel replacement center for the regiment in Puerto Rico. This decision would pay tremendous dividends for the unit once it reached Korea, ensuring it had a steady stream of Puerto Rican recruits during the war. No other U.S. Army unit in Korea enjoyed the same benefit. Between September 1950 and March 1953, the Replacement Training Center at Camp Tortuguero, Puerto Rico, trained some thirty thousand five hundred Puerto Rican replacements, many of whom would serve in the 65th.[31]

In general, Colonel Harris did not seem unduly concerned with the state of combat readiness within the 65th as it prepared to depart. His assistant regimental operations officer, Capt. William A. Friedman, however, was "appalled" by what he considered to be the unit's lack of preparation. This is not surprising, considering Friedman's previous tours of combat duty in North Africa, Sicily, France, and Germany during World War II, including landing on OMAHA Beach on D-Day. "I know that Colonel Harris was more than proud of how his regiment conducted itself in PORTREX and, in fact, overemphasized how well it did," he said, "but an exercise of that type was not combat qualifying. I had the initial impression that the regiment was a two-battalion garrison unit and that our new 3d Battalion, which was to join us en route after relief from duty in Panama . . . was of a similar combat capability."[32]

While Friedman was judging the regiment against the high standards of the wartime 1st Infantry Division, the 65th was actually the only unit

---

[29] Army Svc Questionnaire, 65th Inf, Carl H. Griffin, Veterans Survey for the Korean War, n.d., MHI.

[30] See Ltr, Luis Muñoz Marin, Ofc of the Governor, La Fortaleza, San Juan, P.R., to the Hon Oscar L. Chapman, Secretary of the Interior, Washington, D.C., 18 Jul 50, Ofc of the Governor, RG 96–20, Gen Archives of Puerto Rico, San Juan, P.R. See also "A Joint Resolution of the Insular Legislature Puerto Rico 1950," n.d., in the same packet.

[31] Culp, *Training and Future Utilization*, p. 22.

[32] Interv, author with Lt Col William A. Friedman, 17 Sep 01, Historians files, CMH.

of its size in the U.S. Army to have participated in three large-scale exercises within three years (all alongside U.S. Marine units). The 3d Battalion, 33d Infantry, had also participated in those exercises along with the 65th. Furthermore, the PORTREX maneuvers in 1950 had simulated combat conditions as closely as safety considerations would allow. Finally, the 65th was one of the few infantry regiments to deploy to the theater with its full complement of officers, NCOs, and enlisted men.

The 65th Departs for Asia

Early on the morning of 27 August 1950, Governor Muñoz Marin and General Sibert held a ceremony at Fort Buchanan for the departing regiment. Although the soldiers' families were not allowed on the post for the ceremony, hundreds of spectators jammed the gates. "Our 'secret' movement orders were apparently no secret to the local populace," recorded Harris.[33] Once the ceremony concluded, the men of the 65th Infantry marched to the docks and began boarding the USNS *Marine Lynx*. Loading took six more hours than expected, primarily because of the difficulty in moving equipment-laden men through the ship's narrow stairwells and passageways. "The deployment was pretty chaotic," recalled Captain Friedman long after. "We looked a little like a rock band with all the musical instruments being carried aboard, along with all of the paraphernalia that troops embarking for a long voyage to a combat zone normally carry."[34]

At 0300 on the twenty-eighth, the *Marine Lynx* departed for Panama. "The men had filled the decks, the railings, the lifeboats, and even the superstructure of the ship, including the ladder to the crow's nest, in order to get a last glimpse of their beloved island," recalled Harris. "For the most part, they were silent as we sailed out of San Juan Harbor. . . . As I stood at the railing, I wondered how well these men would fight when they were committed to combat. A commander never really knows until after the first battle what his troops are going to do."[35]

The *Marine Lynx* arrived in Panama on 30 August. There, the 65th Infantry's 3d Battalion and regimental heavy mortar company transferred to the USS *Sergeant Howard E. Woodford* to relieve congestion aboard the *Marine Lynx*. During the night, Captain Griffin oversaw the inprocessing of 449 new NCOs and enlisted men assigned to the 3d Battalion.[36]

The next day, the regiment sailed for Japan aboard the two ships. "Our first concern after leaving Panama was getting ready for combat," Griffin

---

[33] Harris, *Puerto Rico's Fighting 65th*, p. 47.
[34] Interv, author with Friedman, 17 Sep 01.
[35] Harris, *Puerto Rico's Fighting 65th*, pp. 47–48.
[36] Army Service Questionnaire, 65th Inf, Griffin.

Members of the 1st Battalion, 65th Infantry, board the USNS Marine Lynx at the Army terminal in San Juan.

recalled. "We had two battalions and the other special units aboard [our] ship and we knew that we had to keep them busy. To do that we issued detailed directives to all units for basic tasks . . . in addition to classes on how to take care of themselves in cold weather."[37] Colonel Harris directed his regimental operations section to draw up three-month, two-month, and two-week training plans. "If we got the chance to use any of them we felt that the training would be invaluable, but we still felt that we would probably go straight to Korea," remembered Griffin.[38]

Instruction focused on the care, maintenance, assembly, and disassembly of individual and crew-served weapons; basic marksmanship; bayonet training; and squad and platoon tactics. While these were essentially the same subjects the regiment had been tested on the previous year, many of the soldiers who recently joined the 65th needed instruction in these tasks. Officers and NCOs attended day and night classes covering a wide range of military subjects.

The need to train the heavy mortar company in the use of its new 4.2-inch mortars figured prominently on Harris' priority list. This highly accurate and sturdy weapon packed as much punch as a 105-mm. artillery piece. The company was organized and equipped so that it could deploy as a complete

---

[37] Ibid.
[38] Ibid.

Members of the Regimental Headquarters Company, 65th Infantry, attend class aboard the USNS Marine Lynx *en route to Japan.*

unit in support of the entire regiment or as individual platoons in support of each infantry battalion. "It was," wrote Harris, "particularly useful in searching out defiladed areas which could not be hit by low-angle, direct-fire artillery pieces."[39] Having received the mortars in Panama, the men of the company had never fired them on land prior to arriving in Korea. The only live-fire training the heavy mortar company received before entering combat had occurred while the unit was at sea on the *Sergeant Woodford*: the crews fired their mortars off the fantail of the ship.[40]

In the evenings, motion pictures and troop-produced variety shows helped to keep the soldiers entertained. Many men attended religious services. The regimental staff published a newspaper to keep the men abreast of international and sporting events, as well as a bulletin containing lessons learned in Korea.[41] In addition, Harris instituted weekly meetings aboard ship with the senior noncommissioned officers of the regiment. The purpose of these

---

[39] Harris, *Puerto Rico's Fighting 65th*, p. 5.
[40] Ibid., p. 47.
[41] Dolcater, *3d Infantry Division*, p. 59.

gatherings was to solicit their views or complaints on matters of general interest as well as to remind them of their responsibilities as leaders in combat. According to Harris, one of the ideas that sprang from these meetings was to select a nickname for the 65th Infantry. The men of the regiment settled on the Borinqueneers, derived from one of Puerto Rico's indigenous tribes.[42]

On 10 September, the men of the 65th heard via radio that several battalions of the 24th Infantry Division had been overrun at Taejon, ninety miles south of Seoul, and that its commander, General Dean, was presumed killed in action. The regiment received the news with particular sadness because Dean's son-in-law, 1st Lt. Robert C. Williams, was serving as the executive officer of Company E.[43] The younger Williams had twice won the Distinguished Service Cross during World War II.[44]

On 15 September, the day before the 65th Infantry crossed the International Date Line, a tank detachment departed Seattle, Washington, aboard the USS *General A. W. Greely*. Originating at Fort George G. Meade, Maryland, and commanded by Capt. Arthur W. Myers, the unit consisted of eight officers and eighty-one NCOs and enlisted men manning seventeen World War II–vintage M4A3E8 Sherman medium tanks. When it arrived in Korea, it would become the 65th's heavy tank company.[45]

As the regiment continued to make its way across the Pacific Ocean, the 3d Infantry Division headquarters arrived in Japan on 16 September. The division immediately became the theater reserve and began training its two existing regiments for combat. The effort was difficult at best. Although the commissioned ranks of the 3d Division's infantry regiments were close to their full complement of 157 officers and 26 warrant officers apiece, most of the unit's rifle companies had only 40 or 50 troops, rather than the 211 authorized.[46] Indeed, the division, which was supposed to have 18,804 men, had only 7,494 when it arrived in Japan.[47]

In theory, the assignment of eight thousand three hundred South Korean recruits to the division between 19 and 24 September closed most of that gap.[48] U.S. Army losses in Korea and the amount of time required for units and personnel to reach the Orient led to a 15 August agreement between the Far East Command and the South Korean government for the temporary

---

[42] Harris, *Puerto Rico's Fighting 65th*, pp. 49–50.

[43] Ibid., p. 50.

[44] *Official Army Register: Volume I, United States Active and Retired Lists, 1 January 1951* (Washington, D.C.: Government Printing Office, 1951), p. 728.

[45] Co Morning Rpts, Tank Co Detachment, 65th Inf, 15 Sep 50, NPRC.

[46] Dolcater, *3d Infantry Division*, p. 61.

[47] Monthly Cmd Rpt, 3d Inf Div, Nov 50.

[48] Eighth United States Army Korea (EUSAK) War Diary, Sep 50, Table of Contents, 1–20 Sep 50.

assignment of Korean nationals to American combat units. Under what was known as the Korean Augmentation to the United States Army (KATUSA) program, as many as eight thousand South Koreans were to serve in each American division.[49] From the outset, the program was plagued by problems. Language barriers; cultural differences; inadequate preparatory training; and unfamiliarity with U.S. Army organization, weapons, tactics, and procedures on the part of the new recruits all greatly hindered the effectiveness of the South Korean augmentees.[50]

"The Koreans had undergone a confusing experience," the 3d Division's history would later observe. "They had been recruited hastily by the Republic of Korea Army to meet the greedy demands of war for manpower."[51] The account told how the long arm of the South Korean Army's recruiting service had snatched one young man as he was visiting a corner drugstore to buy medicine for his wife:

> He had been taken in tow, hustled aboard ship in Pusan, then had been removed to Japan . . . where he arrived in civilian clothes. . . . Along with his fellows, he had been stripped of his clothes, directed into showers, had a haircut, been dusted with DDT, had chow, been given immunization shots in both arms and received an M–1 rifle. Now he stood in ranks, looking at some crazy Americans who also were looking at him and preparing to move him to some other unknown place.[52]

On 22 September, the 65th Infantry arrived at Sasebo, Japan, where it stopped only briefly before continuing on to Pusan. At that time, Colonel Harris learned that the *Sergeant Woodford* had broken down in the middle of the Pacific and would have to return to Hawaii. The 3d Battalion and the heavy mortar company were thus not expected to arrive in Korea for another week to ten days. Harris also received word that the *General Greely* had broken down at sea and that the 65th Infantry's tank company would not make landfall for another four days.[53]

Despite these incidents, spirits in the regiment were high. A little more than a week earlier, on 15 September, Maj. Gen. Edward M. Almond's X Corps had landed at Inch'on. The amphibious assault came ashore deep in the North Korean rear and cut the enemy's supply lines. Walker's Eighth Army broke out of the Pusan Perimeter three days later. By 23 September, when the bulk of the 65th Infantry arrived in Korea, the enemy cordon

---

[49] 1st Lt Martin Blumenson, "Special Problems in the Korean Conflict," Eighth U.S. Army Korea, 5 Feb 52, p. 64, CMH.
[50] Ibid., pp. 68–69.
[51] Dolcater, *3d Infantry Division*, p. 61.
[52] Ibid.
[53] Harris, *Puerto Rico's Fighting 65th*, p. 52.

around Pusan had been shattered and the North Korean Army ceased to be an effective fighting force.

The Borinqueneers Arrive in Korea

On the day the lead elements of the 65th Infantry went ashore, the regiment numbered 3,920 officers and men, including the 89 troopers of the regimental tank company still at sea on the *Greely*.[54] All three of its infantry battalions were overstrength. The 1st Battalion had 957 personnel, 46 more than its authorization of 911. The 2d Battalion had 941. Colonel Gavin's 3d Battalion was the strongest with 1,056 men. The nine infantry companies were authorized 211 men each but averaged 224 soldiers. The three weapons companies were slightly overstrength. Authorized 165 soldiers each, they averaged 177 apiece.[55]

The 65th was thus a very welcome addition to Eighth Army. It was considerably stronger than the 1st Cavalry Division's 5th, 7th, and 8th Cavalry regiments, which averaged about two thousand five hundred men each.[56] At the same time, the six infantry regiments of the 2d and 25th Infantry Divisions averaged about two thousand four hundred men each.[57] Only the 24th Infantry Division's 19th and 21st Infantries and the separate 5th Regimental Combat Team, all of which averaged about three thousand one hundred fifty men, approached the 65th Infantry in strength.

In terms of U.S. personnel, the 65th Infantry was also larger than the other infantry regiments in General Almond's X Corps. The 7th Infantry Division's 31st Infantry had 3,461 U.S. soldiers, while the 32d Infantry had 3,154.[58] Meanwhile, the 1st Marine regiment of Maj. Gen. Oliver P. Smith's 1st Marine Division (Reinforced), which had conducted the amphibious counterattack at Inch'on, had 3,395 men on 23 September 1950 while the 5th Marines numbered 3,170.[59] Only the 7th Marines, with 3,666 Americans, resembled the 65th Infantry in size and composition.[60]

Finally, the 65th was largest of the three infantry regiments that constituted the theater reserve. The 3d Infantry Division's 7th and 15th Infantries

---

[54] Co Morning Rpts, 65th Inf, 22 Sep 50, Mil Rcds Br, NPRC.
[55] Ibid.
[56] Personnel Daily Sum, 1st Cav Div, 23 Sep 50, Eighth U.S. Army, Rcds of U.S. Army Operational, Tactical, and Support Organizations (World War II and Thereafter), RG 338, NACP.
[57] Personnel Daily Sums, 2d Inf Div, 23 Sep 50, and 25th Inf Div, 23 Sep 50.
[58] Personnel Daily Sum, 7th Inf Div, 24 Sep 50; War Diary, 7th Inf Div, Sep 50.
[59] Lynn Montross and Capt Nicholas A. Canzona, *U.S. Marine Operations in Korea, 1950–1953,* 5 vols. (Washington, D.C.: Headquarters, U.S. Marine Corps, 1955), 2: 303–04.
[60] Ibid.

each had only about 40 percent of its authorized strength, some 1,500 U.S. soldiers, when the 65th arrived. The addition of 1,700 South Korean fillers to each of these regiments raised their numbers to levels acceptable for combat.[61] Only the 4,285-man 187th Airborne Regimental Combat Team, which had just started to arrive in Korea, was larger than the 65th Infantry. This number, however, included all of the unit's attachments. The regiment itself included around 3,400 paratroopers.[62]

Arriving in Korea at virtually full strength, the 65th Infantry had enough officers and men to conduct defensive operations without fear of enemy troops infiltrating through thinly held lines. In addition, the 65th was capable of conducting sustained offensive operations despite the inevitable casualties. The unit's weapons companies had sufficient crews to man all of their heavy machine guns and mortars, which meant that the rifle battalions would enjoy the full firepower of those weapons. All things considered, the 65th arrived in much better shape to weather its first engagement than did many of its predecessors.

After disembarking in Pusan, Colonel Harris made his way to Eighth Army headquarters just north of the city. Following an update on the tactical situation, Harris was escorted into the office of the Eighth Army commander, General Walker. "I soon learned . . . that his reputation for abruptness and short, clipped sentences was well founded," Harris recalled:

> Within seconds after I sat down he asked me if I thought the Puerto Rican soldiers would fight. I minced no words in answering in equally abrupt terms. I told him that I thought they were the best soldiers that I had ever seen. . . . I had no worries about the Puerto Ricans' fighting ability or their courage; furthermore, I was prepared to go with them to do battle with anybody.[63]

Walker appeared satisfied with Harris' answers. Motioning for the regimental commander to follow him to a large window behind his desk, he showed him a number of passenger trains and the marshalling yards below: "Bill, do you see those trains? Get on them and go that way," pointing north.[64] Harris took his leave from General Walker and Eighth Army headquarters and found Colonel Childs, who had already received instructions to move the regiment to Samnangjin, twenty miles northwest of Pusan, and was at that moment marching the first elements of the 65th toward the rail

---

[61] Monthly Cmd Rpts, 7th Inf, Nov 50, and 15th Inf, Nov 50.

[62] Daily Personnel Sum, 31 Oct 50, General Headquarters (GHQ), United Nations Command (UNC), United Nations (UN)/Far East Command (FEC) GHQ, Staff Section Rpts, ann. II, G–1 Sections I–IV, 1 Jan–31 Oct 50, Entry 429, Rcds of the AGO, RG 407, NACP.

[63] Harris, *Puerto Rico's Fighting 65th*, p. 56.

[64] Ibid.

yards. The first train departed the station at 1215 carrying the 2d Battalion; a second train left the yard forty-five minutes later. Motor convoys carrying the rest of the regiment's soldiers and equipment departed Pusan at 1900 that evening and at 0500 the following day.[65]

The first train had gone only ten miles when guerrillas fired on it. The training the men received in Puerto Rico and refined on their sea journey now began to pay off. One element of the 2d Battalion established a base of fire from the stopped train while another drove off the enemy troops. "The entire episode lasted little more than thirty or forty minutes," recalled Harris, "but even in that short period of time, one could see that the Puerto Ricans had no fear whatever. They took to that little skirmish like ducks to water."[66] The battalion, which suffered no casualties in the engagement, proceeded to Samnangjin, which it reached at dusk. The remainder of the regiment continued to arrive throughout the night and into the next morning.

On 25 September, two days after the 65th Infantry arrived in Korea, Eighth Army attached the 65th to Maj. Gen. John B. Coulter's IX Corps. A graduate of the West Texas Military Academy and a veteran of the two world wars, 59-year-old Coulter had spent much of his peacetime career in Texas.[67] The Army had activated Coulter's IX Corps at Fort Sheridan, Illinois, on 10 August 1950. It had become operational in Korea on 23 September with the 2d and 25th Infantry Divisions attached. The corps' mission was to cut off and destroy retreating enemy troops within its assigned zone of operations and to assist the South Korean police in assuming control of liberated areas. Facing it were the remnants of six North Korean infantry divisions, an armored brigade, and a security regiment. The terrain in the IX Corps sector in southwest Korea was rugged and offered the North Koreans an excellent opportunity to avoid entrapment by advancing U.S. and South Korean divisions.

By the time the 65th joined the IX Corps at the end of September 1950, the North Koreans in that sector were operating mostly in small groups that rarely acted in concert. They fought from hastily organized positions and then withdrew or dispersed when faced with a determined attack. "The lack of prepared defensive positions and the lack of heavy artillery and mortar fire indicated that the enemy's supply system was disintegrating," the corps war diary reported. "Ammunition and vehicles were discovered abandoned, [the latter] apparently due to the lack of fuel to operate."[68]

---

[65] Periodic Opns Rpt no. 220, 23–26 Sep 50, EUSAK War Diary, Sep 50.

[66] Harris, *Puerto Rico's Fighting 65th*, p. 58.

[67] *Generals of the Army* (Washington, D.C.: Office of the Chief of Staff of the Army, 1953), pp. 5–6.

[68] IX Corps War Diary, Sep 50.

Intending the regiment to spend two weeks training near Samnangjin before committing to combat, IX Corps initially assigned the 65th Infantry to a relatively quiet sector between the town and the Naktong River. (*Map 1*) On 27 September, the corps attached the 65th to Maj. Gen. Lawrence B. Keiser's 2d Infantry Division. The division had crossed the Naktong on 18 September and was now attacking westward. It had been involved in fierce fighting since its arrival, suffering almost four thousand eight hundred battle casualties and another two thousand nonbattle casualties.[69] The 65th Infantry joined General Keiser's command as the lead elements of the 2d Division were nearing Chonju, an important crossroads one hundred twenty miles northwest of Pusan that was no more than twenty miles from the western coast of Korea. Despite the rapid progress of the 2d Division, however, pockets of enemy resistance remained throughout its sector. The first task of the 65th would be to reduce or eliminate the threat to U.S. supply lines and to the corps rear area.

The Regiment Enters Combat

Harris reported to the division command post, where General Keiser directed him to assemble the 65th's regimental headquarters and support elements near the village of Changyong, twenty-one miles northwest of Samnangjin and eight miles east of the Naktong. The general ordered the 65th Infantry to send a rifle battalion forward to relieve a battalion of the 9th Infantry on Hill 409, some ten miles north of Changyong. A second battalion would secure the bridge at Yuga-myon along the main supply route linking the division with the Eighth Army supply base at Pusan. The regiment was to look for the remains of the North Korean *10th Division*, which meant that the regiment (with only two infantry battalions because the 3d Battalion was still en route to Korea from Hawaii) would have to patrol a forty-square-mile area to locate and destroy whatever enemy troops remained.[70]

To accomplish the mission, General Keiser augmented the 65th Infantry with two batteries from the 15th and 503d Field Artillery Battalions, a platoon of tanks from the 9th Infantry regimental tank company, and a battery from the 82d Anti-Aircraft Artillery (AAA) Automatic Weapons Battalion.[71] It was all the division could spare. The automatic-

---

[69] Personnel Daily Sum, 2d Inf Div, 27 Sep 50.

[70] Monthly Cmd Rpt, 2d Inf Div, Nov 50; Harris, *Puerto Rico's Fighting 65th*, pp. 61–62.

[71] Monthly Cmd Rpt, 2d Inf Div, Sep 50. The 503d Field Artillery Battalion was composed of black enlisted men with mostly white officers. For a history of the battalion in Korea, see William M. Donnelly, *We Can Do It: The 503d Field Artillery Battalion in the Korean War* (Washington, D.C.: U.S. Army Center of Military History, 2001).

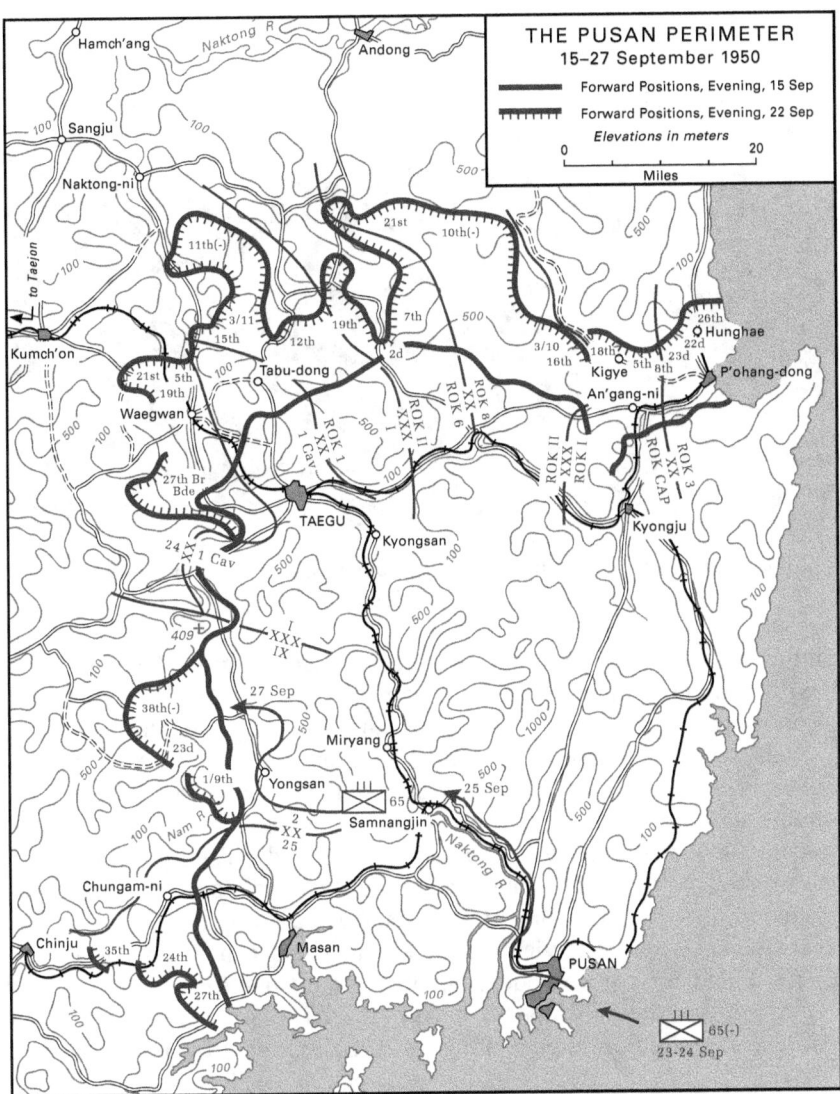

Map 1

weapons battery consisted of quad Browning M2HB .50-caliber machine guns mounted on eight M16 halftracks and eight M19 full-tracked vehicles with twin 40-mm. cannons. With an effective rate of fire up to fifteen hundred .50-caliber or two hundred forty 40-mm. rounds per minute, each of these weapon systems, originally intended for air defense, were capable of

Trucks carrying the 65th Infantry to the front cross a bridge over the Naktong River in October 1950.

putting out a tremendous amount of direct fire against ground targets. With the exception of fighter-bombers using napalm and rockets, no other U.S. weapon could defeat and demoralize enemy troops more quickly.[72]

The regiment's first major tactical mission took place the next day, 28 September. Dammer's 2d Battalion relieved the 9th Infantry's 2d Battalion on Hill 409 and then attacked a nearby hill defended by a small enemy force, taking the objective at a cost of six wounded.[73] The following day, a patrol from the regimental Intelligence and Reconnaissance Platoon, commanded by 1st Lt. Jose Torres-Caban, engaged a group of enemy soldiers near Chang-dong, in the vicinity of Chonju. The patrol, at the cost of one soldier killed and two wounded, captured five prisoners.[74]

Soon after the 65th was attached to the 2d Infantry Division, Eighth Army also assigned a large contingent of Korean recruits to the regiment. "To my absolute disgust, the following morning 1,150 South Korean soldiers arrived at my CP [command post] with orders from Eighth Army assigning them to us," recalled Harris, who made no secret of his disdain for the new recruits. "Having 1,150 South Koreans, or even 50, to watch in addition to our other problems, was all that we needed. If they had been

---

[72] S. L. A. Marshall, *Infantry Operations & Weapons Usage in Korea* (London: Greenhill Books, 1988), pp. 110–11.
[73] Monthly Cmd Rpts, 2d Inf Div, Sep 50, and 3d Inf Div, Nov 50.
[74] Morning Rpt, HQ and HQ Co, 65th Inf, 29 Sep 50, Mil Rcds Br, NPRC.

Staff of the 2d Battalion, 65th Infantry, during a lull in the action near Kumch'on, October 1950

North Koreans, I would have known what to do with them, but South Koreans I wanted no part of."[75]

Regardless, Harris devised a way to make it appear that his unit had tried to integrate the Koreans among its ranks. "We assigned one South Korean soldier to each of our ten-man squads," he wrote:

> With nine of our men watching him all the time, he couldn't do much damage. When one of them committed an offense requiring disciplinary action, and this was frequent, our procedure was to relieve him of his weapons, ammunition, and equipment, lead him out to the road, point him in the direction of Pusan, and motion for him to start walking.

According to Harris, within three months, the original contingent of augmentees had shrunk down to forty or fifty "whom our men felt they could trust, although I never did."[76]

For two reasons, Harris escaped official censure for his decision to turn away large numbers of South Korean soldiers. First, other American

---

[75] Harris, *Puerto Rico's Fighting 65th*, p. 64.
[76] Ibid.

regiment and division commanders were expressing their dissatisfaction with the KATUSA program, viewing the augmentees as burdens rather than as assets.[77] Second, Eighth Army had recently decided to use KATUSAs to reconstitute the shattered South Korean Army. Before the end of the year, over nine thousand were transferred from the American 2d, 3d, and 24th Infantry Divisions and 1st Cavalry Division to the South Korean military.[78]

Although the 3d Division had temporarily relinquished control of the 65th Infantry, it sent reinforcements to Harris in the form of the 58th AFA Battalion, along with Company C, 10th Engineer Battalion, and Battery C, 3d AAA Battalion. Colonel Gavin's 3d Battalion arrived in Pusan at the beginning of October, after transferring from the broken-down USS *Sergeant Woodford* to the USS *General Edwin D. Patrick* in Hawaii, and joined the regiment at Changyong.[79] In light of the new additions, Keiser decided to give the 65th a more prominent role.

Shortly after the arrival of the 3d Battalion, Gavin was promoted to colonel and reassigned. Harris appointed his regimental operations officer, Maj. Edward G. Allen, as the new battalion commander. A graduate of the University of Vermont, 37-year-old Allen had earned two Bronze Stars and a Purple Heart during World War II.[80] Captain Friedman, who had previously worked under Allen as the assistant regimental operations officer, found him to be an outstanding officer. "He was sound, undemonstrative, and tactically capable," he said. "Allen was always deeply involved with his companies, checking weapons emplacements and showing great concern about the troops."[81] Friedman became the new regimental chief operations officer.

With all of its components now gathered together into a full regimental combat team, the 65th began to hunt for the North Koreans in earnest. As the men of the regiment searched for the enemy, they became familiar with enemy tactics and how best to counter them. "We learned . . . that our most effective technique was to hunt out and destroy them during the daylight hours and then to go into an all-around, wagon-wheel, defensive position on the high ground at night," wrote Harris. "We also learned to remain in those defensive positions no matter how many of the enemy attacked us."[82]

---

[77] Blumenson, "Special Problems," p. 71.
[78] Exact figures vary between 9,946 and 13,601 personnel. Ibid., p. 72.
[79] Harris, *Puerto Rico's Fighting 65th*, p. 69.
[80] *Official Army Register, 1 January 1950*, p. 12.
[81] Interv, author with Friedman, 17 Sep 01.
[82] Harris, *Puerto Rico's Fighting 65th*, p. 70.

Colonel Harris (fourth from left) with his commanders and a visiting colonel at Kumch'on, 20 October 1950. Colonel St. Clair is immediately to Harris' right, Colonel Dammer is third from left, and Major Allen is second from left. Below, Sgt. Modesto Cartagena (far left) and M.Sgt. Manuel Freytes (far right) check the identification cards of Korean civilians passing through the 65th Infantry's area of operations.

The good working relationship between the 65th Infantry and the 58th AFA Battalion contributed significantly to the regiment's increasing effectiveness as a combat team. Capt. Robert L. Adams, an artillery liaison officer who met frequently with Harris' staff, observed:

> The infantry battalion commanders were very cooperative and we always coordinated with the mortar company. I believe they were absolutely convinced that the artillery was part of their team. From my observation, I can't think of any time when we could not give them just about what they wanted. . . . I can recall we had patrols staying out all night and we would ring them with an absolute ring of artillery fire and kept the enemy away from the hill all the way around. We did not fire just in front—we made a circle.[83]

On 4 October, the 65th Infantry moved north some thirty-five miles from Changyong to the Waegwan-Kumch'on region, where it relieved the 27th British Commonwealth Infantry Brigade and secured the 2d Division's main supply route. As it had for the previous week, the regiment sought to block the escape routes of retreating North Korean units while overcoming isolated points of resistance and conducting antiguerrilla sweeps.

On 5 October, the regiment left the 2d Division and joined General Kean's 25th Infantry Division. During the second week of October, the unit's regimental tank company and the heavy mortar company joined the 65th in the field.[84] Colonel Harris broke the mortar company into platoons and assigned one to each rifle battalion, which normally operated as self-supporting combat teams. Colonel St. Clair's 1st Battalion fought with Battery A, 58th AFA Battalion, attached. It also had the 1st Platoons of the 65th Infantry's heavy mortar company, medical company, and regimental service company. Colonel Dammer's 2d Battalion fought with Battery B and the 2d Platoons of the same support units, while Major Allen's 3d Battalion fought with Battery C and the 3d Platoons of the support units. Control of the tank company, Company C, 10th Engineers, and Battery C, 3d AAA Battalion, remained with Colonel Harris at regimental headquarters.[85]

While attached to the 25th Division, the 65th fought a number of small actions that gradually developed the regiment's fighting skills. The 65th's most significant battle during the month took place on the morning of 17 October, after an aerial observer from the 35th Infantry detected an estimated four hundred North Korean soldiers near Yongam-ni, a village ten

---

[83] Debfg Rpt no. 71, Capt Robert L. Adams, 58th Armored Field Artillery (AFA) Bn, 3d Inf Div, Sep 50–Dec 51, 26 Feb 52, Dept of Training Publications and Aids, Artillery School, copy in Historians files.

[84] Monthly Cmd Rpts, 2d Inf Div, Sep 50, and 3d Inf Div, Nov 50.

[85] Monthly Cmd Rpt, 65th Inf, Nov 50.

Colonel Harris (left) confers with General Kean (center) and Col. Mariano C. Auzrin of the 10th Philippines Battalion Combat Team near Waegwan, 8 October 1950.

miles west of Hamch'ang.[86] That information put the 65th Infantry on alert, most of all Colonel St. Clair's 2d Battalion located near Hamch'ang.

The North Koreans landed the first blow, targeting 1st Lt. Albert E. Carsely's Company E, which had taken up positions near the village of Sin'gi-dong only a short distance from Hamch'ang. Taking advantage of the predawn darkness, a large North Korean force infiltrated to within yards of the Americans without being detected. At 0615, the enemy launched a surprise attack that quickly penetrated the Company E perimeter. Lieutenant Carsely emerged from his command post and saw a North Korean soldier only seven yards away and running in his direction. The lieutenant shot the man with his carbine and then rallied his soldiers, leading them in a successful counterattack. The North Koreans retreated after losing seventy-eight killed and another sixty-four captured.[87]

The 65th followed that success with smaller sweep operations over the last ten days of the month between Kumch'on and Hamch'ang. The regiment captured 350 North Korean soldiers and killed hundreds more.[88] By

---

[86] Unit Rpt no. 12, HQ, RCT 35, Bk 8, War Diaries—Unit Rpts, 25th Inf Div, Oct 50.

[87] GO no. 337, 25th Inf Div, 15 Nov 50, sub: Award of Silver Star to Lieutenant Albert E. Carsely, in Monthly Cmd Rpt, 65th Inf, Nov 50.

[88] Narr, 18 Oct 50, IX Corps War Diary, Oct 50.

the end of October, the 65th had taken a total of 921 prisoners while killing or wounding more than 600 enemy soldiers. In the process, it sustained thirty-eight battle casualties.[89]

Responding to a query from Puerto Rico on the state and performance of the regiment in Korea, General MacArthur observed that the unit was "showing magnificent ability and courage in field operations" and deemed it a credit to Puerto Rico.[90]

---

[89] Daily Personnel Sum, UN/FEC GHQ, 31 Oct 50, Staff Section Rpts, G–1 Sections I–IV, Rcds of GHQ, FEC, Supreme Cdr Allied Powers, and UNC, RG 554, NACP; Monthly Cmd Rpt, 65th Inf, Nov 50.

[90] Ltr, Gen Douglas MacArthur, to HQ, U.S. Army Forces in the Antilles and in the Mil Dist of Puerto Rico, n.d., RG 96–20, Gen Archives of Puerto Rico.

Chapter 3

WITH X CORPS IN NORTH KOREA NOVEMBER–DECEMBER 1950

At the end of October, the 65th Infantry found itself attached to General Almond's X Corps. The 58-year-old Almond, a graduate of the Virginia Military Institute, was a decorated veteran of World Wars I and II. Before the attack on Pearl Harbor, he had served as the assistant division commander of the 93d Infantry Division; during the war, he had commanded the 92d Infantry Division in Italy. The 92d was the only all-black unit to fight as a complete division in World War II. Its initial battlefield performance, however, left much to be desired and only seemed to confirm many of Almond's deep-seated racial prejudices.

After World War II, Almond served as the chief of staff for personnel of the Army Forces in the Pacific; the deputy chief of staff of the Far East Command; and finally as the chief of staff of the Far East Command under General MacArthur.[1] Impressed with Almond's ability and loyalty, MacArthur handpicked him to plan and execute the Inch'on operation. In addition to his appointment as commanding general of X Corps, originally known as the Far East Command Reserve Headquarters, Almond retained his position as MacArthur's chief of staff and as deputy commander of the Far East Command. This arrangement meant that Almond reported to MacArthur and not to General Walker, the Eighth Army commander.[2]

On 27 September, General MacArthur received a "personal for" message from the Joint Chiefs of Staff authorizing him to conduct military operations north of the 38th Parallel. Two days later, X Corps recaptured Seoul. By 2 October, the American press was reporting that South Korean troops had crossed the 38th Parallel. MacArthur responded by ordering the

---

[1] *Generals of the Army*, pp. 1–3.
[2] Military History Section, FEC, "History of the Korean War," pt. 2, vol. 1, "General Headquarters Support and Participation (25 Jun 50–30 Apr 51)," ch. 5, pp. 16–17, CMH.

General Almond aboard a Navy helicopter, 30 October 1950

entire Eighth Army to begin advancing north while X Corps withdrew from Inch'on and prepared to conduct another amphibious landing on the eastern coast of Korea. Once ashore, General Almond's troops would establish blocking positions between Wonsan and P'yongyang to delay the retreating enemy units long enough to allow Eighth Army to complete their destruction.[3] MacArthur believed that North Korea would capitulate only after its armed forces were eliminated.

The discovery of underwater mines in the North Korean harbor at Wonsan, a city one hundred ten air miles northeast of Seoul and the proposed site of X Corps' second amphibious assault, delayed operations for a week. As X Corps awaited word from the U.S. Navy that the harbor was clear, the South Korean I Corps advanced rapidly northward along the eastern coastline of North Korea against sporadic resistance. The force captured Wonsan on 10 October. Hamhung, an important transportation hub sixty-five miles farther north, fell eight days later.

Regardless of recent successes, MacArthur was determined to maintain pressure on the North Koreans. On 24 October, he removed all restrictions on the use of United Nations (UN) ground forces after determining that "tactical considerations overcame the political aspects of employing only ROK [Republic of Korea, or South Korean] troops in areas contiguous to the border of North Korea."[4] In order to facilitate cooperation between the South Korean and UN units converging on that area, he placed the South Korean I Corps under Almond's command and gave X Corps operational responsibility for northeastern Korea. At that point, Almond's force included the South Korean 3d and Capital Divisions, the U.S. 1st Marine Division, the U.S. 3d and 7th Infantry Divisions, and the South Korean 1st Marine Regiment. All told, X Corps numbered 85,200 men:

---

[3] Ibid., ch. 6, pp. 22–24.
[4] Ibid., p. 34.

51,500 American and 33,700 South Korean soldiers.[5] Elements of X Corps, including Almond's headquarters and the 1st Marine Division, began landing at Wonsan on 26 October 1950. (*See Map 2.*) Three days later, the 7th Infantry Division landed one hundred fifty miles to the northwest at the port of Iwon.[6]

Wonsan had always played an important role in both United Nations and North Korean operational planning. A moderate-size seaport, the city was located at the southern tip of the Hamhung-Hungnam-Wonsan area, which encompassed the industrialized heart of North Korea. It was an important road and rail hub with connections fanning out to other parts of the country. Paved roads led westward to the North Korean capital, P'yongyang, southwestward to P'yonggang, and southward along the coast all the way to Pusan. All those factors made Wonsan a natural focal point for military operations.[7]

Despite the relatively well-developed road network in the area, X Corps had to overcome the extremely rugged terrain that characterized most of northeastern Korea. Even the coastal plain hardly deserved the name. The only level or semilevel land along the coast was limited to isolated pockets extending no more than three to five miles inland. To the west and northwest of the coast lay the T'aebaek Mountains with steep slopes and narrow, twisting valleys. The peaks in the highest part of the range reached six thousand feet or more. Although winter temperatures often dropped to 20 or 30 degrees below zero, snow during October and November was rare; even in December, it would not accumulate to form deep drifts. Beginning forty air miles northward from Hamhung and extending another forty miles north into the heart of the T'aebaeks was the Changjin Reservoir.[8] The smaller Pujon Reservoir was fifteen miles to the northeast. The principal road north from the Wonsan-Hamhung plain climbed the T'aebaek Mountains to the Kot'o-ri plateau and then continued on to Hagaru-ri at the southern end of the Changjin Reservoir. A second major traffic artery curved northeast from Hamhung toward the Soviet border. Secondary routes were extremely rare and in most cases consisted of scarcely more than mountain trails.[9]

The initial X Corps landings on the northeast coast of Korea met with little or no enemy resistance. While the South Koreans continued to advance up the coast to the northeast, the U.S. 1st Marine and 7th

---

[5] Appleman, *South to the Naktong, North to the Yalu*, pp. 684–85.

[6] War Diary, X Corps, Monthly Sum, 1 Oct 50–31 Oct 50, Wonsan-Iwon Landings. Unless otherwise noted, all War Diaries, Cmd Rpts, and Monthly Sums are in Entry 429, Rcds of the AGO, RG 407, NACP.

[7] Dolcater, *3d Infantry Division in Korea*, p. 68.

[8] UN forces usually called the Changjin Reservoir by its Japanese name, the Chosin Reservoir.

[9] Appleman, *South to the Naktong, North to the Yalu*, p. 685.

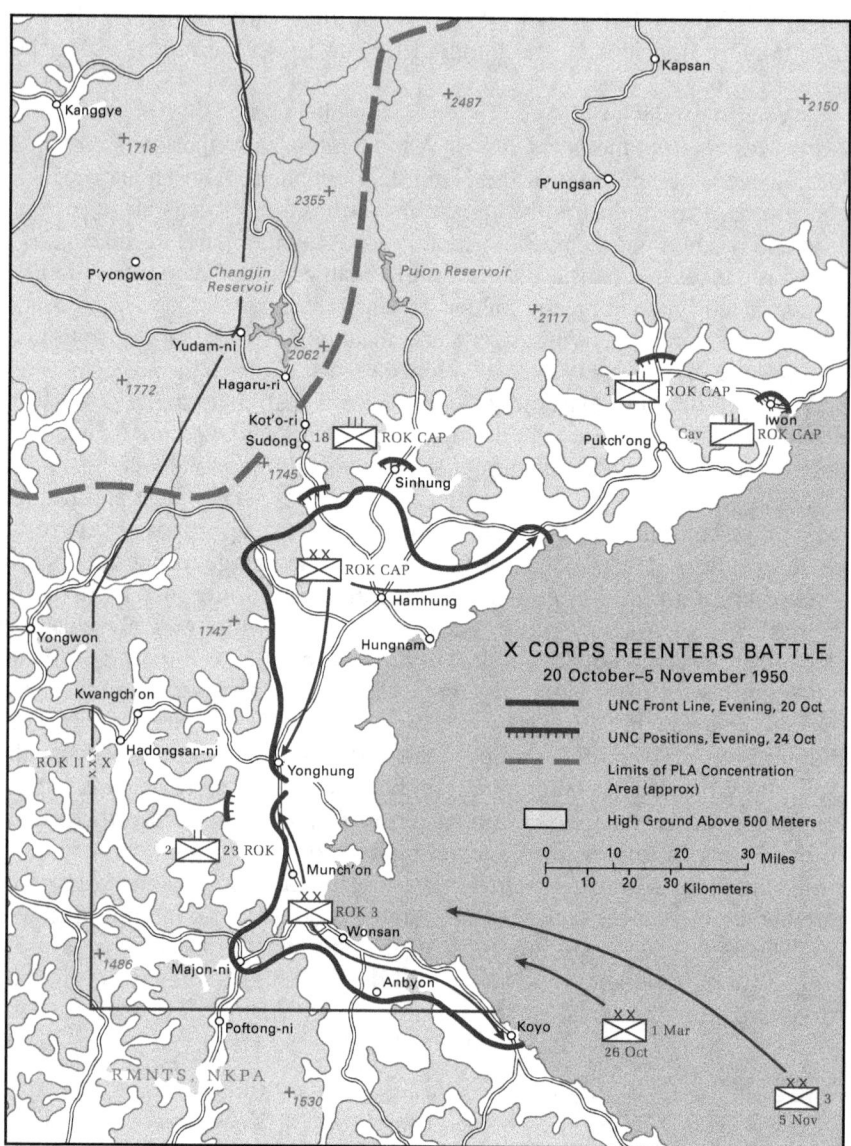

MAP 2

Infantry Divisions headed inland to encircle and destroy the remnants of the North Korean Army gathered in the mountains one hundred miles northeast of P'yongyang. The Eighth Army's pursuit had been temporarily halted until enough supplies could be pushed forward to restart the offensive.[10]

Moving northwest from Iwon toward the Manchurian border, the 7th Division initially reported light opposition from the North Koreans. The 1st Marine Division, on the other hand, encountered resistance south of Wonsan from small, organized groups of retreating enemy soldiers. The marines succeeded in dispersing the enemy after several days of hard fighting. North Korean units operating in the area north of Hungnam, particularly near the Changjin and Pujon Reservoirs, were also putting up a stiff fight. According to intelligence gathered by the South Korean I Corps, the North Korean Army had undergone a major reorganization and was no longer on the verge of disintegrating. Raising another warning flag that the war might continue longer than anticipated, the capture of two Chinese soldiers twenty miles south of the Changjin Reservoir near Sudong on 28 October signaled the presence of Chinese troops in North Korea. Over the next several days, the South Koreans succeeded in capturing twenty-three more Chinese.[11] In return, the Chinese scattered three South Korean regiments and destroyed a fourth.[12]

November opened ominously for the men of the U.S. Eighth Army. Late in the evening of 1 November, the Chinese *39th Army* launched a series of massive attacks against the U.S. 1st Cavalry Division's 5th and 8th Cavalries near Unsan, fifty miles south of the Chinese border. The Communists swarmed over the positions of the outnumbered Americans, inflicting heavy casualties and forcing them to retreat. The 8th Cavalry lost over eight hundred men, almost one-third of its strength, including two- to three hundred captured. Equipment losses included twelve howitzers, ten tanks, and a tank-recovery vehicle. On 3 November, the 8th Cavalry reported that it had only 45 percent of its authorized strength, leading the 1st Cavalry Division to rate the unit combat ineffective.[13]

The Chinese also launched a punishing assault near Chongch'on against the British Commonwealth 27th Infantry Brigade and the U.S. 24th Division's 19th Infantry. These and other elements of Eighth Army fell back ten miles to the southwest to new defensive positions along the Chongch'on River. The Chinese, however, broke off their attacks and by

---

[10] FEC, "History of the Korean War," pt. 2, vol. 1, ch. 7, p. 1.

[11] Appleman, *South to the Naktong, North to the Yalu*, pp. 687–88.

[12] These were the 2d, 7th, 10th, and 19th Regiments. A number of American advisers were also killed or captured during these engagements. Ibid., pp. 673–75.

[13] Ibid., pp. 707–08.

November appeared to have vanished into the hills and valleys of northeastern Korea.[14]

The Chinese offensive came as a shock to the United Nations Command. After the breakout from the Pusan Perimeter and the spectacular success of the Inch'on landings, the war in Korea seemed to have been virtually won. As MacArthur's forces pursued fleeing North Korean troops in mid-October, he held a one-day conference with President Truman at Wake Island to discuss future strategy. Truman cautioned MacArthur to look for indications that the Soviet Union or Communist China might enter the war. Convinced he could reunify Korea in short order, MacArthur paid little heed to the president's caution, moving north until the clashes between Eighth Army and the Chinese brought his advance to a halt.[15]

Advance into Northeastern Korea

The 65th Regimental Combat Team moved to Pusan and prepared to land at Wonsan to support the X Corps and 3d Infantry Division moves into northeastern Korea. Each of the 65th RCT's task-organized battalion combat teams (BCTs) contained a headquarters company, a heavy-weapons company, and three rifle companies, as well as a field artillery battery, an antiaircraft artillery platoon, a medical platoon, and a service section. Colonel Harris also intended to cross-attach platoons from the regimental heavy mortar company to each of his battalions but neglected to issue such orders prior to moving out. Rather than parcel out all of the regiment's supporting elements to each battalion, however, Harris retained control over the 65th's tank company; Company C, 10th Engineer Battalion; and the 3d Platoon, 1st Clearing Company, 3d Medical Battalion.[16]

The regimental command group departed for Wonsan by airplane on 2 November. At X Corps headquarters in Hamhung, the chief of logistics, Col. Aubrey D. Smith, a West Point graduate and an old friend of Harris, briefed the group on the regiment's upcoming mission. He told Harris that after moving to Yonghung (thirty-five miles north of Wonsan) the 65th was to shift seventy miles due west to make contact with the 1st Cavalry Division on Eighth Army's right flank. Once the 65th was in position, Colonel Harris was to find and interdict enemy forces coming from the north and to develop the situation as it arose.

"Now on the face of it, that didn't sound too bad," Harris later wrote, "but when he said that the enemy force consisted of two Chinese armies and

---

[14] Ibid., pp. 712–15.
[15] Schnabel, *Policy and Direction*, pp. 212–13.
[16] Monthly Cmd Rpt, 65th Inf, Nov 50.

that no one really knew even the approximate location of Eighth Army's right flank, those two factors made a difference."[17] Complicating matters were the distances involved and the formidable T'aebaek Mountains, a major obstacle to east-west movement.

Later that evening, at a dinner hosted by the X Corps commander, General Almond asked Colonel Harris about his Puerto Rican soldiers. Harris clearly sensed that Almond harbored deep misgivings about units not composed of white soldiers. "I told him the same things I had said to General Walker and then brought him up to date on our activities since we had been in Korea," remembered Harris.[18]

A staff meeting followed the meal. Almond personally briefed Harris and the commanding general of the 1st Marine Division on their respective missions.[19] As soon as the meeting concluded, Harris departed for his own command post, where he instructed the staff to immediately begin drawing plans for the westward movement.

Eager to show Almond the capabilities of the 65th RCT, Harris was not above giving his regiment a bit of an advantage in carrying out its difficult mission. While waiting the following morning for the main body of his regiment to land at Wonsan, Harris purloined a communications van powerful enough to maintain a radio connection between Korea and Japan. "This was a real find," the regimental commander later acknowledged. "I only hoped that no one discovered that I was stealing it from the corps or that someone decided to give the operators a mission that would prevent them from going with me."[20] The incident illustrates one of Harris' most basic tenets in Korea, namely, a recognition of the need for reliable communications at all times. He was willing to take whatever steps were necessary to maintain contact with higher headquarters.

The 1st and 2d Battalions arrived on 5 November after an uneventful sea journey from Pusan. They were the first troops from the 3d Infantry Division to land in North Korea.[21] Badgered by Almond to keep on schedule, Harris and his battalion commanders worked frantically to offload the troops and to begin moving toward Yonghung. By late evening, Lt. Col. Herman W. Dammer's 2d Battalion departed Wonsan aboard trucks provided by X Corps. The unit rode throughout the night and the following day, arriving at Yonghung on the evening of 6 November. It pitched its camp on the high ground west of the town. Colonel Dammer established radio communications with X Corps as the 2d Battalion began to dig in on

---

[17] Harris, *Puerto Rico's Fighting 65th*, p. 85.
[18] Ibid., p. 88.
[19] Ibid.
[20] Ibid., pp. 89–90.
[21] HQ, X Corps, Nov War Diary Sums, 1 Nov–30 Nov 50.

the high ground. Harris waited for his other battalions to arrive, only to discover belatedly that General Almond had diverted Lt. Col. Howard B. St. Clair's 1st Battalion and Major Allen's 3d Battalion to reinforce the 1st Marine Division near Munch'on, ten miles northwest of Wonsan.[22]

The 2d Battalion was not the only American unit bivouacked at Yonghung. The 96th Field Artillery Battalion established an overnight defensive perimeter near the town en route to the 1st Marine Division. The 96th's assistant operations officer, Capt. Edward F. Gudgel Jr., noted the 65th's arrival: "Late in the evening an infantry battalion and regimental headquarters moved onto the high ground about 800 yards to our rear. However, we did not establish communications or coordinate defense immediately."[23]

Failure to tie in with the infantry would have severe consequences. At 0300, after silently overpowering a security outpost, North Korean troops penetrated the 96th Field Artillery Battalion's perimeter.[24] Armed with rifles, automatic weapons, and at least one small mortar, the enemy set fire to several vehicles. Trucks loaded with fuel and ammunition began exploding, tossing flaming debris and deadly fragments in all directions. Although several 155-mm. howitzers were destroyed, the artillerymen prevented their attackers from inflicting further damage.[25]

The nearby 2d Battalion did not have long to wait for its first taste of combat north of the 38th Parallel. At 0330 on 7 November, elements of the North Korean *11th Regiment, 5th Division*, struck Capt. Antonio Muña's Company G and Capt. Tomas H. Guffain's Company F. The attackers were supported by accurate mortar fire that the Americans were unable to suppress using their own mortars. "In our haste to get on toward our objective, I had frankly overlooked the attachment of the regimental mortar company to the 2d Battalion," Harris admitted. "There are times in combat when a commander wonders just why he did or did not take some particular action, and this was one of those times for me."[26]

After three hours of fighting, the 2d Battalion had dangerously low ammunition reserves because the unit had not been given enough time to pick up extra ammunition from X Corps stockpiles when it debarked at Wonsan. Apprised of the problem, Harris transmitted a priority message to

---

[22] Harris, *Puerto Rico's Fighting 65th*, pp. 91–95.

[23] Capt E. F. Gudgel, Asst S–3, 96th Field Artillery (FA) Bn, Sep 50–Oct 51, Debfg Rpt no. 55, 20 Dec 51, Dept of Training Publications and Aids, Artillery School, Fort Sill, Okla., copy in Historians files, CMH.

[24] Ibid.

[25] Capt Fred Schoomaker, Comdr, B Btry, 96th FA Bn, Oct 50–Dec 50, Debfg Rpt no. 57, 21 Dec 51, Dept of Training Publications and Aids, Artillery School, copy in Historians files.

[26] Harris, *Puerto Rico's Fighting 65th*, p. 98.

X Corps using his recently appropriated communications van. He requested an airdrop of ammunition, medical supplies, and food at first light. As he coordinated the emergency resupply mission, ammunition shortages forced one platoon from Company G to abandon its positions to the enemy. Later, elements of the North Korean *11th Regiment* succeeded in overwhelming a platoon from Company F.

Despite dwindling ammunition supplies, the 2d Battalion counterattacked at dawn to regain the ground it had lost during the night. By 0700, Companies F and G had reoccupied their original positions. Seven C–47 transports delivered two-and-one-half tons of desperately needed ammunition and supplies to Dammer's troops thirty minutes later.[27] "We were now prepared to fight it out on the top of that mountain until doomsday, or at least until we could get our other battalions up with us," recalled Harris, who admitted that the continued survival of the unit had depended on the airdrop.[28]

The 96th Field Artillery Battalion also succeeded in getting one of its observation planes aloft. The pilot lost no time in bringing the unit's surviving howitzers to bear against the enemy troops. The shelling was reported as "very effective" by an American soldier who was briefly held by the North Koreans.[29]

Faced with the prospect of further losses for little gain, the enemy chose to break contact. The 2d Battalion, 65th Infantry, suffered 29 casualties, including 5 Americans and 1 South Korean augmentee killed and 21 Americans and 2 South Koreans wounded. Known North Korean losses totaled 19 killed and 25 captured, but it was widely believed that the retreating Communists also evacuated a number of their dead and wounded from the battlefield.[30]

Since arriving at Wonsan less than forty-eight hours earlier, Harris had made three mistakes, all of which he later acknowledged. First, he had neglected to attach a platoon from the heavy mortar company to the 2d Battalion. This error had deprived the unit of weapons that would have been able to silence North Korean mortars positioned in defilade. Second, Harris had failed to ensure that his troops had sufficient ammunition prior to departing Wonsan. Had it not been for the emergency resupply provided by airdrop, Dammer's battalion would have had to relinquish the high ground west of Yonghung. Third, Harris had failed to order the 96th Field Artillery Battalion to reposition its howitzers so they would have been integrated into the defensive perimeter of the 2d Battalion. These were the sort of

---

[27] William M. Leary, *Anything, Anytime, Anywhere: Combat Cargo in the Korean War*, U.S. Air Force in the Korean War (Washington, D.C.: Air Force History and Museums Program, 2000), p. 12.

[28] Harris, *Puerto Rico's Fighting 65th*, p. 103.

[29] Gudgel, Debfg Rpt no. 55, 20 Dec 51.

[30] Monthly Cmd Rpt, 65th Inf, Nov 50.

Colonel Harris (left) with Maj. Gen. William H. Turner of the Far East Air Force's Combat Cargo Command. Turner's pilots dropped vitally needed supplies to Dammer's 2d Battalion.

mistakes a more-experienced combat commander would never have made and that Harris would not repeat.

Shortly after the fighting concluded, General Almond arrived at Harris' command post to talk with him about the battle. While both were en route to the 2d Battalion aid station, the general remarked to Harris that he had little confidence in these "colored" troops because "he had a bitter experience with them in Italy and . . . didn't trust them." Harris responded that although there were indeed some black Puerto Ricans and Virgin Islanders in the ranks of the 65th, the bulk of his troops were white. "The men of the 65th are white Puerto Ricans," he stressed, "and I might say that the colored troops have fought like real troopers. We haven't had any trouble with them." Almond had nothing more to say on the subject.[31] Later that day, he sent Harris a message complimenting the regiment on a fine job.[32]

---

[31] Harris, *Puerto Rico's Fighting 65th*, pp. 104–05.
[32] Monthly Cmd Rpt, 65th Inf, Nov 50.

Although allied forces had suffered some setbacks in early November 1950, the United Nations Command was still optimistic. Despite the unexpected Chinese riposte, which the Chinese government said was the work of "volunteer" troops acting spontaneously on behalf of the North Korean people, the UNC position as a whole appeared favorable for renewed offensive operations. The North Korean Army had been defeated, with its remnants fleeing into the central mountain range to conduct guerrilla warfare or retreating north toward sanctuary in China. Eighth Army defensive positions along the Chongch'on River, halfway between the 38th Parallel and the Yalu River, appeared formidable. The 1st Cavalry Division had taken a beating, but two of its regiments were still in good condition. Despite earlier trials, the 24th and 25th Infantry Divisions were generally in good condition. On Eighth Army's right flank, the U.S. 2d Infantry Division was in position to backstop the South Korean 6th and 8th Infantry Divisions. Meanwhile, the five divisions of X Corps (the South Korean Capital and 3d Divisions, the U.S. 3d and 7th Divisions, and the U.S. 1st Marine Division) were fresh and, in the case of the 1st Marine Division, at full strength. Many of the UN soldiers were looking forward to attacking north to the Yalu to end the war and return home by Christmas.

The 65th RCT's war in North Korea had nevertheless just begun. At 0630 on 9 November, for the second time, the North Koreans hit the 2d Battalion occupying the high ground west of Yonghung. The Americans repulsed the attack, killing thirty-four of the enemy and capturing forty. Later that day, the 3d Battalion arrived in Yonghung after being relieved from its brief attachment to the marines. On 10 November, the 1st Battalion also arrived, accompanied by the 58th AFA Battalion, which immediately commenced firing missions against known or suspected enemy troop concentrations.[33]

The 3d Division's tactical command post established itself at Wonsan at midnight on 10 November. The 65th Infantry returned to division control the following day. While the remainder of the X Corps advanced north against scattered opposition, the 3d Division received orders to station one infantry battalion in Hamhung as the corps reserve. Overall, the division was to protect X Corps' western flank, to prepare for offensive operations into north-central Korea, to secure the corps' logistical hub at Wonsan, and to relieve the 1st Marine Division north of the 3d Division's area of operations near the Changjin Reservoir. To assist General Soule in carrying out these missions, the 3d Division received operational control of the South Korean 26th Infantry Regiment of the Capital Division.[34]

---

[33] Ibid.
[34] Monthly Cmd Rpt, 3d Inf Div, Nov 50.

Self-propelled 105-mm. howitzer of the 58th Armored Field Artillery Battalion displacing to a new firing position

The 3d Division's newly designated area of operations spanned ninety by thirty-five miles. According to Soule, it was too large to permit effective centralized control. As a consequence, the general decided to fight the division as four semiautonomous regimental combat teams. Col. John S. Guthrie commanded the division reserve, which consisted of his own 7th Infantry along with the 64th Heavy Tank Battalion. The force was to secure the coastal area between the port of Hungnam (five miles southeast of Hamhung) and Wonsan. General Soule divided the rest of the 3d Division zone into southern, western, and northern sections. Col. Dennis M. Moore and his 15th Infantry would secure the region to the south and west of Wonsan. The 65th Infantry would take up positions to the west of Yonghung and Hamhung, while Lt. Col. Suk Jong Chol's South Korean 26th Infantry would take control of the northern sector. The 65th was to patrol aggressively to the west toward the gap that separated the Eighth Army from X Corps.[35]

The 65th's portion of the division sector covered approximately nine hundred square miles. In fact, Harris would later write, "our area was so large that there was no way really that we could patrol it, let alone defend

---

[35] Ibid.

it. And since our principal missions were still to make contact with Eighth Army as well as 'develop the situation,' we continued to stretch out from Yonghung in that direction."[36]

Although the 65th kept moving west, its progress was not fast enough for the corps commander. Flying over the regiment and observing that the lead battalion had stopped, Almond contacted Harris and asked him why. The colonel responded that the unit had reported a break in the road that prevented further advance. Reconnoitering the route himself from the air, the general failed to find any gaps. Landing at Harris' command post, he blasted the colonel for being less than energetic and ordered him to expedite the regiment's movement.[37]

Despite Almond's exhortations, Harris continued to advance with caution. By 12 November, St. Clair's 1st Battalion was occupying a patrol base near Kwangch'on, some thirty miles northwest of Yonghung. Dammer's 2d Battalion stood on the outskirts of Yonghung, while Allen's 3d Battalion positioned itself fifteen miles to the west.[38] In light of the unknown situation and the rough terrain that lay between the Eighth Army and X Corps, those dispositions were extremely prudent. They suggest that Harris suspected he might run into a large enemy force to the west and was prepared to fall back quickly on Yonghung. In effect, the colonel seemed to be doing just enough to keep Almond placated while ensuring the survival of the 65th Infantry in an uncertain situation.[39]

Harris' concern could have been only heightened by an incident that took place on 13 November. A motorized patrol from Capt. George E. Armstrong's Company B, led by 1st Lt. Walter N. Higgins, encountered North Korean troops entrenched on a ridge overlooking the village of Hadongsan-ni, ten miles southwest of Kwangch'on. Both sides opened fire on each other about the same time. In the ensuing skirmish, Lieutenant Higgins charged the enemy position, killing several and forcing the remainder to flee. Although mortally wounded, he led his men back to the company to report the enemy presence.[40]

Company B's encounter was only one indication of the growing strength of the reconstituted North Korean Army. On 13 November, the

---

[36] Harris, *Puerto Rico's Fighting 65th*, p. 114.

[37] HQ, X Corps, Nov War Diary Sums.

[38] Monthly Cmd Rpt, 3d Inf Div, Nov 50.

[39] Maj. Gen. Oliver P. Smith of the 1st Marine Division would have agreed with Harris. He also slowed his troops moving north of the Changjin Reservoir. Appleman, *South to the Naktong, North to the Yalu*, p. 772.

[40] GO no. 139, HQ, 3d Div, 14 May 51, sub: Silver Star Medal, First Lieutenant Walter N. Higgins, in Monthly Cmd Rpt, 3d Inf Div, May 51; Harris, *Puerto Rico's Fighting 65th*, pp. 108–09.

A patrol from Company L, 65th Infantry, brings in captured enemy troops near Yonghung.

North Korean *507th Brigade* and a regiment of the *41st Infantry Division*, reinforced with T–34 tanks, launched a determined attack against the South Korean Capital Division's motorized cavalry regiment near Kilchu, a large town approximately one hundred twenty-five air miles northeast of Hungnam. It took until 16 November for allied ground, air, and naval gunfire to defeat the assault. The South Koreans inflicted 1,858 casualties on their opponents and captured 105. Seven North Korean tanks, two self-propelled guns, and two artillery pieces littered the snow-covered battlefield.[41] At the same time, guerrilla activity intensified in UN rear areas. Combined with the growing resistance offered by conventional North Korean forces, these attacks in rear areas began to slow the progress of X Corps.[42]

The weather also played a part in delaying the United Nations' timetable for victory. Snow and subzero temperatures appeared as early as 10 November in the X Corps area of operations. In very short order, the men of the 65th found themselves suffering because they lacked winter clothing. On 13 November, the 3d Division asked X Corps to expedite the delivery of

---

[41] Appleman, *South to the Naktong, North to the Yalu*, p. 731.
[42] HQ, X Corps, Nov War Diary Sums; Appleman, *South to the Naktong, North to the Yalu*, p. 773.

cold-weather gear to the 65th Infantry.[43] The following day, the command sent to the regiment seven truckloads of winter clothing and three railroad cars filled with other supplies.[44] On 17 November, the 3d Division obtained a shipment of specialized winter footwear for the unit, particularly leather boots with rubber soles and partial rubber uppers designed for cold, wet weather.[45] Although the logisticians tried to satisfy everyone's needs, at the end of the month some members of the 65th still lacked winter jackets, woolen underwear, and winterized boots.[46]

On 18 November, as the 65th struggled with the unexpected advent of subzero weather, Harris ordered his 1st Battalion at Kwangch'on to send a rifle company north to establish contact with the South Korean 26th Infantry Regiment. The unit dispatched Captain Armstrong's recently bloodied Company B to the village of Paek-san, about thirteen miles to the north. After looking for and failing to find the South Koreans, Armstrong and his men made camp for the night on a ridge near the village.

At 0200 on 21 November, a reinforced company of North Koreans supported by mortars and automatic weapons attacked Company B. At the same time, another group of North Koreans ambushed a Company B patrol that was operating outside the unit's defensive perimeter. The fighting grew so intense that Armstrong began to worry about running out of ammunition.[47]

The enemy broke off the attack just before daylight; but at 0630, the North Koreans launched another assault with reinforcements from a second company. Just as Company B's ammunition was about to run out, a U.S. airdrop replenished its stocks. "Our men gained new life and managed to beat off several other attacks before St. Clair was able to get reinforcements," recalled Harris. "It was a close call."[48] The North Koreans retreated shortly thereafter, leaving behind twenty bodies and twenty-five prisoners. Company B sustained three killed and ten wounded.[49] Navy helicopters, a relatively new development in warfare, evacuated the wounded.[50]

On 22 November, Company C of the 64th Heavy Tank Battalion joined the 65th Infantry, giving Colonel Harris two tank companies.[51] Rather than

---

[43] Staff Mtg Notes, 13 Nov 50, in Monthly Cmd Rpt, 3d Inf Div, Nov 50.
[44] Staff Mtg Notes, 14 Nov 50, in Monthly Cmd Rpt, 3d Inf Div, Nov 50.
[45] Ibid.
[46] Staff Mtg Notes, 18 Nov 50, in Monthly Cmd Rpt, 3d Inf Div, Nov 50; Monthly Cmd Rpt, 65th Inf, Nov 50.
[47] Harris, *Puerto Rico's Fighting 65th*, p. 115.
[48] Ibid., p. 116.
[49] Monthly Cmd Rpts, 65th Inf, Nov 50, and 3d Inf Div, Nov 50; Harris, *Puerto Rico's Fighting 65th*, p. 116.
[50] Dolcater, *3d Infantry Division in Korea*, p. 74.
[51] Monthly Cmd Rpt, 65th Inf, Nov 50.

place an additional burden on his logistical system by parceling out the vehicles to each rifle battalion, Harris consolidated the tanks into a single formation that could deliver a concentrated blow when the need arose.

Despite the presence of sizable Chinese Communist forces, General MacArthur continued his planning to consolidate all of Korea under UN control. Plans were laid for a concerted drive by Eighth Army and X Corps to the border starting on 15 November. Logistics problems so hampered preparations, however, that the assault was delayed until 24 November.[52]

General Walker planned to advance along a seventy-mile front with the U.S. I and IX Corps and the South Korean II Corps moving abreast. The initial objective of the I and IX Corps was a road twenty miles beyond their current position, an east-west line about fifty miles north of P'yongyang that would assist lateral communications and provide access to the mountain corridors leading to the border. Once in possession of the road, Eighth Army would have another forty miles to go before it reached the Yalu. The South Korean II Corps would advance on the right flank, moving along the east side of the Chongch'on valley until it met up with Almond's X Corps at Inch'ori, thirty miles west of Hamhung. By so doing, the South Korean II Corps would close the worrisome forty-mile gap between Eighth Army and X Corps.[53]

As of 23 November, the units belonging to X Corps occupied widely separated positions across a 150-mile front. The U.S. 1st Marine Division held the town of Hagaru-ri at the lower end of the Changjin Reservoir. Seventy miles to the northeast, the U.S. 7th Infantry Division occupied Hyesanjin on the Yalu. Thirty miles to the east and slightly south of the 7th Division, a portion of the South Korean 3d Division held the town of Hapsu. Forty miles northeast of Hapsu, the South Korean Capital Division stood on the outskirts of Ch'ongjin—a mere eleven miles from the narrow strip of Chinese territory that separated North Korea from the Soviet Union.

MacArthur directed Almond to help Walker by sending X Corps troops west toward Eighth Army. Since the UN front slanted across the peninsula with the Eighth Army holding a more southerly portion, a westward attack by Almond's forces would put X Corps to the rear of the Chinese and North Korean forces blocking Walker's advance. Although this plan appeared fea-

---

[52] FEC, "History of the Korean War," pt. 2, vol. 1, ch. 7, pp. 20–21.

[53] The I Corps consisted of the U.S. 24th Division, the South Korean 1st Division, and the British 27th Brigade. The IX Corps was organized with the U.S. 2d and 25th Divisions and the Turkish 1st Brigade. The South Korean 6th, 7th, and 8th Divisions comprised the South Korean II Corps. The U.S. 1st Cavalry Division and the British 29th Brigade constituted the Eighth Army reserve. Billy C. Mossman, *Ebb and Flow: November 1950–July 1951*, U.S. Army in the Korean War (Washington, D.C.: U.S. Army Center of Military History, 1990), pp. 45–46.

sible on the map, closer inspection would have revealed impassable terrain. Nonetheless, Almond played the part of loyal subordinate, requesting that MacArthur make only a single change in the plan. Concerned that his supply lines would become overextended if X Corps began its assault from the town of Changjin, twenty miles north of the Changjin Reservoir, Almond proposed that his troops attack into the Eighth Army zone over the road leading from Yudam-ni at the western edge of the reservoir. MacArthur agreed and instructed the general to move as soon as possible.[54]

Almond set 27 November as the opening date for the X Corps attack. He intended the 1st Marine Division at the Changjin Reservoir to advance on Mup'yong-ni, fifty miles to the west, before pressing northwestward to the Yalu and relieving the South Korean II Corps of its frontline responsibilities. The U.S. 7th Division at Hyesanjin would push westward, securing the territory between the Yalu and the reservoir in the area previously assigned to the 1st Marine Division. The South Korean I Corps would continue moving north to the border while the U.S. 3d Division and the South Korean 1st Marine Regiment would protect the corps rear area, especially the airfield and harbor facilities at Wonsan. In addition, the 3d Division was responsible for gaining and maintaining contact with Eighth Army while securing the corps' western flank and, if necessary, lending support to the 1st Marine Division. Faced with a daunting set of operational requirements, Harris was concerned about the 65th's ability to coordinate operations in the rugged terrain of northeastern Korea at the onset of harsh winter weather.

In order to repel a Chinese attack that might hit the yawning gap separating X Corps from Eighth Army, Harris began organizing a mobile force capable of striking out quickly from Yonghung toward any threatened point within the regiment's area of operations. Pessimistic about his ability to maintain uninterrupted links with supporting air and artillery, Harris arranged for his infantry units to carry ten very-high-frequency (VHF) radios as they traveled cross-country. He obtained carts and oxen to ease the burden his troops would face in transporting the bulky radios across mountainous terrain. Recognizing the need for timely engineer support, he requested a bulldozer from the 3d Division so his regiment could clear its own roads if necessary. On 25 November, after weighing the request, General Soule ordered his staff to provide the bulldozer.[55]

That same day, the Intelligence and Reconnaissance Platoon made contact with an entrenched enemy force near Midun-ni and Inhung-ni, some ten to fifteen miles southwest of Yonghung. (*See Map 3.*) Harris dispatched two rifle platoons from Lieutenant Carsely's Company E, augmented by two self-

---

[54] Ibid., pp. 47–48.
[55] Staff Mtg Notes, 25 Nov 50, in Monthly Cmd Rpt, 3d Inf Div, Nov 50.

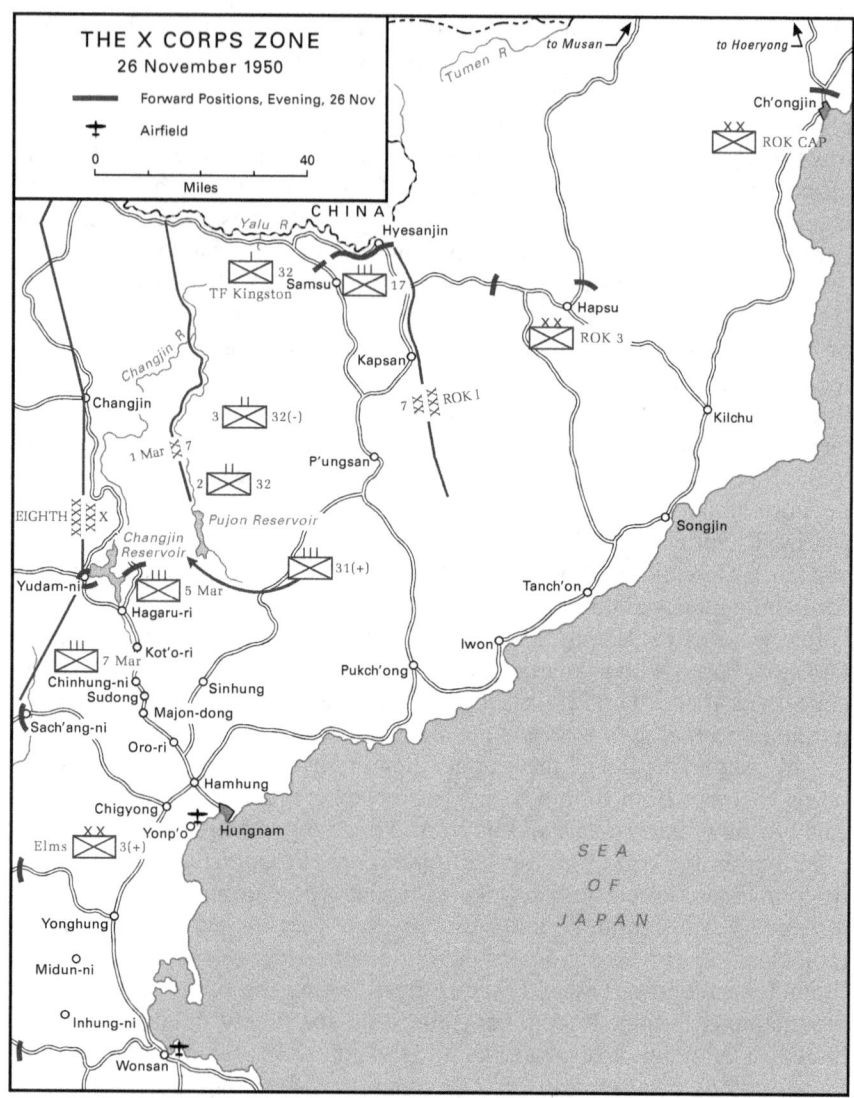

MAP 3

propelled 105-mm. howitzers from the 58th AFA Battalion and a platoon of medium tanks. Harris intended to fix the Communists in place with his infantry and then pound them into submission with his artillery and tanks.[56]

---

[56] Monthly Cmd Rpt, 65th Inf, Nov 50.

That night, a strong Chinese force struck Eighth Army's 2d Division northeast of Kunu-ri along the Chongch'on River, approximately seventy-five miles west of Yonghung. Heavy losses forced the Chinese to suspend their attacks in the early morning hours, but they resumed just before dawn. After launching vigorous counterattacks that regained several key pieces of terrain, the Americans dug in, consolidated their positions, and waited. In the meantime, on 26 November, Carsely's task force swept Midun-ni only to find it empty. The enemy force sighted the previous day had vanished.

To gain a better idea of what was happening to his west, General Soule directed a member of his staff to fly to the 2d Division for an update.[57] Conscious of the vulnerable seam between X Corps and the Eighth Army, a gap too large for the 65th Infantry to close, Soule wanted to know if the enemy was trying to exploit that weakness. The general ordered an intelligence officer from his staff to join Harris' 1st Battalion and then lead the unit west until it made contact with troops from the Eighth Army. Another source of concern to Soule was the region around Paek-san, forty miles northwest of Yonghung, which lay between the 65th Infantry and the South Korean 26th Infantry. Intelligence reports indicated that the bulk of the twenty-five thousand North Korean guerrillas operating in the division's zone were at Yonghung. If they acted in concert, they could seriously disrupt allied supply lines that were growing longer and more tenuous by the day. Even as X Corps prepared to resume its advance toward the Chinese border, signs of trouble abounded for the thinly stretched units.

X Corps in Crisis

The X Corps attack toward the Yalu had barely begun on 27 November when the Chinese launched nearly simultaneous assaults against U.S. units on both sides of the Changjin Reservoir. The Chinese *79th* and *89th Divisions* from the *27th Army* attacked two Marine regiments moving on the west side of the reservoir near Yudam-ni. Although the marines inflicted heavy casualties on the Chinese, they soon found themselves in danger of being cut off from their division headquarters at Hagaru-ri, at the southern end of the reservoir. The Chinese *80th Division* from the *20th Army*, meanwhile, struck the 7th Division's Task Force MACLEAN on the east side of the Changjin Reservoir. (This force would be renamed Task Force FAITH on 29 November when Lt. Col. Don C. Faith assumed command following the capture of Col. Allan D. MacLean.) The Chinese attacked ferociously, forcing the 7th Division soldiers to yield ground in several places; but the Americans regained most of the territory when the enemy withdrew at dawn.

---

[57] Staff Mtg Min, 26 Nov 50, in Monthly Cmd Rpt, 3d Inf Div, Nov 50.

Meanwhile, a crisis was growing within the Eighth Army's area of operations. On the night of 25 and 26 November, Chinese forces attacked the flank of the South Korean 16th Infantry, 8th Division, which guarded the right end of the Eighth Army line some thirty-five miles west of Yonghung. A stronger Chinese force then infiltrated through the sector held by the South Korean 7th Division, ten miles to the northwest, and along the seam between the South Korean 7th and 8th Divisions five miles closer in. By the next morning, the Chinese were placing heavy pressure along the entire front held by the South Korean II Corps. One South Korean regiment sought safety by sliding westward into the U.S. 2d Division's sector. Two other South Korean regiments hastily retreated after discovering that the Chinese had established roadblocks behind them along their main supply line. With that, the entire South Korean II Corps on Eighth Army's right wing began to collapse. By the evening of 26 November, it was no longer a cohesive military organization.[58]

With that obstruction out of the way, the Chinese sought to outflank and then curl behind the Eighth Army. As the Chinese *39th* and *40th Armies* pressed against the U.S. 2d and 25th Divisions from the north, the Chinese *38th Army* exploited its earlier success against the South Korean II Corps by attacking the now-exposed right flank of the 2d Division. The Chinese *39th Army* moved south astride the Kuryong River and then concentrated its might on the U.S. 25th Division holding the center of the Eighth Army line. Facing overwhelming pressure, the 25th Division withdrew several miles on the morning on 27 November. Within a day, the entire allied line was in retreat; the Chinese began sending forces around the right flank of Eighth Army to envelop it from the east. Walker's only hope for his army was to pull back far enough to deny the Chinese any opportunity to isolate the UN forces.[59]

The losses of the American 2d Division are indicative of the ferocity and power of the enemy offensive. Over a four-day period, the U.S. unit lost five thousand soldiers killed, wounded, and missing; almost 50 percent of its communications equipment; 45 percent of its mortars, recoilless rifles, and machine guns; all but eight howitzers; 30 percent of its wheeled and tracked vehicles; and 90 percent of its engineer equipment while holding off attempts by five enemy divisions to turn the Eighth Army flank.[60]

As Eighth Army began its retreat on the evening of 28 November, the Chinese struck X Corps again, hitting widely dispersed U.S. units with waves upon waves of infantry and shattering the trio of battalions compris-

---

[58] Mossman, *Ebb and Flow*, pp. 69–70.
[59] Ibid., p. 83.
[60] FEC, "History of the Korean War," pt. 2, vol. 1, ch. 8, p. 2.

ing Task Force FAITH on the east side of the Changjin Reservoir. On the morning of 1 December, having suffered almost one thousand five hundred killed, wounded, and missing out of an original complement of two thousand five hundred personnel, the 7th Division task force ceased to exist.[61] General MacArthur reported to the Joint Chiefs of Staff that Eighth Army and X Corps would assume a defensive stance until the Chinese broke off their attacks.[62]

In General Almond's area of operations, the U.S. 1st Marine and 7th Infantry Divisions and several South Korean divisions were scattered in relatively small groups separated by extremely rugged terrain and dependent on poorly maintained secondary roads for supplies and reinforcement. There was no ground contact between Eighth Army and X Corps. Regardless, General Soule continued to look for ways to use the 3d Division to relieve some of the pressure on the Eighth Army's right flank.[63] That was difficult to arrange, however, because fierce guerrilla attacks against the 7th and the 15th Infantries and the division's supply lines had tied up most of his forces. It was only in the 65th's sector to the west that things remained relatively quiet. The 3d Battalion continued its advance toward Yongsan, five miles to the west of Midun-ni and twenty miles southwest of Yonghung, without making enemy contact. That evening, the battalion shifted ten miles to the northwest to support St. Clair's 1st Battalion, which had begun to report increased enemy activity near Hadongsan-ni.

By 30 November, General Walker had pulled the Eighth Army back to the Chongch'on, significantly reducing the likelihood that his troops would be cut off and destroyed by the Chinese. Although the marines and Army troops near the Changjin Reservoir came under attack, the enemy did not make an all-out effort against General Almond's entire X Corps, giving its widely scattered units an opportunity to withdraw and to regroup. General MacArthur directed Almond to pull his far-flung forces into a defensive perimeter around Hamhung and Hungnam. Almond in turn ordered X Corps to establish the enclave on the coast and to secure its western flank against further enemy inroads. This meant that the South Korean I Corps would have to backtrack 300 miles along the northeastern coast while the main body of the U.S. 7th Division faced a 200-mile southerly retreat through the mountains.[64] Fortunately for these units, the desperate fight put up by

---

[61] Marine casualties from 27 November–10 December 1950 totaled 2,621 killed, wounded, and missing; while the 7th Division had 2,760 dead, wounded, and missing. Mossman, *Ebb and Flow*, p. 147.

[62] FEC, "History of the Korean War," pt. 2, vol. 1, ch. 8, p. 4.

[63] Staff Mtg Min, 26 Nov 50, in Monthly Cmd Rpt, 3d Inf Div, Nov 50.

[64] Mossman, *Ebb and Flow*, p. 128.

the 1st Marine Division and Task Force FAITH at the Changjin Reservoir delayed the enemy long enough for the maneuver to succeed.[65]

During the first part of December, the 3d Division fought guerrilla groups that ranged in size from a few men to as many as four thousand. Consisting mainly of former North Korean soldiers, these forces were spread across the division sector from Paek-san in the north to Singosan in the south. The guerrillas raided villages, harassed supply lines, and sometimes attacked division outposts. "The enemy was dangerous and defended his assembly areas vigorously," General Soule reported. "He seemed determined to remain in the Division zone for the winter. His equipment [was] inadequate, however, and there appeared to be no resupply."[66]

The harsh December weather and the rough terrain made operations difficult for the 65th. Temperatures dropped below freezing every night. Since the division was now well-supplied with winter clothing and equipment, however, many officers believed that the bad weather was more damaging to the morale and efficiency of the enemy than it was to the Americans. The terrain was another matter. Steep mountains restricted vehicular traffic to the limited road network. Complicating matters, American forces were so thinly spread that some battalions were operating as much as twenty-five road miles from their parent units. The supply routes connecting them usually consisted of single-lane highways, a fact that facilitated enemy roadblocks and ambushes.[67]

During the first three days of December, the 3d Division and the 65th Infantry received a series of contradictory orders, reflecting the confusion at X Corps headquarters about the enemy situation and intentions. On 1 December, the 65th received instructions to move the 1st Battalion to a piece of high ground thirty miles west of Yonghung. The regiment quickly cancelled the orders, however, when it received new instructions to move the entire unit to Hamhung. An advance detachment of the 65th departed for the city on 1 December. The next day, the division recalled the detachment and ordered the regiment to proceed to Wonsan instead. Only St. Clair's 1st Battalion had reached Wonsan when Colonel Harris received a fourth order directing the 65th to move to Hamhung.[68]

Other units belonging to the 3d Division were also converging on Hamhung as fast as railroad, shipping, and the unit's own vehicles permitted. By 2200 on 4 December, the entire 65th Infantry had closed on the town, relieving the 7th Division's 32d Infantry. Operations Order no. 9 from X Corps, published the following day, directed the 3d Division to

---

[65] HQ, X Corps, Nov War Diary Sums.
[66] Monthly Cmd Rpt, 3d Inf Div, Dec 50.
[67] Ibid.
[68] Monthly Cmd Rpt, 65th Inf, Dec 50.

Generals Almond (center) and Soule (right) enter the 3d Division command post for a briefing on 3 December 1950. Below, a patrol from the 3d Infantry Division advances to relieve a convoy pinned down by enemy fire just north of a Korean village.

organize and defend the Hamhung-Hungnam area, to cover the withdrawal of the 1st Marine Division, and to provide a regiment that would serve as corps reserve.

The 65th Infantry had two specific tasks to perform. The first was to stop a large enemy force that was moving southeast in the direction of Hamhung. For this mission, Colonel Harris gained control of the 3d Battalions of the 7th and 15th Infantries. Both units, along with St. Clair's 1st Battalion, occupied defensive positions on a line running generally east-west through the town of Oro-ri, fourteen miles northwest of Hungnam.

The regiment's second mission was more complex. It was to defend the town of Majon-dong, eight miles northwest of Oro-ri; to clear enemy forces from the four-mile stretch of road between Majon-dong and Sudong to the north; and to safeguard the withdrawal from Hagaru-ri of the 1st Marine Division, which was surrounded by elements of four Chinese armies. To accomplish these demanding tasks, Harris formed Task Force CHILDS under the command of his regimental executive officer, Colonel Childs. A formidable force, it consisted of the regiment's 2d and 3d Battalions; Batteries A and B of the 58th AFA Battalion; Company C, 73d Engineer Battalion; Company A, 4th Marine Tank Battalion; and the bulk of the 4th Chemical Company.[69] All told for both missions of the 65th, Harris found himself in command of a force equivalent to two reinforced infantry regiments.

On 5 December, General Smith of the 1st Marine Division asked General Almond to furnish a relief force that would help the 1st Battalion, 1st Marines, to clear the road from Hagaru-ri to Kot'o-ri, a town ten miles to the south. In response, the 3d Division assembled Task Force DOG, led by the assistant division commander, Brig. Gen. Armistead D. Mead, to aid the marines. Task Force DOG consisted of the 3d Battalion, 7th Infantry; the 92d AFA Battalion equipped with 155-mm. howitzers; the 52d Transportation Truck Battalion; the 3d Platoon, 3d Reconnaissance Company; Company A, 73d Engineer Battalion; and numerous other detachments including a tactical air control party. Its mission was to establish a defensive line in the vicinity of Chinhung-ni, nine miles south of Kot'o-ri, to facilitate the initial stages of the 1st Marine Division's move south from Hagaru-ri. (*Map 4*)

Supporting Mead was the 7th Infantry Division's 31st Field Artillery Battalion, which had been attached to the 3d Division, as well as X Corps' 96th Field Artillery Battalion and 999th Field Artillery Battalion. Two liaison aircraft from the division's artillery would provide aerial observation support.[70] Task Force DOG would help the marines fight their way out of

---

[69] Monthly Cmd Rpts, 3d Inf Div, Dec 50, and 65th Inf, Dec 50.

[70] Task Force DOG Opns Order no. 1, 6 Dec 50, in Monthly Command Rpt, 3d Inf Div, Dec 50.

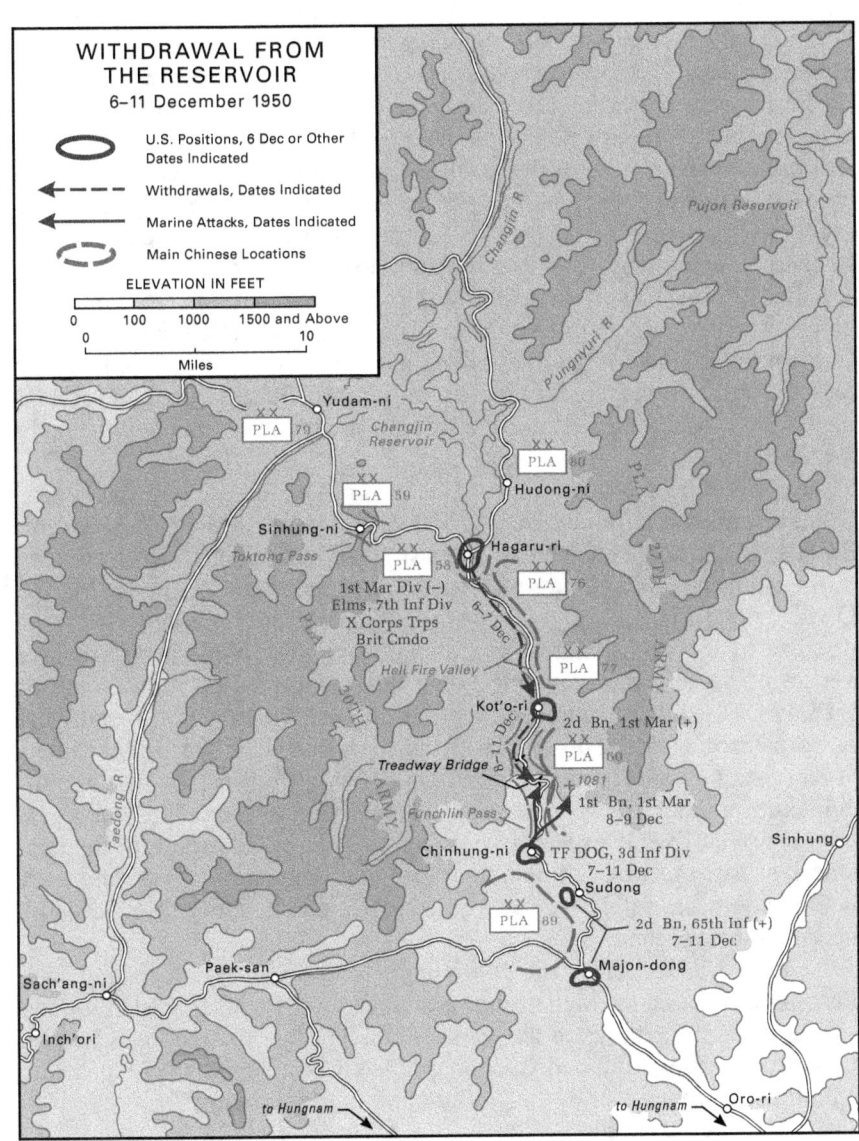

Map 4

Hagaru-ri while Task Force CHILDS secured the high ground farther south along the withdrawal route.[71]

While Harris and Mead were organizing Task Force CHILDS and Task Force DOG, the Chinese were massing four infantry divisions from the *20th, 26th,* and *27th Armies* southwest of the reservoir. The *58th* and *76th Divisions* were poised to strike the main body of the 1st Marine Division concentrated at Hagaru-ri. The Chinese also positioned the *77th* and *60th Divisions*, respectively, to the northeast and southeast of Kot'o-ri on the road leading away from the Changjin Reservoir. In the event the Americans fought their way out of the trap at Hagaru-ri, those forces were in position to intercept them when they headed south toward Hungnam.

Task Force CHILDS occupied defensive positions near Majon-dong early in the evening of 5 December. The next day, the Chinese attacked Companies L and M but the Americans threw them back with heavy losses. As that engagement tapered off, the 2d Battalion began to clear the Chinese-occupied hills north of Majon-dong that overlooked the main supply route.

Shortly after midnight on 6–7 December, Almond ordered Task Force DOG at Hamhung to relieve the 1st Battalion, 1st Marines, at Chinhung-ni. By late afternoon that same day, the task force had reached Oro-ri, twenty miles southeast of Chinhung-ni. By 2200, the main body of the 1st Marine Division had successfully withdrawn approximately two-thirds of the distance to Kot'o-ri, where Marine engineers were preparing to replace a blown bridge over a yawning gorge three-and-one-half miles south of the town. The division engineer, Lt. Col. John H. Partridge, requested that X Corps drop eight 2,500-lb. Treadway (portable vehicular bridge) spans at Kot'o-ri. On 7 December, eight C–119 Flying Boxcar transport aircraft delivered the materiel, along with plywood centerpieces that would permit all types of vehicles to use the span, to a drop zone south of the gap. One Treadway section fell in Chinese territory and another was damaged; but the engineers safely recovered the remaining six. Only four would be needed to bridge the gap.[72]

Early on 8 December, the 2d Battalion, 65th Infantry, attached to Task Force DOG, cleared the high ground along the road connecting Majon-dong and Sudong, three miles to the north. Confident that the road was secure, Colonel Dammer stationed Captain Muña's Company G in Sudong and withdrew the remainder of the 2d Battalion to Majon-dong.[73]

---

[71] Although Task Force DOG and the Army's role in supporting the withdrawal of the marines is well known, little has been published on Task Force CHILDS and its crucial role in holding the route open against sustained Chinese attacks.

[72] Mossman, *Ebb and Flow*, p. 141.

[73] Monthly Cmd Rpts, 3d Inf Div, Dec 50, and 65th Inf, Dec 50.

The remainder of Task Force DOG passed through Sudong and closed on Chinhung-ni at 1420 without encountering any opposition. The 3d Battalion, 7th Infantry, relieved the 1st Battalion, 1st Marines, along the town's perimeter that evening. The Marine battalion then began preparing for the push north toward Kot'o-ri to open the withdrawal route for the marines and their attached Army units, which were still slowly fighting their way southward.

On 8 and 9 December, against unexpectedly light resistance, the men of the 1st Battalion, 1st Marines, supported by engineer, artillery, and self-propelled antiaircraft guns detached from Task Force DOG, cleared the road north of Chinhung-ni up to the gorge with the blown bridge. There, it met up with elements of the 7th Marines positioned on commanding terrain overlooking the approaches to the blown bridge. By 1800 on 9 December, Army and Marine engineers had installed the portable Treadway spans over the gorge. This permitted the 1st Marine Division to continue its way south. Led by the 1st Battalion of the 7th Marines, the divisional trains, the remainder of the 7th Marines, and then the 5th Marines passed over the span during the night and throughout the next day. After the last elements had crossed over the bridge, Marine engineers demolished the span.

In an attempt to cut the main supply route south of Kot'o-ri and to trap the withdrawing U.S. forces, the Chinese initiated a series of attacks against Company G of the 65th Infantry west of the village of Sudong during the late afternoon of 10 December. Although the Communist troops attacked in strength, heavy U.S. artillery and small-arms fire repulsed the effort and inflicted many casualties.

During the night of 10–11 December, the tail of the combined Marine and Army column was passing through Sudong when Company G found itself under attack once more. With the assistance of artillery fire, Captain Muña's men threw the enemy back, inflicting some one hundred fifty casualties without sustaining any friendly losses. During the predawn hours of 11 December, Chinese soldiers attacked Company G three more times, finally breaking through its defensive positions and swarming onto the road as the 1st Marines regimental train was passing through the village. A counterattack by marines and Task Force DOG cleared the road and bordering buildings by daybreak. Bringing up the rear from Chinhung-ni, Task Force DOG reached Majon-dong at 2000. After the Army and Marine units had passed through its defensive positions, Task Force CHILDS also joined the column moving south toward Hungnam.

On 12 December, the 3d Division dissolved Task Forces DOG and CHILDS.[74] While covering the withdrawal of the 1st Marine and 7th Infantry

---

[74] Ibid.

General Almond (left) commends General Mead (center) upon the successful completion of Task Force Dog's mission to assist the withdrawal of the 1st Marine and 7th Divisions.

Divisions from the Changjin Reservoir, the 3d Division had lost 50 killed, 206 wounded, and 147 missing.[75] Colonel Childs, the commander of Task Force CHILDS, and Sfc. Felix G. Nieves of Company G both won Silver Stars for gallantry in action at Sudong.[76]

Evacuation from Hungnam to Pusan

On 11 December, as the first elements of the 1st Marine Division reached Hungnam after their harrowing journey from the Changjin

---

[75] Mossman, *Ebb and Flow*, p. 147.

[76] GO no. 27, HQ, 3d Inf Div, 20 Jan 51, sub: Award of the Silver Star Medal to Lieutenant Colonel George W. Childs, in Monthly Cmd Rpt, 3d Inf Div, Jan 51; GO no. 71, HQ, 3d Inf Div, 22 Mar 51, sub: Award of the Silver Star Medal to Sergeant First Class Felix G. Nieves, in Monthly Cmd Rpt, 3d Inf Div, Mar 51.

Reservoir, General Almond announced the evacuation plan for X Corps. Allied troops under his command would establish a defensive perimeter around Hungnam through which all UN personnel, equipment, and supplies remaining in northeastern Korea were to be evacuated through the port. The 3d Infantry Division was to defend the western perimeter around Hungnam while the 7th Infantry Division guarded the northern sector along the Changjin Reservoir road. The three regiments of the South Korean I Corps would protect the northeastern sector along the coast.

Within the 3d Division sector, the attached South Korean 1st Marine Regiment was positioned on the left flank, the 65th Infantry held its center, and the 7th Infantry guarded the right wing. The 15th Infantry was in the rear serving as X Corps reserve. The 7th and 65th were to surround the city with six successive delaying lines: Charlie, Mike, Peter, Tare, Able, and Fox. The first unit slated for evacuation was the South Korean 1st Marine Regiment, which was to release its sector to the 7th Infantry and embark whenever division headquarters issued the order.

Farther north, the 3d Reconnaissance Company was to screen the roads leading to Hamhung from Oro-ri and Sinhung. It would also protect lines of communication against sabotage. The 64th Heavy Tank Battalion meanwhile became part of the 3d Division reserve, along with the 3d Battalion, 7th Infantry, whose commander, Lt. Col. Thomas A. O'Neil, was directed to prepare a variety of counterattack plans, giving particular attention to the center sector occupied by the 65th Infantry. Every man was to hold his position until otherwise instructed. Withdrawals through delaying lines would be on division order only.[77]

Colonel Harris' plan called for the 65th Infantry's battalions to leapfrog from the outer defensive lines toward the harbor as Chinese pressure increased. The 1st and 3d Battalions would make the initial move, covered by the 2d Battalion. Once the secondary line had been occupied, the 2d Battalion would move back, covered both by supporting artillery fire and by the 1st and 3d Battalions. This process would be repeated until the regiment reached Line Fox, the main line of resistance, where it would make its final stand.[78]

The 65th Infantry would not get its orders to evacuate until several intervening events took place. First, the 1st Marine Division would need to board vessels destined for Pusan. Second, several hundred thousand tons of supplies, ammunition, and equipment would have to be evacuated along

---

[77] Monthly Cmd Rpt, 3d Inf Div, Dec 50; Dolcater, *3d Infantry Division in Korea*, pp. 96–97.

[78] Monthly Cmd Rpt, 65th Inf, Dec 50.

with tens of thousands of Korean refugees. Finally, the 7th Division would have to withdraw completely from the line and be in the process of boarding ships. "As I saw it," remembered Harris, "this would leave only us chickens of the 3d Division to man the Line Fox perimeter. When we got to that point, anything could happen."[79]

As X Corps began evacuating men, equipment, and supplies from Hungnam, the tempo of contact with the enemy along the outer perimeter began to increase. In these initial engagements, fighting the bitter cold and numbing weariness, the division's artillerymen played an essential role: sending tons of shells screaming into Chinese positions. According to the division history of the war, "They laid down curtains of fire around friendly defensive positions, shot up enemy supply columns, broke up Red attacks and, all in all, killed Communists by the hundreds."[80] Naval gunfire, guided by naval control parties, added to the enemy's woes. Tactical air support also devastated the Communists as they tried to break through the line around Hungnam.

The Chinese for their part landed some of their heaviest blows against units of the 65th Infantry. At 0139 on 14 December, four hundred Chinese soldiers attacked St. Clair's 1st Battalion on Line Charlie in the Oro-ri area. Moving from the north, the assault collided with Captain Armstrong's Company B, overrunning two platoons and forcing the remainder of the company to withdraw across a small tributary of the Songch'on River west of Oro-ri. Supported by artillery and air strikes, a counterattack that included Capt. George J. Magner's Company C, the remainder of Company B, and a platoon of tanks from the regimental tank company forced the Chinese to withdraw with heavy losses. The defenders lost four killed and fourteen wounded.[81]

The 3d Division had scheduled the 7th and 65th Infantries to withdraw from Lines Peter and Able beginning at 0800 on 16 December. The withdrawal to a more compact perimeter was necessary because the South Korean 1st Marine Regiment was scheduled to be pulled off the line and evacuated. Yonp'o airfield, west of Hungnam, became a key position within the new perimeter because a considerable quantity of supplies located there remained to be flown or shipped out. Possession of the airfield by the Chinese would also give the enemy a clear view of allied loading operations within Hungnam harbor and make the port an easy target.[82]

---

[79] Harris, *Puerto Rico's Fighting 65th*, pp. 128–29.
[80] Dolcater, *3d Infantry Division in Korea*, p. 97.
[81] Monthly Cmd Rpt, 65th Inf, Dec 50.
[82] Monthly Cmd Rpt, 3d Inf Div, Dec 50.

The line forms to the right for UN equipment and vehicles being loaded onto a landing ship, tank, during the evacuation from Wonsan. Below, M.Sgt. Cesar Melendez and Cpl. Andelmo Irizarry, both members of Headquarters Company, 1st Battalion, 65th Infantry, lay a 120-lb. demolition charge on a bridge near Oro-ri.

Heavy Chinese pressure on the 7th and the 65th Infantries commencing on the night of 14 and 15 December resulted in the 3d Division withdrawing sooner than expected. A platoon outpost on Line Charlie several miles northeast of Oro-ri was the first to fall back. At 0100 on 15 December, a platoon belonging to Capt. Vincent J. O'Reilly's Company I directed artillery fire on an enemy column, destroying several vehicles. The Chinese responded with a company-size assault against the outpost. After a brief firefight, Captain O'Reilly ordered the platoon to fall back to positions on Line Tare.

During the morning, other outposts along Line Charlie were ordered to fall back as a result of similar engagements. As the Chinese pressure increased, the 3d Division instructed the 7th and the 65th Infantries to fight delaying actions as long as possible before withdrawing. Throughout 15 December, the regimental commanders requested permission to withdraw more quickly in the face of what they believed to be large concentrations of Chinese troops. Division, however, turned down the requests, attempting to trade time for space.[83]

Chinese pressure tapered off on 16 December, with the enemy launching only two attacks in the morning and one smaller probe later in the day. Even so, one of the morning attacks, carried out by a reinforced Chinese company against the newly promoted Lt. Col. Edward G. Allen's 3d Battalion, succeeded in penetrating Line Mike. A counterattack restored the line and resulted in heavy Chinese losses, including twenty-seven soldiers taken as prisoners. The 3d Battalion had seven killed and twenty wounded.

Later in the day, the 2d Battalion, 65th Infantry, moved back from Line Mike to Line Peter with the mission of covering the eventual withdrawal of the 1st and 3d Battalions. In turn, those two units withdrew at 1500 to relieve the 1st and 3d Battalions of the 17th and 32d Infantries, respectively. The 2d Battalion remained at Line Peter. That evening, the division ordered the 7th and the 65th to pull back to Line Fox at 0900 the next day, 17 December. Both regiments were to maintain strong outposts facing toward the enemy.[84]

The 65th remained on Line Fox for the next six days. The Chinese continued to probe the regiment; but mortar and artillery fire, along with naval gunfire from the destroyers and cruisers, repulsed them. On 18 December, the 3d Division assumed the entire responsibility for the defense

---

[83] Ibid.
[84] Monthly Cmd Rpt, 3d Inf Div, Dec 50.

of Hungnam and took control of all UN units that remained ashore. The following day, Harris received a welcome surprise in the form of a letter of commendation from General Coulter, the commander of IX Corps, who expressed his appreciation for the 65th Infantry's hard work earlier that year.

By 22 December, all of the 3d Infantry Division's subordinate regimental headquarters, service companies, medical companies, and advance groups from each rifle battalion had finished boarding Navy ships in preparation for movement to Pusan. Despite the strain on shipping capacity and the impediments the enemy's efforts posed to the orderly evacuation of UN personnel and equipment, approximately one hundred thousand civilians also boarded the departing vessels.

On 23 December, air reconnaissance and agent reports revealed that a massive enemy buildup was in progress near Hagaru-ri and along the Sach'ang-ni–Chigyong road.[85] That day, the remaining elements of the 3d Division fell back to Line Fox, the last defensive ring around Hungnam. Anticipating the final evacuation of Hungnam, the 3d Division headquarters published Operations Instructions no. 7 that evening, directing that upon arrival in Pusan all units were to replace damaged and missing equipment; incorporate whatever replacements were available; hold training exercises based on lessons learned in combat; and perform maintenance on weapons, vehicles, and equipment. General Soule expected the division to regain full combat readiness within ten days of landing.[86]

At 0930 on 24 December, the remaining elements of the 3d Division began withdrawing from Line Fox and boarding the Navy ships. The 7th

Colonel Harris at his regimental command post, 18 December 1950

---

[85] HQ X Corps, Cmd Rpt, Dec 50.
[86] Monthly Cmd Rpt, 3d Inf Div, Dec 50.

Generals Soule (left) and Mead confer outside the 3d Division command post during the final days of the Wonsan evacuation.

Infantry cleared the beach at 1230, the 65th Infantry at 1245, and the 15th Infantry at 1400. During this final phase, Dammer's 2d Battalion covered the final withdrawal and embarkation of the 65th Infantry's 1st and 3d Battalions. Then the 2d Battalion, the last unit of the 65th Infantry to leave North Korea, withdrew under the cover of a machine-gun strongpoint. The soldiers of the 65th Infantry boarded the USS *Freeman* and *Henrico*, the SS *Hunter Victory* and *Carleton Victory*, and LST Q0134. The regiment's bulk cargo and most of its vehicles had been loaded earlier. At 1400, the 3d Division command post became operational aboard the USS *Bayfield*.[87]

Although thousands of enemy troops ringed the Hungnam perimeter, the Chinese did not launch any major assaults against the steadily shrinking lodgment during the final days of the evacuation. Artillery and naval fires succeeded in thwarting every enemy attempt to organize an attack.[88] In all,

---

[87] Ibid.
[88] Ibid.

corps and division artillery units fired more than forty-six thousand rounds between 19 and 24 December, including almost eleven thousand rounds on the last day alone. In addition, naval guns averaged more than two thousand rounds per day under the direction of the division fire-support coordination center.[89]

The 3d Infantry Division had played a central role in protecting the largest beachhead evacuation in U.S. military history. Under the division's protection, X Corps had evacuated 17,500 military vehicles, 350,000 tons of bulk cargo, 105,000 troops, and 100,000 refugees. The allies had destroyed all installations of military value in Hungnam when the United Nations force departed.[90]

Colonel Harris called the evacuation "a logistical and strategic miracle." Even so, he added, "we soon forgot all about the Chinese, the cold weather, and the other hardships of combat, for the navy went out of its way to make all of the creature comforts available to us during the five days we were aboard ship."[91] The men of the 65th luxuriated in hot showers; clean sheets and bunks; and hot meals at the mess tables, where they enjoyed a traditional Christmas feast.

Throughout December 1950, the 65th Infantry had suffered 139 battle and 212 nonbattle casualties. Respiratory ailments had accounted for a large number of the nonbattle casualties. Severe colds and pneumonia-like symptoms that began in Hungnam spread quickly aboard the overcrowded ships going to Pusan. Self-inflicted injuries, attributed to the "improper handling of weapons and vehicles," accounted for another twenty-one casualties, prompting Harris to institute a training program to reduce accidents. Since cold-weather injuries accounted for fifty-seven of the regiment's nonbattle casualties, Harris also reemphasized training in the proper use of cold-weather garments, the employment of warming tents when possible, and the need to change socks and clothing frequently. To replace the month's losses, the regiment received 372 Puerto Rican enlisted replacements on 30 December.[92]

Overall, Colonel Harris was pleased with his soldiers. "The results of the different operations of the 65th RCT during this period can be classified as excellent," he reported. "The morale and combat efficiency of the unit is also excellent."[93] The X Corps and 3d Division commanders commended

---

[89] Ibid.
[90] Ibid.
[91] Harris, *Puerto Rico's Fighting 65th*, p. 132.
[92] Monthly Cmd Rpt, 65th Inf, Dec 50.
[93] Ibid.

the unit for its outstanding performance. General Almond presented the officers and men of the regiment with eleven of the forty-two Silver Stars awarded by X Corps during combat operations in North Korea. General Soule awarded thirteen more Silver Star medals to Borinqueneers during December.[94]

Since its arrival in Korea, the 65th Infantry had suffered a total of 714 casualties and had participated in several difficult operations.[95] The 65th had played a critical role in the expansion of the X Corps bridgehead at Wonsan during November, in the withdrawal of the 1st Marine Division and remnants of the 7th Infantry Division from the Changjin Reservoir during the first part of December, and in the defense of Hungnam that followed. "The record speaks for itself," wrote Harris, in a memorandum he issued aboard ship on Christmas Eve. "But that record stems from the specific part which each officer and man of the regiment has played in these military campaigns; and without whose loyal and tireless efforts this regiment could not have carried on. With humble sincerity, I congratulate and thank all of you."[96]

---

[94] See "65th Infantry Regiment in Korea Silver Star Recipients" prepared by author based on Silver Star citations in records maintained at National Archives II and Dolcater, *3d Infantry Division in Korea*.

[95] HQ, X Corps, Nov 50 War Diary Sums and Dec 50 Cmd Rpt; Monthly Cmd Rpts, 3d Inf Div, Dec 50, and 65th Inf, Dec 50, Jan 51. Battle casualties during September totaled 1 killed and 2 wounded. Losses for October (149) were not delineated. November figures included 11 killed, 32 wounded, 2 missing, and 104 nonbattle casualties. Combined losses in December 1950 and January 1951 totaled 36 killed, 86 wounded, 17 missing, and 212 nonbattle casualties. A Company A motorized patrol disappeared on 8 December, resulting in 13 missing. The Chinese repatriated 1 officer and 9 enlisted men from the patrol at the end of the conflict.

[96] Harris, *Puerto Rico's Fighting 65th*, pp. 136–37.

Chapter 4

FROM PUSAN TO THE IMJIN
JANUARY–MARCH 1951

The 3d Division finished disembarking at Pusan during the first two days of January 1951. As personnel, equipment, and supplies came ashore, its units moved to assembly areas in the vicinity of Toji-ri and Ulsan (thirty-five miles north of Pusan). There, the units repaired worn equipment, replenished basic ammunition loads, and integrated new replacements. Organized once again as a regimental combat team with the additions of the 10th Field Artillery and 92d AFA Battalions as well as Company C of the 10th Combat Engineer Battalion, the 65th Infantry then went to Yongjang-ni, thirty-five miles southeast of Taegu.[1]

In addition to gaining several hundred Puerto Rican replacements, the 65th still had 572 of its original complement of South Korean augmentees, which gave it an effective strength of 4,008, considerably in excess of its authorized strength of 3,797 officers and men. By way of comparison, the 7th and 15th Infantries, respectively, numbered 2,600 and 2,826 officers and men. Those figures included 800–900 Korean augmentees apiece and were representative of many U.S. infantry regiments in Eighth Army during that time.[2] The 65th was twice as strong as its sister regiments in terms of American soldiers. Because of this, Colonel Harris encountered little difficulty in returning 460 augmentees to the South Korean Army during January 1951.[3]

As the 65th Infantry refitted and reorganized, its officers made an effort to collect and disseminate vital combat lessons that the troops had learned during the previous several months. At division level, General Soule appointed a board, headed by the assistant division commander,

---

[1] Monthly Cmd Rpt, 65th Inf, Jan 51. Unless otherwise noted, all Cmd Rpts are in Entry 429, Rcds of the AGO, RG 407, NACP.
[2] Monthly Cmd Rpt, 3d Inf Div, Jan 51.
[3] Monthly Cmd Rpt, 65th Inf, Jan 51.

General Mead, to evaluate the 3d Division's combat performance to date. The group interviewed individuals of all ranks in a search for information that would improve future combat effectiveness. Some of the key lessons were the needs for accurate intelligence reporting, vigorous patrolling of the battlefield, greater integration of fire and maneuver at all levels, and the importance of integrated security and defense.[4]

On 3 January, Lt. Gen. Frank W. Milburn's I Corps took operational control of the 3d Division and ordered it to move to Ch'onan, fifty miles south of Seoul. The I Corps, which consisted of the 25th Infantry Division, the South Korean 1st Division, the Turkish Brigade, and the British 29th Infantry Brigade, had fought valiantly but unsuccessfully to prevent the Chinese from capturing the South Korean capital. Badly bruised, I Corps was in dire need of reinforcements. The 3d Division immediately began moving north, completing a 230-mile trek by 4 January under extremely adverse weather conditions, including a 22-hour blizzard.[5]

Between 1 and 5 January 1951, Chinese pressure had compelled the United Nations forces to withdraw from north of Seoul to new positions along the southern bank of the Han. When the frozen river proved to be little or no barrier to the advancing Chinese armies, Milburn abandoned Seoul after a brief rearguard action. On 5 January, elements of the 3d Division moved to a spot just north of Suwon, a city twenty miles south of Seoul, while the 25th Division and the South Korean 1st Division occupied blocking positions near the town of Anyang about ten miles south of the capital. Eighth Army directed General Milburn to protect Suwon until the huge cache of supplies there could be safely evacuated. When allied personnel accomplished that task on 6 January, the I Corps units near Suwon and Anyang pulled back to rejoin the main body of the Eighth Army.

The new line of resistance for I Corps ran from P'yongt'aek on the western coast twenty-eight miles south of Seoul to a point just beyond Ansong, sixteen miles to the east, where it joined up with IX Corps. (*Map 5*) The British Commonwealth 29th Brigade and the attached Thai Battalion occupied Milburn's left flank astride Route 1, which ran north to south through P'yongt'aek. The 3d Division's 15th Infantry occupied high ground on the right flank of the British brigade. The South Korean 1st Division, situated to block Route 17, which passed through Ansong, was positioned on the right flank of the 15th Infantry. The 3d Battalion of the 65th Infantry, as well as the 35th Infantry of the 25th Division, lay behind the 15th Infantry's main line of resistance. The remainder of the 25th Division, along with the

---

[4] Monthly Cmd Rpt, 65th Inf, Dec 50; Monthly Cmd Rpt, 3d Inf Div, Jan 51, Entry 429; Cmd Rpt, X Corps, Dec 50; Dolcater, *3d Infantry Division in Korea*, p. 127.

[5] Monthly Cmd Rpt, 65th Inf, Jan 51.

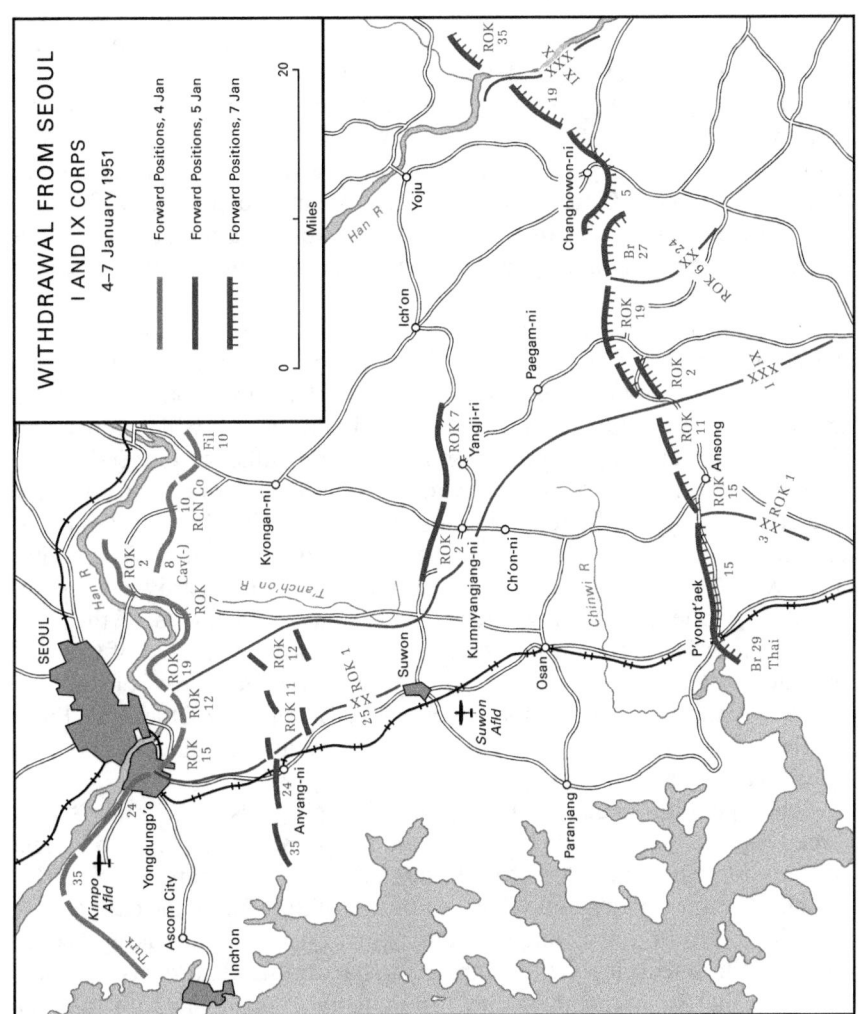

Turkish 1st Brigade, served as I Corps reserve at Ch'onan, thirteen miles south of P'yongt'aek.

Operations WOLFHOUND and THUNDERBOLT

Between 7 and 13 January, Eighth Army detected a growing enemy buildup between Suwon and Osan eight miles to the south. General Ridgway, the new Eighth Army commander, directed I Corps on 15 January to "investigate" with a force that included at least one tank battalion and "punish" any enemy he located. Ridgway had replaced Lt. Gen. Walton H. Walker in late December when the latter died in a traffic accident fourteen miles south of Seoul. Ridgway was certain that the Chinese troops would be caught off guard by a sudden thrust supported by artillery and airpower.[6]

On 14 January, General Milburn initiated Operation WOLFHOUND, spearheaded by the 25th Infantry Division, to conduct a reconnaissance-in-force in the Suwon-Osan area. The 3d Infantry Division would protect the 25th Division's right flank while it advanced to Route 20, which connected Suwon with Kumyangjang-ni ten miles to the southeast. General Soule ordered the formation of two battalion combat teams, one from the 65th Infantry, which would operate in close proximity with the 25th Division, and the other from the 15th Infantry, which would move on the right wing and screen the area to the east.[7] The 65th had orders to destroy any enemy it located while maintaining contact with adjacent elements of the 25th Division moving northward. The 65th's contribution consisted of Colonel Dammer's 2d Battalion, supported by the regimental tank company, a platoon of the regimental mortar company, Battery C of the 10th Field Artillery Battalion, Company C of the 10th Combat Engineer Battalion, and a tactical air control party.

The operation began on 15 January. The progress of Dammer's task force was soon halted by icy weather and the primitive road network. The 2d Battalion was forced to detour through the 25th Division sector until it reached Mangp'o-ri, a small village southeast of Suwon. To the east, the 1st Battalion, 15th Infantry, entered Kumyangjang-ni without making enemy contact. While securing the high ground to the north and northeast of town, however, the Americans took fire from enemy troops. The 15th Infantry task force mounted a hasty assault that killed fifty Chinese and forced the remainder to flee. On 16 January, the 3d Division ordered both battalions to return to friendly lines. A covering force from the 2d Battalion, 15th

---
[6] Mossman, *Ebb and Flow*, p. 228.
[7] Monthly Cmd Rpt, 3d Inf Div, Jan 51.

Infantry, killed thirty-five members of an enemy detachment attempting to follow the withdrawing units.[8]

"Operation WOLFHOUND was mounted so quickly that there was not time for adequate reconnaissance," General Soule reported. "As a result the mission of the 2nd Battalion . . . was not completed. The poor road net and icy condition of the road made the mission impractical with the heavy equipment with which it was attempted."[9] Even so, Operation WOLFHOUND lifted the morale of the 3d Division by placing the force back onto the offensive. More important, the operation had determined that the enemy was not active along the division front except for the concentration near Kumyangjang-ni.[10]

General Ridgway

Overall, General Milburn estimated that WOLFHOUND had inflicted fourteen hundred casualties on the enemy, most the result of air strikes. American losses came to three killed and seven wounded.[11] While most of the I Corps units that fought in the two-day operation returned to their original positions, some stayed behind to man an outpost line along the Chinwi River, five miles south of Osan.

Commending Milburn's force for its fighting spirit, General Ridgway instructed his other corps commanders to devise similar operations. General Milburn, meanwhile, built on his initial success by ordering a reconnaissance-in-force in the Kumnyangjang-ni area, where an estimated enemy battalion was thought to be operating. In response, the 65th Infantry formed a battalion combat team from Colonel St. Clair's 1st Battalion supported by the regimental tank company, a platoon of heavy mortars, an engineer company, a field artillery battery, and a tactical air control party. The task force was attached to the 25th Division's 35th Infantry for the duration of the operation.

---

[8] Monthly Cmd Rpt, 65th Inf, Jan 51.
[9] Ibid.
[10] Ibid.
[11] Mossman, *Ebb and Flow*, p. 238.

The one-day operation on 22 January resulted in only two small skirmishes during which the Americans killed three enemy soldiers and captured one. There were no friendly losses. Despite its limited duration, the effort confirmed the absence of strong enemy forces within ten miles of the I Corps front. This encouraged General Ridgway to expand his plans for an Eighth Army drive to the north.[12]

On 23 January 1951, Eighth Army's intelligence staff reported that the bulk of the Chinese *XII Army Group* was located within an area bounded by Route 20 to the south and the Han to the east and north. When air reconnaissance missions could not confirm that information, Ridgway mounted Operation THUNDERBOLT to drive the enemy into the open if he was there. The advance was limited in nature, including only a small portion of Milburn's I Corps and Coulter's neighboring IX Corps. Both commanders had instructions to probe as far as the Han, neither using more than one American division reinforced by armor and, at the discretion of each corps, one South Korean regiment. This approach, making limited advances while holding large forces in reserve, was one of the key lessons allied commanders had learned from the Chinese. It would become a standard feature of UN operations for the remainder of the war.[13]

Led by reconnaissance elements moving along a wide front, the Turkish Brigade and the 35th Infantry covered four miles on the opening day of THUNDERBOLT, 25 January, without meeting significant opposition. As the Americans continued their advance, however, enemy resistance began to stiffen. The 35th Infantry fought an enemy force at Suwon and took the city at 1300 on 26 January. The Turks encountered a strong force of Chinese troops at Kumyangjang-ni, nine miles to the east, who held the town until 1930 that evening.

Anticipating the probability of even stronger resistance nearer the Han, Ridgway authorized Milburn on 28 January to add the 3d Division to the I Corps thrust. That same day, I Corps published its order for Operation EXPLOITATION. The operation was meant to consolidate the gains of THUNDERBOLT and to advance I Corps to the high ground just south of the Han. Milburn's plan called for three divisions to occupy positions along the river with the 25th Division on the left, the 3d in the center, and the South Korean 1st Division on the right. The British 29th Brigade would act as the corps reserve. Contesting the effort was the Chinese *50th Army*, composed of the *148th*, *149th*, and *150th Divisions*, each with an estimated strength of seven thousand eight hundred men.[14]

---

[12] Monthly Cmd Rpt, 65th Inf, Jan 51; Mossman, *Ebb and Flow*, p. 238.
[13] Mossman, *Ebb and Flow*, p. 240.
[14] Staff Bfg Min, 26 Jan 51, in Monthly Cmd Rpt, 3d Inf Div, Jan 51.

M4A3E8 medium tanks of the 65th Heavy Tank Company await orders to move against dug-in Communist troops near Suwon, 27 January 1951.

Preparatory to the attack ordered by Operation EXPLOITATION, the 3d Division began to move northward on 27 January along the axis of Route 55 with the 65th Infantry on the left and the 15th Infantry on the right. At first, the Americans encountered only light resistance; but enemy opposition gradually stiffened as Chinese reinforcements began deploying in the path of the 3d Division. Hastily laid minefields covered by small-arms, machine-gun, mortar, and artillery fire slowed the American troops. The Chinese defensive layout, featuring mostly company-size positions, suggested to General Soule that he was still facing only a screening force. This led U.S. commanders to question whether the Chinese had established a main line of resistance south of the Han. Neither prisoner interrogation nor air reconnaissance provided any answers.

During the early morning of 29 January, the Chinese made their first concentrated effort to block the 3d Division. At 0200, a battalion from the Chinese *447th Regiment*, blowing whistles and bugles and supported by concentrated machine-gun and mortar fire, hurled itself at the 1st Battalion, 65th Infantry, encamped several miles northeast of Suwon. Surrounding the Company A command post, the enemy soldiers pinned down the company commander and his headquarters platoon. The unit's executive officer, 1st Lt. Paul Lavergne, then charged the Communists while blazing away with his automatic rifle. His bold and unexpected maneuver sent the enemy running and bought enough time for Colonel St. Clair to organize a counterattack with Company C.

The Chinese also struck 1st Lt. Rafael A. Serra's Company B, which was located in a defensive perimeter on nearby Hill 270. Confronted by an estimated three hundred enemy troops armed with grenades, automatic weapons, and mortars, Company B found itself in danger of being overrun. Seeing a gap develop in his perimeter, Lieutenant Serra repositioned his men to plug the hole and then called for mortar and artillery fire as close to his troops as safety would allow. Their attack disrupted by the incoming shells, the Chinese soon retreated.

Meanwhile, Company C from the 1st Battalion launched a counterattack against the enemy soldiers besieging Company A. The commander of Company C, Captain Magner, "had ordered his men to fix bayonets," remembered Harris, "and when they landed in the middle of two hundred Chinese, the fur began to fly. In short order it became a rifle-butt swinging, bayonet jabbing, close-range shootout, where it was difficult to distinguish friend from foe."[15] Meanwhile, elements of the 65th's tank and headquarters companies, located with the regimental command post on an adjoining hill five hundred yards to the south, targeted several Chinese heavy-weapons teams with tank cannons and machine guns.

As a result of the regiment's quick reaction, the Borinqueneers were able to regain the initiative and prevent the enemy from making further inroads against the 1st Battalion's defensive perimeter. M.Sgt. Juan Cordero of Company B, 1st Battalion, for example, led a platoon-size counterattack against the Chinese. Using grenades and small arms, he forced the enemy back and restored the line in his sector. After he reorganized his men, his company repulsed all subsequent Communist attacks and infiltration attempts. For leadership and courage under fire, Sergeant Cordero received the Bronze Star for valor.[16]

While most of the soldiers in the 1st Battalion were busy repelling the Chinese onslaught, others, such as Sgt. Victor G. Colon-Mateo, an aid man in the 65th's Medical Company, worked to save the lives of wounded comrades. "[When] heavy enemy mortar fire wounded several men," the sergeant's Bronze Star citation read, "Sergeant Colon-Mateo immediately went to the wounded and administered first aid in the midst of the heavy mortar barrage. Then he assisted in evacuating the wounded through intense enemy action."[17]

Sometimes the actions of a single soldier turned the momentum of battle. The commander of the 1st Battalion's Headquarters Company, 1st Lt. Julian F. Lockerman, responded to the Chinese attack by laying down a withering fire with a jeep-mounted .50-caliber machine gun. The weapon's throaty

---

[15] Harris, *Puerto Rico's Fighting 65th*, p. 153.

[16] GO no. 92, HQ, 3d Inf Div, 11 Apr 51, sub: Award of Bronze Star Medal to Master Sergeant Juan Cordero, in Monthly Cmd Rpt, 3d Inf Div, Apr 51.

[17] GO no. 86, HQ, 3d Inf Div, 2 Apr 51, sub: Award of Bronze Star Medal to Sergeant Victor G. Colon-Mateo, in Monthly Cmd Rpt, 3d Inf Div, Apr 51.

As an L-19 observation plane circles overhead, men of the 65th Infantry enter a newly recaptured village just west of Suwon during Operation EXPLOITATION.

blast—accompanied by the loud screams of seriously wounded Communist soldiers—nearly drowned out the other sounds of the fight. Golf-ball-size tracers were clearly visible as they streaked through the enemy formation, silhouetting the attackers. In the end, Lockerman's fire was so intense and destructive that the enemy became demoralized and withdrew. In return, Headquarters Company sustained only a single casualty.[18]

When the fighting was over, more than 100 dead Communist soldiers lay on the battlefield. In all, the 65th sustained 3 killed, 15 wounded, and 1 missing. One of the dead was Lieutenant Lavergne, the executive officer of Company A. "He had been in the thick of the fighting from the beginning," wrote Harris, "and was the rallying point around which our men made their stand. Had it not been for his heroic leadership, the enemy might have overrun the entire A Company position."[19] For his role in the action, Lieutenant

---

[18] Harris, *Puerto Rico's Fighting 65th*, p. 153.
[19] Ibid.

Lavergne received a posthumous Silver Star. A second Silver Star went to Lieutenant Lockerman of Headquarters Company.[20]

Despite the gutsy performance of the 1st Battalion, General Soule criticized the Borinqueneers because of their failure to detect the attack until too late. "Undoubtedly some of the men fell asleep and permitted the enemy to get too close before fire could be placed upon them," the division commander remarked to his staff later that evening. "Outposts should be in operation . . . and booby traps should be employed. The attack upon the 65th came in the direction in which they had expected it and was partially successful due to the fact that the men just were not alert."[21]

Always sensitive to the needs of his soldiers, Soule angrily noted that the division's efforts to evacuate the 65th's casualties had been "hardly satisfactory." Furthermore, the division surgeon had failed to request helicopter evacuation. Soule ordered his chief of staff, Col. Oliver P. Newman, to emphasize to the regiment the importance of evacuating seriously wounded soldiers immediately. At the conclusion of the meeting, Soule speculated that some Chinese were probably hiding out to the rear of the 3d Division's position and so ordered a search of all villages and areas within fifteen hundred yards of each unit.[22]

The Chinese were having problems of their own, especially when conducting offensive operations. "The weak point of our division at the present time is its combat ability," reported one of the Chinese *50th Army*'s division commanders:

> This is due to the lack of know-how and experience. Company commanders and platoon leaders lack experience and knowledge of military matters and are poor leaders. There are many soldiers who never received adequate training and they don't know how to conduct themselves in combat. We must overcome these defects and cooperate with each other in making them first class soldiers.[23]

As a result of the surprise predawn assault on the positions of the 65th Infantry, the 3d Division delayed an attack it had scheduled for the morning of 29 January in order to collate and analyze intelligence it had gathered on the battlefield.[24] The 65th's Intelligence and Reconnaissance Platoon had found a map overlay and a field order on a dead Chinese soldier. The

---

[20] GO no. 69, HQ, 3d Inf Div, 20 Mar 51, listing Award of Silver Medal (Posthumously) to 1st Lieutenant Paul Lavergne and Award of the Silver Star Medal to 1st Lieutenant Julian F. Lockerman, Monthly Cmd Rpt, 3d Inf Div, Apr 51.

[21] Staff Bfg Min, 29 Jan 51, in Monthly Cmd Rpt, 3d Inf Div, Jan 51.

[22] Ibid.

[23] Chinese *50th Army*, trans. of "References for Night Combat for Small Units," 28 Jan 51, in ann. 2, Monthly Cmd Rpt, 65th Inf, Jan 51.

[24] Staff Bfg Min, 29 Jan 51.

map revealed the organization, dispositions, and locations of the forces opposing the 3d Division. A regiment of eighteen hundred to two thousand troops blocked the way of the 65th and another three Chinese regiments opposed the remainder of the 3d Division.[25]

Indeed, when the division launched its attack later that afternoon, the 65th and 15th Infantries soon encountered heavy resistance. The Chinese fought from stout emplacements on commanding terrain, amply supported by mortars and artillery. On the right, the 15th Infantry stalled in the face of Chinese field fortifications on Hill 425 located five miles north-northwest of Kumnyangjang-ni. On the left, the 65th encountered similar resistance north of Suwon on Hills 449 and 262, in the 1st and 2d Battalion sectors, respectively.

Aware that it had engaged the Chinese *149th* and *150th Divisions*, the 65th put the intelligence to good use. "When one of our battalions hit some resistance, and the commander determined that it was from one of the positions on the map, he would call for mortar and artillery fire and attack in accordance with plans already worked out," Harris related.[26] In effect, using the enemy's own maps, Harris was able to pinpoint and eliminate Communist entrenchments without throwing his battalions headlong into the teeth of the enemy's defenses.

On 30 January, the 65th Infantry set out to take Hills 449 and 262. St. Clair's 1st Battalion on the left assaulted the higher of the two peaks, while Dammer's 2d Battalion on the right headed for the smaller elevation. Colonel Allen's 3d Battalion remained in reserve. In addition to the artillery units attached to the regiment, three battalions of 155-mm. howitzers supported the attack, an indication that both I Corps and the 3d Division considered Colonel Harris' assault to be their main thrust. So did General Ridgway, who came to the 65th's sector to observe the assault in person.

The regimental tank company and the mortar company worked closely with the 1st and 2d Battalions, as did the rapid-firing automatic weapons of the 3d Anti-Aircraft Artillery Automatic Weapons Battalion, which peppered enemy positions with thousands of .50-caliber and 40-mm. rounds. "Knowing beforehand where each strong point was located," Harris remembered, "gave us a greater advantage and, more important, saved many lives."[27] By nightfall, the regiment had seized the better part of Hills 449 and 262 at a cost of five killed and thirty-three wounded.[28]

After watching the initial phase of the attack, Ridgway spent the remainder of 30 January visiting uncommitted elements of the 65th Infantry:

---

[25] Harris, *Puerto Rico's Fighting 65th*, p. 145.
[26] Ibid., p. 145.
[27] Ibid., p. 147.
[28] Monthly Cmd Rpts, 65th Inf, Jan 51, and 3d Inf Div, Jan 51.

A light machine-gun team from the 65th Infantry engages Communist troops holding out on a nearby hilltop.

"When I heard that he was coming to visit us, I selected the two tallest Puerto Rican soldiers I could find, over six feet, tied several dummy hand grenades to their field jackets, and then gave each of them a long knife," recalled Harris. "I smeared some black soot on their faces and posted them as guards to the entrance of my command post."[29]

Ridgway also spent the next day with the regiment and received a briefing from Colonel Harris.[30] No one noticed if the Puerto Rican soldiers posted at the entrance of Harris' command post elicited a favorable remark from Ridgway. However, the Eighth Army commander clearly made a favorable impression on the men of the 65th. "He was an exceptional leader and enjoyed the widest admiration from the units in the field," remembered the regiment's assistant intelligence officer, Capt. Charles E. Boyle. "For those of us aware of the defeatist attitude of Eighth Army under General Walker, General Ridgway was a breath of fresh air and changed our whole perspective. We became accomplished fighters with the intention of winning."[31]

Upon returning to his headquarters, Ridgway sent a thank-you to Harris:

---

[29] Harris, *Puerto Rico's Fighting 65th*, p. 156.
[30] CG's Jnl, 31 Jan 51, in Monthly Cmd Rpt, 3d Inf Div, Jan 51.
[31] Interv, author with Charles E. Boyle, 15 Feb 01, Historians files, CMH.

What I saw and heard of your regiment reflects great credit on you, the regiment, and the people of Puerto Rico, who can be proud of their valiant sons. I am confident that their battle records and training levels will win them high honors. . . . Their conduct in battle has served only to increase the high regard in which I hold these fine troops.[32]

Harris remarked that Ridgway's two-day visit was "quite an unusual amount of time for an army commander to spend with one regimental combat team."[33] He could not have been more correct. Ridgway was not only assessing the Puerto Ricans' combat performance but was also contemplating the future integration of Puerto Rican troops throughout Eighth Army. Having watched the 65th in action on 30 January, that very evening Ridgway directed General Soule to use Puerto Rican replacements throughout the 3d Division rather than assign them specifically to the Puerto Rican regiment.

There appear to have been two major considerations behind Ridgway's instructions to Soule. The first and more important had to do with maintaining the combat efficiency of units fighting in Korea. Ridgway believed that segregation was a highly inefficient use of manpower and thus staunchly supported integration. Confronted with growing battle losses in white infantry units and an increasing surplus of African American replacements arriving in Japan, in August 1950, Eighth Army began sending individual black soldiers to understrength white units just as it had been assigning individual Korean soldiers.[34] This process accelerated during early 1951. Viewed in this light, Ridgway's orders for Puerto Rican soldiers to be used throughout the 3d Division appears to have been part of his strategy to make the most of the manpower available to the Eighth Army.

A second, lesser circumstance that influenced the Eighth Army's shift in assignment policies had to do with the growing surplus of Puerto Rican soldiers slated to arrive in Korea in 1951. By the end of December 1950, several thousand Puerto Ricans had entered the military and were training on the island. Over half were slated to go to Far East Command.[35] At this point in the war, with few exceptions, Puerto Ricans could serve only in

---

[32] Harris, *Puerto Rico's Fighting 65th*, p. 157.

[33] Ibid., p. 156.

[34] Morris J. MacGregor Jr., *Integration of the Armed Forces, 1940–1965* (Washington, D.C.: U.S. Army Center of Military History, 1989), p. 433.

[35] HQ, USARFANT [U.S. Army Forces, Antilles], Ltr, ANTAG [Antilles Adjutant General] 312 to Col Culp, 15 October 1952, in Culp, *Training and Future Utilization*, p. 22. During 1951, a total of 9,346 enlisted men graduated from basic training in Puerto Rico. Of this number, 8,946 were shipped overseas to Korea, the U.S. Caribbean Command, and Europe. Cmd Rpt no. 2, 1 Dec 51–30 Nov 52, dtd 10 Dec 52, HQ, U.S. Army Forces Antilles, pp. 2, 8.

Puerto Rican units, a policy that benefited the 65th Infantry by providing it with ample replacements at a time when many combat units were facing manpower shortages. Not until 1952 would the Army amend its assignment policies to allow Puerto Rican enlisted soldiers fluent in English to be assigned anywhere in the Army.[36]

The number of Puerto Rican trainees indicated that the 65th Infantry, which had arrived in Korea with a 10 percent surplus of personnel, would remain overstrength through the summer of 1951. Although the regiment was authorized 3,614 enlisted personnel, it would have some 4,000 men by February 1951.[37] In comparison, the other infantry regiments of the 3d Division averaged 1,800 American soldiers apiece and had to incorporate 800 to 900 South Koreans each to attain authorized manning levels.[38]

In a word, the need for men, combined with the forecast surplus of Puerto Rican soldiers, had convinced Ridgway to include Puerto Ricans in the Eighth Army's integration plans. Although General Soule initially resisted on the grounds that language difficulties would otherwise result, he conceded that "if the present high percentage of Puerto Rican replacements continues, however, it will be necessary to assign them to other units."[39]

The 3d Division would need all the help it could get. At the end of January 1951, the Chinese still continued to cling to their positions despite the immense concentrations of air and artillery fire leveled against them. On 31 January, the 7th Infantry took the 15th Infantry's place on line while the 15th reverted to division reserve. The 65th Infantry remained on station, renewing its attacks north of Suwon against increasingly bitter Chinese resistance. "The nature of the terrain and the defense put up by the enemy," reported Soule, "leads to the conclusion that the enemy MLR [main line of resistance] has been reached."[40]

Five men of the 65th won the Silver Star for gallantry in action on 31 January. Among them were Colonel Allen, the 3d Battalion's commander, and 2d Lt. Pablo Ramirez of Company A, who was killed in the fighting. "Lieutenant Ramirez led his platoon in an assault on Hill 499 in the vicinity of Kalgok, Korea," the citation read:

---

[36] Entry dtd 15 Apr 52, HQ USARFANT and MDPR [Military District of Puerto Rico] Daily Jnl. See also entry dtd 20 Mar 52. In anticipation of this change, an experiment held in March 1952 sent 100 non–English speaking Puerto Rican recruits to the English Qualification Unit at Fort Devens, Massachusetts, for thirteen weeks of language training. They later received basic and advanced training at a Replacement Training Center in the continental United States.

[37] Monthly Cmd Rpt, 3d Inf Div, Jan 51.

[38] Ibid.

[39] Monthly Cmd Rpt, 3d Inf Div, Feb 51, sec. IV.

[40] Staff Bfg Min, 31 Jan 51, in Monthly Cmd Rpt, 3d Inf Div, Jan 51.

In the initial phase of the assault an enemy artillery barrage killed one of his men and wounded two others. The platoon was scattered by the shelling, but Lieutenant Ramirez immediately reorganized his men and continued to attack the hill despite the Chinese artillery and small arms fire. He discovered two wounded soldiers and evacuated them. Upon reaching a third man, he was killed by an exploding shell.[41]

In addition to the five men who earned Silver Stars, numerous others in the unit received several Bronze Stars for valor.[42]

The 65th Infantry ended the month having established a solid record as the 3d Division's assault regiment. Between 23 and 31 January, its officers estimated, it had killed 307 Chinese and North Korean soldiers, wounded an estimated 900, and captured 23. In turn, the unit had suffered 92 battle casualties and 275 nonbattle casualties, most of the latter being cold-weather injuries.[43]

Preparing to Liberate Seoul

At the beginning of February 1951, the Chinese *149th Division* remained north of Suwon in a position to block the advance of the 3d Division. The 65th, operating on the division's left flank, confronted the Chinese *447th Regiment* while the 15th Infantry, operating on the right, faced the *445th*. Due to heavy losses, cold weather, and an unreliable replacement system, enemy strength had fallen from an average of six hundred men per battalion to somewhere between two hundred and two hundred fifty soldiers in each unit. The enemy was also suffering from low morale due to a lack of food, clothing, and supplies. Even so, the *149th Division* stood firm while the bulk of Chinese forces withdrew to new positions on the north side of the Han, where they were preparing a last-ditch line to defend Seoul.[44]

Despite its weakened state, the *447th Regiment* that stood opposite the 65th remained a dangerous and unpredictable foe. During the second day of General Ridgway's visit to the regiment, the Chinese raided Company G. "About two o'clock in the morning the Chinese counter-attacked," recalled Sgt. Alfonso Garcia. "They infiltrated our position and Lieutenant [Fernando] Vasaldua was killed by a grenade. One of the fragments hit me above the right eyebrow and I killed the Chinese who threw it. Meanwhile

---

[41] HQ, 3d Inf Div, GO no. 92, 11 Apr 51, sub: Award of Silver Star (Posthumous) to 2nd Lieutenant Pablo Ramirez, in Monthly Cmd Rpt, 3d Inf Div, Apr 51.

[42] GO nos. 67, 73, 74, 83, Mar 51, in Monthly Cmd Rpt, 3d Inf Div, Mar 51; GO no. 92, Apr 51, in Monthly Command Rpt, 3d Inf Div, Apr 51.

[43] Monthly Cmd Rpt, 65th Inf, Jan 51.

[44] Monthly Cmd Rpt, 3d Inf Div, Feb 51.

the Reds overran our position and Corporal [Gonzalez S.] Centeno and I were captured."[45]

After four hours of intense fighting, the men of the 65th repulsed the enemy and restored the line.[46] The captured Puerto Ricans joined a group of sixteen U.S. and British captives healthy enough to travel on foot. Before setting out on their journey north, the prisoners witnessed the Chinese execute one American who was too weak to walk. "One month was spent marching north from one Prisoner of War cage to another in freezing weather without enough clothes to stay warm, because the Chinese had taken most of them away from us," remembered Sergeant Garcia. At one point when the enemy became careless about security, the two Puerto Ricans killed a guard and escaped. In the month that followed, the pair worked their way back to allied lines. "Although we came close to both freezing and starving to death," Garcia commented, "we managed to survive."[47]

February began with the 65th Infantry continuing its effort to seize the high ground that dominated the southeastern approaches to Seoul. On 1 February, backed by the 10th and 92d Field Artillery Battalions, tanks, and air support, the 65th launched a coordinated three-battalion attack against a range of hills north of Suwon.[48] The regiment made steady gains despite strong enemy resistance. As the Americans neared the crest of one objective, the 1st and 2d Battalions fixed bayonets and charged the Communists, driving the enemy off the summit. "Apparently the sight of cold steel in the hands of the Puerto Ricans so unnerved some of the Chinese that they made the fatal mistake of starting to run down the far side of the hill," Harris said. "When they did, our men just picked them off like cottontails in a corn field."[49]

After the battle, Harris and his men surveyed the positions the Chinese had abandoned. "There was no doubt that we had captured their defensive plans," the colonel remarked:

> Our mortars and artillery had literally lifted the ground from a depth of about three or four feet and turned it over like a cook would flip pancakes on a griddle. And what the mortars and artillery did not accomplish, the foot troops completed. The whole area was a shambles of tangled barbed wire, broken logs, busted equipment, and dead bodies.[50]

---

[45] Harris, *Puerto Rico's Fighting 65th*, p. 150.
[46] Monthly Cmd Rpt, 65th Inf, Feb 51.
[47] Harris, *Puerto Rico's Fighting 65th*, p. 151.
[48] Monthly Cmd Rpt, 65th Inf, Feb 51.
[49] Harris, *Puerto Rico's Fighting 65th*, p. 147.
[50] Ibid.

The Chinese, despite their losses, were not willing to abandon Seoul without a major fight. Starting on the night of 2 February, when an enemy company raided Dammer's 2d Battalion, the Chinese increased the size and frequency of their attacks during the hours of darkness. They also adjusted their tactics to confuse allied intelligence. "During the early hours of each night the enemy would pull back some ten or twelve miles so that we were unable to locate them," Harris noted. "Then several hours before daybreak, down the ridges they would come, hundreds of them running at top speed."[51] The Chinese deception ploy ended up having little or no effect. Over the next several days, the 65th continued to grind forward, smashing one fiercely contested enemy strongpoint after another.

During this period, each regiment of the 3d Division formed an armored task force for the purpose of raiding the Communist rear area. In the 65th Infantry, Colonel Harris created Task Force MYERS, led by Capt. Arthur W. Myers, former commander of the regimental tank company who had become the regimental operations officer. The armored group consisted of the 65th's tank company, its headquarters company, the regimental Intelligence and Reconnaissance Platoon, an artillery battery accompanied by a forward observer, and a tactical air control party.

On 2 February 1951, Task Force MYERS made a thrust into enemy territory with the goal of destroying a Chinese command post thought to be operating in the area. While the tanks never located the well-camouflaged enemy headquarters, they did encounter and engage a force of three hundred Chinese infantry, killing an estimated one hundred fifty without suffering any losses.[52]

Over the days that followed, all three of the 65th Infantry's battalions continued to push northward between Routes 1 and 55 toward the Han. On 8 February, the 1st and 3d Battalions seized a series of hills just a few miles from the river with support from the regimental tank company. Opposition was so insignificant that Colonel Harris ordered Task Force MYERS to attack northward to prevent the Chinese from retreating across the Han. He reinforced the task force with Company G, 2d Battalion; Company C, 10th Combat Engineers; Battery D, 3d AAA Battalion; and a forward observer team from the 58th AFA Battalion.

On 9 February, Task Force MYERS reached Sokchon-ni, a ferry crossing on the south bank of the Han, without making contact with the enemy. In doing so, it became the first unit of I Corps to reach the river. The next day, the task force worked its way westward to the town of Majukko-ri,

---

[51] Ibid., p. 154.
[52] Monthly Cmd Rpt, 65th Inf, Feb 51; Dolcater, *3d Infantry Division in Korea*, p. 140.

Tanks and troops from the 15th Infantry battle Chinese troops south of the Han River.

where it engaged fifty Chinese soldiers. It killed twenty of them in a sharp fight before returning to Sokchon-ni to rejoin the 65th Infantry. Meanwhile, the rest of the 3d Division moved forward to join the regiment on the south bank of the Han.[53]

On 10 February, the 15th Infantry relieved the 65th, which assumed the duties of division reserve after having endured fourteen continuous days of combat. General Soule decided "to give the 'Borinqueneers' a breather . . . so that fresh troops could drive into the withdrawing Reds with all possible vigor."[54]

The period in reserve gave Harris and his officers an opportunity to boost the morale of the regiment with some rare creature comforts. The men took showers and visited a mobile post exchange, where they bought more than $8,000 in merchandise in February alone. In addition, morale officers showed movies using portable projectors and generators and provided tape recorders with Puerto Rican music tapes. The Red Cross and Army chaplains provided assistance visits and religious services. The chaplains particularly were important in sustaining the morale of the mostly Catholic unit. Finally, Harris and his officers saw to it that the exploits of the 65th Infantry were widely publicized in the Army newspaper *Stars and Stripes*.[55]

---

[53] Monthly Cmd Rpts, 65th Inf, Feb 51, and 3d Inf Div, Feb 51; Dolcater, *3d Infantry Division in Korea*, p. 143.

[54] Dolcater, *3d Infantry Division in Korea*, p. 143.

[55] Monthly Cmd Rpts, 65th Inf, Jan–Mar 51.

The 65th also took heart from the widespread support lavished upon its members by the citizens of Puerto Rico. News dispatches, pictures, and letters from the unit's soldiers appeared daily in the island's press. Radio programs and baseball games were dedicated to the troops, and editorial writers expressed the highest praise and appreciation for the regiment's efforts and sacrifices. Harris informed the troops that the island's legislature had approved a joint resolution of gratitude "to the men of the 65th Infantry Regiment for their heroic tasks on the battlefields of the Korean peninsula in defense of the principles of democracy." He added that fifty new buses serving the island's metropolitan area between San Juan and Rio Piedras had been decorated with the regimental crest.[56] For many Puerto Ricans, the successes and failures of the 65th Infantry reflected upon the entire island's reputation.

Around the time that the 65th Infantry went into reserve, both I Corps and IX Corps wrapped up Operation THUNDERBOLT by completing their advance to the Han. Meanwhile, General Almond's X Corps farther inland was in the process of chewing up North Korean forces near Chip'yong-ni, twenty-two miles east-southeast of Seoul. The X Corps thrust, known as Operation ROUNDUP, was designed to protect the advance of IX Corps but had the unintended effect of drawing enemy forces into the west central region, away from the forces involved in Operation THUNDERBOLT.

On the night of 11–12 February, the enemy struck back at X Corps with five Chinese armies and two North Korean corps, approximately one hundred thirty-five thousand soldiers in total. His main effort fell upon the South Korean 3d and 8th Divisions near Changbong, eighteen miles northeast of Chip'yong-ni, and Hoengsong, twenty miles east of Chip'yong-ni. The attack penetrated the South Korean line, inflicted almost ten thousand casualties, and forced the defenders to retreat to the southeast. Their precipitous withdrawal created a large gap in the center of the X Corps.

South Korean units were not the only allied forces to give way. The Chinese overran a U.S. field artillery battalion supporting the South Korean 8th Division and inflicted heavy losses on the U.S. 38th Infantry from the 2d Infantry Division and its attached Dutch Battalion. Under pressure, the 2d Division that was holding the left flank of X Corps withdrew some seven miles. There, it established a new line that ran east from Chip'yong-ni to the region just north of Wonju, a distance of twenty miles. Concurrently, the 7th Division took position east of Wonju to protect the 2d Division's right flank. Knowing that the two divisions lacked sufficient strength to hold

---

[56] Matthew T. Kenny, "65th Reg't Puerto Rico's Pride and Joy," *Stars and Stripes*, 13 January 1951; Cpl Neil Mellblom, "PR Reg't Gets News by Proxy," *Stars and Stripes*, 8 February 1951; "Puerto Ricans Show Pride in Their Men in Korea," *Stars and Stripes*, 2 April 1951; all in Historians files, CMH.

such a long front indefinitely, General Almond ordered the 2d Division to pull its 23d Infantry out of Chip'yong-ni to create a more compact line south of the city. Before the American unit could comply, however, elements of four Chinese divisions surrounded the regiment.

Just as the situation began to look desperate, the allies once again regained their footing. The isolated 23d Infantry valiantly held its ground, and within a few days it became clear that the Communist offensive had spent itself. By 18 February, enemy forces had begun retreating north rather than trying to hold what they had taken. The stubborn stand the 23d Infantry made at Chip'yong-ni, the tremendous losses the enemy had suffered at the hands of the allies, and a pressing need to resupply and reorganize ultimately forced the Communists to break contact and withdraw. The success enjoyed by X Corps in repulsing the Communist offensive helped convince General Ridgway that the Eighth Army had fully regained the confidence it had lost in the wake of earlier defeats and was now prepared to undertake even more ambitious offensive efforts in the near future.[57]

The I Corps area of operations had not remained idle when the enemy had tried to roll back X Corps. Even though the bulk of the 65th Infantry was busy training in small-unit tactics and the employment of flamethrowers while serving as division reserve, the regiment was never completely out of the fighting. On 12 February, Dammer's 2d Battalion and the regiment's tank company supported an attack spearheaded by the 7th Infantry.[58] Then, at 0230 on 13 February, a force of fifteen hundred North Korean soldiers smashed into St. Clair's 1st Battalion and Allen's 3d Battalion. The fighting that followed was brutal; but by daylight, the 65th had repulsed the enemy.[59]

The next day, the Puerto Ricans laid on a pursuit and caught up with the enemy force before it could slip back across the Han. Captain Boyle, the assistant intelligence officer, spent much of the day in an L–16 light observation aircraft in constant communication with Harris and the battalion commanders, U.S. Air Force fighter-bombers, and the supporting artillery and regimental mortar company. He took turns with the regimental chief operations officer, Captain Myers, in surveying the situation from aloft. Calling in air power, artillery, and mortars, the pair wreaked havoc on the enemy. When the dust settled, the 65th was credited with killing 537 North Koreans and capturing 268 more. Losses within the regiment totaled one man killed and six wounded. The rest of the 3d Division killed 463 of the enemy and captured 150, annihilating what was left of the Communist

---

[57] Mossman, *Ebb and Flow*, p. 300.
[58] Monthly Cmd Rpt, 65th Inf, Feb 51.
[59] Ibid.

force. Only a few survivors managed to escape. The enemy unit was later identified as the *1st Infantry* of the North Korean *8th Division*.[60]

The 3d Division later received a commendation from I Corps for its role in the fight.[61] General Soule distributed a memorandum that heartily endorsed General Milburn's recognition of his division: "Each and every one of you participated in this action and fully performed your duty as a member of the division fighting team. I am proud of you and the division's record on this occasion."[62] Taking the narrowest viewpoint, Harris was angered by the commendation: "I was slightly amazed to receive such a general commendation because the 65th was just about the only unit of the division which had participated in the fight."[63]

The 65th Infantry continued to see action in midmonth despite officially being in division reserve. On 16 February 1951, Colonel Allen's 3d Battalion relieved a battalion of the 7th Infantry that had recently experienced three concerted Chinese attacks. That night, the Borinqueneers drove off the fourth and final assault. Sporadic enemy activity continued in the regiment's sector.

On 19 February, the 65th sent a task force composed of elements of the regimental tank company, a platoon from the 64th Heavy Tank Battalion, and Battery C of the 3d Anti-Aircraft Artillery Automatic Weapons Battalion on a northward foray. Supported by Company B from St. Clair's 1st Battalion and the 58th AFA Battalion, the armored vehicles attacked toward the Han against stiff enemy resistance and seized a series of intermediate objectives in the process. While this was happening, the 2d Battalion became embroiled in several skirmishes of its own. The unit captured 16 enemy soldiers while killing 125 and wounding 50 more. By 20 February, the entire regiment was once again in action, taking up positions just south of the Han on Line Boston with the 2d and 3d Battalions on line and the 1st Battalion in reserve.[64]

At that point, the 3d Division had a frontage of over fourteen miles, which left each of its regiments responsible for an unusually wide sector. Since it was impossible to hold the entire line in strength, each regiment stationed outposts along the southern bank of the Han, installed barbed

---

[60] Monthly Cmd Rpts, 65th Inf, Feb 51, and 3d Inf Div, Feb 51; Dolcater, *3d Infantry Division in Korea*, pp. 145–48.

[61] Ltr, Lt Gen F. W. Milburn, CG, HQ, I Corps, to Maj Gen Robert H. Soule, CG, 3d Inf Div, 15 Feb 51, in Monthly Cmd Rpt, 3d Inf Div, Feb 51.

[62] Ltr, HQ, 3d Inf Div, 17 Feb 51, sub: Commendation, in Monthly Cmd Rpt, 3d Inf Div, Feb 51.

[63] Harris, *Puerto Rico's Fighting 65th*, p. 168. The 15th Infantry also played a major part in the engagement and inflicted only slightly fewer casualties on the North Korean unit.

[64] Monthly Cmd Rpt, 65th Inf, Feb 51.

wire and trip flares, and patrolled its sector aggressively. Mobile task forces waited in reserve, ready to move quickly to any threatened point along the river. While developing and rehearsing its counterattack plans, the 3d Division waited to see what the enemy would do.

On to Seoul and the Imjin

While the left flank of the Eighth Army remained anchored along the south side of the Han, General Ridgway scheduled Operation KILLER to begin on 21 February. The operation would use the right wing of the Eighth Army to destroy enemy units in the Chech'on salient, a bulge in the allied line southeast of Wonju thirty miles across and fifteen miles deep that contained the North Korean *V Corps*. Ridgway also intended KILLER to wear down the Chinese *66th Army Group* defending the sector between Chip'yong-ni and Wonju. He directed the IX and X Corps to advance northward between ten and fifteen miles to Line Arizona, which extended east from Yangp'yong (five miles west of Chip'yong-ni) to a point three miles north of Hoengsong and then along the highway linking Wonju and Kangnung (fifty miles to the northeast). The 24th Division of IX Corps, along with I Corps, would protect the western flank of the advance while the South Korean III Corps covered the eastern flank.[65]

The operation got off to a slow start. It took Eighth Army three days to move its forces into position for the attack. Meanwhile, the Chinese, who had detected the United Nations' buildup, made good use of the delay to begin evacuating the Chech'on salient. The weather then began to conspire against the operation. For the first twenty days of the month, temperatures remained within their normal range. When the operation began on 21 February, however, they rose dramatically, creating a sudden thaw that turned roads, trails, and rice paddies into swamps. Rain fell intermittently, making even more of a mess. During daylight hours, trucks and jeeps continually bogged down and landslides blocked highways. After dark, temperatures dropped below freezing, turning the muddy roads into solid sheets of ice.

Aided by the miserable weather, the Chinese and North Koreans retreated northward, pursued slowly by the rain-sodden and mud-encumbered Eighth Army. The allied pace quickened in the second week of the operation, when the weather finally improved. In the end, Operation KILLER lasted fourteen days, during which IX Corps alone claimed to have killed 7,819 enemy soldiers. Nevertheless, the rain and mud ensured that KILLER was only partially successful. Deprived of its advantage in mobility by the

---

[65] Mossman, *Ebb and Flow*, pp. 302, 306–07.

weather, Eighth Army failed to overtake and destroy any large formation of enemy troops.[66]

For its part, the 65th Infantry viewed KILLER as an opportunity to at last cross the Han because the enemy might be distracted by the operation to the east. Each battalion in the regiment vied for the honor of being the first unit across the river. A patrol from Company L, 3d Battalion, made the first attempt on 20 February with help from the regimental tank company but fell back in the face of heavy enemy fire. Four days later, however, two small patrols from the 2d Battalion succeeded in getting across. One three-man patrol established an observation post in enemy territory for two-and-a-half hours while a squad-size detail from Company E scouted the north side of the river.[67]

The 65th Infantry remained on the Han through the end of February 1951. Tallying the results for the month, the regiment had killed 1,505 enemy soldiers, wounded several times that number, and captured 316 prisoners. In return, it suffered 99 battle and 190 nonbattle casualties. "It is believed," wrote Harris, "that the *esprit* of the regiment was the highest that it has ever been since its arrival in Korea."[68]

The 65th Infantry had been in almost nonstop combat, prompting some of the troops to remark that they were doing all of the 3d Division's fighting. When asked by officers of the regiment why the 65th spent so much time at the front, the assistant division commander, General Mead, replied that the unit was the strongest in the division because it had arrived in Korea overstrength at a time when the other regiments were understrength. The Puerto Ricans had also preceded the main body of the division by two months and thus had more combat experience than any of the other regiments.[69]

At the beginning of March, Ridgway began planning a continuation of Operation KILLER. Codenamed RIPPER, the effort sought to preempt a possible Communist counteroffensive by destroying enemy forces in west-central Korea and demolishing their supplies. It also sought to outflank the enemy troops holding Seoul and the area north of the city as far as the Imjin, twenty-five miles away. (*See Map 6.*) If things went well, Ridgway also intended to push forward the eastern flank of the UN line to keep pace with the forces advancing near Seoul. Although aware of MacArthur's interest in recapturing the South Korean capital, Ridgway preferred to avoid a direct assault. He hoped to seize the city and the commanding terrain to

---

[66] Ibid., pp. 308–11.
[67] Monthly Cmd Rpt, 65th Inf, Feb 51.
[68] Ibid.
[69] Army Svc Questionnaire, 65th Inf, Griffin, n.d.; Ltr, Col George W. Childs to Clay Blair, 12 Nov 84, Clay and Joan Blair Collection, MHI.

General Mead (far left) conferring with Colonel Harris (second from left)

its north either through a flanking attack or by grinding down the opposing enemy forces to the point where retreat was their only option. According to Ridgway, neither the capture of new ground nor the retention of old was essential to the operation. He was much more interested in inflicting maximum losses on the enemy at minimum cost to friendly units.[70]

The orders for Operation RIPPER arrived at I Corps on 2 March. The 3d Division was to relieve elements of the 25th Division so they could cross the Han some eight to twelve miles east of Seoul. Once the entire 25th Division had forded the river and Ridgway had given Soule permission to advance, the 3d Division would also cross the Han to expand the breakthrough.

On 5 March, the 1st Battalion of the 7th Infantry relieved the 65th so Colonel Harris and his men could prepare to lead the 3d Division across the Han. Since rice paddies bordered the river, confining all traffic to roads, and aerial reconnaissance had revealed that all of the most obvious crossing sites near ferries and bridges were heavily mined and defended, the

---

[70] Mossman, *Ebb and Flow*, pp. 310–11.

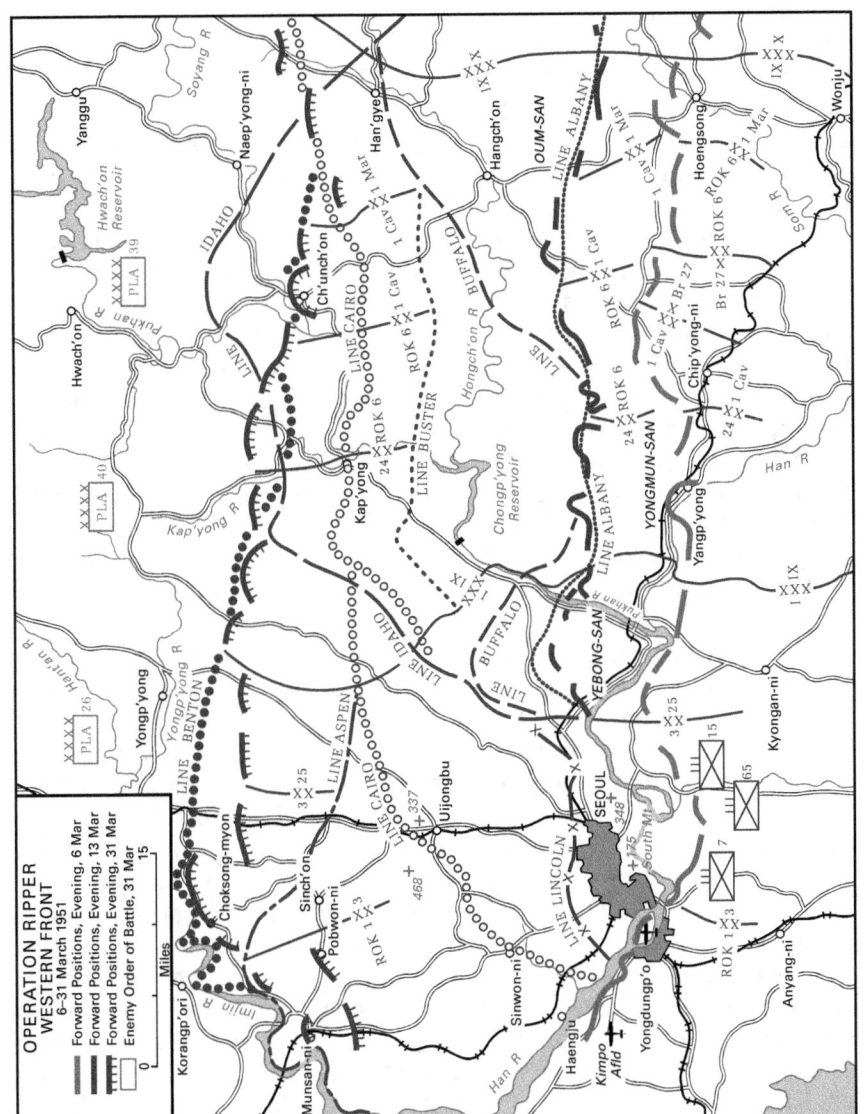

MAP 6

regiment spent the next ten days learning how to cross a contested river under the tutelage of the 10th Combat Engineer Battalion.[71]

To distract the enemy's attention from the place on the river where the 25th Division was to cross, the 15th Infantry conducted a demonstration near Seoul along the south bank of the Han in full view of the Communist troops on the opposite side. This diversion, as well as one by the 7th Division sixty-five miles to the east, apparently worked. At 0615 on 7 March, following an artillery preparation by the 3d Division, the 25th Division began to cross the river farther upstream with little trouble from the Chinese.[72]

Following the successful river crossing by the 25th Division, the four divisions of IX Corps to its east began advancing across a 35-mile front. They made steady gains against moderate to light resistance, with the enemy becoming more disorganized with each passing day. On the right flank of the UN line, the X Corps and South Korean III Corps met with greater opposition; but both still won sizable gains. Between 11 and 13 March, the 25th Division reached its first phase line, Albany, about five to seven miles from the division's starting point. By that time, most of IX Corps had also reached Line Albany, as had X Corps and the South Korean III Corps. After Ridgway spent a few days to consolidate his gains and to bring supplies forward, he ordered the next phase of Ripper—an advance by IX Corps toward Hongch'on, forty-five miles northeast of Seoul—to begin on 14 March.

Ridgway planned to sweep around Seoul from the east and isolate the city rather than attack it head-on. This flanking maneuver would almost certainly force the enemy to withdraw from the capital once the Communists realized that their forces there were in danger of being trapped. Even before Ripper began, however, the allies detected signs that the enemy might have already decided to forfeit the city. On 12 March, aerial reconnaissance detected a group of six hundred Communist soldiers marching away from Seoul to the northwest. That night, patrols from the 3d Division operating on the north bank of the Han failed to make contact with the enemy and reported that the Chinese had apparently abandoned their positions.

Over the next two days, patrols from the 3d Division continued to see signs that the Communists had withdrawn from the city. Meeting no resistance, a South Korean reconnaissance platoon attached to the 15th Infantry set up an outpost on Hill 175 on the southern outskirts of the capital. Likewise, the 7th Infantry's Intelligence and Reconnaissance Platoon set up an observation post on Hill 348 two miles east of Seoul after finding

---

[71] Monthly Cmd Rpt, 3d Inf Div, Mar 51.
[72] Ibid.; Dolcater, *3d Infantry Division in Korea*, pp. 153–54.

it undefended. Shortly thereafter, patrols from the 15th entered Seoul itself and others from both the 7th and the 15th moved freely to the east and north of the city without encountering enemy opposition. As Ridgway had intended, the Communists had given up the capital once they recognized the danger of it being encircled by UN forces. Seoul had changed hands for the fourth and final time of the war.[73]

Seeing that the enemy had evacuated the capital, General Soule asked General Milburn for permission to put a larger force across the Han to reinforce the Intelligence and Reconnaissance Platoon on Hill 348. Permission was forthcoming, but I Corps specified that Soule should use only one battalion and that the unit should avoid becoming heavily engaged because the lack of a bridge in the area would hamper any effort to provide reinforcements. On 16 March, Dammer's 2d Battalion, augmented by an engineer platoon, a heavy mortar platoon, a medical platoon, and a tactical air control party, crossed the Han into Seoul. The 58th AFA Battalion, two platoons of tanks, and the remainder of the heavy mortar company took up positions on the southern bank to provide supporting fires. Company C, 10th Combat Engineer Battalion, also backed the effort, sweeping the crossing area for mines and then operating two rafts and a large ferry to move Dammer's task force over the Han. The 2d Battalion completed its mission to relieve the Intelligence and Reconnaissance Platoon on Hill 348 without a shot being fired.

The next day, while 2d Battalion patrols worked their way five thousand yards to the north without making enemy contact, St. Clair's 1st Battalion crossed the Han and occupied positions between Hill 348 and Seoul along Line Lincoln, several miles to the north of the city.[74] The next day, the remainder of the 65th crossed the river using a newly built bridge and then took up defensive positions on the northern bank. The regiment stayed there for the next four days, sending out patrols to locate any enemy forces that might remain in the area.[75]

After abandoning Seoul, the Communists continued their northward retreat, conducting skillful delaying actions that exploited the rugged, muddy terrain to maximum advantage. The Eighth Army forces involved in RIPPER pressed on doggedly, finishing the operation with the unopposed capture of Chunchon on 21 March. In all, Eighth Army's formations had advanced an average of thirty miles but had been unable to deliver a fatal blow to the Communist armies facing them. Although 7,151 Chinese and

---

[73] Monthly Cmd Rpt, 3d Inf Div, Mar 51; Dolcater, *3d Infantry Division in Korea*, p. 156.

[74] Monthly Cmd Rpts, 65th Inf, Mar 51, and 3d Inf Div, Mar 51; Dolcater, *3d Infantry Division in Korea*, p. 156.

[75] Monthly Cmd Rpt, 65th Inf, Mar 51.

North Korean soldiers had been killed and thousands more captured, the enemy had time and again pulled back before the allies could inflict crippling damage.[76]

As a result, even as Operation RIPPER wound down, Ridgway was planning a new attack. Codenamed COURAGEOUS and spearheaded by I Corps, it was designed to trap the Chinese *26th Army* and the North Korean *I Corps* in the region north of Seoul between the Han and the Imjin. The centerpiece of the operation would be an airborne assault, code-named TOMAHAWK, by the reinforced 187th Airborne Regimental Combat Team near the town of Munsan-ni, on the Imjin some twenty-four miles northwest of Seoul. Task Force GROWDON, consisting of Lt. Col. John S. Growdon's 6th Medium Tank Battalion (borrowed from the IX Corps) and the 3d Division's 2d Battalion, 7th Infantry, as well as the 58th AFA Battalion (minus Battery C), would act as hammer to the 187th's anvil.[77] As soon as the airborne troops had landed, the task force would press forward to the drop zone to destroy the large number of enemy soldiers Ridgway expected to be trapped between the two units.

While COURAGEOUS unfolded, the 65th RCT would not remain idle. At 0800 on 22 March, the regiment found itself on the offensive once more, this time attacking toward Uijongbu, an important road hub ten miles north of Seoul. The 65th was configured as a regimental combat team with the addition of the 39th Field Artillery Battalion, Battery C of the 58th AFA Battalion, and Lt. Col. Dionisio S. Ojeda's Philippine 10th Battalion Combat Team.

On the surface, the Filipino unit was an especially welcome addition because it included a headquarters company, three rifle companies, an armored company without tanks that had been converted into a heavy weapons company, and a reconnaissance company with seven M24 Chaffee light tanks. Numbering almost thirteen hundred men, the 10th Battalion Combat Team increased the strength of the 65th Regimental Combat Team to some fifty-three hundred officers and men.[78] However, the 10th Battalion Combat Team's arrival was preceded by speculation and rumors, many of them negative.

The 10th BCT had arrived in Korea on 19 September 1950.[79] It was initially attached to the 25th Division, whose American leaders observed, "The [10th BCT] commander remained uncooperative with the American

---

[76] Mossman, *Ebb and Flow*, p. 334.
[77] Ibid., p. 337.
[78] Monthly Cmd Rpts, 65th Inf, Mar 51, and 3d Inf Div, Mar 51.
[79] "South Korean and United Nations Ground Forces Strength in Korea, 31 Jul 50–31 Jul 53," and Sitrep, GHQ, FEC, 29–30 Sep 50, both cited in Appleman, *South to the Naktong, North to the Yalu*, p. 606.

Paratroopers of the 187th Airborne Regimental Combat Team make final preparations before boarding C–119 Flying Boxcar planes bound for Munsan-ni.

command, apparently refusing to make allowances for the difficulties of a fast moving military situation."[80] The relationship between the 10th BCT and American units deteriorated further when the Filipinos were transferred to the 187th Airborne RCT.[81] On 16 November, Col. Mariano C. Azurin transmitted to the commanding general of the Philippine Army a message accusing the Americans of acting in bad faith. The Filipino commander was upset because his men had yet to receive cold-weather clothing. Additionally, only seven out of twenty-eight promised light and medium tanks had been delivered.[82] To make matters worse, Azurin was left with

---

[80] Memo, CMH to Chief of Staff of the Army (CSA), 23 Nov 65, sub: Philippine Contributions in Korea, encl 3, Evaluation and General Background Information (Extract from Historical Manuscript "History of the Korean War, Inter-Allied Cooperation During Combat Operations" covering June 1950–July 1951), pp. 5–8, copy in CMH.

[81] Ibid., p. 8.

[82] "Philippine Officer Complains Cold Hurts Troops in Korea," *New York Times*, 20 November 1950, copy in Historians files.

Colonels Allen (left) and Ojeda near Sansong-ni

no one to command because all of his companies had been parceled out to American units. Four days later, he dispatched a similar message to Elpidio R. Quirino, President of the Philippine Republic.[83] Although winter clothing arrived and the detached companies were returned, Azurin was soon replaced by Colonel Ojeda.[84] In that sense, it was fortunate that Harris received the 10th BCT after the controversy had subsided.

Operation COURAGEOUS began on 23 March 1951, when paratroopers from the 187th Airborne RCT jumped from more than a hundred C–119 Flying Boxcar transports into Munsan-ni. The Americans secured their objectives in a matter of hours and linked up with Task Force GROWDON later that night. Enemy resistance proved to be light as most of the Chinese *26th Army* and the North Korean *I Corps* had already moved north of the

---

[83] Memo, CMH to CSA, 23 Nov 65, encl. 3, p. 8.

[84] Harris erroneously states that the Filipinos were assigned to the 65th RCT prior to this period. See Harris, *Puerto Rico's Fighting 65th*, p. 70.

Infantrymen of the 2d Battalion, 7th Infantry, negotiate a steep hillside trail near Uijongbu, 23 March 1951.

Imjin. As the 65th soon discovered, however, some Communist troops remained in place to fight a rear-guard action. Fifteen miles to the southeast of Munsan-ni, the regiment attacked a series of enemy-held hills near Uijongbu. All three battalions of the 65th became engaged in prolonged firefights. Among the heroes of the day was 1st Lt. Richard W. Durkee of Company L, 3d Battalion. As his citation for the Distinguished Service Cross later read, he "single-handedly assaulted an enemy position and killed the occupant with a bayonet. Unable to remove his bayonet from the body of the dead soldier, he went unarmed to another hostile position, seized an enemy soldier's rifle by the bayonet, wrested the weapon from his hands and clubbed him to death." Inspired by the fearlessness of their leader, the men moved forward to secure their objective.[85]

As the 3d Division closed on Uijongbu, it became clear to the Americans that the enemy did not intend to hold the city itself but only to delay the allied advance as long as possible. The division's Task Force HAWKINS, consisting of the 64th Tank Battalion and two tank platoons each from the 15th and 65th Infantries, entered Uijongbu and then reconnoitered north

---

[85] This was the first DSC awarded to a member of the 65th Infantry in Korea. GO no. 522, HQ, Eighth United States Army Korea, 7 Jul 51, sub: Award of Distinguished Service Cross to 1st Lieutenant Richard W. Durkee, Rcds of U.S. Army Operational, Tactical, and Support Organizations (World War II and Thereafter), RG 338, NACP; See also Dolcater, *3d Infantry Division in Korea*, p. 159.

several miles along Route 33 before returning to town. Mines disabled two tanks; but otherwise, the force made no contact. When the 3d Division resumed its advance the next day, it discovered that the Chinese had organized strong positions on Hill 468, three miles northwest of Uijongbu, and on Hill 337, about a mile northeast of the town. From these positions, the Communists could block Route 33 heading north from the city and Route 3 branching to its northeast. While the 15th Infantry succeeded in clearing Hill 337 on the division's right, the Borinqueneers could make no headway at all against the Chinese on Hill 468 despite a daylong effort.[86]

Sensing an opportunity, General Milburn ordered the commander of the 187th Airborne Regimental Combat Team, Brig. Gen. Frank S. Bowen, to prepare his unit for an eastward attack from Munsan-ni to seize high ground abutting Route 33 some ten miles north of Uijongbu. The purpose of the assault was to get behind the Chinese, cut off their retreat, and destroy them in detail by trapping them between the 187th Airborne RCT and the advancing 3d Division.

When the operation began on 25 March, an armored task force from the 65th Infantry, consisting of all seventeen medium tanks from the regimental tank company and a supporting engineer section, moved north to link up with the 187th. The force lost five tanks to mines and failed to reach its objective.[87] It took until 27 March for elements of the 15th and 65th Infantries to finally rendezvous with the paratroopers. By then, the Chinese on Hill 468 had escaped.

Informed of the Chinese withdrawal from Uijongbu, General Ridgway ordered I and IX Corps to advance to Line Benton. The limit of advance for COURAGEOUS, Line Benton originated east of Munsan-ni, followed the upstream course of the Imjin to a point where it intersected the 38th Parallel and then ran generally due east to Ch'unch'on. The two allied corps began pushing forward around daybreak on 31 March. In the I Corps sector, the 65th Infantry attacked with two battalions abreast near Choksong-myon, an area ten miles northeast of Munsan-ni that was a mile or so south of the winding Imjin. The Chinese troops who were stationed there as a rear guard put up a tough fight. Complicating matters further, the assault took place under extremely poor weather conditions over muddy hills and roads that combined with the heavy vehicular traffic on the limited transportation network to slow the unit's movement. At the end of the day, nonetheless, patrols from the 65th Infantry were roaming the southern bank of the Imjin.

---

[86] Monthly Cmd Rpt, 65th Inf, Mar 51.
[87] Ibid.

Filipino troops move up to relieve elements of the 3d Battalion, 65th Infantry, 26 March 1951.

In all, by the end of March 1951, Eighth Army was once again closing on the 38th Parallel. With growing indications that the Communists were regrouping for a spring offensive, however, Ridgway requested permission to move even farther north to secure more geographically defensible positions. When President Truman and General MacArthur agreed, United Nations forces stood poised to continue their offensive.

Chapter 5

FROM THE IMJIN BACK TO SEOUL APRIL 1951

The Eighth Army's advance toward the 38th Parallel was code-named RUGGED. The operation established a new phase line, Kansas, which stretched across the Korean peninsula just north of the 38th Parallel. Two corps, I and IX, would secure the western end, taking possession of the land from the mouth of the Imjin to the western edge of the Hwach'on Reservoir, a distance of sixty-five miles. The X Corps would pick up at that point, securing the remainder of the reservoir's shoreline and extending allied control eastward to Route 24 in the Soyang Valley. The South Korean I and III Corps would occupy the mountainous terrain between Route 24 and Yangyang on the eastern coast. Once Kansas was secure, General Ridgway planned to pull a substantial number of units off line to prepare for a possible Chinese counteroffensive. To that end, he intended to man his forward defenses with a minimum number of ground units strongly supported by artillery and airpower. The bulk of Eighth Army would stand in reserve to the south to counterattack once the Chinese had made their move. Ridgway's goal was to inflict heavy losses on the enemy rather than merely to hold terrain.[1]

Eighth Army would not remain idle while the enemy gathered his strength for another offensive. Ridgway planned a spoiling attack known as Operation DAUNTLESS to threaten the enemy's logistical hub in the Iron Triangle, an area bounded by the railroad town of P'yonggang, thirty-five miles northwest of the Hwach'on Reservoir; the town of Ch'orwon, thirteen miles southwest of P'yonggang; and the town of Kumhwa, an equal distance southeast of P'yonggang. The operation would begin on 9 April, with I and IX Corps attacking in the west and elements of the South Korean

---

[1] Mossman, *Ebb and Flow*, pp. 348–49.

I Corps in the east. Once allied forces reached Line Wyoming, which ran in a northeastern arc from the junction of the Imjin and Hantan Rivers to Kumhwa and then southeast to the Hwach'on Reservoir, they would establish a heavily defended outpost line. The advance to Wyoming would create a dent in the enemy line approximately fifteen miles deep and forty miles wide. When the Communists opened their next offensive, the forces along Wyoming would conduct a fighting withdrawal to Kansas while inflicting the maximum damage and disruption on the enemy with artillery and close air support. The main battle would occur along Line Kansas.[2]

Facing I and IX Corps between the Imjin and the Hwach'on Reservoir were, from west to east, elements of the Chinese *26th*, *40th*, and *39th Armies*. In front of the X Corps and the South Korean III and I Corps farther east were elements of the North Korean *69th Infantry Brigade* and the North Korean *1st*, *15th*, and *45th Divisions*. Intelligence indicated that the Communists were constructing and occupying a chain of fortified positions rather than massing their troops in forward assembly areas. Based on these reports, the Eighth Army's chief of intelligence, Col. James C. Tarkenton, concluded that an enemy offensive was not imminent, leaving time for Ridgway to launch Operations RUGGED and DAUNTLESS before the Chinese were able to preempt them.[3]

Operation RUGGED got underway with a staggered start during the first five days of April, with each corps and division moving forward when its preparations had been completed. On 1 April, the 3d Division's 65th Infantry and British Commonwealth 29th Infantry Brigade began moving north along the axis of Route 33, the Americans on the right and British on left, toward Line Kansas. (*Map 7*) The Philippine 10th Battalion Combat Team and the Belgian Battalion reinforced the 29th Brigade. Three of the 3d Division's four field artillery battalions (the 9th, 39th, and 58th Armored) supported the assault. The 65th Infantry, with the 2d and 3d Battalions in the vanguard, soon made contact with the *232d* and *233d Regiments* of the Chinese *78th Division*. On the left, the British 29th Brigade hit the *228th* and *229th Regiments* of the Chinese *76th Division*. The attack continued on 2 April against moderate Chinese resistance, with the 65th killing forty enemy soldiers while incurring no friendly losses. At the end of the day, the 7th Infantry relieved the 65th, which moved into division reserve.[4]

To the west, I and IX Corps continued moving north until 5 April, when they reached Line Kansas. General Ridgway wanted the follow-on

---

[2] Ibid., pp. 349–50, 361–62.

[3] Eighth Army Priority Intelligence Requirement 266, 4 Apr 51, cited in Mossman, *Ebb and Flow*, p. 351.

[4] Monthly Cmd Rpts, 65th Inf, Apr 51, and 3d Inf Div, Apr 51. Unless otherwise noted, all Cmd Rpts are in Entry 429, Rcds of the AGO, RG 407, NACP.

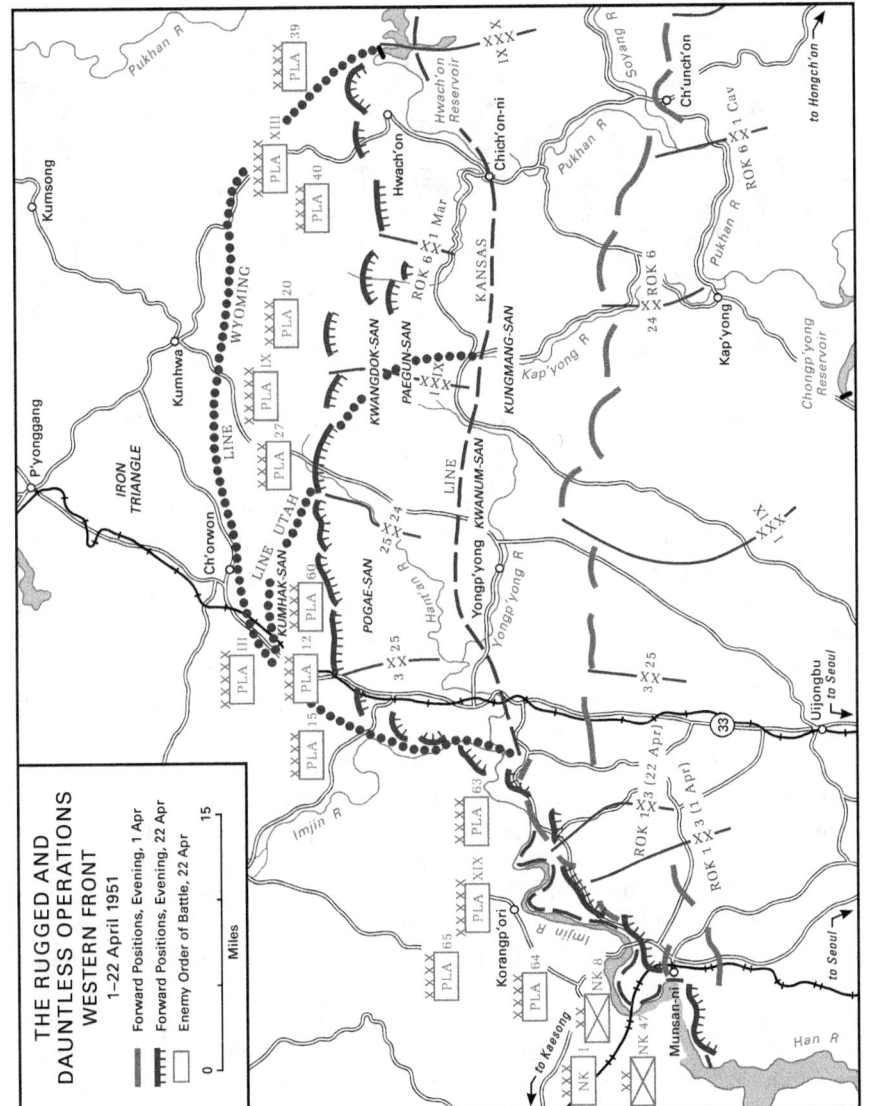

An American M4A3E8 medium tank engages Communist troops near the 38th Parallel.

operation, DAUNTLESS, to begin late on 9 April; but by that date, X Corps and the South Korean III Corps still had not reached Line Kansas. On 11 April, while those two formations continued to struggle with the terrain as much as with the North Koreans, Ridgway ordered I and IX Corps to start toward the Iron Triangle. The intermediate objective line, Utah, carved a semicircle eleven miles above Kansas between the Imjin and the eastern slopes of Kungmang Mountain, its trace crossing the Kumhak, Kwangdok, and Paegun mountain masses. At the top of its arc, Utah lay only a few miles short of Ch'orwon. Although the British Commonwealth 27th Brigade on the far left flank of IX Corps would make a short advance, the opening phase of the attack would be primarily an I Corps operation involving the U.S. 3d, 24th, and 25th Infantry Divisions.

At that point, the 65th Infantry had been holding in division reserve for seven days, fully absorbed in the task of training the first contingent of what would become an influx of 33 officer and 1,078 enlisted replacements during April. Since an equal number of the regiment's seasoned veterans would rotate back to Puerto Rico, the month would be an important milestone in the history of the regiment: fully one-fourth of the unit would turn over within a thirty-day period. Given the short time allotted, it remained to be seen how effectively the 65th could integrate the new arrivals into its ranks.

On the morning of 10 April, the 1st and 3d Battalions, the Philippines 10th Battalion Combat Team, and the regimental tank and heavy mortar

American engineers construct a bridge across the Hantan River in early April 1951.

companies moved into forward positions. The 2d Battalion remained in regimental reserve conducting squad and platoon exercises and test-firing small arms.[5] The next day, the regiment, minus the 2d Battalion and the Filipino unit, attacked through the 7th Infantry along the axis of Route 33, seizing and occupying high ground near the Hantan against sporadic Chinese resistance.

As Eighth Army launched Operation Dauntless, important changes were taking place at the highest levels of the United Nations Command. General of the Army Douglas MacArthur had long chafed at the strategic limitations President Truman had imposed on him, especially those restricting military action against mainland China. He expressed those frustrations in a letter to Speaker of the House of the U.S. Congress Joseph W. Martin, who later released it to the press. Truman viewed the whole episode as an act of defiance. After consulting with selected members of his cabinet and the Joint Chiefs of Staff, Truman decided to remove MacArthur. The action created a furor at home, but it had little impact on combat operations in Korea. The president appointed General Ridgway to take MacArthur's place as

---

[5] Ibid.

General Van Fleet

head of the Far East Command and immediately designated Lt. Gen. James A. Van Fleet as the new commander of Eighth Army.[6]

Van Fleet was a worthy successor to lead the UN forces. A 1915 West Point graduate, he had commanded a machine-gun battalion with the 6th Infantry Division during World War I. Between the wars, he commanded a battalion in the 42d Infantry, a predominately Panamanian and Puerto Rican unit, in the Panama Canal Zone from 1925 to 1927.[7] Advancing through multiple levels of command during World War II, he had landed with the 8th Infantry at UTAH Beach on D-Day and later led the 90th Division and III Corps in combat. Army Chief of Staff General J. Lawton Collins considered him one of the best of the U.S. Army's field commanders in Europe during World War II. Prior to taking charge of Eighth Army, Van Fleet had headed a joint U.S. military advisory and planning group in Greece and the Second Army at Fort Meade, Maryland. Van Fleet was a highly decorated officer whose awards for valor included three Distinguished Service Crosses all won during World War II.[8]

In notifying General Ridgway of his successor in Korea, the Joint Chiefs of Staff had authorized him to employ Van Fleet in some other capacity if Ridgway wanted to remain in temporary command to handle the expected enemy offensive. Ridgway chose not to do that, officially relinquishing command of Eighth Army to Van Fleet on the afternoon of 14 April. Even so, he reserved the right to approve major moves above Line Utah. Prior to departing, Ridgway instructed Van Fleet to notify him before crossing that line. Although Ridgway did not tell Van Fleet at that time, he intended to restrict combat operations north of Line Wyoming also, once he had established himself in Tokyo.

---

[6] Mossman, *Ebb and Flow*, pp. 362–65.

[7] Paul F. Braim, *The Will to Win: The Life of General James A. Van Fleet* (Annapolis, Md.: Naval Institute Press, 2001), pp. 48–52.

[8] *Generals of the Army* (Washington, D.C.: Office of the Chief of Staff of the Army, 1955), pp. 26–27.

Colonel Harris had more immediate challenges to face. On 14 April, the 65th Infantry secured its objective on Line Utah with assistance from the divisional artillery, the Philippine 10th BCT, and the 10th Combat Engineer Battalion.[9] The regiment's arrival was marred by an unfortunate accident. Several soldiers from the 65th were severely wounded when a shell fired by the 58th AFA Battalion exploded near a friendly outpost. The error was attributed to a misunderstanding between the battalion fire-direction center and a firing battery.[10] That night, the Chinese began challenging the regiment's patrols while probing the 3d Division's defensive line.

Three days later, a Chinese infantry company attacked a scout party from Company C, forcing it to withdraw. Shortly thereafter, an armored patrol from the 65th's tank company temporarily abandoned three tanks after encountering obstacles in its path and coming under attack. In the ensuing battle, the tank company killed thirty Chinese soldiers and recovered the abandoned vehicles. Unfortunately, the 58th AFA Battalion fired a high-explosive shell that landed near the patrol, wounding six Puerto Ricans. Although the incident was traced to an incorrect target location provided by an infantry platoon leader, after the two misfire incidents, the 58th was replaced by the 10th Field Artillery Battalion and sent to the rear for retraining.[11]

On 19 April, the Borinqueneers continued to pressure the Chinese by attacking three hills on Line Utah between the Imjin and Route 33. Those particular pieces of terrain offered a commanding view of the surrounding countryside and would prove useful in blocking the expected Chinese counteroffensive. For this mission, the 65th received assistance from the 10th Combat Engineer Battalion and Company B of the 64th Heavy Tank Battalion. Despite numerous obstacles that delayed the armor, the regiment took all three hills against a "well entrenched" and "fanatically determined enemy."[12] During the fighting, two Puerto Rican soldiers from Company C, Sgt. Modesto Cartegena and Cpl. Fabian Nieves-Laguer, won the Distinguished Service Cross for charging and knocking out a series of enemy dugouts. Their actions enabled the company to seize its objective and to hold that ground against several enemy counterattacks.[13]

---

[9] Monthly Cmd Rpts, 65th Inf, Apr 51, and 3d Inf Div, Apr 51.
[10] Cmd Rpt no. 4, 58th Armd Field Arty Bn, 10 May 51.
[11] Ibid.
[12] Monthly Cmd Rpts, 65th Inf, Apr 51, and 3d Inf Div, Apr 51.
[13] GO no. 635, HQ, EUSAK, 12 Aug 51, sub: Award of Distinguished Service Cross to Cpl. Fabian Nieves-Laguer; GO no. 698, HQ, EUSAK, 16 Sep 51, sub: Award of Distinguished Service Cross to Sgt. Modesto Cartegena; both in Entry 429, Rcds of the AGO, RG 407, NACP.

The Chinese grew increasingly restive as a result of the Eighth Army's advance across the 38th Parallel. By 19 April, U.S. intelligence estimated that the Communists had positioned elements of the Chinese *XIX Army Group* in the west and the *III Army Group* in the east opposite the U.S. 3d and 25th Infantry Divisions. The front ran some twenty miles in width, and the combined strength of the two Communist army groups seemed to be about two hundred thousand men. "Based on past experience," General Soule, the 3d Division commander, wrote, "It was estimated that this disposition in depth on a narrow front indicated an offensive attitude. The Chinese had achieved numerical superiority on a limited front" and "were capable of mounting a formidable offensive down the Uijongbu corridor toward Seoul." On 21 and 22 April, aerial and ground reconnaissance revealed increasing numbers of Chinese troops marching south toward the sector held by the 3d Division. Moving in groups that were as large as a battalion, some approached within one-and-a-half miles of the division's outpost line.[14]

The men of the 65th spent the next several days reconnoitering to the north and west while improving their defensive positions on Line Utah. Mounted patrols continued to lose armored vehicles, often to the muddy terrain instead of to enemy fire, prompting the 2d Battalion to conduct a limited attack on 22 April to recover two bogged-down tanks. During the operation, the Puerto Ricans encountered three entrenched Chinese companies. They recovered the vehicles, but only after an extended firefight. The battalion killed an estimated sixty Communist soldiers during the engagement.[15]

As the Chinese buildup continued, it was mirrored on a smaller scale by a growing surplus of Puerto Ricans within the 65th Infantry. What to do with all the Puerto Rican replacements had become a key issue for Eighth Army. Of the 4,047 troops forecast to arrive at the 3d Division during April 1951, 2,400 (60 percent) were Puerto Ricans. At that rate, the 65th would soon find itself overstrength by 30 percent, some 1,400 men.

In addition to the contingent due in April, another 2,300 Puerto Rican soldiers were en route to Korea. Knowing that the Eighth Army would not assign new men to the already overstrength regiment, General Soule sought to create additional units to absorb that excess. On 22 April, he wrote to Ridgway recommending the formation of an all–Puerto Rican regimental combat team. The force would consist of the 65th Infantry regiment, the 504th Field Artillery Battalion then stationed in Panama, an engineer company, and an antiaircraft artillery battery. It would number almost 5,000

---

[14] Monthly Cmd Rpt, 3d Inf Div, Apr 51.
[15] Monthly Cmd Rpts, 65th Inf, Apr 51, and 3d Inf Div, Apr 51.

men: 3,800 infantrymen, 700 artillerymen, 200 engineers, and 200 antiaircraft soldiers. Soule argued, "The formation of an all Puerto Rican Combat Team will provide for the best utilization of Puerto Rican manpower."[16] He also recommended that Colonel Harris be responsible for organizing and commanding the proposed organization.

There is no indication that Ridgway seriously contemplated the proposal. The new head of the Far East Command strongly believed that segregation was an inefficient means of managing personnel during wartime.[17] In addition, Ridgway felt segregation was impeding Eighth Army's efforts to "assure the sort of *esprit* a fighting army needs, where each soldier stands proudly on his own feet, knowing himself to be as good as the next fellow and better than the enemy. Besides it had always seemed to me both un-American and un-Christian for free citizens to be taught to downgrade themselves this way, as if they were unfit to associate with their fellows or accept leadership themselves."[18]

Creation of a new segregated unit would have clearly undermined Ridgway's commitment to integration. Indeed, Soule's letter may have encouraged the Far East Command to assign Puerto Rican personnel to units outside the 3d Division, for it revealed that the growing surplus of Puerto Rican personnel was large enough to form a separate regimental combat team and perhaps even a division. In the context of the infantry shortages then prevalent throughout Eighth Army, this was a truly telling disclosure.

Soule's memorandum also acknowledged that the assignment of Puerto Rican personnel to units in the 3d Division other than the 65th was already well underway. The general had ordered the integration of 650 surplus Puerto Rican replacements throughout the division: 400 to the field artillery, 150 to the engineers, and 100 to the antiaircraft artillery. According to Colonel Newman, the division's chief of staff who later became the assistant division commander, this was part of an experiment aimed at assigning 1,000 Puerto Rican soldiers to combat and support units throughout the division in order to assess the impact of integration on the force.[19]

Commanders within the 3d Division initially resisted the move, but opposition soon subsided. "The fact that so many men were so readily

---

[16] Ltr, HQ, 3d Inf Div, 22 Apr 51, sub: Utilization of Puerto Rican Personnel, in Monthly Cmd Rpt, 3d Inf Div, Apr 51.

[17] On 24 May 1951, Ridgway forced the issue by formally requesting authority to abolish segregation within the Far East Command. MacGregor, *Integration of the Armed Forces*, p. 442.

[18] Matthew B. Ridgway, *The Korean War* (New York: Doubleday & Co., 1967), p. 193.

[19] Ibid. The 10th Field Artillery Battalion, for example, received 107 Puerto Rican replacements on 7 Apr 50. Monthly Cmd Rpt, 10th FA Bn, Apr 51.

absorbed," wrote Col. William W. Culp in a 1953 study that examined the use of Puerto Rican troops in the Korean War, "indicated that integration would present no difficult problems."[20] The 3d Division's regimental commanders agreed with this assessment. "They were integrated into the units as any normal replacements," recalled the commander of the 15th Infantry, Col. Thomas R. Yancey:

> I remember that certain individuals who had previous experience in civilian life as mechanics became particularly adapt [sic] as members of the maintenance crews of the heavy tank company. The men were placed in slots where it was estimated that they could best perform their duty. Some, of course, were sent to squads where they became proficient as riflemen. They worked well with the American soldier and I believe, although there is no definite proof, the typical Puerto Rican soldier replacement probably performed better with the 15th Regiment than if he had been assigned to a unit of his own nationality. I am of the opinion that the Puerto Rican soldier can be integrated through[out] our continental units.[21]

Shifts in existing personnel policies, in addition to integration, were also being considered by the Army. The Korean conflict posed a unique challenge to the Army because only a small percentage of its soldiers were involved in actual combat. World War II experience indicated that after long periods of sustained combat soldiers became careless and even indifferent to their own safety. The Army leadership regarded relief of combat veterans from the pressure of lengthy duty on the front line as a means of conserving manpower and bolstering morale. As early as 10 August 1950, Chief of Army Field Forces General Mark W. Clark stated that "a rotation policy must surely be established in all fairness to those now fighting in Korea."[22]

When formulating a theaterwide rotation policy, the dual aims of employing available manpower in the most economical fashion possible and ensuring individuals were sent home before falling victim to "battle exhaustion" were accorded equal consideration. This philosophy resulted in the adoption of both command and individual rotation programs. The latter was geared toward sending a soldier home once he was exposed to combat for a predetermined period of time. Command rotation involved the temporary withdrawal of entire units from the front line for rest, reha-

---

[20] Culp, *Training and Future Utilization*, p. 28.

[21] In fact, Puerto Ricans had been granted U.S. citizenship in 1917. Ltr, Col T. R. Yancey to Col W. W. Culp, 19 Jan 53, Thomas R. Yancey Papers, MHI.

[22] Ltr, Gen Mark W. Clark, OCAFF [Office, Chief of Army Field Forces], to Lt Gen E. H. Brooks, Army G–1, 10 Aug 50, cited in Maj Elva Stillwaugh, "Personnel Policies in the Korean Conflict," Historical Resources Collection, CMH.

bilitation, and training. Command rotation also allowed units to retain individuals for longer periods before they reached the maximum number of days of combat exposure.

The Chinese intervention in November 1950 prompted the Army to postpone implementation of the rotation program until the situation in Korea stabilized. Things had improved sufficiently by March 1951 to allow General MacArthur to send a proposed rotation plan to the Department of the Army for approval. Under this proposal, the commanding general of Eighth Army would ultimately decide who was to rotate on a "most-deserving-first" basis.[23] A soldier would be eligible for rotation after he spent six months with a combat division or similar unit in Korea, twelve months in Korea with a support unit, or any combination of the two.

On 9 March 1951, General MacArthur informed all members of the Far East Command of his proposed rotation policy. Since many soldiers already exceeded the guidelines, personnel who spent considerable time in close proximity to the enemy or who performed extremely hazardous service were given a higher priority than other soldiers. The first shipload of "combat rotation personnel," 109 officers and 1,392 enlisted men, left the Far East Command on 22 April 1951.[24]

On the same day the first soldiers departed Korea, the bulk of the Eighth Army stood astride or slightly north of Line Kansas, which extended 116 miles from the confluence of the Han and Imjin Rivers to the town of Yangyang on the east coast of Korea. The leading elements of I and IX Corps had advanced beyond Line Kansas to Line Utah and were well on their way to Line Wyoming. That afternoon, however, the Turkish Brigade captured a Chinese eight-man forward observer team. The Chinese captain in charge of the group revealed that three enemy divisions were assembled directly in front of the 25th Division and would attack that night.

The capture of this group, along with a sudden rise in the number of enemy patrols and skirmishes that day, suggested that a major offensive was imminent.[25] That evening, General Van Fleet warned all units in the Eighth Army to be prepared for a massive Communist assault.[26]

Van Fleet's analysis was correct. To attack the U.S. I and IX Corps, the enemy had gathered a North Korean corps with 2 divisions and 4 Chinese army groups with 14 armies and 42 infantry divisions supported by 4 artillery divisions and 2 separate artillery regiments. The Communist order of battle included, from west to east, the North Korean *I Corps*; the Chinese

---

[23] Stillwaugh, "Personnel Policies in the Korean Conflict," ch. 3, p. 5.

[24] Staff Section Rpt, G–1, GHQ, FEC, 1–30 Apr 51, ann. 2, ch. 2, cited in Stillwaugh, "Personnel Policies in the Korean Conflict," ch. 3, p. 7.

[25] Monthly Cmd Rpt, I Corps, Apr 51.

[26] Monthly Cmd Rpt, 3d Inf Div, Apr 51.

XIX Army Group consisting of the *64th, 65th,* and *63d Armies*; the *III Army Group* consisting of the Chinese *15th, 12th,* and *60th Armies*; the Chinese *IX Army Group* consisting of the *27th* and *20th Armies*; and the Chinese *XIII Army Group* composed of the *40th* and *39th Armies*. Their goal was to break through to Seoul, whose capture the commander of the Chinese People's Volunteers in Korea, Péng Déhuái, had promised to Mao Zedong as a May Day gift. The offensive was to have been supported by the Chinese Air Force, but preemptive U.S. air strikes beginning on 17 April against the enemy's forward airfields had neutralized that threat.[27]

The Chinese Spring Offensive of 1951

The enemy offensive, the fifth of the war, began with an attack during the night of 22–23 April against the South Korean 6th Division, which held the center of the allied line just west of the Hwach'on Reservoir. Preceded by a massive artillery barrage, the attackers soon broke through the South Koreans, exposing the right flank of the U.S. 24th Division to the west and the left flank of the U.S. 1st Marine Division to the east. A follow-on attack the next day completed the destruction of the 6th Division. Although the Chinese advanced some twenty miles southwest of the reservoir, elements of the 27th Commonwealth Infantry Brigade and the U.S. 72d Heavy Tank Battalion held them off long enough to enable an orderly withdrawal of UN forces.[28]

Despite the devastation wrought upon the South Korean 6th Division, Eighth Army's I and IX Corps were in fact the main targets of the Chinese offensive. Milburn's I Corps was arrayed with the 3d Division on the left and the 25th Division on the right. General Soule considered his twelve-mile sector between Korangp'ori, ten miles northeast of Munsan-ni, and Route 33 to be particularly vulnerable. The 3d Division deployed two of its infantry regiments to defend the main line of resistance, with Harris' 65th Infantry on the right and Brig. Thomas Brodie's attached British 29th Independent Infantry Brigade Group on the left. Soule strengthened this line by positioning his 3d Division reserve, the 7th Infantry and the 64th Heavy Tank Battalion, in a central location just north of the Hantan, where it could be employed against a Chinese penetration. The 15th Infantry was not available to Soule because it had been designated as the I Corps reserve.

---

[27] Mossman, *Ebb and Flow*, pp. 325, 378–81.

[28] Impression of the British Commonwealth Part in CCF [Chinese Communist Forces] Offensive on 22–26 April 1951 as seen by Lt Gen H. C. H. Robertson KBE [Knight Commander of the British Empire], DSO [Distinguished Service Order], who was in the area, WO 216/345, The National Archives (TNA), Kew, London.

For its part, the 65th Infantry deployed its own 3d and 2d Battalions on line, facing west and northwest, respectively, along the Imjin, while the attached Philippine 10th BCT held the regiment's right flank astride Route 33. The Turkish Brigade, which was attached to the 25th Division, was just east of the Filipino unit. The Belgian Battalion, attached to the British 29th Brigade Group, anchored the left flank of the 65th Infantry next to the 3d Battalion. The regiment's 1st Battalion remained in reserve.[29]

Brigadier Brodie

As dusk approached, the soldiers of the 3d Division checked their weapons and ensured that they had plenty of ammunition and grenades within reach. Platoon leaders and noncommissioned officers moved from position to position to check fields of fire and to make certain that their units had both flanks securely tied. Out on the listening posts screening the front line, a handful of men waited silently as darkness settled in. They strained their ears for any sounds that might betray the beginning of the Chinese assault. The listening posts were not expected to hold but rather to fade back to the main defensive line with word that the Chinese were coming.[30]

The attack began at 2000 on 22 April when the enemy hit the Turkish 1st Brigade with a powerful artillery barrage. Shortly after midnight, an artillery and mortar barrage followed by intense small-arms and machine-gun fire struck the entire 3d Division line. At 0030, a vast wave of screaming Chinese soldiers hit the division's outposts and drove them back. Twenty minutes later, in an attempt to split the position held by the 65th Infantry's 2d Battalion, a Chinese force launched an assault along the seam between Companies E and F. The attack was so intense that the unit's new commander, Lt. Col. Lawrence A. Johnson, had to pull his battalion back several hundred yards to regroup. A World War II Bronze Star winner, 36-year-old Johnson had replaced Dammer earlier in the month.

---

[29] Monthly Cmd Rpts, 65th Inf, Apr 51, and 3d Inf Div, Apr 51; Mossman, *Ebb and Flow*, pp. 385–86.

[30] Dolcater, *3d Infantry Division in Korea*, p. 195.

Shortly after attacking the 2d Battalion, the Communists slammed into Allen's 3d Battalion and the Filipino soldiers of Ojeda's 10th Battalion Combat Team. Although the 3d Battalion held its position, Company B of the 10th Battalion had to pull back because of overwhelming Chinese strength. The commanding officer of the 10th's Heavy Weapons (Tank) Company, Capt. Conrado D. Yap, ignored orders to withdraw and instead led a daring counterattack to regain a key piece of terrain. Though Yap was mortally wounded, his men succeeded in recapturing the objective.[31] Yap posthumously received the Philippine Medal of Valor and U.S. Distinguished Service Cross.

The troops of the *34th Division* of the Chinese *12th Army* and *29th Division* of the Chinese *15th Army* continued their assault against the 3d Division despite taking grievous losses from American machine-gun, mortar, and artillery fire. "The enemy attack," wrote General Soule, "was characterized by the 'conveyor belt' tactics which he had used on previous occasions to exploit his superiority in numbers."[32] Soule was referring to the Chinese use of successive echelons of infantry attacking on a narrow front. The Communists used these tactics to maintain forward momentum and to rapidly exploit success in the face of concentrated American firepower.

Colonel Harris committed the 65th Infantry's reserve, Lt. Col. Howard B. St. Clair's 1st Battalion; but it could not entirely stop the enemy's advance. At 0345, the regimental command post came under intense artillery and mortar fire. "It was as though the enemy had laid their hands on our defensive plans," recalled Harris, "just as we had theirs at an earlier date."[33] As a result, the command post was forced to displace to the rear in haste and in near-total darkness. Fortunately for the 65th, the enemy divisions failed to exploit the temporary disruption in its command and control system. "I believe that the main enemy attack bounced off us, spilled over on both sides of us, and then concentrated on the British and the Turks," remembered a relieved Harris.[34] The fighting subsided somewhat after another early-morning counterattack by the Philippine 10th Battalion Combat Team recovered some of the ground lost in the initial Chinese assaults.

The 65th Infantry's assistant intelligence officer, Captain Boyle, and regimental operations officer, Capt. Arthur Myers, went aloft at the crack of dawn in an L–16 liaison aircraft to direct air attacks and artillery fire against the Chinese. Piloted by the division air officer, Capt. Daniel C.

---

[31] Ibid., p. 196.
[32] Monthly Cmd Rpt, 3d Inf Div, Apr 51.
[33] Harris, *Puerto Rico's Fighting 65th*, p. 182.
[34] Ibid.

Prescott, the aircraft remained in the air for most of the day, playing a vital role in fending off further assaults. The heavy mortar and artillery fire they called in had a 90 percent success rate in hitting enemy targets, Boyle recalled.[35] A tally later disclosed that the 3d Division had expended nineteen thousand rounds of 105-mm. and 155-mm. high-explosive shells in the 24-hour period ending at 1800 on 23 April. The artillery proved to be devastating given the echeloned formations the Chinese commanders had used. Surprisingly, the 65th was the only regiment in the division that used liaison aircraft in such a manner.[36]

Despite losing many troops, the enemy succeeded in establishing a regiment-size bridgehead south of the Imjin on the morning of 23 April. In light of the punishment received from the 65th Infantry, however, the Communists modified their plan, concentrating their attacks against the units on either side of the regiment. Attacking the Belgian Battalion on the left flank, the Chinese headed for two key bridges over the Hantan. The 29th Brigade dispatched a mechanized patrol from the 1st Royal Ulster Rifles, reinforced by engineers, to secure the bridges. Enemy soldiers ambushed the patrol on the northern bank of the river and forced it to retreat across the bridges after losing a dozen men and two Oxford armored personnel carriers.[37]

At 0730, General Soule rushed a rifle company from the 7th Infantry and two tank platoons to assist the Belgian troops, most of whom were still fighting on the north bank of the Imjin. The task force came under heavy fire when it reached the two spans, a sign that the enemy was now only a short distance away from the bridges. By 1330, the commander of the Belgian Battalion, Lt. Col. Albert Crahay, informed the 3d Division that his unit would soon have to withdraw without its vehicles because enemy forces had blocked its only highway route across the Imjin. The division dispatched Lt. Col. Fred C. Weyand's 1st Battalion of the 7th Infantry to assist Crahay. Supported by British armor and artillery units, at 1800 Weyand launched a furious assault that diverted Chinese attention long enough for the Belgians to pull back across the river with the loss of only seven vehicles.[38]

As bad as the situation was on the left flank of the 65th, the situation on its right had grown to critical proportions by the morning of 23 April. A predawn attack by the Chinese *179th Division* had shattered the Turkish Brigade, opening a gap between I Corps and IX Corps. In the resulting

---

[35] Interv, author with Boyle, 15 Feb 01.

[36] Monthly Cmd Rpt, 3d Inf Div, Apr 51.

[37] Anthony Farrar-Hockley, *The British Part in the Korean War*, 2 vols. (London: Her Majesty's Stationary Office, 1995), 2: 116.

[38] Monthly Cmd Rpt, 3d Inf Div, Apr 51.

British troops from the 29th Independent Brigade Group rest for a moment before pulling back in the face of unrelenting Chinese attacks. Below, looking northwest, the positions of the Gloster Battalion south of the Imjin River.

melee, the Chinese had become so intermingled with the Turks that allied artillery units stopped firing lest they hit friendly troops. As the situation degenerated, the commander of the 25th Division, Brig. Gen. J. Sladen Bradley, ordered the 24th and 27th Infantries on the right flank of the Turkish brigade to withdraw two miles. The Turks—minus one company that had been virtually wiped out—fought their way south and assembled below the Hantan in better condition than anyone expected. Their withdrawal, however, exposed the 65th Infantry's right flank.[39]

Meanwhile, the British 29th Independent Infantry Brigade Group on the left flank of the Belgian Battalion faced a crisis that was nearly equal to that of the Turkish Brigade. Facing the heaviest attacks in the 3d Division's sector, all elements of the brigade were forced to yield ground, although they did so in an orderly manner. During the morning, nonetheless, elements of the Chinese *187th Division* found and breached the thinly held seam between the 1st Battalion, Gloucestershire Regiment (the "Glosters"), and the 1st Royal Northumberland Fusiliers.[40] The Communist troops steadily poured through the narrow gap, slowly encircling two companies belonging to the Glosters while continuing to exert steady pressure all along the front.[41]

At 0900 on 23 April, General Van Fleet ordered a withdrawal to Line Kansas after concluding that many units in I and IX Corps were in danger of being enveloped. In the 3d Division sector, the 7th Infantry already occupied a portion of Kansas astride Route 33 because Soule had kept the unit there as the division reserve. The 65th Infantry and its attached units leapfrogged back to Kansas at 1330, passing through the 7th Infantry via Route 33 before assembling in a reserve position near the junction of Routes 33 and 11. An L–16 liaison aircraft covered the withdrawal, ready to call in air and artillery strikes if the enemy attempted to pursue. With the 65th out of immediate danger, the 3d Division attached the 3d Battalion of the 65th Infantry to the 7th Infantry in place of Weyand's 1st Battalion, which had been committed to support the Belgians. The Philippine 10th Battalion Combat Team went to the hard-pressed British 29th Brigade Group to act as a reserve force.

The Plight of the Glosters

Meanwhile, the encircled Glosters spent the night of 23–24 April fighting off repeated Chinese attacks. Soule and Brodie knew they had to reach those troops quickly if they were to have any chance of escape. Brigadier

---

[39] Mossman, *Ebb and Flow*, pp. 384–85.

[40] The 29th Brigade deployed a third infantry battalion, the Royal Ulster Rifles, on the right flank of the 1st Royal Northumberland Fusiliers.

[41] Monthly Cmd Rpt, 3d Inf Div, Apr 51.

Brodie arrived at the division command post before dawn on 24 April. Soule urged Brodie to employ the 10th BCT aggressively to link up quickly with the Glosters. Additionally, Soule informed Brodie that he planned to use the 65th Infantry to restore the 29th Brigade's main line of resistance the following day. When Soule asked if Brodie was satisfied with the timing, objectives, and scope of both attacks, he answered affirmatively.[42]

A task force consisting of Company C of the 10th Battalion Combat Team; three M24 Chaffee light tanks from the 10th's reconnaissance company; and ten Centurion medium tanks from C Squadron, 8th King's Royal Irish Hussars, moved out early on the morning of 24 April to link up with the Glosters.[43] The isolated British unit was located beyond a gorge two-and-one-half miles to the north near Solma-ri. (*Map 8*) The task force encountered heavy resistance but succeeded in reaching the entrance to the gorge. Suddenly, a mortar round damaged the lead Filipino M24 Chaffee, halting the column.[44] The official British history summarized the rapid unraveling of the relief effort:

> As no one else was helping, two of the Centurions squeezed past the other light tanks and, under their covering fire, the [crew of the disabled Chaffee] were able to join the main body. The 10 BCT's commanding officer proposed to Major [Henry] Huth [the British tank company commander] that his Centurions should assume the leading role, an offer wisely declined. The Centurions were too heavy and too wide for the track through the gorge, but even if, in this emergency, they attempted to move down it, the sides were so steep that they would be unable to apply fire effectively.... At this point the relief operation on 24th April came effectively to an end."[45]

The American liaison officer at the British brigade command post reported to Soule at 1845:

> GLOS [Glosters] still in Psn [position]—fairly safe. Have had some Equip[ment] and Weapons shot up. Don't believe their casualties to be heavy considering their situation.... Relief force of 10th BCT and T[an]ks have been ordered back because leading T[an]k became immobilized in a ravine blocking road completely about 2,000 y[ar]ds short of GLOS Psns—further progress of 10th BCT was considered by Brigadier to be unwise."[46]

---

[42] Memo, Brig Gen A. D. Mead to Maj Gen Soule, n.d., encl 6, Rpt of Gloucestershire Bn, 22–25 Apr 51, EUSAK, 26 May 51, Historical Resources Collection.

[43] *History of the United Nations Forces in the Korean War*, 6 vols. (Seoul, Korea: Ministry of National Defense, 1977), 6: 315.

[44] Sum of the 29th BIB [British Infantry Brigade] Opns, encl. no. 1, in Monthly Cmd Rpt, 3d Inf Div, Apr 51.

[45] Farrar-Hockley, *The British Part in the Korean War*, 2: 127.

[46] Entry dtd 241845 Apr 51, 3d Div G–3 Jnl, encl 7, Rpt of Gloucestershire Bn, 22–25 Apr 51.

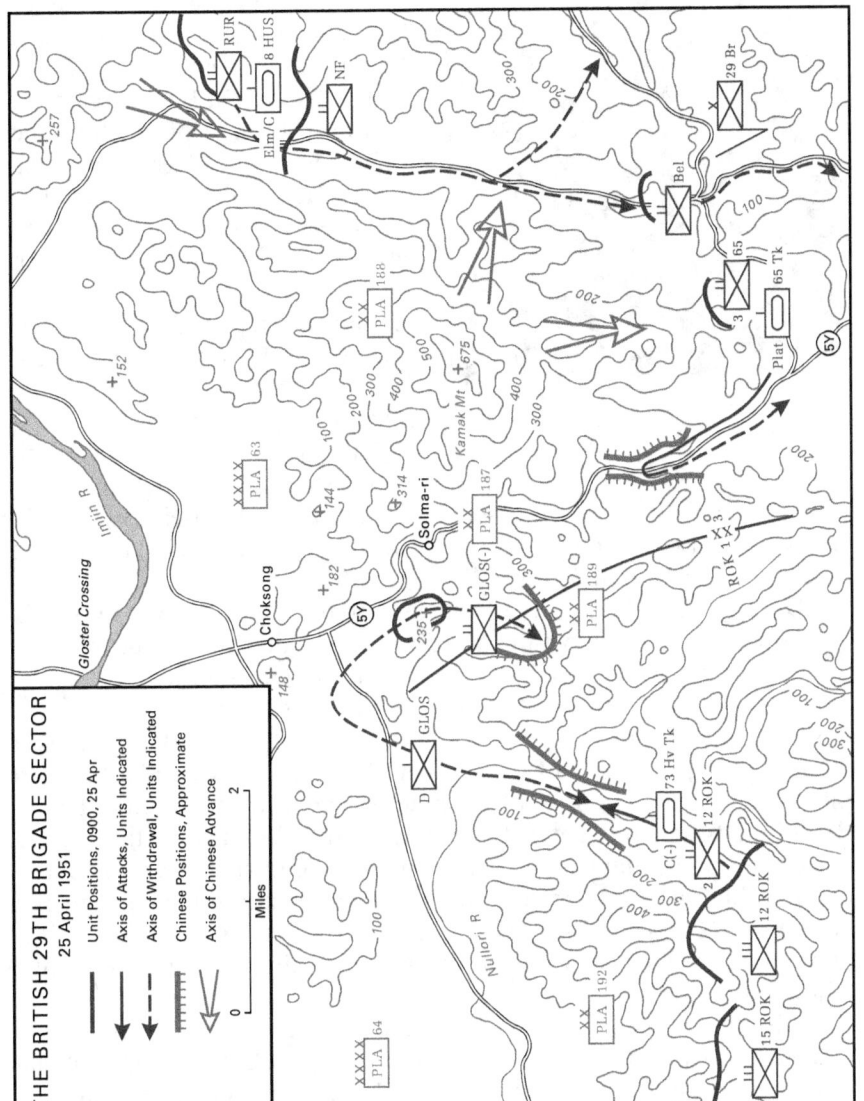

Map 8

Colonel Carne

General Soule decided to mount a second and stronger relief effort using two battalions of the 65th Infantry, the bulk of the 64th Heavy Tank Battalion, and the 10th Field Artillery Battalion. The plan called for the 1st and 3d Battalions of the 65th to evict the Chinese from the high ground on either side of the gorge leading to the Glosters. The 64th Heavy Tank Battalion was to advance through the gorge and then assist the 1st and 3d Battalions in rescuing the trapped British soldiers. The 10th BCT, which had reverted to Harris' control, was to occupy a blocking position near the gorge until the task force had returned with the Glosters in tow. After conferring with Brigadier Brodie, who assured him that Lt. Col. Joseph P. Carne's Glosters could hold out until relieved, General Soule scheduled the second relief effort for 0630 on 25 April.[47]

During the night, however, the Chinese infiltrated the 3d Division's front line to such an extent that the division's main supply route seemed to be in jeopardy. By daylight, enemy forces were also placing small-arms and mortar fire on the positions of the 1st and 3d Battalions of the 65th Infantry, the Philippine 10th BCT, the Belgian Battalion, and the remaining elements of the British 29th Infantry Brigade. Later in the morning, one hundred fifty Chinese infantrymen attacked the 1st Battalion, which prevented the regiment from launching the second relief mission as planned. Consequently, the 65th spent 24 April fending off Chinese attacks instead of coming to the aid of the beleaguered Glosters.[48] That same day, General Milburn directed I Corps to withdraw southward to Line Delta, which lay approximately ten miles above Uijongbu.

Still, the problem of the Glosters remained unsolved. General Soule ordered Colonel Harris to go to the British brigade's command post and discuss with Brodie what steps to take. "I reminded Soule," remembered Harris, "that everything I had was already engaged, and that we were fight-

---
[47] Monthly Cmd Rpt, 3d Inf Div, Apr 51.
[48] Ibid.

The 10th BCT M24 Chaffee light tank knocked out by Chinese mortar fire during the initial relief attempt seen here several months after the ground was recaptured by UN forces

ing for our lives"; but the division commander persisted.[49] Accompanied by his artillery and air liaison officers, Harris attended a planning session near Brodie's headquarters. The commander of the 64th Heavy Tank Battalion, Lt. Col. Wilson M. Hawkins; Brigadier Brodie; and several other British officers were also present.

Brig. Gen. Armistead D. Mead arrived soon after the planning session started. When Mead asked for an update on the situation, he learned that the composition of the task force was still under discussion, that a British armored unit commander had recommended a small number of tanks, and that one platoon of the 65th Tank Company was being considered. Mead interrupted the update to emphasize "the need for speed." Harris responded that he understood his mission perfectly and that he and Brodie would handle the matter if left alone. Brodie nodded in agreement.[50]

After Mead departed, Major Huth tried unsuccessfully to convince Harris that tanks alone would not succeed unless accompanied by infantry. The tanks would also have to be accompanied by engineers to clear mines

---

[49] Harris, *Puerto Rico's Fighting 65th*, p. 182.
[50] Memo, Mead to Soule, n.d., encl. 6.

from the narrow gorge that led to the Glosters. A strong force of supporting infantry was necessary to clear the high ground flanking the narrow road to allow the engineers to work effectively. Harris' final decision, to which Brodie assented, was that only a small group of tanks could be spared for the relief mission. Brodie also authorized the withdrawal of the Gloster battalion at this time.[51]

Capt. Claude Smith, the commander of the 65th Infantry's regimental tank company, drew the mission. Although Smith wanted to employ his entire unit, Harris directed him to use only a single tank platoon because of the narrow gorge through which the vehicles would have to pass. However, he assured General Mead, who had accompanied Harris to his regimental command post, that the 65th was prepared to follow up with a larger force if that became necessary.[52]

At 0900, the tank platoon, short one vehicle left behind for maintenance, started up Route 5Y toward the Glosters. By this time, substantial elements of the Chinese *187th* and *189th Divisions* stood between the American tank platoon and the encircled Brits. Although a forward observer from the 10th Field Artillery Battalion was to have accompanied the tanks, he did not arrive in time to join the platoon. Due to the hilly terrain blocking the signals of their lower-powered radio, the tankers were unable to remain in communication with the 65th's command post for very long. The sole source of information on the relief effort originated from visual observation reports by an L–16 spotter plane flying overhead.

About the time Captain Smith's tanks began advancing toward the Gloster Battalion, Brig. Gen. Moon Bong Kang, commanding the 1st South Korean Division immediately to the west, dispatched a task force of his own to rescue the British unit. Kang's force consisted of the 2d Battalion of the South Korean 12th Infantry Regiment aided by two tank platoons from Company C of the U.S. 73d Heavy Tank Battalion. Intense Chinese fire brought the column to a halt, however, after it had advanced but a single mile.[53] Meanwhile, the Glosters had begun a breakout attempt, moving on foot through the hills while leaving their seriously wounded behind for the Chinese.

Captain Smith's tank platoon advanced only a mile before becoming bogged down in a firefight with a large Chinese force. Concerned that the enemy occupying the high ground on his flanks might encircle and destroy his unit and aware that his men were running low on ammunition, Smith ordered his small force to pull back, and it reached its company area at

---

[51] Farrar-Hockley, *The British Part in the Korean War*, 2: 130.
[52] Monthly Cmd Rpts, 65th Inf, Apr 51, and 3d Inf Div, Apr 51; Mossman, *Ebb and Flow*, p. 422.
[53] Mossman, *Ebb and Flow*, pp. 422–24.

about 1300. Still under orders to relieve the British unit, Harris ordered another attempt by a different tank platoon. It headed out along the same route at approximately 1400. This second force was marginally stronger than the first because it contained an artillery observer and was escorted overhead by four fighter-bombers and a liaison aircraft. A mile out of the company area, the British tank company commander, Major Huth, flagged the U.S. tank platoon to a halt and convinced its commander that his vehicles would never be able to reach the Glosters. At that point, realizing that more rescue attempts would be futile, Harris withdrew his tanks. He had nothing left to commit.

In retrospect, Huth acted correctly in halting the second relief attempt by the 65th Infantry's tank company. The majority of the Glosters attempting to stealthily make their way back to allied lines found themselves pinned down by Chinese fire. Most were taken prisoner that afternoon, while others were captured over the next few days. Two small groups were able to bypass the Chinese and make their way back to friendly forces. Brigadier Brodie ordered the remaining elements of his brigade to pull back before they also were encircled. "It was a heartbreaking decision," the 3d Division's historian later noted, "but the brigade commander believed his position permitted no other course of action."[54]

After heavy fighting and the loss of several Centurion tanks, the main body of the 29th Brigade was finally able to break contact with the Chinese to reach Line Delta. As for the Glosters, the Chinese took 21 officers and 501 men, including 153 wounded, into captivity. The prisoners included Colonel Carne, who voluntarily remained with the wounded rather than escape. Fifty-eight Glosters were killed, and only forty-one survivors made it back to their brigade.[55]

Concerned about possible international repercussions, the Far East Command directed Eighth Army to conduct a full investigation of the events leading to the loss of the Gloster battalion. In a personal letter to General Van Fleet dated 7 May, Ridgway remarked, "I cannot but feel a certain disquiet that down through the channel of command, the full responsibility for realizing the danger to which this unit was exposed, then for extricating it when that danger became grave, was not recognized nor implemented."[56]

After reviewing all of the reports collected by Eighth Army investigators, Van Fleet responded to Ridgway's concerns:

---

[54] Dolcater, *3d Infantry Division in Korea*, p. 198.

[55] Farrar-Hockley, *The British Part in the Korean War*, 2: 136; Col E. D. Harding, *The Imjin Roll* (Rushden, Northamptonshire: Force & Corporate Publishing, 2000), p. 88.

[56] Farrar-Hockley, *The British Part in the Korean War*, 2: 135.

Members of the 1st Battalion, Gloucestershire Regiment (the "Glosters"), taken prisoner during the battle

It is my opinion that all reasonable and possible courses of action open to the responsible commanders concerned were initiated in an effort to extricate the Gloucestershire Battalion. . . . The overwhelming strength and determination of the enemy's attacks, together with his initial capability to exploit early penetrations by infiltration and enveloping actions, taxed the Corps, Division, and Brigade Commanders' limited reserves to the maximum. . . . The loss of this gallant fighting unit will continue to be felt with deep regret by myself and members of this command. Its magnificent stand in the face of overwhelming odds contributed immeasurably to the maintenance of the tactical integrity of the entire I US Corps.[57]

Eighth Army Regroups

On 25 April 1951, the 65th Infantry began a fighting withdrawal toward Seoul as Eighth Army fell back under heavy pressure from the enemy. Combat film footage shows the regiment's unshaven and exhausted soldiers retreating beneath dark, overcast skies in a constant drizzle.[58] "I

---

[57] Memo to Commander-in-Chief, FEC, 26 May 51, sub: Rpt of Gloucestershire Battalion, 22–25 Apr 51.

[58] "Retreat, Uijongbu," Motion Picture ADC-8852, Rcds of the Ofc of the Ch Signal Ofcr, RG 111, NACP.

became particularly concerned about having one of our units cut off as had happened to the Glosters," remembered Harris. "The timing of our battalion withdrawals became highly important to insure [*sic*] that we didn't leave one of them hanging out in the breeze. In fact, at one point it took an actual bayonet charge by the combined forces of B and K Companies before the 1st and 3d Battalions could continue their moves to the rear."[59]

During the evening of 25 April, the 3d Division began regrouping along Line Delta. The 65th Infantry, with the Philippine 10th BCT attached, stood on the division's left flank while the 15th Infantry took its right. The 7th Infantry waited in reserve. During the early morning hours of 26 April, an enemy assault rocked the 65th's 2d Battalion so sharply that Soule committed the 3d Reconnaissance Company to reinforce the unit. The Chinese assault succeeded in isolating one company and battalion headquarters while forcing the other two companies and the regimental heavy mortar platoon to retreat. The latter unit was so hard pressed that it had to leave behind all weapons and vehicles.[60]

Capt. Thomas J. Sanders, the 2d Battalion's artillery liaison officer, brought in a curtain of high-explosive shells to protect the surrounded Puerto Ricans and kept it up throughout the night. Temporarily attached to the 3d Division, the 7th Cavalry also rushed forward to repel the assault. Bolstered by fresh troops, the 65th drove off the enemy when morning came. The arrival of supporting tanks and self-propelled antiaircraft guns enabled the mortar company to recover its temporarily abandoned weapons and vehicles.[61] Soon thereafter, the exhausted Borinqueneers shifted to division reserve. The following day, the 3d Division fell back to occupy Line Golden, two miles south of Uijongbu.[62]

On 28 April, Eighth Army attached the 65th Infantry's 2d and 3d Battalions and the 10th Battalion Combat Team to the 25th Division while keeping the 1st Battalion in reserve. On that day, Eighth Army completed its retrograde movement to No Name Line six miles north of Seoul.[63] The new defensive line started at the Han estuary and made an arc above Seoul before continuing twenty miles due east. There, it angled sharply to the northeast and continued across the Korean peninsula to Taep'o-ri on the coast.[64]

On the night of 28 April, a reinforced Chinese battalion attacked Company C of the 65th Infantry's 1st Battalion as it defended No Name

---

[59] Harris, *Puerto Rico's Fighting 65th*, p. 185.
[60] Monthly Cmd Rpt, 10th Field Arty Bn, Apr 51, RG 407, NACP.
[61] Ibid.
[62] Monthly Cmd Rpt, 3d Inf Div, Apr 51.
[63] Ibid.
[64] Mossman, *Ebb and Flow*, p. 380.

Elements of the 65th Infantry moving south near Uijongbu

Line a few miles northeast of the capital. The attackers, who were being pounded by eight American artillery battalions, suffered tremendous losses.[65] Although the enemy overran part of the American line, M.Sgt. Juan E. Negron refused to withdraw. Encircled, he held his position throughout the night and into the morning, almost singlehandedly halting the Communist attack. Negron personally killed fifteen Chinese soldiers and enabled his company to reorganize. He received a Silver Star that was later upgraded to a Distinguished Service Cross.[66]

The next day, the 1st Battalion launched a counterattack that killed one hundred fifty enemy soldiers, captured fifty, and drove the surviving Chinese back. The entire regiment then reverted to division reserve in Seoul. Harris, for one, was grateful for the respite. "When we finally arrived at the outskirts of the city," he said, "we were able to breathe more easily because some rather extensive defensive emplacements had been set up there. We had sent a few troops back there even before we arrived

---

[65] Monthly Cmd Rpt, 10th Field Arty Bn, Apr 51.

[66] GO no. 588, HQ, EUSAK, 21 Jun 53, sub: Award of Distinguished Service Cross to Master Sergeant Juan E. Negron, Rcds of U.S. Army Operational, Tactical and Support Organizations (World War II and Thereafter), RG 338, NACP.

and they had already started on these fortifications. . . . I believe that those emplacements were worthy of any built during World War II."[67] The 65th Infantry's well-earned stay in the rear would be relatively brief. Even at that moment, the Communist armies were gathering their strength for another grand offensive.

---

[67] Harris, *Puerto Rico's Fighting 65th*, p. 185.

Chapter 6

FROM SEOUL TO THE CH'ORWON VALLEY: MAY–JULY 1951

From the very beginning of the Chinese spring offensive in 1951, General Van Fleet felt that the United Nations forces had to retain possession of Seoul. Not only would the UN forces gain a tactical advantage by maintaining a foothold above the Han, but retention of the capital would also prevent additional psychological damage to the South Korean populace. To give up Seoul for a third time, he believed, "would ruin the spirit of the nation."[1] His order on 23 April to defend Line Kansas despite the tremendous pressure the enemy was exerting on Eighth Army reflected that resolve. While the UN troops had been forced to withdraw from Line Kansas, he considered that situation temporary; he would no longer permit Eighth Army to give up defensible ground without concrete justification.

Convinced by the morning of 28 April that the main enemy effort was slowing down, Van Fleet informed his corps commanders that he intended to hold No Name Line indefinitely. He instructed them to use an active defense, making full use of artillery and armored forces to spoil or to rebuff enemy attacks. Though members of his staff considered it too risky to station significant numbers of troops north of the Han, the general insisted there would be no pullback without his personal authorization.

Arrayed north of Seoul, General Milburn's I Corps had six regiments on line and the same number assembled in and on the edges of the city. The British 29th Infantry Brigade was positioned below the Han at the base of the Kimpo Peninsula to prevent enemy attempts to envelop the South Korean capital from the west. The Turkish Brigade was to do the same job on the eastern flank of the city. With adequate reserves, well-constructed defenses, and a narrow front that allowed concentrated artillery

---

[1] Mossman, *Ebb and Flow*, p. 434; Braim, *The Will to Win*, p. 249.

Soldiers of the 3d Reconnaissance Company rest near Chip'yong-ni.

fire, Milburn's corps was in a defensive position far stronger than any it had occupied since the beginning of the Chinese offensive.

The 65th Infantry, meanwhile, acted as the division reserve on the outskirts of Seoul. During the first two weeks of May, assisted by Company C of the 10th Combat Engineer Battalion, the regiment fortified its sector by stringing barbed wire and digging foxholes, constructing weapons emplacements, and building command and observation posts. Korean laborers did most of the hard work. These efforts yielded for the 65th's area of operations four successive defensive lines: Silver, Iron, Lead, and Wood. At the same time, Harris' staff drew up a number of counterattack plans in case the enemy broke through to the city.[2]

Battle Below the Soyang

On 11 May, Eighth Army intelligence officers concluded that the Communists were once again ready to renew their offensive.[3] Aerial sightings of large bodies of troops moving east, usually at night or dur-

---

[2] Monthly Cmd Rpt, 65th Inf, May 51. Unless otherwise noted, all Cmd Rpts are in Entry 429, Rcds of the AGO, RG 407, NACP.

[3] Mossman, *Ebb and Flow*, p. 440.

ing cloudy days, suggested that major enemy formations were repositioning for a wide, flanking attack around Seoul. General Van Fleet paid particular attention to reports from prisoners and spies that the Chinese *12th, 15th, 20th, 27th,* and *60th Armies* were massing in west-central Korea. In response, he ordered the No Name fortifications improved and directed that the area between Ch'unch'on, forty miles northeast of Seoul, and the Hwach'on Reservoir, another fifteen miles away, receive special attention because the bulk of the Chinese formations were assembling there.[4]

The enemy struck on 16 May 1951, slamming into the right flank and the center of Almond's X Corps. The Chinese sent their first wave across the Soyang against the South Korean 5th and 7th Divisions, which were holding the line some fifteen to twenty miles east of Ch'unch'on. (*See Map 9.*) Almond authorized the two divisions to withdraw to No Name Line around midnight. While the 5th Division successfully occupied new positions on the right flank of the American 2d Infantry Division, the South Korean 7th Division completely fell apart when it pulled back. The South Korean III Corps on the 2d Division's right wing also pulled back, and its 3d and 9th Divisions lost the bulk of their artillery when they encountered roadblocks established by the Chinese to their rear. By 18 May, the enemy had created a deep salient in the right wing of the Eighth Army and had advanced as far as Soksa-ri, twenty-five miles south of No Name.

The U.S. 2d Division fought ferociously to contain the western shoulder of the Chinese thrust. Facing fierce enemy attacks to its front, the division also had to contend with the collapse of most of the South Korean units on its right flank. Despite heavy losses, the Americans held their ground. At midnight on 18 May, Van Fleet attached the 3d Infantry Division to X Corps to cover the retreat of the South Korean III Corps and to assist in retaking No Name. Mindful that a full division moving at once would overwhelm the region's limited road network, Eighth Army directed General Soule to send the 7th Infantry out on 19 May with the 65th to follow the next day. General Van Fleet sent the 15th Infantry to the U.S. 2d Division so it could help protect the eastern flank of X Corps.

The 65th for its part would counterattack the enemy salient. On 21 May, General Almond directed Soule to secure a critical mountain pass midway between Soksa-ri and Habae-jae (ten miles to the northwest) as well as a road junction four miles east of Habae-jae. Possession of those conduits would isolate the lead Chinese units that were continuing to push

---

[4] Ibid., p. 441.

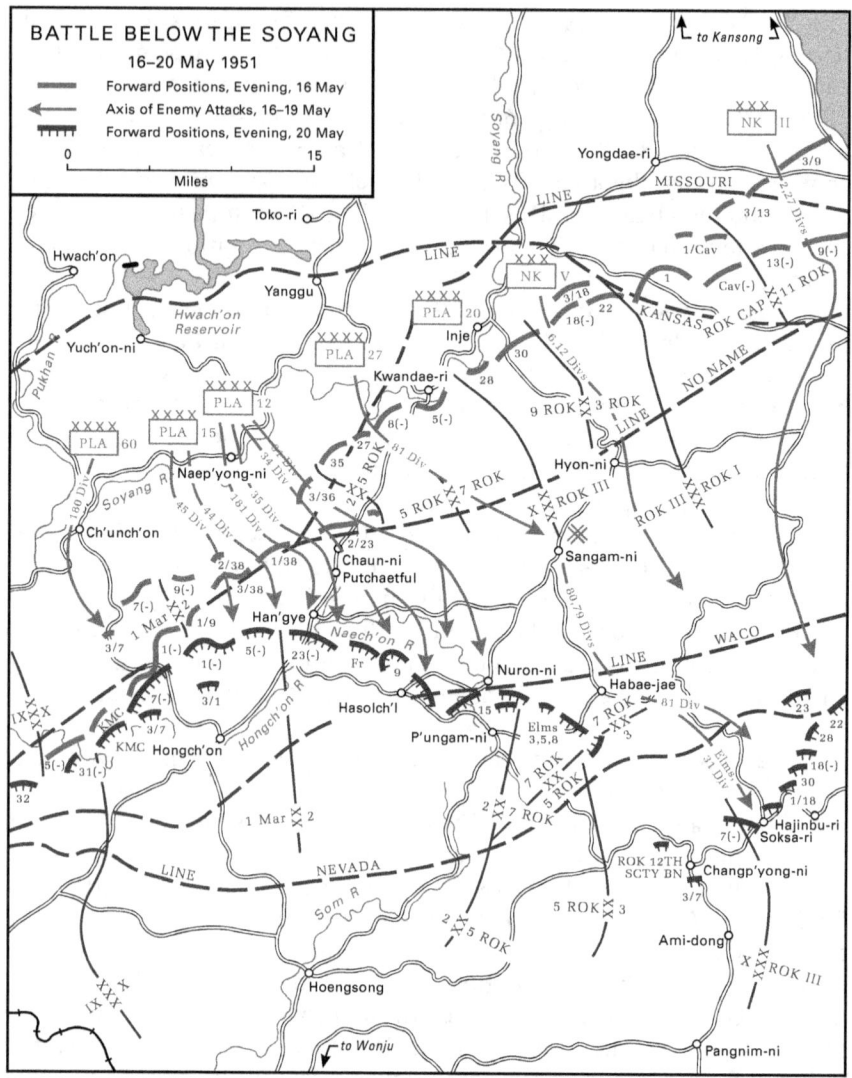

Map 9

south. Knowing that the enemy might bypass those two chokepoints by infiltrating troops over the mountains on the right flank of the 3d Division, Almond gave Soule operational control over the South Korean 8th and 9th Divisions. Soule instructed the 9th Division to guard the mountain pathways while the U.S. 7th and 65th Infantries seized the pass and the road junction near Habae-jae. He ordered the 15th Infantry, now under X Corps control, to secure the town of Habae-jae itself. The untried South Korean 8th Division would stand in reserve.[5]

From 22 to 29 May, the 7th and 65th encountered moderate enemy resistance as they slowly but steadily drove toward their objectives. The timing of the 3d Division's attack could hardly have been more fortuitous because it caught the North Koreans off guard as they attempted to change places with the exhausted Chinese. The enemy lost what little tactical cohesion he still possessed as intermingled Chinese and North Korean units tried unsuccessfully to fend off the allied advance. Although the mountainous terrain, fog, and adverse weather conditions slowed the American advance, the 7th and 65th Infantry regiments covered forty miles in eight days. As the enemy's supply and command problems multiplied, he was forced to give up the territory he had won at the beginning of the offensive.[6] In the end, the failed Communist attack along the Soyang turned out to be the last major Chinese offensive of the Korean conflict.

On 27 May, General Van Fleet laid out a new plan, codenamed PILEDRIVER, to expand the Eighth Army's counterattack across the whole Korean peninsula. The U.S. I and IX Corps would push north to Line Wyoming so they could cut enemy lines of communication at the base of the Iron Triangle and block the main roads running southeast toward the Hwach'on Reservoir and Ch'unch'on. Once this was done, X Corps and the South Korean I Corps to the east would establish defensive positions along a newly redrawn portion of Line Kansas that ran northeast from the Hwach'on Reservoir to the coastal town of Kojin-ni, thirty-five miles away.

Van Fleet intended to pause only briefly at Line Kansas before launching another attack with his right wing on 6 June to defeat enemy forces located between Kumhwa and the coastal town of T'ongch'on, twenty-three miles north of Kojin-ni. He needed the approval of Far East Command, however, before moving beyond Kansas and Wyoming. Ridgway turned down the request because he did not believe the risks were worth the potential benefits. Instead, Ridgway reminded Van Fleet that the Eighth Army's mission "was to exact maximum enemy losses at minimum cost while maintaining UNC forces intact, and this mission could best be carried out by a gradual advance to lines Kansas and Wyoming." Conforming to Ridgway's guidance, Van Fleet instructed his commanders to fortify Lines Kansas and Wyoming upon reaching them and to conduct only limited operations to the north from then on.[7]

---

[5] Ibid., pp. 461–63, 473; Dolcater, *3d Infantry Division in Korea*, pp. 208–09.

[6] Mossman, *Ebb and Flow*, pp. 469–70; Monthly Cmd Rpt, 3d Inf Div, May 51.

[7] Mossman, *Ebb and Flow*, p. 487.

American troops make their way forward under enemy fire, 26 May 1951.

On the evening of 29 May, the South Korean 16th Regiment, 8th Division, relieved the 65th Infantry in the South Korean III Corps sector. Early the following morning, the regiment moved west, covering a road distance of more than one hundred sixty miles before returning to the I Corps zone on 31 May.[8] For the month, the 65th was credited with killing almost five hundred enemy soldiers and capturing eighty-one others. In addition, the regiment had seized large stocks of ammunition and small arms along with Russian- and Japanese-made mortars and artillery pieces.[9] Eleven battle casualties was a relatively small price to pay for the unit's successes.[10]

Enemy activity in the 65th's new sector proved to be light, a boon to the exhausted men. "We took the opportunity to celebrate our fifty-second anniversary," Colonel Harris recalled, "A one-battalion parade, a holiday, some special food, and the last of our Don Q rum were the principal items on the program."[11] The unit also received a congratulatory message from General Milburn, who noted: "The Regiment has been assigned one important role after another since the Third Division joined the Corps and has carried out these assignments in an exemplary manner. It has established a fighting reputation and a standard of combat leadership of which it can be proud."[12]

---

[8] Monthly Cmd Rpt, 65th Inf, May 51.
[9] Ibid.; Monthly Cmd Rpt, 3d Inf Div, May 51.
[10] Ibid.
[11] Harris, *Puerto Rico's Fighting 65th*, p. 191.
[12] Ibid., p. 213.

In May 1951, 30 officers and 688 enlisted men from the 65th Infantry rotated back to the United States. The group, which represented almost 20 percent of the regiment's authorized strength, formed the bulk of the 800 troops who rotated home from the 3d Division during the month. While the Eighth Army rotation plan gave priority to frontline soldiers in all units, the 65th had been fighting longer and had far more eligible personnel than its sister regiments. Although General Soule previously decreed that monthly rotations would be reduced if they resulted in a unit dipping below 85 percent of its authorized strength, the arrival of 9 officer and 155 enlisted replacements permitted the Borinqueneers to release all eligible personnel on time.[13]

Among the departing leaders was Colonel Allen, the commander of the 3d Battalion. Lt. Col. Thomas O'Neil replaced him. The 40-year-old O'Neil had graduated from West Point and had won a Bronze Star during World War II. He had previously led the 3d Battalion of the 7th Infantry and was assigned to the 3d Battalion, 65th Infantry, on a temporary basis while waiting to take command of the 15th Infantry. Only Colonel St. Clair remained from the original group of battalion commanders that sailed from Puerto Rico in August 1950.[14]

Toward the Iron Triangle

The 65th had little time available to orient new leaders and integrate enlisted replacements before it took to the field once again. Eighth Army launched Operation PILEDRIVER on 3 June 1951 to regain Lines Wyoming and Kansas. Van Fleet "expected that PILEDRIVER would prove to be a fast, easy march. He was mistaken. It proved to be slow and arduous." Several factors, to include the rotation of many experienced leaders, rumors of an impending cease-fire, heavy rain, unexpected resistance, and the widespread effects of physical and mental fatigue resulting from six weeks of nonstop combat would combine to significantly dilute the power of the Eighth Army's latest offensive.[15]

In a preliminary move on 1 June, the 7th Infantry succeeded in transporting two companies to the northern bank of the Hantan using a temporary bridge constructed in the face of intense enemy fire. Emboldened by success, the unit launched an attack against Chinese positions dominating the only road leading from the crossing site. A second American battalion was able to cross the river, whereupon it turned west in a maneuver

---

[13] Ltr, HQ, 3d Inf Div, 6 May 51, sub: Officer and Enlisted Rotation Implementation, in Monthly Cmd Rpt, 3d Inf Div, May 51; Monthly Command Rpt, 65th Inf, May 51.

[14] *Register of Graduates and Former Cadets, 1802–1980*, p. 394.

[15] Blair, *The Forgotten War*, pp. 912–13.

designed to strike the rear of the enemy force guarding the only approach to the Hantan on the regiment's western flank. By the following morning, the 7th Infantry had succeeded in clearing out all the enemy positions in its zone of operations on the northern bank of the river.

The 3d Infantry Division began its main assault for PILEDRIVER at 0600 on 3 June. Plans called for the 65th and 7th Infantries to attack abreast with the 15th Infantry remaining in reserve. The assault regiments, with the 65th on the right and the 7th on the left, would try to take the high ground below Ch'orwon while the 64th Heavy Tank Battalion would conduct a reconnaissance in force along the road that led north to Kumhwa.[16]

The armored unit sent its Company C, supported by an engineer squad, to reconnoiter crossing points over the Hantan. The operation began when the tank company detached one of its platoons to check out a ford that the map located near the village of Tongdong-ni. The platoon swung west of the main north-south valley, which allowed it to bypass enemy resistance, but was unable to locate a suitable river crossing.

After waiting for the platoon to return, the entire company began moving up the main north-south valley paralleling the Hantan to locate a second crossing site reported in the vicinity of Oumsong. The company had covered two of the nine miles to its objective when two batteries of enemy 57-mm. antitank guns fired on the lead M46 platoon near the village of Chail-li. One of the tanks immediately burst into flames while two others were damaged and several crewmembers wounded. After futilely spending three hours trying to pinpoint the enemy weapons, the tank company finally requested the assistance of a light observation plane. While the aircraft was able to locate the Chinese weapons, however, artillery fire and air strikes failed to destroy them. When Company C moved forward again, enemy fire damaged another pair of M46 vehicles. In exchange, the tankers were able to claim the destruction of only one of the enemy 57-mm. guns. The armored force, less four damaged vehicles temporarily left behind, returned to friendly lines.[17]

As the day wore on, the 65th Infantry also began to encounter heavy resistance. On the right flank, St. Clair's 1st Battalion attacked two hills known as the Twin Peaks that lay two miles to the southeast of Chail-li. The unit led with Company B on the right and Company C on the left, trailed by Company A. The Puerto Ricans made good progress initially, moving deeper into enemy territory for two hours until they finally encountered the enemy. One soldier was killed and another wounded in Company B by the opening bursts of mortar and automatic-weapons fire, while two men from

---

[16] Monthly Cmd Rpt, 3d Inf Div, Jun 51.
[17] Monthly Cmd Rpt, 64th Tank Bn, Jun 51.

Puerto Rican infantrymen seek cover in an enemy trench captured during Operation PILEDRIVER.

Company C were also hit.[18] The battalion continued to push forward doggedly regardless of mounting losses.

By 1700, Company C had seized the western hillock after a short bout of hand-to-hand combat. Although Company B had killed twenty Chinese, it was unable to secure the other peak. As evening approached, friendly losses stood at eight killed and twelve wounded.[19] The Chinese also suffered numerous casualties.

Approximately two miles to the west, Johnson's 2d Battalion was fighting fiercely to maintain a new bridgehead it had established across the Hantan. The 3d Platoon of Company E, led by 1st Lt. Smith B. Chamberlain, had waded across the flooded river under intense enemy artillery, mortar, and small-arms fire, using only a rope as a guideline. During the crossing, a soldier lost his footing and was swept away by the swift current. A West Point graduate and World War II veteran, Chamberlain rescued the man as well as three others who encountered similar mishaps. Several other soldiers, unable to swim, disappeared forever in the swirling waters.

After assembling his bedraggled soldiers on the far bank, Chamberlain led them in an assault against a Chinese-occupied hill overlooking the

---

[18] Entries 030635 through 030920 Jun 51, Unit Jnl, 1st Bn, in Monthly Cmd Rpt, 65th Inf, Jun 51.

[19] Entry dtd 032025 Jun 51, Unit Jnl, 1st Bn, in Monthly Cmd Rpt, 65th Inf, Jun 51.

crossing site. After a three-hour struggle during which their lieutenant suffered repeated wounds, the platoon succeeded in capturing its objective.[20]

Once Chamberlain reported that his men had seized the hill, the rest of the 2d Battalion began battling its way across the river to reinforce the slender bridgehead on the northern bank. Because the lodgment was confined between two bends in the river, only a limited number of troops could be ferried across. This forced Company F to remain south of the Hantan until the companies on the other side could gain more ground. The Chinese launched a series of counterattacks against the American lodgment during the night.[21]

On the morning of 4 June, the 1st Battalion continued its fight for the Twin Peaks. It made only slow progress against the well-entrenched enemy. St. Clair committed Company A in support of the stalled attack on the right. The combination of fresh troops and additional firepower carried Companies A and B almost to the crest of their objective before a Chinese counterattack held them in place for the remainder of the night. Company A had sustained four wounded while Company B lost six killed and five wounded.[22]

That same day, the 65th lent a platoon from Company L to the 64th Tank Battalion when the latter unit sent a task force northward to retrieve the vehicles left behind at Chail-li. Minutes after arriving, the Americans encountered intense mortar and artillery fire that ultimately prevented towing away the stricken M46s. The recovery team stripped the disabled vehicles of classified items before abandoning all recovery efforts.[23]

In the meantime, the 2d Battalion again found itself in serious trouble. The Chinese reacted violently to the unit's crossing of the Hantan by launching a battalion-size counterattack supported by heavy concentrations of mortar and artillery fire. The intensity of the attack proved too much for the beleaguered defenders, so Harris and Soule decided to pull them back to the southern bank of the river. The withdrawal took place under the protective fire of three battalions of artillery and the guns of Company A of the 64th Heavy Tank Battalion, but it was not without mishap. As the men started across a footbridge installed by the 10th Combat Engineer Battalion, they bunched up and caused it to collapse. A number of soldiers,

---

[20] Monthly Cmd Rpt, 65th Inf, Jun 51; *Register of Graduates and Former Cadets, 1802–1980*, p. 483; GO no. 684, HQ, EUSAK, 23 Jul 53, sub: Award of Distinguished Service Cross to 1st Lt Smith B. Chamberlain, Entry 429, Rcds of the AGO, RG 407, NACP.

[21] Entries 031245 to 041920 Jun 51, 2d Bn Opns Jnl, in Monthly Command Rpt, 65th Inf Rgt, Jun 51.

[22] Entries 041405 and 041625 Jun 51, 1st Bn Opns Jnl, in Monthly Cmd Rpt, 65th Inf Rgt, Jun 51.

[23] Entry 031800 Jun 51, Bn Opns Jnl, in Monthly Cmd Rpt, 64th Tank Bn, Jun 51.

Engineers probing for hidden mines ahead of a slowly moving M4A3E8 medium tank near Ch'orwon

several of whom were wounded, tumbled into the current. Many were rescued, but some drowned. With the footbridge unserviceable, the engineers sought an alternative means to get the rest of the 2d Battalion across the river to safety.

"After all that rain, those damn rice paddies were hip-deep in mud and water," recalled Sfc. Tom N. Simonson of Company C, 10th Combat Engineer Battalion. "We finally got some boats down to the river, but it was too high and swift for them."[24] An L–16 aircraft towed a line across at low altitude, releasing it as the aircraft reached the far bank. The engineers on the southern bank attached a rope to their end of the line and then a string of boats to the rope. By pulling the craft across one at a time, the engineer detachment on the northern bank began evacuating the men. "We made several trips," remembered Simonson, "with the Chinese dropping artillery all over the place, but the 65th all wound up on the south bank."[25] By 2330, the surviving members of the 2d Battalion were safe. The ferocity with

---

[24] Dolcater, *3d Infantry Division in Korea*, p. 263.
[25] Ibid.

which the Chinese had contested the river crossing deterred the division from making another attempt in the same area.[26]

The 65th persevered, however, and renewed the contest for the Twin Peaks on the morning of 5 June. Following closely behind a thirty-minute artillery and mortar preparation, Company A quickly seized a small hillock just south of Twin Peaks. Soon afterward, Company B surged forward at 1020 intent on securing the easternmost peak. Enemy resistance proved spotty, enabling the unit to secure its objective by early afternoon. As both companies consolidated on the newly won ground, they discovered unopened crates of antitank and antipersonnel mines, abandoned weapons, and a hidden stockpile containing two thousand rounds of mortar ammunition. In addition to material losses, the enemy unit defending Twin Peaks had also suffered one hundred fifty to two hundred casualties.[27]

Resuming its advance on the following day, St. Clair's battalion bypassed Chail-li before continuing on two miles to the north and finally halting near the town of Chip'o-ri. With the 7th Infantry to the west already in possession of a firm foothold across the Hantan, the 3d Division directed the 65th to halt its crossing attempts. Reinforced by Company I, the 2d Battalion remained in place to prevent the Chinese from striking a blow against the 7th Infantry's deep right flank.

On 7 June, the 15th Infantry replaced the 65th, which went into reserve for rest and refitting. The 3d Division continued its advance to Line Wyoming on 8 June in the general direction of Ch'orwon. With the attached South Korean 9th Division on the left flank, the 7th Infantry, the Philippine 10th Battalion Combat Team, and the 15th Infantry moved abreast against moderate to heavy resistance. One of the South Korean regiments was hit by a Chinese counterattack later that day and fell back two thousand yards. In response, Soule repositioned the 65th Infantry's 3d Battalion forward where it could reinforce either the 7th Infantry or the South Korean 9th Division as needed. The following day, the South Korean unit regained the ground it had lost. In the meantime, the 15th Infantry advanced so rapidly that the 1st Battalion of the 65th was deployed to protect the division's newly exposed right flank.

During the I Corps advance to Line Wyoming, Communist forces had tenaciously defended key terrain during the day, often counterattacking at night and then withdrawing during the predawn hours. In the early days of the operation, allied troops were subjected to heavy mortar and artillery fire. As the attack progressed, however, the volume of that fire slack-

---

[26] Monthly Cmd Rpts, 65th Inf, Jun 51, and 3d Inf Div, Jun 51.

[27] Entries 051235, 051245 Jun 51, 1st Bn Opns Jnl, in Monthly Cmd Rpt, 65th Inf Rgt, Jun 51.

Soldiers from the 7th Infantry use a captured enemy footbridge to make their way rearward after being relieved by the 65th Infantry.

ened, indicating that the enemy had either withdrawn his heavy weapons to prevent capture or had suffered severe losses from friendly counterbattery fire.[28]

By 10 June, the 15th Infantry had occupied its final objective along Line Wyoming. Facing stiff opposition, the 7th Infantry regiment and South Korean 9th Division made slower progress, however, and did not come up alongside the 15th until two days later. The 7th Infantry later recorded:

> Eleven inches of rain fell between 1 June and 12 June. . . . The HANTAN was a constant obstacle to both attacking elements and logistical support. The terrain was rugged, rocky, heavily vegetated and wooded. Roads were in terrible condition and the enemy had sown mines indiscriminately. This campaign was fought under the worst imaginable conditions and against a determined, aggressive, and well-supported enemy.[29]

The 3d Reconnaissance Company and foot patrols of the 7th Infantry entered Ch'orwon on the morning of 12 June. Residents informed them that ten thousand Chinese had withdrawn north through the city on 9 June and that the last enemy troops had left on 11 June. The 3d Division

---

[28] Monthly Cmd Rpt, 3d Inf Div, Jun 51.
[29] Monthly Cmd Rpt, 7th Inf, Jun 51.

consolidated its positions along Wyoming while sending patrols northward to regain contact with the enemy. Later that afternoon, the 65th relieved the 7th Infantry and went back into the line.[30]

Even before the 65th began relieving the 7th Infantry, General Milburn ordered the 3d Division to conduct an armored thrust from Ch'orwon to P'yonggang to link up with a 25th Division tank column that was coming from the direction of Kumhwa. The thrust, codenamed Operation GOOSE, would be a one-day mission with all units returning to friendly lines by dark. Milburn intended the reconnaissance in force to disrupt enemy operations throughout the Iron Triangle, a prime Communist logistical zone. To carry out the mission, General Soule formed Task Force HAWKINS, consisting of the 64th Heavy Tank Battalion, Company I of the 7th Infantry in M39 personnel carriers, a battery from the 58th AFA Battalion, two tank platoons from the 65th Tank Company, and a squad from the 10th Combat Engineer Battalion.[31] The 65th Infantry and the South Korean 9th Division would deploy several infantry battalions to protect the task force's flanks and rear.

Covered by artillery fire and airstrikes, the 3d Division's portion of Operation GOOSE went off without a hitch. Tank platoons from the 65th Infantry patrolled and kept the road open behind the advancing task force, which entered P'yonggang without opposition. One tank platoon from the neighboring 25th Division actually linked up with Task Force HAWKINS in P'yonggang; but roadblocks, mines, and stiff enemy resistance along the Kumhwa road prevented the remainder of the 25th Division task force from reaching its goal.[32]

On 16 June, the chief personnel officer of the Eighth Army, Col. Edgar T. Conley, informed Colonel Harris that Brig. Gen. Bryan L. Milburn, the chief personnel officer for the Far East Command, wanted to transfer him to Tokyo. On 20 June 1951, as a result, Harris relinquished command to Col. Erwin O. Gibson. "Leaving the 65th was a bit emotional," he remembered. "We had a small parade as a departing ceremony . . . then I said a few words to the assembled noncoms and quickly jumped into my jeep and departed for Seoul."[33]

Colonel Gibson, a 44-year-old reserve officer who transitioned to the Regular Army in 1946, had served with the 39th Infantry during World War II, winning three Bronze Stars. Prior to taking command of the 65th Infantry, he had been the chief of logistics for the 3d Division and then,

---

[30] Monthly Cmd Rpt, 65th Inf, Jun 51.
[31] Monthly Cmd Rpts, 3d Inf Div, Jun 51, and 7th Inf, Jun 51.
[32] Ibid.
[33] Harris, *Puerto Rico's Fighting 65th*, p. 197.

briefly, the chief of logistics for X Corps.[34] Gibson may have owed his new assignment to General Almond, who habitually rewarded members of his staff with regimental commands.[35] Shortly before Gibson took over, General Soule presented him with a Legion of Merit for his exemplary service during the evacuation of Hungnam and the attack to the Han.[36] "I liked Gibson," remembered Capt. Charlie Boyle:

> He took command at a time when not much was happening but he certainly gave the impression that he knew what he was doing. He did not interfere with the way things were going and pretty much accepted the fact that the regimental operations officer and I had more first hand [sic] knowledge of the situation than he did, so he simply let us carry on as we had been doing.[37]

Fighting for the Sobang Mountains

The 3d Division maintained its positions directly south of the Iron Triangle throughout June. The legs of the triangle, anchored on the towns of Ch'orwon, Kumhwa, and P'yonggang, encompassed virtually all of the major rail and road networks in north-central Korea. While Ch'orwon and Kumhwa were firmly under UN control, the Sobang Mountains north and west of the Hantan and south of P'yonggang remained in Communist hands. The keys to controlling this enemy-occupied area were Hills 717 and 682.

By the third week of June, the Chinese were actively patrolling throughout the Sobang Mountains. This prompted Soule to begin planning an attack designed to push back the Chinese in that sector. The primary aim of the operation was to destroy the enemy defenders and then, if all went well, to establish outposts on each hill. The ultimate decision as to what to do with the hills depended upon the outcome of the operation. After learning that intelligence estimates placed two enemy platoons on Hill 682 and a single reinforced Chinese platoon on Hill 717, Soule decided to employ a single infantry battalion for the operation.[38] Col. Thomas R. Yancey's 15th Infantry drew the assignment. Soule instructed Yancey to launch the attack at 0700 on 23 June.

Yancey gave the mission to Lt. Col. Julius W. Levy's 1st Battalion of the 15th Infantry. While the American unit succeeded in taking Hill 682

---

[34] GO no. 36, HQ 65th Inf, 20 Jun 51, in Monthly Cmd Rpt, 65th Inf, Jun 51; *Official Army Register, 1 January 1951*, p. 244. Gibson was commissioned in the infantry.

[35] Blair, *The Forgotten War*, p. 917.

[36] Staff Bfg Min, 18 Jun 51, in Monthly Cmd Rpt, 3d Inf Div, Jun 51.

[37] Ltr, Boyle to author, 10 Apr 01, Historians files, CMH.

[38] Capt William J. Fox, "Hills 717 and 682 in the 'Iron Triangle' Area," Jun 51, pp. 1–3, 7th Historical Detachment, Eighth U.S. Army, CMH.

and the southern half of Hill 717, it was forced to abandon its gains in the face of Chinese counterattacks.

Although the Chinese were not expelled from the Sobang Mountains, the battle provided the 3d Division an opportunity to assess the performance of Puerto Rican soldiers diverted from the 65th to other units. The chief personnel officer of the 1st Battalion, 15th Infantry, reported that "his unit was composed of colored troops, ROK [South Korean], Hawaiian and Puerto Rican soldiers." He singled out the Puerto Ricans for special praise, rating them as excellent soldiers.[39]

The month of June 1951 ended on a disappointing note for the 65th Infantry. On the evening of 28 June, a motorized patrol from the regiment's Intelligence and Reconnaissance Platoon left their jeeps and three guards at a prearranged dismount point prior to continuing the rest of the way on foot. A reinforced enemy squad attacked the guards, who abandoned the jeeps and fled. In the meantime, the rest of the patrol had gotten into a firefight and reported three of its men missing. An aerial search the following morning failed to locate either the missing personnel or the vehicles.[40]

The incident was overshadowed by personnel readiness issues that began to crop up in the 65th. By late June 1951, the strength of the regiment dropped below its authorized level of 3,794 for the first time during the war.[41] To remedy the problem, General Soule temporarily curtailed further rotation from the regiment. As a result, although two thousand two hundred soldiers left the division by the end of the month, only forty-four came from the 65th Infantry.[42] Many of the remaining men clearly met the criteria for rotation, having accrued on average forty-six more days in combat than their counterparts in the 7th Infantry and forty more than those of the 15th.[43] Not surprisingly, Soule's decision proved very unpopular with the men who were not allowed to leave Korea.

General Soule's second step to maintain the strength of the 65th Infantry entailed transferring Puerto Rican soldiers from the 7th and 15th Infantries. Although the commanders of those units had resisted when Puerto Ricans were originally assigned to their units, the transfers to the 65th were accomplished only after significant foot dragging. In part, this attitude stemmed from a marked reluctance on the part of the losing units who wanted to retain combat-proven soldiers. Also, some Puerto Ricans

---

[39] Fox, "Hills 717 and 682," app 4.
[40] Staff Bfg Min, 29 Jun 51, in Monthly Cmd Rpt, 3d Inf Div, Jun 51.
[41] Personnel Daily Sum, 30 Jun 51, in Monthly Cmd Rpt, 3d Inf Div, Jun 51.
[42] Monthly Cmd Rpt, 65th Inf, Jun 51.
[43] Personnel Daily Sum, 30 Jun 51.

asked to remain in other units rather than transfer over to the 65th.[44] The realignment took place, however, despite the chorus of dismay that greeted the directive.

Finally, General Soule pressured Eighth Army for additional Puerto Rican replacements and was promised two hundred fifty per month. As a result, the strength of the 65th began to rise. By the beginning of July 1951, it had grown to three thousand seven hundred eighty men.[45] Even so, Eighth Army decided to divert eleven hundred Puerto Rican replacements to units other than the 65th Infantry and the 3d Infantry Division.[46]

The month of July began with the 65th continuing to improve its defenses, patrolling, training new replacements, and cleaning and repairing its weapons.[47] A number of personnel received temporary assignments to serve as interpreters with a newly arrived Colombian infantry battalion. They would remain there until Eighth Army was confident the newly arrived Latin American soldiers had attained "satisfactory combat efficiency."[48] Colombia would be the last allied nation to contribute ground combat forces to Eighth Army. With the addition of this troop contingent, Eighth Army consisted of 3 U.S. and 1 South Korean corps, 17 American and South Korean divisions, 4 UN brigades, 1 separate infantry regiment, and 9 separate infantry battalions.[49] A total of 554,500 allied soldiers, including 253,000 Americans, 273,000 South Koreans, and 28,000 men from fourteen other countries, were in Korea. Approximately 569,200 enemy soldiers, more than half of them Chinese, faced them.[50]

The 3d Infantry Division's inability to take Hills 682 and 717 remained a source of concern. The Chinese in that sector were now strong enough to pose a serious threat to the American main line of resistance. The enemy also deployed strong security detachments atop dominant terrain to prevent the Americans from establishing outposts and conducting patrols. Soule conceived Operation DOUGHNUT to redress this unsatisfactory situation.

---

[44] The 10th Engineers, for example, did not send its quota to the 65th Infantry until late on 4 July. Monthly Cmd Rpt, 10th Engrs C Bn, Jul 51.

[45] Monthly Cmd Rpt, 3d Inf Div, Jul 51.

[46] Staff Mtg Notes, 28 Jun 51, in Monthly Cmd Rpt, 3d Inf Div, Jun 51. Many were National Guardsmen from the 296th Infantry called to active duty.

[47] Monthly Cmd Rpt, 65th Inf, Jun 51.

[48] Staff Bfg Min, 27 Jun 51, in Monthly Cmd Rpt, 3d Inf Div, Jun 51.

[49] These totals do not reflect the impending formation of the British Commonwealth 1st Division. It was slated to absorb the Canadian 25th and British Commonwealth 28th and 29th Brigades in late July, leaving the Turks as the only separate brigade. Mossman, *Ebb and Flow*, p. 502.

[50] Ibid. North Korean forces included 7 corps, 23 divisions, and 2 brigades; the Chinese deployed 5 army groups, 17 armies, and 51 divisions in Korea.

DOUGHNUT called for a double envelopment of Hills 682 and 717 by an armor-infantry task force in conjunction with an attack by an infantry regiment (minus one battalion). The elements of the Chinese *233d* and *234th Regiments* defending the main objective had a combined strength equivalent to one full regiment. A total of twenty-four Communist artillery pieces were in position to support the defenders.[51] Although planned for 30 June, the attack was temporarily postponed because the weather was too overcast for air support.[52]

After several days of work by his staff, General Soule invited Generals Van Fleet and Milburn to a briefing on the proposed operation. Accompanied by two Air Force generals, the Eighth Army commander and I Corps commander flew to the 3d Division command post for the meeting. Having spent several hours questioning Soule on specific aspects of the proposed operation, both Ridgway and Milburn voiced their approval. After making a few minor adjustments, the 3d Division distributed the operations order to participating units by the following morning.[53]

Task Force HAWKINS, which had been assembled for Operation GOOSE in mid-June, formed the primary armored component of DOUGHNUT. It consisted of the 64th Heavy Tank Battalion (less one company), Maj. John E. Harris' 3d Battalion (less one company), a detachment from the 10th Combat Engineer Battalion, and a tactical air control party. Major Harris had assumed command of the 65th Infantry's 3d Battalion from Colonel O'Neil earlier in the month. A 35-year-old reserve officer on extended active duty, Harris had served in World War II.[54]

Task Force KNAPP, a subordinate element of Task Force HAWKINS, comprised the second armored column slated to make the thrust against the Chinese defending Hills 682 and 717. Task Force KNAPP consisted of the 64th Heavy Tank Battalion's Company C; Company K from the 3d Battalion, 15th Infantry; a detachment of engineers; and a tactical air control party.

DOUGHNUT began on 1 July, when Task Force HAWKINS moved northeast from Ch'orwon in the direction of P'yonggang. Task Force KNAPP, which attacked northwest along the road from Kumhwa, also headed toward P'yonggang. (*Map 10*) Neither of the groups made significant contact with the enemy. The 65th Infantry tank company and the 3d Battalion's Company I, with the assistance of a neighboring South Korean unit, secured the roads behind HAWKINS and KNAPP.[55]

---

[51] Monthly Cmd Rpt, 3d Inf Div, Jul 51.

[52] Ibid.

[53] Capt William J. Fox, "Operation DOUGHNUT," Mil Hist Sec, Eighth U.S. Army, copy at CMH.

[54] *Official National Guard Register for 1943* (Washington, D.C.: National Guard Bureau, 1943), p. 513.

[55] Monthly Cmd Rpt, 3d Inf Div, Jul 51.

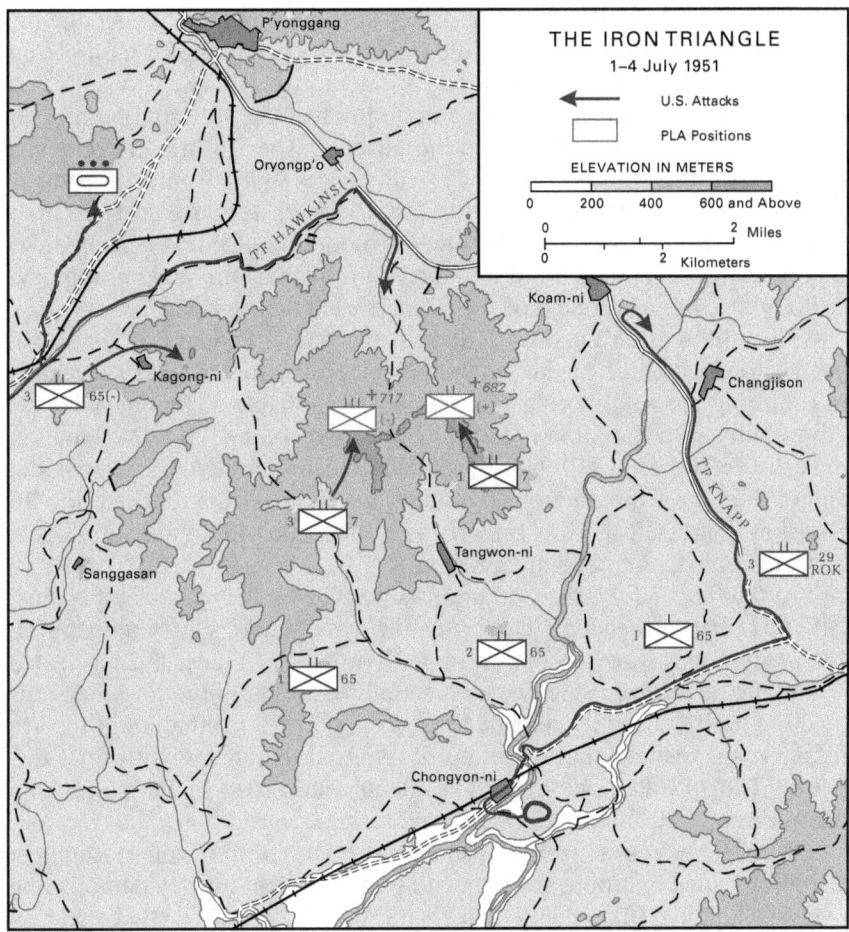

Map 10

Two battalions of the 7th Infantry assigned to take Hills 717 and 682 encountered stiff resistance. A pair of enemy battalions held the first while a third defended the slightly shorter of the two peaks. The Chinese troops fought from mutually supporting bunkers, directing intense artillery, mortar, automatic-weapons, and small-arms fire against the Americans. The 3d Infantry Division responded with fifteen thousand rounds from the light and medium howitzers of the 9th, 10th, 90th, and 159th Field Artillery Battalions. In addition, U.S. fighter-bombers flew eighty-six close air support missions during the assault.

Although the artillery and air strikes failed to completely dislodge the enemy by nightfall, the troops of the 7th Infantry had gained a foothold on both objectives. During the night, the 1st Battalion on Hill 682 was subjected to a pair of enemy counterattacks and both it and the 3d Battalion on Hill 717 endured Chinese artillery and mortar fire.[56] The 7th Infantry renewed its attack on the morning of 2 July. Although a squad from Company K managed to secure the crest of Hill 717, the men were driven from their position by an enemy mortar barrage. A platoon from Company A made its way to the top of Hill 682, but was forced off by machine-gun, mortar, and artillery fire. For a second day, the Chinese held their ground.

To reinforce the push on Hill 717, the 65th Infantry's 3d Battalion passed to the control of the 7th Infantry the next morning. It succeeded in capturing the neighboring Hill 608 but was unable to link up with the 7th Infantry's 3d Battalion at Hill 717. Meanwhile, the 7th's 1st Battalion took the defenders of Hill 682 by surprise when it circled to the west and approached the Chinese from the rear.[57] As darkness approached, the 3d Division instructed the 7th Infantry to "button up" in anticipation of an almost certain Chinese counterattack.

At 0300 on 4 July, the Communists launched a furious assault against Hill 682 that succeeded in overrunning two platoons of Company B. Company C was struck from three directions by the Chinese but succeeded in holding its ground. Shielded by a curtain of artillery fire, the Americans held out until the enemy retreated at daylight. The 3d Battalion of the 7th Infantry was also hit that night, but it repulsed the enemy with little difficulty. The 3d Battalion of the 65th Infantry succeeded in linking up with the troops on Hill 717 shortly after daybreak.

With both peaks secure, elements of the 10th Combat Engineer Battalion, aided by troops from the 7th Infantry, spent the day demolishing over two hundred fifty enemy bunkers on Hills 682 and 717. Once that task was complete, the 7th Infantry and its supporting units withdrew to the main line of resistance. Meanwhile, the 65th Infantry's 3d Battalion also fell back to Line Wyoming, double-checking that all villages along the way were free of enemy forces.[58]

General Soule considered Operation DOUGHNUT an unqualified success. In its wake, attacks against the neighboring South Korean 9th Division diminished in scope and severity and the security of the 3d Infantry Division grew. Furthermore, friendly patrols were at last able to operate freely anywhere in the Iron Triangle. In all, allied forces had 196 casualties compared

---

[56] Monthly Cmd Rpt, 7th Inf, Jul 51.
[57] Ibid.
[58] Monthly Cmd Rpt, 3d Inf Div, Jul 51.

Riflemen of the 7th Infantry, 3d Division, moving out to attack Hill 717 on the morning of 3 July

to an estimated 2,200 Communist losses. The 3d Division also captured large quantities of enemy weapons, ammunition, and equipment.[59]

As DOUGHNUT wound down, the Chinese and North Korean leaders agreed to hold cease-fire talks at Kaesong, a small village eight miles northwest of Munsan-ni. The initial round of negotiations brought a temporary end to major offensive operations by both sides. This announcement was greeted with mixed feelings by U.S. and UN troops. Many commanders began to notice a disquieting change in the attitudes of their soldiers. Brig. Gen. Hayden L. Boatner later observed: "The hoped for success for the truce talks caused undue optimism that the 'war was over.' Officers and men 'let up,' dug in on the Kansas Line, and when battle was [later] renewed many did not display the 'élan' of previous months because of that 'war is over' attitude."[60]

As the conflict entered its second summer, Eighth Army's line was anchored in the west along the Han estuary and extended to just below the southwestern corner of the Iron Triangle before curving around the Hwach'on Reservoir and rising steeply northeast to meet the Sea of Japan forty-two

---

[59] Ibid.

[60] Ltr, Maj Gen (Ret) Hayden L. Boatner to Ch of Mil Hist, 3 Jan 67, sub: Comments on "Truce Tent and Fighting Front," Ofc of the Ch of Mil Hist, Rcds of the Army Staff, RG 319, NACP.

miles above the 38th Parallel. With minor modifications, this would become the boundary between the two Koreas following the armistice in 1953.

Heavy rains fell in late July, putting a halt to large-scale military activity. Some units suffered equipment losses when rain-swollen streams flooded bivouac areas. The torrential downpour also washed out some bridges and roads. Although neither Eighth Army nor the Communists mounted any major operations, the 3d Division and the 65th Infantry continued to patrol aggressively with varying degrees of enemy contact.[61]

During July 1951, the 65th Infantry endured 18 battle and 157 nonbattle casualties. This constituted a small percentage of the 229 battle and 718 nonbattle casualties incurred by the entire 3d Division that month. During July, the 65th had also contributed 522 officers and men to the 2,156 3d Division personnel rotated home. Despite the relatively small number of battle losses, the regiment's frontline units remained understrength even though they had received 611 replacements, almost half of the 1,271 assigned to the entire 3d Division.[62] There were simply not enough replacements coming into Korea to offset the combination of stateside rotation losses and nonbattle casualties. Furthermore, the majority of new soldiers had received only basic training and would require additional instruction before they could go into combat.[63]

Given the growing personnel shortfalls, it appeared that future rotations from the regiment might have to be curtailed again. "The shortage of Puerto Rican replacements remains a problem," Soule observed at the time. "Unless replacements for combat arms officers also arrive, it is quite possible a serious morale problem will arise."[64] The abundance of experienced career NCOs who had served in World War II offset the shortage of officers to a degree; however, many of those NCOs were "short timers" due to return home soon.

Among those who rotated to the United States in July 1951 was Colonel St. Clair, the last of the 65th's original battalion commanders. St. Clair had received two Silver Stars and a Bronze Star for valor during his tour in Korea.[65] Lt. Col. Franklin B. Simmons Jr. replaced him as the 1st Battalion commander. Thirty-four-year-old Simmons was a World War II veteran who had been commissioned from the ranks.[66] Simmons had served as the

---

[61] Ibid.; Monthly Cmd Rpt, 65th Inf, Jul 51, Entry 429.

[62] Personnel Daily Sum, 20 Jun 51, in Monthly Cmd Rpt, 3d Inf Div, Jun 51; Personnel Daily Sum, 31 Jul 51, in Monthly Cmd Rpt, 3d Inf Div, Jul 51.

[63] Monthly Cmd Rpt, 65th Inf, Jul 51.

[64] Ibid.

[65] *Register of Graduates and Former Cadets, 1802–1980*, p. 422.

[66] *Official Army Register, Volume I, United States Army Active and Retired Lists, 1 January 1952* (Washington, D.C.: Department of the Army, 1952), p. 684.

division's chief logistical officer for four months before being assigned to the regiment.[67]

In the span of ninety days, the regimental commander and all three battalion commanders had departed the 65th Infantry. In addition, a total of 40 officers, all seasoned combat veterans, had departed along with 1,244 sergeants and enlisted soldiers. Combined with battle casualties, this was more than a third of the regiment's authorized strength. Just three months old, Eighth Army's rotation policy had already deprived the 65th of a large number of its combat-experienced leaders and soldiers.

The 65th Infantry was hardly alone in this. An Army-wide shortage of officers had existed since the beginning of the conflict, mainly because the reserve officer recall programs had not produced the required number of men. As a result, officer rotations lagged seriously behind those of enlisted men. In a 3 June 1951 cable to the Department of the Army, General Ridgway reported that Eighth Army's combat effectiveness of was in jeopardy because of his inability to replace the large numbers of company- and field-grade officers who were departing. Although the general could have declined to rotate many of the seasoned veterans, both he and his commanders felt the move would be counterproductive—many of the men in question had reached their breaking points. After long periods in combat, they had nothing more to give.[68]

Ridgway recognized the urgent need to rotate burned-out officers and to find more enlisted men to keep Eighth Army up to strength. He also noted that the current rotation system in the view of General Van Fleet had a beneficial effect on morale. In that light, he proposed that the Army increase replacement shipments for July, August, and September to twenty-five hundred officers and thirty-eight thousand five hundred enlisted men per month.[69] In a response dated 22 June, Army Chief of Staff General J. Lawton Collins approved Ridgway's proposal but cautioned that full implementation would have a serious effect on planned Army deployments to Europe.[70]

As a result of the growing rotation backlog, the Army decided to institute a new policy on 21 July.[71] The plan, which would go into effect on 1 September 1951, was based on "Constructive Months Service" points. Rotation would be contingent on meeting a set number of points established

---

[67] Simmons was the assistant chief logistical officer until he replaced Gibson when the latter was promoted to colonel and sent to X Corps. Dolcater, *3d Infantry Division in Korea*, p. 25.
[68] Stillwaugh, "Personnel Policies in the Korean Conflict," ch. 3, p. 10.
[69] Ibid.
[70] Ibid., p. 12.
[71] Ibid., p. 13.

by the Far East Command. The command decided initially that individuals would need to earn thirty-six points for rotation, which translated into a tour of nine to eighteen months in Korea depending on the length of time an individual's unit spent in combat. Men were to receive four points for each month spent on the line and two points for each month spent in reserve or rear areas. An infantryman who earned four points for each month his unit was in contact with the enemy would find that number reduced to two per month whenever his unit was placed in reserve.

All rotations would be based upon the ability of Department of the Army personnel managers to support the new policy. This meant that the number of troops being rotated per month would have to equal the number of replacements that arrived. As with the first rotation scheme, certain critical categories of personnel were exempt from the new plan. Any individual that accrued enough constructive service credits to meet the rotation criteria, however, could not be retained more than sixty days after becoming eligible except by approval of the Far East Command.[72] This was the rotation policy that Eighth Army, and the 65th Infantry, would follow for the remainder of the war.

---

[72] Ibid., pp. 24–25.

Chapter 7

OPERATIONS IN THE IRON TRIANGLE AUGUST–DECEMBER 1951

August opened with the 3d Division still occupying Line Wyoming from Ch'orwon to Kumhwa. Attached to the division were the South Korean 9th Division and the Philippine 10th Battalion Combat Team. The Chinese *77th* and *78th Divisions, 26th Army*, opposed the 3d Division; elements of the Chinese *80th Division, 27th Army*, were arrayed opposite the South Korean 9th Division. On 1 August, I Corps directed General Soule to establish a series of patrol bases forward of the main line of resistance. Corps headquarters also ordered the 3d Division to send a small task force into P'yonggang, a mission that Soule gave to the 65th Infantry.[1]

Eighth Army had employed forward patrol bases extensively since the spring of 1951. Located as far as eight to ten miles in front of the main line, they accommodated units ranging in size from a single company to regimental combat team. Most often, they were positioned on commanding terrain covering the main avenues of approach to friendly lines. During daylight hours, when allied air and artillery support was most effective, foot and mounted patrols traversed the areas between the bases. The forward outposts also facilitated offensive action because they denied key terrain to the enemy in front of the allied line. This allowed UN troops to jump off from positions on the main line without being detected or fired on by Communist forces.[2]

On 2 August, the 65th Infantry's 2d Battalion established a company patrol base a little over two miles north of Line Wyoming to protect elements of the 10th Combat Engineer Battalion working on the road running

---

[1] Monthly Cmd Rpts, I Corps, Aug 51, and 3d Inf Div, Aug 51. Unless otherwise noted, all Cmd Rpts are in Entry 429, Rcds of the AGO, RG 407, NACP.

[2] Monthly Cmd Rpt, 3d Inf Div, Aug 51.

northeast from Ch'orwon. In preparation for the raid on P'yonggang, the 2d Battalion established a two-company patrol base nearly nine miles north of the line to facilitate observation of the roads and trails into the city. The following day, relieved of its sector by the 7th Infantry, the remainder of the regiment moved to a forward assembly area.

At 0715 on 8 August, the 1st Battalion, 65th Infantry; elements of the 65th's tank company; and Battery B, 3d AAA Battalion, moved north from Ch'orwon in the midst of a heavy rainstorm. Companies A and B reached P'yonggang ninety minutes later, sweeping through the town and high ground to the north without encountering opposition. The next day, the 2d Battalion, minus Company G, which remained in position overlooking P'yonggang, pulled back as the regiment went into division reserve. During the following week, the men of the 65th Infantry patrolled into enemy territory from both the main line of resistance and from the forward patrol bases, frequently encountering squad and platoon-size groups of Chinese soldiers. The Americans typically dispersed these small units with artillery and tank fire.[3]

It rained almost incessantly from 3 to 13 August, seriously hampering operations. Many roads became impassable when culverts and low bridges washed out. The muddy conditions severely curtailed cross-country travel by vehicle and even by foot. From 11 to 14 August, the main supply route of the 3d Division ceased to function because rising waters washed away a bridge across the Hantan. By the last week in August, however, the 10th Combat Engineer Battalion succeeded in restoring all principal roads in the division sector.[4]

The poor weather did not entirely stop combat operations. On the morning of 19 August, some three hundred Communist soldiers attacked the 2d Battalion's Company F and the regimental tank company while they were engaged in mopping-up operations between Ch'orwon and P'yonggang. With their outposts overrun and the main body of the company beginning to fall back, M.Sgt. Pedro J. Zayas rallied the men. Exposing himself to enemy fire and then leveling devastating machine-gun fire and hurling hand grenades at close range, he inflicted heavy casualties on the Communist troops, forcing them to abandon their attack. For his actions, Sergeant Zayas received the Silver Star.[5]

On 25 August, Major Harris' 3d Battalion, reinforced by other elements of the regiment, staged a live-fire training demonstration, Operation ANNIHILATION, for a large group of VIPs. In order to get the maximum train-

---

[3] Ibid.; Monthly Cmd Rpt, 65th Inf, Aug 51.
[4] Monthly Cmd Rpt, 3d Inf Div, Aug 51.
[5] GO no. 546, HQ, 3d Inf Div, 30 Nov 51, in Monthly Cmd Rpt, 3d Inf Div, Nov 51.

Flash floods washed pontoon bridges in the 3d Division sector several hundred yards downstream. During August, heavy torrential rains bogged down lines of communication to the front.

ing advantage, all of the replacements that the regiment had received in August 1951—a total of 11 officers and warrant officers and 685 enlisted men, as well as all of the battalion NCOs and company-grade officers that could be spared—participated in the live-fire rehearsals. The demonstration went off without a hitch.[6] The VIPs attending the exercise included General Van Fleet; famed news commentator H. V. Kaltenborn and his wife; the IX Corps commander, Lt. Gen. William M. Hoge; and the new I Corps commander, Maj. Gen. John W. "Iron Mike" O'Daniel.

A highly decorated veteran of both World Wars, O'Daniel was a living legend within the 3d Division. During World War I, he had participated in the St. Mihiel and Meuse-Argonne campaigns. During World War II, O'Daniel had fought with the 3d Division as the assistant division commander and later as the division commander. Following World War II, O'Daniel had gone on to command the Infantry School at Fort Benning, Georgia, and later served as military attaché in Moscow. Prior to assuming command of I Corps, he had been the infantry inspector for the chief

---

[6] Monthly Cmd Rpt, 65th Inf, Aug 51.

of Army Field Forces.[7] An aggressive leader and a close friend of General Ridgway, he had gone to Korea at the latter's personal request.[8]

Operation CLEANUP I and II

In early September 1951, General Soule ordered the 65th Infantry to begin planning for a demonstration along the road between Ch'orwon and Sibyon-ni, thirty miles to the west. The regiment would also scour the high ground to the south of the road. Soule intended this spoiling operation to disrupt enemy supply and communications channels, destroy Chinese forces in the area, and knock out artillery and mortar positions. One of the mission's specific goals was to seize and occupy a ridgeline west of Ch'orwon that extended along the same latitude for several miles and included Hill 487, one of the tallest peaks in the region. Codenamed CLEANUP, the attack was scheduled for 17 September.

Task Force CUTTHROAT, consisting of the 65th Infantry, the 64th Heavy Tank Battalion (less one company), and a detachment from the 10th Combat Engineer Battalion, took on the mission. The 9th, 10th, and 58th Field Artillery Battalions deployed to firing positions west of Hill 487 while the 7th and 15th Infantries occupied new patrol bases from which they could support the 65th's attack. A specially modified M4A3 Sherman tank would use a flail (revolving drums with chains attached to detonate hidden mines) to clear the roads in advance of the remainder of the armored column. Finally, the 7th Infantry and the 3d Reconnaissance Company would mount a vigorous sweep north of Ch'orwon to mask preparations for the attack.[9]

Task Force CUTTHROAT began its mission on the morning of 17 September, with the 1st and 3d Battalions leading and the 2d Battalion in reserve. Originally scheduled to begin at 0545, the attack was delayed for thirty minutes by heavy fog. Company E of the 15th Infantry, however, used the cover provided by the fog to launch a diversionary attack against Hill 487 to draw attention away from the 65th's advance.[10]

When the poor visibility showed no signs of improving, the column moved forward nevertheless. The flail vehicle's commander, Sgt. Augustine O. Green Jr., later recorded:

> After five yards from the starting point we detonated a mine. I stopped the vehicle, cut the flail engine, and raised the flail. I found the dif-

---

[7] *Generals of the Army* (Washington, D.C.: Office of the Chief of Staff of the Army, 1953), pp. 21–23.
[8] Blair, *The Forgotten War*, p. 573.
[9] Monthly Cmd Rpt, 3d Inf Div, Sep 51.
[10] Monthly Cmd Rpt, 15th Inf, Sep 51.

ferential shield completely blown off. The flail had detonated a mine on the right side, leaving a crater about two and a half feet in diameter. Looking to the left, I noticed the flail had failed to detonate another mine but defused it by tearing off the whole top of the mine. I remounted, started the flail engine, engaged the flail, and started down the road again.[11]

The flail tank somehow missed detonating a third antitank mine as it resumed clearing the road. An M46 Patton medium tank from the 3d Platoon of Company A, 64th Tank Battalion, hit the overlooked mine and was immobilized.[12] The remainder of the tanks shoved the disabled vehicle aside and continued. The flail tank resumed operation, detonating three more mines before the revolving drum was rendered inoperative by the shock of repeated explosions.

At 0800, the fog finally began to dissipate. Incoming enemy mortar and artillery fire increased as visibility improved. As the lead elements of the 65th Infantry continued forward, a steady rain began to fall. The advance briefly halted when Company E deployed to both sides of the road to give protection to an engineer mine-clearing detail that took over from the damaged flail tank. Even though the precipitation persisted, the infantry and tanks slowly pushed on, leading Colonel Gibson and General Soule to believe that Hill 487 and the ridgeline to the west would soon fall to their men despite the conditions. An increasing amount of small-arms, mortar, and artillery fire targeted the engineer detail, eventually forcing them to halt operations and seek cover.

The Americans responded by employing their own artillery to pummel Chinese positions visibly contesting the advance. Although the engineers were unable to resume their mine-clearing duties, the lead tank company moved forward once again. At 1300, a pair of M46s from Company A, 64th Tank Battalion, struck mines in rapid succession. A Chinese antitank gun engaged one of the disabled Patton tanks and another M46 directly behind it, knocking out both vehicles.[13] Soon afterward, an aerial observer located the emplacement housing the enemy gun. A rain of high-explosive shells succeeded in knocking out the Chinese antitank weapon, killing its seven-man crew, and suppressing three other guns located nearby. Two of the three damaged M46s were retrieved under cover of the friendly barrage before the lead tank company began pulling back. A fourth tank struck a mine during the

---

[11] Memo, Sgt Augustine O. Green Jr., Co A, 64th Heavy Tank Bn to Ordnance Ofcr, 703d Ordnance Co, 20 Sep 51, sub: Combat Operation of Flail Tank, in Monthly Cmd Rpt, 64th Tank Bn, Sep 51.
[12] Entry 180430 Sep 51, Monthly Cmd Report, 64th Tank Bn, Sep 51.
[13] Entry 181300 Sep 51, Unit Opns Jnl, 64th Tank Bn, Sep 51.

withdrawal. Intense enemy fire forced the Americans to abandon their efforts to recover the vehicle.[14]

By this time, the 15th Infantry's diversion had also been halted by enemy fire.[15] As the supporting tanks pulled back, Companies L and K of the 65th Infantry secured the northern half of Hill 487 but reported that the enemy continued to resist on its southern half. The precipitation, as it turned out, delayed the American advance just long enough for the Chinese to bring up additional men and guns. Facing intense enemy fire, the Americans on the hill broke contact later that day and withdrew. Although unsuccessful in the first attempt to take Hill 487, the 65th had inflicted an estimated one hundred seventy casualties on the Chinese while noting that "resistance offered by the enemy was much greater than had been expected."[16]

For much of the day, those back at regimental headquarters were only vaguely aware of what was happening at the front. During the late morning, General Soule had visited the 65th Infantry command post, where Colonel Gibson assured him that his men were advancing to the objective without any enemy contact. Soule then departed Gibson's command post to meet General O'Daniel, who was arriving at the division airstrip via light aircraft to observe the attack. The division commander soon learned of the true situation; none of the attacking units had actually reached their assigned objectives as previously reported and were in fact pinned down by enemy fire. What was worse, the troops were occupying positions that would be untenable once night fell.

"Quite evidently," observed Capt. John T. Daniels, the division's secretary of the general staff, "the Task Force Commander [Gibson] had not been forward to accurately determine the location of his troops, and Battalion Commanders were not in positions to [accurately] determine where their troops were [and inform the regimental commander accordingly]."[17]

Colonel Gibson went forward in a tank after Soule left, belatedly discovering that his troops had not reached their objectives. Gibson then recommended to division that, in light of the intensity of the Chinese artillery and mortar fire and the untenable positions held by his men, his infantry should pull back to safer positions for the night. The division gave him permission to withdraw; with that, the operation effectively came to an end.[18]

At an Operation CLEANUP after-action meeting on 19 September, the regimental commanders involved in the mission complained that the division had never given their units the support they had been promised.

---

[14] Entry 181630 Sep 51, Unit Opns Jnl, 64th Tank Bn, Sep 51.
[15] Monthly Cmd Rpt, 15th Inf, Sep 51.
[16] Monthly Cmd Rpt, 65th Inf, Sep 51.
[17] Monthly Cmd Rpt, 3d Inf Div, Sep 51.
[18] Staff Bfg Min, 19 Sep 51, in Monthly Cmd Rpt, 3d Inf Div, Sep 51.

Tanks had found it difficult to maneuver because of the poor weather conditions and the profusion of mines. The heavy mortars did not reach their forward positions on schedule because the flail tank was disabled early on and enemy fire prevented the engineers from clearing the roads. In addition, the early morning fog and rain hampered aerial observation of fires. Topping it all off, enemy resistance had been much stiffer than expected and the Chinese had come out in greater strength than intelligence had predicted.

Dissatisfied with the whole operation, Soule questioned Gibson and his subordinate commanders closely on all aspects of the assault. Colonel Simmons, for one, pointed out that by the time his 1st Battalion assaulted its initial objective the enemy presence there had grown from a reinforced platoon to several companies. Chinese commanders had also supported their troops with a heavy volume of artillery and mortar fire, which accounted for the bulk of the 1st Battalion's ten killed and eighty wounded.[19] The 65th, for its part, suffered a total of sixteen battle deaths in the action.[20]

General Soule informed the commanders present and his staff that for the record the division had suffered its worst day ever in combat. "We have had units that had greater casualties, but today we failed to take an objective and had to withdraw without being 'kicked out,'" he observed. "Bad weather, incorrect reports of troop location, and lack of aggressiveness on the part of the tanks all contributed to this."[21]

In retrospect, Soule's criticism ignored dramatic changes taking place in the basic nature of the Korean conflict. An assessment of Chinese tactics in the autumn of 1951 reveals:

> The enemy had used the period of relative inactivity, during the "peace talks," to occupy, organize, and fortify all key terrain features in his area. These defensive installations included covered communications trenches and foxholes, bunkers for crew-served weapons, [and] caves for supplies and living quarters.... Antitank and antipersonnel mines combined with booby traps and powerful demolition charges were employed extensively on critical avenues of approach. Bunkers were unusually strong, in some instances having 12 layers of logs 10–12 inches in diameter, covered by dirt up to 18 feet deep. They proved to be impervious to all except direct hits by medium or heavy artillery or 1000-pound bombs.[22]

The 3d Division had never encountered such sophisticated defenses during its previous battles.

---

[19] Monthly Cmd Rpt, 3d Inf Div, Sep 51.
[20] Staff Bfg Min, 20 Sep 51, in Monthly Cmd Rpt, 3d Inf Div, Sep 51.
[21] Staff Bfg Min, 18 Sep 51, in Monthly Cmd Rpt, 3d Inf Div, Sep 51.
[22] AAR, HQ I Corps, n.d., sub: Operation Commando, p. 4, copy in CMH.

As it was, the ridgeline west of Hill 487 remained to be taken and Soule believed that the terrain was vital to the security of a proposed railhead in Kumhwa. As such, it could not be allowed to remain in enemy hands. Operation CLEANUP II was his response. The new plan called for the 15th Infantry to seize Hill 487 while the 65th seized Hills 292 and 477 to the west. The 7th Infantry would remain in division reserve along with a tank company from the 64th Heavy Tank Battalion, the 3d Reconnaissance Company, and the Philippine 20th (formerly 10th) Battalion Combat Team.[23]

Although the 65th Infantry went into reserve as preparations for Operation CLEANUP II gained momentum, the 65th's 2d Battalion under Lt. Col. Lawrence A. Johnson remained in place under the 15th Infantry's control. On 20 September, a patrol from Company F reported that the Twin Peaks hill mass, which dominated the approaches to Hill 487, was deserted. Accordingly, the commander of the 15th Infantry ordered Johnson's unit to seize the Twin Peaks before the Chinese reoccupied them.

Company F of the 65th drew the mission. On the morning of 21 September, the company departed the main line of resistance intent on securing the Twin Peaks. The lead platoon had almost reached the crest of the hill mass when it encountered intense small-arms and automatic-weapons fire. One squad managed to battle its way forward in the face of severe resistance before being compelled to fall back. When Company E advanced to support the attack, enemy fire quickly pinned it down. After suffering thirty-nine casualties by midafternoon, both units returned to their original positions. On 22 September, the 1st Battalion of the 65th Infantry relieved the 2d Battalion, which returned to the regiment to prepare for CLEANUP II. Two days later, the 65th assumed responsibility for the 15th Infantry's entire sector to permit the latter unit ample time to prepare for a coordinated assault on Hill 487.[24]

In response to the rebuff suffered at Twin Peaks, Soule redoubled efforts to saturate the Chinese opposing his division with napalm and high explosives.[25] He also deployed several tanks on commanding terrain opposite the division's objective where they could shoot directly into the enemy defenses. The 15th Infantry initiated its own "bust the bunker" program, employing tanks, recoilless rifles, mortars, and a dedicated 8-inch howitzer against enemy defensive positions.[26] In the nine days before CLEANUP II began, more than forty-five thousand rounds of artillery, recoilless rifle,

---

[23] The 10th BCT was redesignated the 20th BCT on 6 Sep 51. Monthly Cmd Rpt, 3d Inf Div, Sep 51.

[24] Monthly Cmd Rpt, 15th Inf, Sep 51.

[25] Staff Bfg Min, 19 Sep 51, in Monthly Cmd Rpt, 3d Inf Div, Sep 51.

[26] Monthly Cmd Rpt, 15th Inf, Sep 51.

mortar, and tank fire blanketed the area.[27] This was despite a dire shortage of 4.2-inch mortar ammunition.[28]

On 23 September, General Soule informed his staff that the 23d Infantry of the U.S. 2d Division in the X Corps sector had failed to take an objective after meeting heavy resistance.[29] That setback, combined with the shortcomings exhibited by his division during Operation CLEANUP, convinced Soule that planning at the company and battalion level was not being done thoroughly. "An attack should not be made or a patrol should not be sent out unless a careful, detailed plan is made and everyone knows exactly what to do," he said. "Sending a man into action without careful, thorough planning can only result in heavy casualties. Plans must include fire plans, methods and routes of approach, and a means for extraction of a force. Planning has been too superficial and has not gone all the way down."[30]

The division commander also expressed his concern that some officers were submitting inaccurate reports on troop locations, noting that it could result in fratricide by friendly mortars and artillery. "Individuals not knowing where they are and making inaccurate reports of locations," he warned, "should be relieved from command and sent to the rear for additional training in map reading."[31] Taking personal interest in the preparatory phase of the operation, he repeatedly visited each regiment and battalion to check on the status of preparations and to ensure that each commander understood his mission.[32]

The enemy on and around Hill 487, meanwhile, was preparing for an American attack. Just before CLEANUP II began, responsibility for defending the ridgeline that included the Twin Peaks and Hills 292, 487, and 477 passed from the Chinese *141st Division* to the fresh *140th Division*. The *140th* inherited a stoutly constructed series of mutually supporting bunkers located near the crest of each hill. The emplacements were well dug in and covered with alternating layers of logs and dirt that provided strong overhead cover. The enemy also deployed his mortars in reverse slope positions to shield them from detection and counterfire. Positioned near the crest of each hill, the bunkers and supporting weapons proved very difficult targets for allied artillery.[33]

---

[27] Monthly Cmd Rpt, 3d Inf Div, Sep 51. The 15th Infantry's contribution included 20,187 mortar, 1,987 recoilless-rifle, and 1,930 76-mm. tank gun rounds for a total of 24,104. Monthly Cmd Rpt, 15th Inf, Sep 51.
[28] Staff Bfg Min, 21 Sep 51, in Monthly Cmd Rpt, 3d Inf Div, Sep 51.
[29] Staff Bfg Min, 22 Sep 51, in Monthly Cmd Rpt, 3d Inf Div, Sep 51.
[30] Staff Bfg Min, 23 Sep 51, in Monthly Cmd Rpt, 3d Inf Div, Sep 51.
[31] Ibid.
[32] Ibid.
[33] Monthly Cmd Rpt, 3d Inf Div, Oct 51.

The western half of Hill 487 after it had been secured by American troops. The soldier standing in the foreground is looking north, toward the Chinese main line of resistance.

Cleanup II kicked off at 0230 on 29 September when elements of the 1st and 2d Battalions of the 15th Infantry attacked Hill 487. While incessant rain and limited visibility hampered the initial American advance, the poor weather also served to shield the attackers from detection. Around 0600, a reinforced platoon from Company E stormed the top layer of the enemy trenches and bunkers, leading to a grenade-throwing contest "which the Reds lost."[34] Spearheaded by Company A, the 1st Battalion overcame enemy resistance on the northern peak. General Soule remarked that the troops had performed "exceptionally," showing a great deal of aggressiveness by going in "hard and fast" to seize their objective."[35] Total friendly casualties amounted to three killed and thirty-six wounded.[36] That evening, the 15th Infantry employed small-arms fire and grenades to repel three Chinese counterattacks on Hill 487.[37]

---

[34] Dolcater, *3d Infantry Division in Korea*, p. 249.
[35] Staff Bfg Min, 30 Sep 51, in Monthly Cmd Rpt, 3d Inf Div, Sep 51.
[36] Monthly Cmd Rpt, 15th Inf, Sep 51.
[37] Lt Bevin R. Alexander, "The Battle of Bloody Angle—Sept to Oct 1951," 5th Historical Detachment, EUSAK, pp. 34–35, CMH.

As planned, Harris' 3d Battalion had begun a supporting attack on the Twin Peaks at 0530, supported by a portion of the 64th Heavy Tank Battalion and the 58th Armored Field Artillery Battalion. The Americans secured the eastern summit by 0630, but the 3d Battalion struggled unsuccessfully for the next nine hours to dislodge elements of the *141st Division* from well-fortified positions on the western peak. The neighboring 15th Infantry observed that "the fanatical enemy . . . denied every attempt of the Puerto Ricans to enlarge this foothold. Very steep slopes resulting from the truly conical shape of these peaks greatly aided the enemy in impeding progress."[38] Deteriorating weather and poor visibility forced the 3d Battalion to call off the attack and remain in place for the night.

On the morning of 30 September, the 65th Infantry resumed the contest for the western summit. Company G of the 15th Infantry moved off Hill 487 and took up firing positions from which it could support the assault. Aided by the additional fire support, the 3d Battalion secured the western rise of the Twin Peaks by midafternoon.[39] Soule's extra preparations appeared to have paid off; CLEANUP II emerged as a relative success story for the 3d Division.

Into the Iron Triangle Once Again

By the end of September, the 65th Infantry's strength had dropped to 3,678 personnel, slightly below its authorization of 3,686. By comparison, the strength of the 7th and 15th Infantries stood at around 4,000 each, although this figure included a number of KATUSA soldiers.[40] During September, the 65th sustained 236 battle casualties and rotated 8 officers and 252 enlisted men while receiving 43 officers and 352 enlisted men as replacements—too few to bring the unit up to the strength of its sister regiments.[41] As a consequence, Soule temporarily stopped the rotation home of Puerto Rican personnel, "the most eligible in the Division." This was a blow to the more than 600 Puerto Rican enlisted men who had already earned enough points to leave.[42] Fearing a deterioration of the regiment's morale, the division commander urgently requested that the Army fill requisitions for all categories of Puerto Rican personnel at the earliest possible date.

Complicating matters, while the influx of replacements during September 1951 had relieved the chronic shortfall of officers to a degree,

---

[38] Monthly Cmd Rpt, 15th Inf, Sep 51.
[39] Monthly Cmd Rpts, 65th Inf, Sep 51, and 3d Inf Div, Sep 51.
[40] Personnel Daily Sum, 29 Sep 51, in Monthly Cmd Rpt, 65th Inf, Sep 51; Monthly Cmd Rpt, 3d Inf Div, Sep 51.
[41] Monthly Cmd Rpt, 65th Inf, Sep 51.
[42] CG's Jnl, 22 Sep 51, in Monthly Cmd Rpt, 3d Inf Div, Sep 51.

many of the newly assigned lieutenants and captains lacked combat experience and few veteran NCOs remained to teach the newcomers. Gibson recommended to Soule:

> that more experienced Puerto Rican Non-Commissioned Officers be assigned to the 65th Infantry Regiment. This regiment is limited to Puerto Rican enlisted personnel and although enlisted replacements have been fairly adequate there have been practically no NCO replacements. This has placed a terrific strain on this regiment in attempting to maintain a proper or even minimum level of experienced NCOs.[43]

Gibson recognized that the number of sergeants in his regiment, those men who performed the vital function of transmitting orders and providing leadership to the enlisted ranks, was quickly becoming a critically weak link in the unit's chain of command.

Soule took Gibson's recommendations under advisement, but the general was busy planning a mission given to him by I Corps to build on the success of CLEANUP II. The new operation, codenamed COMMANDO, had the 3d Division attacking north to establish Line Jamestown five miles beyond Line Wyoming. The new line was situated far enough forward to shield the Uijongbu-Kumhwa rail line from Chinese artillery fire or from ground attack. Occupying the 3d Division's left flank, the 15th Infantry would attack north along a ridgeline that ran from Hill 487 through Hill 477 until it reached Line Jamestown. In the center, the 7th Infantry was to secure Hills 281 and 395, just a few miles north of the Twin Peaks. On the right, the 65th Infantry was to advance northward until it secured an area of high ground southwest of P'yonggang. The starting date for COMMANDO was to be 3 October 1951.[44]

Before the attack could begin, however, the 3d Division had to capture the remaining objectives of CLEANUP II. Permission to do so was granted by I Corps.[45] The 15th Infantry was directed to seize Hill 460, an unnumbered peak midway between Hills 487 and 477, which the Chinese still occupied in some strength, while the 65th Infantry's 3d Battalion was to take possession of Hill 292, a mile north of Hill 487. Taking those two objectives would permit COMMANDO to proceed without leaving behind pockets of enemy troops who might cause trouble.

The attacks of the 15th and 65th Infantries began at 0730 on 1 October. Both assaults began well against sporadic small-arms fire; but as Harris' 3d Battalion approached the summit of Hill 292, artillery, mortar, and automatic-weapons fire forced it to halt. At that point, Pvt. Badel Hernandez-Guzman

---

[43] Monthly Cmd Rpt, 65th Inf, Sep 51.
[44] Monthly Cmd Rpt, 3d Inf Div, Oct 51.
[45] AAR, HQ I Corps, n.d., p. 7.

of Company I took matters into his own hands. Seizing a flamethrower and advancing across open terrain, he engaged an enemy machine-gun position that posed the greatest threat to his unit. Their attention drawn to the flamethrower operator, the Chinese focused all of their firepower on the private, hurling numerous grenades in an attempt to halt his singlehanded assault. Even so, Hernandez-Guzman charged across twenty yards of open ground to destroy the strongpoint, enabling his company to move forward. For his efforts, he became the sixth member of his regiment to receive the prestigious Distinguished Service Cross.[46] Despite Hernandez-Guzman's heroism, enemy resistance remained strong and the 3d Battalion made little further progress that day.

The following morning, Harris and his men launched three more unsuccessful attacks before finally pulling back in late afternoon.[47] As for the other 3d Division attack that day, the 3d Battalion of the 15th Infantry failed to secure Hill 460. "The enemy defended from well prepared bunkers, so sited that they were mutually supporting," reported General Soule. "The terrain was so precipitous that maneuver was severely limited. The attack was necessarily one of slow, methodical destruction of enemy bunkers by infantry assault teams."[48] Since the 65th Infantry's 3d Battalion had not yet secured Hill 292, Soule decided to attach it to the 15th Infantry, which relieved the 65th of its CLEANUP II sector so the 3d Battalion could finish its mission while the rest of the regiment carried out COMMANDO.

The 3d Infantry Division's participation in COMMANDO began on 3 October when the 65th Infantry, minus its 3d Battalion, moved forward to Line Jamestown on the right flank of the 3d Division without encountering enemy resistance. The 1st Battalion took up positions along the left half of the 65th's sector while the 2d Battalion took up positions along the right. The Philippine 20th Battalion Combat Team, attached to the 65th Infantry, occupied outpost positions forward of the main line of resistance. A short while later, the 7th Infantry's 1st Battalion relieved the 65th Infantry's 1st Battalion, which went into division reserve alongside the main body of the 64th Heavy Tank Battalion.

That same day, 3 October, the 15th Infantry relieved its 3d Battalion at Hill 460, replacing it with the 2d Battalion.[49] A two-company assault succeeded in capturing the crest just before darkness.[50] The 3d Battalion of the 65th Infantry, meanwhile, attacked Hill 292 but made little progress. The commander of the 15th sent two companies from his 3d Battalion against

---

[46] Dolcater, *3d Infantry Division in Korea*, p. 253.
[47] Monthly Cmd Rpt, 65th Inf, Oct 51.
[48] Monthly Cmd Rpt, 3d Inf Div, Oct 51.
[49] Alexander, "Battle of Bloody Angle," p. 48.
[50] Ibid., p. 58.

Hill 477, but they were halted by enemy fire just short of the crest. The 7th Infantry's planned assault against Hill 281, a mile northeast of Hill 292, was postponed for twenty-four hours because of supply and transportation difficulties.[51]

All units returned to the attack on 4 October, resulting in the capture of Hills 281 and 292. While five successive assaults brought the Americans almost to the top of Hill 477, a portion of that critical hill mass remained in enemy hands. At 1700, an estimated two hundred Chinese utilized communications trenches on the reverse slope of Hill 477 to launch a counterattack against Company I of the 15th Infantry.[52] The Communists succeeded in pushing the allied unit back down the hill.

Shortly afterward, the 15th Infantry's Company L received the mission to retake a prominent rock outcropping located midway up Hill 477. The position would serve as a jumping-off point for a full-scale assault against the crest the following morning. Company C conducted a secondary attack against the eastern slope of Hill 477 in an effort to divert attention from the assault. Assisted by elements of Company K, the soldiers of Company L succeeded with relatively few losses in regaining a foothold on Hill 477. The company making the diversionary attack suffered heavy casualties.

For the remainder of the afternoon and during the following morning, the Americans pounded Hill 477 using a 155-mm. gun positioned to fire directly into the enemy bunkers along its crest. Following an intense preparatory bombardment by mortars and 105-mm. howitzers, the 3d Battalion of the 15th Infantry launched its final assault on Hill 477. The enemy force on the hilltop remained in place long enough to inflict two minor casualties before retreating. That same day, the 20th Battalion Combat Team relieved the 65th Infantry's 3d Battalion, which then moved to the Ch'orwon area to serve as the division reserve.[53]

With most of Line Jamestown secure, the infantry regiments of the 3d Division set about securing replacements for their five hundred casualties and improving their new positions.[54] From 5 to 13 October, the 1st and 2d Battalions of the 65th Infantry constructed trenches and bunkers while sending patrols up to three miles to the north. While the scouting parties had only light contact with the enemy, the men on the line suffered con-

---

[51] Monthly Cmd Rpt, 7th Inf, Oct 51.
[52] Alexander, "Battle of Bloody Angle," p. 66.
[53] Monthly Cmd Rpt, 3d Inf Div, Oct 51.
[54] The 7th Infantry sustained 23 killed, 81 wounded, and 2 missing while figures for the 65th totaled 12 killed and 46 wounded. The 15th Infantry suffered 53 killed, 289 wounded, and 1 missing during the fighting for Hills 460 and 477. "Battle of Bloody Angle," app. dtd 27 Feb 52, sub: Friendly Casualties During the Battle of Bloody Angle of 2d Bn, 15th Infantry.

tinually from artillery fire during the day and from numerous squad- and platoon-size attacks at night. On 14 October, the 3d Battalion relieved the 2d Battalion on Jamestown. The 2d Battalion then established a patrol base on Hill 391, just to the north of the main line of resistance.

That same day, the 3d Division began preparing to turn its sector over to the South Korean 9th Division and then go into I Corps reserve. The South Korean 30th Regiment relieved the 65th Infantry between 16 and 18 October. On 19 and 20 October, the 65th Infantry, with Company C of the 10th Combat Engineers attached, moved to the division reserve area fifteen miles northeast of Uijongbu. There, it began an intensive training program that continued through the end of the month. The exercises included firing of individual and crew-served weapons, day and night small-unit infantry tactics, and the reduction of fortified positions.[55]

While in reserve, the 65th Infantry's tank company exchanged its M4A3E8 Shermans for M46 Pattons. With a 90-mm. gun, improved fire control, heavier armor, and a superior engine system, the new Patton tank was a major improvement over the World War II–vintage Sherman. The tank company, aided by instructors from the 64th Tank Battalion, then began conducting gunnery and driver training with the new vehicles.[56]

Other changes took place as the 3d Division implemented General Ridgway's integration policy. The 64th Tank Battalion exchanged personnel with similar units within Eighth Army and with the 7th and 15th Infantries' tank companies. The 58th Field Artillery Battalion swapped out with other divisional field artillery units while the 3d Battalion of the 15th Infantry exchanged with its sister battalions in the 7th and 15th Infantries.[57]

On 15 October, the assistant division commander, Brig. Gen. Armistead D. Mead, rotated back to the United States. His position went to Col. Oliver P. Newman, who had been the division chief of staff since late 1946. Lt. Col. Wilson M. Hawkins, former commander of the 64th Heavy Tank Battalion, became the new chief of staff. Five days later, Brig. Gen. Thomas J. Cross assumed command of the 3d Division from General Soule, who returned to the United States to become the new infantry inspector for U.S. Army Field Forces. A little more than two months after returning to the United States, Soule suffered a fatal heart attack and died on 19 January 1952.[58]

General Cross was not a stranger to the 3d Infantry Division, having previously served as a lieutenant with the 7th Infantry during World War

---

[55] Ibid.; Monthly Cmd Rpt, 65th Inf, Oct 51.

[56] Monthly Cmd Rpt, 3d Inf Div, Oct 51.

[57] Ibid.; The 58th had converted from self-propelled to towed howitzers, therefore it was no longer designated as "Armored" Field Artillery. Capt William N. Kiser, Fort Sill Debfg Rpt no. 71, 26 Feb 52, p. 7, copy in CMH.

[58] Dolcater, *3d Infantry Division in Korea*, p. 19.

I. He had also been assigned to the 33d Infantry in the Panama Canal Zone in the four years after that war. During World War II, he had commanded the 8th Division's 121st Regimental Combat Team. In Korea, he had served both as deputy commander of IX Corps and as commanding general of the Field Training Command, U.S. Military Advisory Group.[59]

At his initial commander's meeting on 31 October 1951, Cross made it clear that his priorities were discipline and training. He stressed the importance of neatness in bivouac areas, fresh unit markings on all assigned vehicles, personal appearance of officers, smartness when saluting, and enforcement of division off-limits areas and speed directives. Switching to the subject of combat training, Cross emphasized the need for detailed operational planning, teamwork, individual marksmanship, and small-unit demonstrations and exercises. "All training must be actively supervised by officers who will stress exactness of detail," he ordered. "Anticipate going back on line, develop battle patrols, and prepare for battalion-size raids."[60]

As Cross was educating the 3d Division on his personal command philosophy, United Nations and Communist negotiators reconvened truce talks at a new location, the village of Panmunjom six miles east of Kaesong. One factor that may have helped persuade the enemy to return to the bargaining table was the determination that Eighth Army had shown in fighting for the commanding terrain to the north of its current line. In doing so, the allies had made it clear they possessed both the strength and the will to defend every inch of Korean soil they now occupied. After some initial sparring, the Communists dropped their original demand for a restoration of the 38th Parallel as the boundary between warring sides and accepted the United Nations' position that a cease-fire would take place along the current front line, which was situated a short distance above the prewar border. In exchange, UN negotiators acceded to Communist demands that an agreement on an official truce line would precede the resolution of other outstanding issues.

To prevent the Communists from ending negotiations once a truce line was in place, the Americans insisted that both sides should conduct combat operations until all outstanding questions on the war had been resolved. The two sides also agreed that the proposed armistice line would be valid for only thirty days. Failure to arrive at a final truce within that time would invalidate the agreement. The willingness to accept the current line of contact as the final demarcation line represented a significant windfall for the

---

[59] *Generals of the Army*, 1953, pp. 20–21; Dolcater, *3d Infantry Division in Korea*, p. 16.
[60] CG's Jnl, 31 Oct 51, in Monthly Cmd Rpt, 3d Inf Div, Oct 51.

Communists, for it indicated that the United Nations had no desire to press deeper into North Korea.

At the end of October, the 65th and 15th Infantries were still training in the rear of the I Corps zone, paying special attention to weapons firing and small-unit field problems. The 7th Infantry was attached to the 25th Division; the 3d Division's artillery and a company of the 64th Heavy Tank Battalion were operating with the South Korean 9th Division.[61] Tallying the results of the 65th for the entire month, the regiment had killed 18 enemy soldiers and captured 18 while sustaining 75 battle and 255 nonbattle losses.[62] The arrival of 26 officer and 969 enlisted replacements offset the unit's 330 casualties and another 178 departures due to rotation.

Among the departing officers was the 2d Battalion commander, Colonel Johnson. Maj. George H. Young Jr. replaced him. The 30-year-old major was a 1942 graduate of the Citadel. A veteran of the 45th Division during World War II, he held the Bronze Star and the Purple Heart. Prior to joining the 65th, Young had been the chief operations officer of the 15th Infantry's 2d Battalion.[63]

The termination of the UN offensive and the resumption of the truce talks had a calming effect on the front. The 65th Infantry began November with training designed to familiarize replacements with the employment of supporting weapons. The 2d Battalion ended training early when I Corps temporarily attached the unit to the British Commonwealth 1st Division. More elements of the 65th left the rear area on 10 November when the 3d Battalion, along with a platoon of tanks and a platoon of mortars, took up blocking positions behind the 1st Cavalry Division that was defending the line northwest of Yonch'on.

Defending Line Jamestown

On 12 November, Ridgway instructed Van Fleet to assume an "active defense." The order meant that Eighth Army would carry out offensive operations only to preserve the existing main line of resistance. That same day, Van Fleet's headquarters notified General Cross that his division would relieve the 1st Cavalry Division on Line Jamestown northwest of Yonch'on, a town some twelve miles southwest of Ch'orwon. The 3d Division's right flank would be held by the South Korean 9th Division and its left flank by the Commonwealth 1st Division. In the zone he was to occupy, Cross decided to place the 15th Infantry on the left wing, the 65th in the center,

---

[61] Monthly Cmd Rpt, 3d Inf Div, Oct 51.

[62] Monthly Cmd Rpt, 65th Inf, Oct 51.

[63] *Official Army Register, 1952*, p. 824; Interv, author with George H. Young, 10 Sep 01, Historians files, CMH.

and the 8th Cavalry (which had been attached to the 3d Division) on the right. The 7th Infantry would become the division reserve.

At a meeting on 17 November, Cross outlined to his subordinate commanders his plan for occupying Line Jamestown. "The defense will be active and aggressive," he noted, "with full use of patrols and raids to keep the enemy engaged." He went on:

> It is desired that all officers of your command particularly [the] Unit Commander, thoroughly understand the importance of careful planning and skilled execution of such plans in preparing positions for defense, regardless of time involved and work required. Nothing less than an impregnable defense will be acceptable. The full efforts of yourself and your command will be directed to this end.[64]

On 19 November, the 65th relieved the 5th Cavalry on Line Jamestown, taking over a sector that was just east of the Imjin and approximately eight miles northwest of Yonch'on. Colonel Gibson put the 3d Battalion on the left, the 1st Battalion in the center, and the 2d Battalion—recently released by the Commonwealth 1st Division—on the right. The Chinese immediately began to probe the regiment at night with squad- and platoon-size raiding parties. During the early morning of 21 November, a patrol from Company F picked up a Chinese deserter who informed his interrogators that his division intended to launch a two-regiment attack at 2000 that night against Hills 346 and 287, both of which were located within the 65th's sector.[65] The enemy also intended to launch a simultaneous assault against the neighboring 8th Cavalry regiment.[66] Various documents the soldier brought with him lent his story credibility.

All units of the regiment went on immediate alert while U.S. artillery pounded suspected enemy assembly areas. The artillery also registered its howitzers on likely avenues of approach leading into the 65th's sector. At 1845, numerous red flares were observed along the regiment's front. Fifteen minutes later, a Chinese machine gun opened fire on an observation post occupied by the artillery forward observer attached to Company F. A similar message was received a few minutes later by the forward observer with Company I. Two artillery batteries shelled the enemy engaging Company F while three more batteries began firing at the Chinese opposing Company I.[67]

---

[64] Monthly Cmd Rpt, 3d Inf Div, Nov 51.
[65] Ibid.
[66] "Narrative Account of the 58th FA Battalion's Participation in the Engagement between the 65th Inf Regiment and Enemy, 21 November 1951 to 22 November 1951," in Monthly Cmd Rpt, 58th Field Arty Bn, Nov 51.
[67] Ibid.

At 2000 on 21 November, the 2d Battalion's outpost line came under attack by an enemy platoon supported by unusually heavy artillery, mortar, small-arms, and automatic-weapons fire. A battery apiece from the 9th and 10th Field Artillery Battalions took the enemy platoon under fire.[68] About the same time, two enemy platoons assaulted an outpost manned by Company C. The size of the attacking force grew as the night wore on; by 2210, no less than a battalion of Chinese soldiers were attacking the outpost line. Forty minutes later, a second Chinese battalion joined the assault. "It was obvious that the enemy was well stocked with artillery and mortar ammunition," wrote Colonel Gibson, "as demonstrated by his willingness to use as many as 1,000 rounds to support his local attacks."[69]

By 2300, the enemy had forced his way to within a short distance of the 2d Battalion's main defensive line. The fighting was intense enough to produce an erroneous report that one platoon of Company C was surrounded by enemy troops. Shortly after midnight, however, the Chinese assault subsided; by 0300, the enemy had withdrawn completely.

During the morning of 22 November, the 8th Cavalry captured a wounded Chinese soldier. The prisoner stated that of his company of approximately ninety men, at least eighty-five had been killed or wounded.[70] Other patrols reported finding grisly evidence confirming that the divisional artillery had seriously disrupted the attack by inflicting heavy casualties on the Communists as they moved forward from their assembly areas. The 65th suffered fifteen killed or wounded compared to an estimated two hundred fifty Chinese casualties.[71]

Having failed against the 65th, the Chinese switched their efforts to another part of the 3d Division's line. On the night of 22 November, supported by an artillery barrage that "pulverized" the 2d Battalion of the 7th Infantry, they succeeded in securing a key hill. Heavy fighting followed in the 7th Infantry sector for the next two days with both sides attacking and counterattacking to regain control of the hill.[72]

On 24 November, Col. Julian B. Lindsey replaced Gibson as commander of the 65th Infantry. A 1929 West Point graduate, 46-year-old Lindsey had commanded the 515th Parachute Infantry during World War II but had not seen combat. After the war, he had commanded the 26th Infantry Division's 101st Infantry in Austria; between 1948 and 1951, he

---

[68] Ibid.

[69] Monthly Cmd Rpt, 65th Inf Rgt, Nov 51.

[70] "Narrative Account of the 58th FA Battalion's Participation."

[71] Monthly Cmd Rpt, 3d Inf Div, Nov 51. Other estimates placed enemy casualties at 100 killed and 500 wounded. See Monthly Cmd Rpt, 58th Field Arty Bn, Nov 51.

[72] Monthly Cmd Rpt, 3d Inf Div, Nov 51.

had served in the Office of the Secretary of Defense.[73] The new regimental commander settled in during the remaining days of November as the 65th continued to patrol north of Line Jamestown. "During the daylight hours the enemy was very sensitive to our patrols," Lindsey noted. "All patrols approaching his battle positions were taken under vigorous artillery, mortar, and small arms fire."[74]

On 27 November, the United Nations and Communist negotiators at Panmunjom established a tentative demarcation line in anticipation of an armistice. Thereupon, General Van Fleet ordered Eighth Army to cease all aggressive patrolling and to avoid contact with the enemy. On 28 November, a high-priority message from I Corps to all subordinate units forbade any offensive action, including intelligence-gathering raids, without express permission from the corps commander. The purpose of the order was to demonstrate "a willingness to reach an agreement."[75] The new orders also limited the use of artillery, tank, mortar, and recoilless-rifle fire in harassing the enemy.

The Communists seemed unwilling to adopt an identical mode of operation. After the enemy pounded the allied line with several intense artillery barrages, the I Corps commander issued a new directive on 29 November that authorized the use of harassing fires, vigorous patrolling, and air and artillery strikes but still prohibited major ground attacks. "Fire five rounds for every one received," it directed. "These fires should be [targeted against] all known enemy locations. This is in addition to artillery fire. We must keep the enemy from building his forces in the front lines."[76] The message also contained the warning that all commanders should remind their men not to expose themselves to enemy view and thus invite hostile fire.

The 65th benefited perhaps a bit more than other regiments from this relative pause in the fighting. In addition to a new regimental commander, the unit also gained two new battalion commanders during the month. Lt. Col. William T. Gleason took over the 1st Battalion, while Lt. Col. John D. Austin replaced Major Harris in the 3d Battalion. Gibson and Harris had led their units for five months, while Simmons had commanded for four. Their command tours ended when all three officers amassed enough points to rotate back to the United States.[77]

---

[73] *Register of Graduates and Former Cadets, 1802–1980*, p. 369.

[74] Monthly Cmd Rpt, 65th Inf, Nov 51.

[75] Msg, 271339Z Nov 51, from CG, I Corps, in Monthly Cmd Rpt, 3d Inf Div, Nov 51.

[76] Msg, 2923251Z Nov 51, from CG, I Corps, in Monthly Cmd Rpt, 3d Inf Div, Nov 51.

[77] Walter G. Hermes, *Truce Tent and Fighting Front*, U.S. Army in the Korean War (Washington, D.C.: U.S. Army Center of Military History, 1988), p. 350. As Army strength increased in the autumn of 1951, the criteria for rotation was lowered to 40 for officers and 36 for enlisted men. In December 1951, the point requirement for officers was raised to 45 in anticipation of an expected shortage of replacements in early 1952. Both officers in question were also eligible for rotation after serving one winter in Korea.

Each of the newcomers possessed varying degrees of combat experience. The 34-year-old Colonel Gleason, a 1941 West Point graduate, had served with the 65th Division in Europe during World War II, earning a Bronze Star. After the war, he had remained in Germany with the 3d Armored Division.[78] The 37-year-old Colonel Austin was also a World War II veteran and had won a Silver Star and a Purple Heart. Originally entering the military as a reservist, Austin was integrated into the Regular Army in 1947.[79]

In all, November 1951 was a relatively quiet period for the 65th Infantry. The regiment suffered 28 battle and 266 nonbattle casualties during the month while inflicting an estimated 264 casualties on the Communists.[80] This amounted to less than 7 percent of the 3d Division's 446 battle losses and just over 25 percent of its 1,020 nonbattle casualties. The unit sent home 627 officers and men while receiving only 23 officers and 272 enlisted replacements.[81] One reason for this disparity in numbers was the Eighth Army policy to rotate back to the United States men who had already endured one winter in Korea, regardless of points.[82]

Colonel Lindsey

In December, the 3d Division focused on small-unit patrols and raids while General Cross and his staff prepared plans to defeat "any aggressive action or treachery by the enemy" during the supposed cease-fire period.[83] Facing the division were elements of the Chinese *39th Army*. Allied intelligence considered the *39th Army* an above-average unit and knew it had received replacements and new equipment prior to its move to the

---

[78] *Register of Graduates and Former Cadets, 1802–1980*, p. 439.
[79] *Official Army Register*, 1951, p. 27.
[80] Monthly Cmd Rpt, 65th Inf, Nov 51.
[81] Ibid.
[82] On 31 October 1951, there were 1,179 enlisted personnel in infantry units and 561 in artillery units of the division who had spent one winter in Korea. A massive influx of replacements in December 1951 permitted all but 44 to rotate before the end of January 1952. Monthly Cmd Rpts, 3d Inf Div, Oct–Jan 52.
[83] Monthly Cmd Rpt, 3d Inf Div, Dec 51.

front lines. It had replaced the Chinese *47th Army*, which had been badly mauled during Operation COMMANDO and in various operations prior to the Panmunjom agreement. Eighth Army made it a top priority to capture prisoners from the *39th Army* in order to confirm its capabilities and intentions.[84]

The 65th had little success in December capturing Chinese soldiers for questioning. Patrols burned all villages along the regimental front to deny the enemy concealment and shelter during the harsh winter months. By the same token, however, loss of those villages made it harder for U.S. patrols to sneak into enemy territory without being seen. Sometimes American patrols got caught out in the open. A raiding party from Company E lost thirteen men on 12 December after being shelled for more than an hour. Four nights later, raiding parties from the 1st and 2d Battalions suffered a combined total of twenty-six casualties in unsuccessful attempts to penetrate Communist lines to capture a prisoner.

Toward the end of the month, Colonel Lindsey decided to switch tactics and employ a much larger force than was usual. On the night of 23 December, the 2d Battalion launched a two-company raid supported by artillery and tanks. The effort failed to secure a single prisoner although the battalion claimed that it inflicted more than two hundred casualties on the Chinese and destroyed numerous bunkers and installations. "Every attempt was made to capture prisoners," wrote Lindsey. "However, the enemy reacted fiercely to all efforts to penetrate his counter reconnaissance screen."[85]

On 25 December, the Chinese erected three signs that were clearly visible to the 3d Division. One depicted an artillery shell with the caption: "Your Christmas Present." Another asked: "Where will you spend your Christmas?"[86] A third depicted an American soldier holding a cup of coffee as he shivered on the frozen ground, accompanied by the caption: "This Christmas at frozen Korea. What For?"[87] The Chinese also strewed thousands of Christmas cards over the ground in front of the American positions. They contained the inscription "Greetings from the Chinese People's Volunteers, Korea 1951" and featured a short poem urging American soldiers to "Demand Peace!" and "Stop the War!"[88]

At the end of December 1951, the 45th Division, a recently deployed National Guard division, assumed control of a portion of the 3d Division's

---

[84] Monthly Cmd Rpt, 65th Inf, Dec 51.
[85] Ibid.
[86] Monthly Cmd Rpt, 3d Inf Div, Dec 51.
[87] See photo in Dolcater, *3d Infantry Division in Korea*, p. 310.
[88] Former 1st Lt. Richard A. Madden, who served with the regimental tank company during the Korean War, provided the author with one of the Christmas cards. Historians files.

sector, enabling General Cross to return the 8th Cavalry to its parent division. The 7th and 65th Infantries remained on line with the 15th Infantry rotating to division reserve. The 65th Infantry had sustained 129 battle and 77 nonbattle casualties during the month while inflicting 389 casualties on the enemy and taking 1 prisoner. Reversing the trends of the previous month, the 65th's battle casualties comprised almost half of the 3d Division's monthly total of 267 combat losses and only 11 percent of the 715 nonbattle casualties.[89] Over the same period, the Chinese had captured at least 6 Puerto Rican soldiers from the 1st and 2d Battalions.[90]

By 31 December, the strength of the 65th had fallen to 3,693 troops, well below the 3,917 soldiers it was authorized. In comparison, the 7th Infantry counted 4,089 officers and men while the 15th Infantry had 3,813.[91] The decrease had occurred even though the 3d Division had received 1,200 Puerto Rican replacements that month. While General Cross reported that the Puerto Rican replacements "could only be assigned to the 65th Infantry," it is clear he did not assign all 1,200 to the regiment.[92] Had he done so, the 65th would have been significantly overstrength and the 7th and 15th Infantries considerably undermanned. Instead, Cross assigned approximately 400 Puerto Rican replacements to each of his infantry regiments.

As 1951 drew to a close, examination of the 65th Infantry's performance since its deployment to Korea revealed that it had been in combat for a total of 460 days and had suffered 1,535 battle and 2,795 nonbattle casualties while taking 2,133 enemy prisoners. In comparison, the 7th had been in combat for 424 days, suffering 2,220 battle and 3,007 nonbattle casualties and capturing 595 prisoners. The 15th Infantry, which had been in combat 419 days, had suffered 2,009 battle and 2,515 nonbattle casualties with 1,076 prisoners taken.[93] Despite those telling numbers, however, the toughest days of the 65th still lay in the future.

---

[89] Monthly Cmd Rpt, 65th Inf, Dec 51; Personnel Daily Sum, 30 Nov 51, in Monthly Cmd Rpt, 3d Inf Div, Nov 51; Personnel Daily Sum, 31 Dec 51, in Monthly Cmd Rpt, 3d Inf Div, Dec 51.

[90] See Personnel Missing—Korea, Rpt for Puerto Rico, Defense Prisoner of War/Missing Personnel Office (DPMO), 12 Jun 2000, pp. 2–4, Historians files.

[91] Personnel Daily Sum, 31 Dec 51, in Monthly Cmd Rpt, 3d Inf Div, Dec 51.

[92] Monthly Cmd Rpts, 3d Inf Div, Dec 51, and 65th Inf, Dec 51.

[93] Personnel Daily Sum, 31 Dec 51.

Chapter 8

IN RESERVE: JANUARY–JUNE 1952

As 1952 opened, the 3d Division continued to bombard Communist positions with mortars and artillery. Each night, the regiment mounted platoon-size ambush patrols in no-man's-land and quick raids against Chinese outposts. The artillery supported these efforts, seeking to destroy any enemy units the patrols had located. The Chinese responded by using machine-gun and mortar fire to "warn" away approaching American patrols and by counterattacking quickly when U.S. raiding parties threatened their positions. The enemy's security was "superior both day and night," wrote the division commander, explaining the 3d Division's difficulty in penetrating the enemy outpost line.[1]

The 65th Infantry received no replacements in January, but 51 officers and 750 enlisted men rotated back to the United States.[2] Among those departing was Colonel Austin, who left after two months in command of the 3d Battalion. His replacement was Lt. Col. Charles H. Kederich, a 38-year-old Regular Army officer who had earned two Bronze Stars and a Purple Heart during World War II.[3] In addition to the soldiers who rotated out, the 65th also sustained eighty-one battle and eighty-seven nonbattle casualties that month.[4]

Like the 65th, many combat units at this stage of the war were facing manpower problems. In fact, the entire Eighth Army was suffering from an exodus of experienced soldiers, a problem further exacerbated by a steady stream of combat casualties. "Recent rotation of large numbers of veterans left the regiment with many leaders unfamiliar with combat conditions and procedures peculiar to Korea," wrote Col. William T. Moore, the commander of the 15th Infantry. "The consensus of officers who have been in

---

[1] Monthly Cmd Rpt, 3d Inf Div, Jan 52. Unless otherwise noted, all Cmd Rpts are in Entry 429, Rcds of the AGO, RG 407, NACP.
[2] Ibid.
[3] *Official Army Register*, 1952, p. 393.
[4] Personnel Daily Sums, 1, 31 Jan 52, both in Monthly Cmd Rpt, 3d Inf Div, Jan 52.

the regiment longest is that while replacements are adequately trained in basic subjects, there is a definite and measurable lowering of combat efficiency during the past six months."[5]

Unable to secure enough seasoned officers and NCOs from the total U.S. Army to make up the shortfall and with the number of enlisted replacements coming to Korea growing smaller, Eighth Army resorted to a bureaucratic fix. General Van Fleet's headquarters directed subordinate commanders to certify in writing that the rotation system was not degrading unit efficiency and to submit those reports on a regular basis. Colonel Moore regarded the policy as a face-saving façade. It was "self evident," he observed, that, "no soldier who has completed only basic training can be expected to equal the fighting qualities of a seasoned veteran."[6] Some officers also became unhappy because a number of higher-ranking commanders used the certify-in-writing policy to justify their relief of subordinate officers whose units did not perform to expectation. "If something goes wrong in a unit of any size, the lowest commander who cannot produce a certificate from his subordinates to the effect that the sin will not be committed is hanged for the crime, regardless of the actual location of the responsibility," wrote one veteran.[7]

Col. Edward A. Walker, the commander of the 7th Infantry, strongly supported Moore's observations regarding the decline in officer quality. "Many reserve officers ordered to active duty and received as officer replacements by the regiment are lacking recent experience in troop leading positions," he wrote. "Although the majority [of them] have attended refresher courses, in the case of recalled officers, a definite minority has had troop experience in the recent past and practically none have had tactical training in recent years."[8] Colonel Lindsey, the 65th Infantry commander, refrained from formally voicing whatever misgivings he might have had.

Lindsey did not have to concern himself with the regiment's manpower problems for much longer. On 1 February 1952, Col. Juan C. Cordero-Davila assumed command of the 65th. The 47-year-old Cordero-Davila was a resident of San Juan and a career officer in the Puerto Rican National Guard. He had previously served for three-and-a-half years with the 65th Infantry during World War II as its chief logistics officer, as executive officer and then as commander of the 3d Battalion, and finally as the regimental executive officer. Following World War II, Cordero-Davila had commanded the Puerto Rican National Guard's 296th Regimental Combat

---

[5] Monthly Cmd Rpt, 15th Inf, Jan 52.
[6] Ibid.
[7] See, for example, "Faithful to Our Trust," *The Army Combat Forces Journal* (December 1954): 18–21, copy in CMH.
[8] Monthly Cmd Rpt, 7th Inf, Jan 52.

Team, which consisted of the 296th Infantry, the 482d Field Artillery Battalion, and the 225th Combat Engineer Company.[9] Stationed at Camps Tortuguero, Salinas, and Losey, and Henry Barracks, its members formed a large proportion of the first group of Puerto Rican replacements sent to Korea in early 1951. A well-known and popular figure in island politics, Cordero-Davila was employed in civilian life as the director of the Puerto Rican Housing Authority, which was responsible for building low-income homes throughout the island.[10]

Cordero-Davila had initially requested a transfer to Korea in a 20 November 1951 letter to Brig. Gen. Robert M. Bathurst, the commanding general of U.S. Army Forces in the Antilles and of the Military District of Puerto Rico. "In view of the fact that a high percentage of my enlisted men have been and are being transferred to the 65th Infantry," he wrote, "I desire to be transferred . . . to command these men in combat."[11]

On 2 January 1952, Cordero-Davila solicited Army Chief of Staff General J. Lawton Collins' support during the general's visit to Puerto Rico. "I explained to Colonel Cordero," Collins told Lt. Gen. Matthew B. Ridgway two days later, "that he might not be assigned to command the 65th, as this would be a matter for determination by the Army Commander."

> He understood this, but nevertheless insisted that he would like to go with his men to Korea and take his chances there. I was so impressed with the logic of Cordero's arguments and with his own personal enthusiasm that I had [the necessary] orders issued. . . . I believe that from a long-range point of view it would be of great value to the future of the National Guard of Puerto Rico if Colonel Cordero could be assigned to the regiment, perhaps as executive officer. Later, if he demonstrates to Van Fleet's satisfaction that he is capable of commanding the regiment in action, it would be a fine thing if he could be given this opportunity.[12]

By sending Cordero-Davila to Korea, Collins left Ridgway little choice but to recommend him for command of the 65th. "Dear Joe," the chief of Far East Command responded on 14 January, "I think your decision was

---

[9] The 296th RCT entered federal service on 10 September 1950. Cmd Rpt no. 2, HQ, U.S. Army Forces Antilles, 10 Dec 52.

[10] *Official National Guard Register (Army), 1951* (Washington, D.C.: National Guard Bureau, 1951), p. 212; *Guardia Nacional de Puerto Rico* (San Juan, Puerto Rico: Guardia Nacional de Puerto Rico y Puerto Rico National Guard Fund Inc., 1987), pp. 476–79; "65th Puerto Rican Regiment Gets New CO," *Pacific Stars and Stripes*, 8 February 1952; Ltr, Cordero to CG, U.S. Army Forces Antilles and Mil Dist of Puerto Rico, Fort Brooke, P.R., 20 Nov 51, file 30, box 77, James A. Van Fleet Papers, George C. Marshall Library (GML), Virginia Military Institute (VMI), Lexington, Va.

[11] Ltr, Cordero to CG, U.S. Army Forces Antilles and Mil Dist of Puerto Rico, 20 Nov 51.

[12] Ltr, Gen J. Lawton Collins to Ridgway, 4 Jan 52, Van Fleet Papers.

Colonel Cordero-Davila (right) receives a decoration from General Cross.

definitely in the best overall interests of the Army and our relations with Puerto Rico. I am at once sending it on to General Van Fleet . . . confident he will feel much the same."[13] The choice for Van Fleet, however, appears not to have been difficult, as both Generals O'Daniel and Cross favored replacing Colonel Lindsey. "In talking to Tom Cross, I feel that Cordero-Davila will in all probability be what is needed for the 65th Infantry," he told Van Fleet. "Cross has not been any too happy with Lindsey. He thinks Lindsey is too soft in handling the men and I am inclined to agree with him."[14] Lindsey left the 65th to become the 3d Infantry Division's chief of staff.[15] Cordero-Davila's appointment to command the 65th made him one of the highest-ranking ethnic officers in the entire Army.

[13] Ltr, Ridgway to Collins, 14 Jan 52, Van Fleet Papers.
[14] Ltr, Lt Gen John W. O'Daniel to Van Fleet, 17 Jan 52, Van Fleet Papers.
[15] Dolcater, *3d Infantry Division in Korea*, p. 20.

The 65th Infantry spent February 1952 improving its positions on Line Jamestown, patrolling, and organizing raids against the Chinese. Still eager to get enemy prisoners, Eighth Army directed all frontline divisions to mount Operation SNARE in midmonth. Suddenly concealing all movement along American lines, Eighth Army expected the enemy to send out patrols to investigate. The scheme worked in the 65th Infantry's sector. Company A captured an enemy soldier on the night of 15 February after the unit repulsed a Communist probe meant to gather intelligence on the 65th. Mortally wounded, the man died shortly after interrogation. SNARE concluded on 16 February with a raid by Company L against a local strongpoint, Hill 143, which inflicted eighty casualties on the enemy and destroyed numerous defensive emplacements. At the end of the operation, the regiment went into I Corps reserve.[16]

During Cordero-Davila's first month in command, the 65th had suffered 42 battle and 161 nonbattle casualties while inflicting 163 casualties on the enemy. The regiment had also captured a Chinese prisoner, albeit at the cost of 10 friendly soldiers missing in action.[17] During the month, the regiment sent 723 personnel back to the United States while receiving 20 officers and 1,057 enlisted men as replacements.[18] In addition to the departure of Colonel Lindsey, officers leaving the 65th included Colonel Young, who had commanded the 2d Battalion for three months. Lt. Col. Clayton C. Craig took his place. A Regular Army graduate of the Infantry and the Artillery Advanced Courses, the 36-year-old officer had earned the Silver Star, two Bronze Stars, and a Purple Heart in World War II.[19]

Major Changes Within the 65th Infantry

The reminiscences of two junior officers who joined the regiment in early 1952, 1st Lt. Walter B. Clark and 1st Lt. Winfred G. Skelton Jr., provide revealing snapshots of the 65th. Clark, a 1951 graduate of the Citadel and the Company Officers Course (a forerunner of the Infantry Officer Basic Course), did not consider his own "limited time with troops following commission [to be] adequate preparation for command in combat." Moreover, upon his arrival at Camp Drake, Japan, in February 1952, he began hearing that the 65th Infantry was "somehow inferior to other units." Once in Korea, he joined the regiment's 1st Battalion where he served as a platoon leader in Company C. "My early impressions were of the poor quality and poor personal conduct of the officers and the deplorable lack

---

[16] Monthly Cmd Rpt, 65th Inf, Feb 52.
[17] Personnel Daily Sums, 1, 29 Feb 52, both in Monthly Cmd Rpt, 3d Inf Div, Feb 52.
[18] Monthly Cmd Rpt, 65th Inf, Feb 52.
[19] *Official Army Register*, 1952, p. 160.

Colonel Gleason, early April 1952

of training and discipline of the enlisted men," he recalled. "I was favorably impressed with the professionalism of the senior non-commissioned officers."[20]

Clark had a lukewarm opinion of Colonel Gleason, his battalion commander, whom he described as adequate but lacking in charisma and personality: "I recall [him] not being especially sensitive toward his Puerto Rican soldiers." He described his company commander, however, as "adequate, hard working, conscientious," and "not ethnically insensitive." As for the unit's other platoon leaders, Clark regarded them as "generally reliable" and "experienced."[21] Most were Reserve Officer Training Corps graduates with varying degrees of courage, tactical competence, and leadership abilities. Clark recalled that most were World War II veterans and a number were former NCOs with reserve commissions.

"Certainly there were exceptions," he went on, "but many of the veterans showed a marked proclivity to not exposing themselves in combat." Language posed another problem, since few continental officers spoke Spanish. Many of the unit's young lieutenants quickly became frustrated with the lack of training and discipline among the Puerto Rican troops. Hispanic officers from the island were probably better equipped to relate to the enlisted men because they shared a common linguistic and cultural heritage; but at that time, there were only a handful of Puerto Rican officers serving in the regiment. Clark could recall meeting only two during his four months with the battalion: "One, an excellent lieutenant rotated shortly after I arrived. The other had been given a battlefield commission for his excellent work as a draftsman in the battalion operations section. He proved inadequate as a rifle platoon leader and was relieved."[22]

In general, Clark viewed the NCOs in his unit as reliable and experienced. While courageous, however, they were more compassionate

---

[20] Interv, author with Walter B. Clark, 17 Jun 00, Historians files, CMH.
[21] Ibid.
[22] Ibid.

than demanding. As for the soldiers themselves, they seemed "young, carefree, ill-trained, not amenable to strong discipline," and "happy-go-lucky." But for all that, they were also "responsive to leadership" and "fiercely loyal to those leaders they believed in." Few spoke English well.[23]

The other junior officer who later provided a wealth of observations about the 65th, Lieutenant Skelton, was a 1950 West Point graduate who had served for a year as a platoon leader in the 82d Airborne Division at Fort Bragg, North Carolina, before joining the regiment. Prior to leaving for Korea, Skelton felt he was "about as good as anybody as a junior officer having participated in the unit training, recruit training, and the numerous exercises."[24]

Upon getting his unit assignment, Skelton was pleasantly surprised to find himself a part of the 65th Infantry, a unit his father had served with in the 1920s. "He had a good impression of the regiment and so did I," Skelton remembered. The young lieutenant had studied Spanish at West Point but was hardly fluent. "I did not learn Spanish in the regiment since the policy was English was the official language and all business was done in English," he recalled. "I knew a few words and in emergencies had to use them such as 'fuego!' [fire!] and 'medico' [medic!]."

When Skelton joined the unit in April 1952, he was made a rifle platoon leader in Company K. He described the battalion commander at the time, Lt. Col. Thomas J. Gendron, who had just replaced Colonel Kederich as commander of the 3d Battalion, as "good." But he considered most of the company commanders "retreads" from World War II who spoke little Spanish and often failed to exhibit high professional standards. As a result, "platoon leaders ran the training [while the company was] in reserve." The fact that officers were solely responsible for training, however, is also a telling comment on the inability of the unit's noncommissioned officers to plan, conduct, and supervise training.

As had Clark, Lieutenant Skelton rated platoon-level leadership in the Puerto Rican regiment as "a step below" that of purely continental units. Having come from a division where the NCOs were "tops," he thought the Puerto Rican NCOs were "reasonably good." Many spoke English even though most of the regiment's enlisted soldiers did not.[25] "You

---

[23] Ibid.

[24] Interv, author with Winfred G. Skelton Jr., 23 Aug 00, Historians files.

[25] This may have been the case in Skelton's unit, but other sources suggest that English-speaking NCOs were not present in great numbers. In the section of its 1952 command report entitled Bilingual Instructors, U.S. Army Forces Antilles commented that its training cadre consisted of "many replacements . . . rotated from Korea, returning with the rank of the first three grades [staff sergeant through master sergeant]. . . . The majority of them had

communicated by repeating important words and gesturing."²⁶ Although Skelton's description was somewhat more positive, taken together, the two officers' remarks describe a unit suffering from deficiencies in training, leadership, and discipline.

A February 1952 newspaper story detailing an incident involving the 65th's "Raider Platoon" reveals that all was not right within the regiment. The concept of Raider Platoons originated with the attachment of a separate Ranger company to each U.S. Infantry division in late 1950. Rangers were highly trained and motivated soldiers who specialized in night operations, patrolling, and raids. Although Ranger companies normally operated at division level, in many instances they were broken down even further, with platoons being assigned to a regiment. A shortage of trained infantrymen forced many units to utilize the rangers for conventional tasks. As a result, these elite units suffered heavy casualties.

On 14 July 1951, Eighth Army dispatched a message to the commanding generals of the 1st Cavalry Division and the 2d, 3d, 7th, 24th, and 25th Infantry Divisions directing them to inactivate their Ranger companies.²⁷ Division and regimental commanders, however, realized the usefulness of having their own specially trained small unit to carry out difficult missions. As a result, a number of provisional Raider Platoons or Regimental Battle Patrols were formed using highly motivated and aggressive soldiers who volunteered for hazardous duty.

According to the *Pacific Stars and Stripes*, a patrol from the 3d Battalion's Company K had gotten pinned down on the frozen banks of the Imjin with four men wounded and with its escape route blocked by exploding enemy shells. A group of elite Raiders from the same battalion came to their aid but chose not to attack the Chinese force that was the source of the problem. Instead, the Puerto Rican lieutenant in charge of the Raiders decided to save the Company K patrol by using his own men to draw away the enemy's fire. "The bold decision made," ran the story, "the Raiders stripped off their heavier garments and began running across the frozen rice paddies, in full view of the Chinese gunners. . . . Stopping

---

also served with the 65th Infantry Regiment (Puerto Ricans) and had used English very little. To resolve the problem, the RTC [Replacement Training Command] established a Cadre Refresher Course [conducted entirely in English] for those personnel." Cmd Rpt no. 2, HQ, U.S. Army Forces Antilles, 10 Dec 52.

²⁶ Interv, author with Walter B. Clark, 17 Jun 00, Historians files. Gendron was not the commander when Clark first arrived. He took over the 3d Battalion after first serving as the 3d Division's chief operations officer.

²⁷ Field Manual (FM) 7–85, *Ranger Unit Operations* (Washington D.C.: Department of the Army, 1987), app. F.

only for the wounded—there were three minor casualties—the Raiders finally reached the cover of a hill and fell gasping for breath to the frozen ground."[28]

As described, the incident was a case of supposedly "elite" soldiers abandoning their fellow comrades or an example of gross tactical incompetence. In either case, the story, which was probably the source of great amusement to *Pacific Stars and Stripes* readers, did little to enhance the regiment's reputation.

The 65th spent the first two weeks of March 1952 training while in division reserve near Tongduch'on-ni, ten miles north of Uijongbu. On paper, everything sounded very impressive. "Training," stated a regimental memorandum, "will be conducted with a minimum amount of formal instruction and a maximum amount of demonstration and practical work. Maximum realism will be introduced into all problems."[29]

The program sought to sharpen the combat skills of the regiment and to help replacement soldiers integrate more quickly into their new units. Scouting, patrolling, ambushes, and assaults on fortified positions were thus the order of the day.[30] Given the observations of Clark and Skelton, however, it seems unlikely that company commanders "lacking the highest orders of professional knowledge" could meet the desired standard of training. The lack of noncommissioned officers able to plan and conduct training also throws doubt on the effectiveness of the unit's training regimen.

During March, the 65th rotated home 4 officers and 799 enlisted soldiers and received 1,001 new men. Most of the troops who arrived had been in the service no more than six to seven months. They had gone overseas shortly after completing nineteen weeks of basic training. Almost 900 of them were draftees, while only 21 were Regular Army volunteers. Enlisted reservists and members of the National Guard made up the remainder.[31]

The 65th Infantry continued training near Tongduch'on-ni through April. Colonel Cordero-Davila tried to improve discipline within the regiment and to instill better leadership qualities in his subordinates. In one instance, he stipulated that "when troops are being marched to and from the training areas an officer will march at the end of the column to eliminate straggling." Cordero-Davila also ordered that individual platoons would never sit idle while others were busy. "Platoons will either be preparing

---

[28] "Puerto Rico Raiders Make Exposed Dash to Save Harassed," *Pacific Stars and Stripes*, 15 February 1952, copy in Historians files.
[29] Training Memo no. 10, 11 Mar 52, in Monthly Cmd Rpt, 65th Inf, Mar 52.
[30] Monthly Cmd Rpt, 65th Inf, Mar 52.
[31] Personnel Staff Jnl, Entry for 1800, 28 Mar 52, in Monthly Cmd Rpt, 65th Inf, Mar 52.

to conduct maneuver training or be participating in some type of related training to the subject being taught."[32]

Cordero-Davila sought to develop each man into a "well trained" and "aggressive" soldier "capable of defeating the enemy under any conditions." Among his goals: his companies needed to become "smoothly operating" formations; his heavy weapons crews had to improve their ability to support assaults; and his soldiers had to become confident to operate even on the darkest night.[33] Cordero-Davila devoted sixteen training hours for each platoon to practice attacks on defensive positions and bunkers. Night operations took another twenty hours of training time. Another eight hours went toward teaching each rifle company how to operate with the regimental tank company.

Cordero-Davila also stressed communications training because that skill was particularly crucial in Korea, where the terrain and the cold winter weather often made it hard for units to stay in radio contact. To that end, select individuals within each company received some eighty hours of training under the guidance of regimental and battalion communications personnel.[34] Taking advantage of a relative lull in combat at the front, Cordero-Davila got permission to extend the 65th's training cycle, originally scheduled to end on 12 April, for an additional two weeks.

Although the colonel stated in March and April that combat training was his top priority, this was not entirely the case. Cordero-Davila arranged several time-consuming unit reviews and command inspections. One inspection in mid-April took three days, for example, and required displays of vehicles, kitchens, crew-served weapons, individual equipment, and unit records. To prepare, soldiers used a detailed manual that included diagrams specifying how equipment, tools, kitchen utensils, and clerical files would be organized and displayed.[35] The inspections brought the regiment's weapons, equipment, and records up to accepted standards but cut down on the time available for training.

This development was hardly surprising given that Cordero-Davila possessed a solid background in staff positions but had rather less experience in the field. To prepare for inspections, a company or battalion had to spend up to a week accounting for, servicing, and painting equipment as well as updating records. Follow-up visits came after the main inspection, eating up more time but prompting Cordero-Davila to write: "Three command inspections of personnel and equipment were conducted . . . which

---

[32] Training Notes, 4 Apr 52, in Monthly Cmd Rpt, 65th Inf, Apr 52.
[33] Training Notes, 9 Apr 52, in Monthly Cmd Rpt, 65th Inf, Apr 52.
[34] Ibid.
[35] Memo no. 28, 15 Apr 52, sub: Command Inspection, in Monthly Cmd Rpt, 65th Inf, Apr 52.

Colonel Kederich (left) poses with the incoming 3d Battalion commander, Colonel Gendron.

were very beneficial to the improvement of the supply status of the unit."[36] It remained to be seen, however, if the time spent on inspections would have been better used for combat training.

In the meantime, the 3d Division had gained a wider sector after Eighth Army reorganized the I Corps front. As a result, Colonel Gleason's 1st Battalion and one platoon of Capt. Carl M. Burns' heavy mortar company moved from the division training area to reinforce the 7th Infantry on Line Jamestown. Departing on 11 April, the 1st Battalion remained on Jamestown for seventeen days before returning to the regiment.[37]

While the regiment saw relatively little action in April, the 65th was busy during the month in terms of gaining two battalion commanders. Colonel Gendron, the 3d Division chief operations officer, replaced Colonel Kederich as commander of the 3d Battalion. The 34-year-old Gendron was a World War II veteran and had earned two

---

[36] Monthly Cmd Rpt, 65th Inf, Apr 52.
[37] Ibid.

Major Davies   *General Dulaney*

Silver Stars, two Bronze Stars, and a Purple Heart.[38] Colonel Gleason moved on after a five-month stint to become the chief personnel officer of the 3d Division. Maj. Albert C. Davies replaced him as 1st Battalion commander. British by birth and a World War II veteran, 40-year-old Davies had earned two Silver Stars during that war.[39] In the view of Lieutenant Clark, "Major Davies was an excellent leader and skilled infantry commander."[40]

Other important personnel changes were taking place within the 3d Division. On 29 April 1952, Maj. Gen. Robert L. Dulaney assumed command from General Cross. The 50-year-old Dulaney had served his first tour with the 3d Division after graduating from West Point in 1923. During World War II, he had commanded the 45th Division's 180th Infantry in Sicily, Italy, France, and Germany. In September 1950, Dulaney had returned to the 45th Division as assistant division commander. In March 1951, he had left the United States with the unit bound for Hokkaido, Japan, and in November had deployed with the 45th Division to Korea.[41]

---

[38] *Official Army Register*, 1952, p. 266.
[39] Ibid., p. 117.
[40] Interv, author with Clark, 17 Jun 00.
[41] *Register of Graduates and Former Cadets, 1802–1980*, p. 343. See also Dolcater, *3d Infantry Division in Korea*, pp. 14–16.

Korea 1952: The Outpost War

By the time Dulaney assumed command of the 3d Division, the war had come to resemble the static situation that had prevailed on the Western Front during much of World War I. By May 1952, Eighth Army's main line of resistance consisted of a nearly unbroken string of bunkers, trenches, and artillery emplacements stretching over one hundred fifty miles across the peninsula. The Chinese and North Korean defenses were even more impressive. The enemy had burrowed deep into the sides of mountains, creating intricate warrens of tunnels and caves capable of housing entire infantry battalions. Arrayed in depths up to twenty miles, the enemy frontline positions were manned by four hundred fifty thousand men. A like number of Communist troops were being held in immediate reserve. The combined Chinese and North Korean armies thus totaled two hundred thousand more troops than the United Nations forces possessed. The Communists also had a large and growing artillery force to call upon, most of the weapons being of recent Soviet manufacture. By the spring of 1952, Eighth Army faced a well-trained, battle-hardened, and numerically superior opponent possessing modern arms and equipment.[42]

Since political leaders on both sides had already indicated their willingness to settle the conflict roughly on the basis of status quo, neither the allied nor the Communist commanders had any reason to launch a major offensive. This was especially true for Generals Van Fleet and Ridgway, who also had to keep American public opinion in mind. Too many casualties for no apparent gain would feed rising discontent at home and result in a loss of popular support for the war. General Clark, who succeeded General Ridgway as head of the Far East Command in May 1952, inherited this policy. The Communists, for whom human casualties were of less consequence given the nature of their culture, avoided large attacks in the belief that they could just as easily achieve their objectives through raids, patrols, bombardments, and limited assaults designed to sap the willpower of their opponents.[43] Limited warfare was the order of the day.

Even though the front remained relatively static, Communist and UN soldiers routinely clashed with one another as they fought for control of no-man's-land. Allied infantrymen also raided enemy lines on a regular basis to capture Chinese and North Korean soldiers for interrogation. These snatch-and-grab operations usually occurred at night and were extremely dangerous. During these raids, American infantry units lost dozens of soldiers, many of whom were taken captive. At this level, the war was a very personal affair,

---

[42] Hermes, *Truce Tent and Fighting Front*, pp. 283–84.
[43] Ibid., p. 507.

and small-unit fights required a great deal of courage. This was especially true for those soldiers and squads assigned to the outpost line—a string of strong points several thousand yards to the front of the main line.

The allied forward positions typically consisted of bunkers and interconnecting trenches perched precariously on top of a barren, rocky hill ringed with barbed wire and mines. These outposts functioned as patrol bases and early-warning stations. They also guarded key terrain features overlooking the main line of resistance. As a consequence of their value to both allied and Communist commanders, they were often the scene of vicious fighting. While most of these engagements were on a small scale, some of the bloodiest battles of 1952 revolved around efforts to establish, defend, or retake hills.

Communist guns hurled over sixty-eight hundred shells a day at Eighth Army positions; during particularly intense engagements, that number could rise to twenty-four thousand rounds a day. Earlier in the war, allied artillerymen had responded to enemy fire with overwhelming force, returning five, ten, and sometimes even twenty times the number of artillery shells they had received.[44]

Owing in part to a logistical pipeline that stretched across the Pacific Ocean, Eighth Army had seen its ammunition situation in Korea go from bad to worse. As the war lengthened into mid-1952, Eighth Army stockpiles dwindled to 25 percent of the required amount of 155-mm. rounds while lighter caliber shells were reduced to 50 percent of the number previously available.[45] The problem was one of the primary reasons for Eighth Army's increasing number of requests for, and growing dependency on, close air support.[46]

Besides the long logistical pipeline, there were several reasons for the shortage. First and foremost was a directive issued by General Van Fleet in early 1951 mandating high rates of fire to offset the enemy's quantitative superiority in foot soldiers. Van Fleet directed commanders to employ five times the normal rate of artillery fire to ease the tactical burden the allied infantry bore. What became known as a "Van Fleet day of fire" for a typical corps in Korea amounted to 250 rounds of 75-mm. howitzer ammunition, 300 rounds of 105-mm. howitzer ammunition, 250 rounds of 155-mm. howitzer ammunition, 200 rounds of 155-mm. gun ammunition, and 200 rounds of 8-inch howitzer ammunition per tube.[47] Although the fighting in

---

[44] Ibid., p. 352.

[45] Ibid., pp. 224–30; James A. Huston, *The Sinews of War: Army Logistics 1775–1953* (Washington, D.C.: U.S. Army Center of Military History, 1966), pp. 630–34.

[46] Conrad Crane, *American Airpower Strategy in Korea, 1950–1953* (Lawrence: University Press of Kansas, 2000), pp. 128–29.

[47] Mossman, *Ebb and Flow*, pp. 441–42.

Soldiers of the 3d Infantry Division constructing new bunkers

1952 generally occurred on a smaller scale, American units still required a significant amount of artillery support to neutralize enemy units defending fortified positions.

Second, American industry had not been producing sufficient quantities of ammunition to keep up with demand. Given a prevailing opinion early in the conflict that World War II stocks would suffice, the decision to open a new production line came only in late 1951. Even then, it would take eighteen months to restart production. As a result, shipments of new artillery shells were not expected to reach Korea until early 1953. In order to bridge the gap between decreasing stockpiles and future production, Eighth Army had to mandate a reduction in the daily expenditure of artillery ammunition.[48]

Third, the stockpile of ammunition remaining at the end of World War II was neither balanced nor well maintained. The official history notes: "There were enormous quantities of some types of ammunition and only small amounts of others. . . . The Army [during the interwar years] drew

---

[48] Hermes, *Truce Tent and Fighting Front*, pp. 224–30; Huston, *The Sinews of War*, pp. 630–34.

freely upon the big stockpile for training purposes yet made no real effort to replace consumption or to balance the items in stock."[49]

Ammunition still needed in Korea during 1952 did not mirror the inventory remaining from World War II. After the Chinese suspended large-scale offensive operations, they turned to positional defense conducted from bunkers capable of withstanding mortar fire and light artillery. The change in enemy strategy placed a premium on heavier guns, such as 155-mm. and 8-inch howitzers, while relegating 105-mm. howitzers, 81-mm. mortars, and 60-mm. mortars to a less useful role when compared to the earlier phases of the Korean conflict.

Against a backdrop of the ammunition shortages, the 65th Infantry spent the first week of May 1952 preparing for and undergoing another series of self-imposed inspections. After inspections were completed, Colonel Cordero-Davila instituted an athletic program aimed at increasing esprit de corps, encouraging a competitive spirit among the men, and improving their physical conditioning. Each battalion and separate company constructed a softball diamond, a volleyball court, and a horseshoe court; all soldiers were encouraged to participate in the games. Sundays and Wednesday afternoons were completely devoted to athletics, as were the late afternoon and early evening of each training day.[50]

Between regular softball and volleyball tournaments, the men of the 65th Infantry participated in a series of rifle-squad exercises between 5 and 15 May. The first exercise, which lasted from 0700 to 1600 on any given day, included a live-fire segment. The second, of the same duration, required each squad to attack a simulated enemy bunker with live ammunition. The third and fourth exercise consisted of day and night patrols without the use of live ammunition. The fifth, lasting from 1900 to 2300 on any given evening, was a nighttime live-fire exercise.[51]

At the conclusion of the training, the regimental operations officer circulated a memorandum that disclosed various problems that remained in the 65th. Some of the men, it indicated, had been unaccountably absent from training while others still lacked the proper equipment. More important, and perhaps a reflection on the language barrier that existed between Puerto Rican enlisted soldiers and continental officers, most company commanders had failed to debrief their soldiers thoroughly after the field problems.[52]

Overall, the training program for the 65th Infantry that spring had yielded mixed results, largely because many veteran NCOs had rotated stateside without being replaced. Inexplicably, neither the regiment nor the division

---

[49] Hermes, *Truce Tent and Fighting Front*, p. 224.
[50] Athletic Memo no. 1, 5 May 52, in Monthly Cmd Rpt, 65th Inf, May 52.
[51] Training Memo no. 22, 2 May 52, in Monthly Cmd Rpt, 65th Inf, May 52.
[52] Memo no. 32, 9 May 52, in Monthly Cmd Rpt, 65th Inf, May 52.

Soldiers of Company G listen to Latin American music played by members of the regimental orchestra known as the Mambo Boys.

attempted to bridge the language barrier by teaching English to Spanish-speaking enlisted soldiers. Instead, many newly arrived Puerto Rican junior enlisted men were assigned to leadership positions and given NCO ranks they would normally have earned only after many months of experience.

On 24 May 1952, Cordero-Davila obtained approval from the 3d Division to extend the 65th's training program once again, this time through 15 June. The focus of this cycle was on company and battalion exercises, including several to be performed at night. To assess the proficiency of the 65th when carrying out an attack, Cordero-Davila arranged a proficiency test for the unit, known as Exercise KAISER I, which employed umpires and colored maneuver flags.[53] Cordero-Davila placed special emphasis on platoon and company troop leadership, indicating that he placed great importance on refining those skills. "Tactical exercises," he pointed out, "should be prepared in a manner which will afford leaders adequate time to make reconnaissance, formulate a plan, and issue adequate orders."[54]

---

[53] Training Memo no. 25, 25 May 52, in Monthly Cmd Rpt, 65th Inf, May 52.
[54] Training Memo no. 27, 14 May 52, in Monthly Cmd Rpt, 65th Inf, May 52.

On 10 June, the 65th moved to the field for a division-directed maneuver exercise. Codenamed SEEK, the effort was designed to duplicate as closely as possible the tactical disposition and circumstances along Line Jamestown. It called for two battalions of the regiment to face off against the remaining battalion, which the 3d Division reinforced for the exercise. The two forces conducted day and night combat as well as reconnaissance patrols and ambushes against each other. They also established and maintained combat outposts forward of their defensive lines.[55]

Although Cordero-Davila had secured additional time for the 65th in the rear, the benefits gained during this period were diluted as the high rate of personnel turnover continued. In May 1952, for example, 9 officers and 700 enlisted men, the majority of them National Guardsmen, returned home. The mandatory release of the National Guard personnel after twenty-four months of service accounted for the mass exodus.[56] Incoming replacements numbered 25 officers and 519 enlisted men, the latter primarily draftees.[57] Only the senior leadership remained fairly constant: the one change during this period came in June when the regimental operations officer, Maj. Clarence F. Stoeckley, assumed command of the 2d Battalion from Colonel Craig, who became the 65th's new executive officer.[58] By that point, the high rate of turnover was such a problem that the regimental commander asked the 3d Division for permission to enlarge the 65th's personnel section to deal with the exodus. "The replacement problem for this organization is . . . similar to that faced by [other] units having a high percentage of National Guard personnel," Cordero-Davila observed in his monthly command report. "The large number of men leaving the unit under the phase out system generally includes the most experienced personnel. . . . It is recommended that groups [of replacements] for units faced with this problem include among them proportional numbers of NCO replacements."[59]

Eighth Army could do little in the near term to address Colonel Cordero-Davila's concern. It faced a situation in which a large number of those who had entered the Army during a relatively short buildup period in late 1950 were scheduled to be released from military service. Because legislation decreed the separation dates for National Guard and certain categories of reservists, the Army had no choice but to let them go. The relatively small Selective Service callup in the spring of 1952 would provide

---

[55] Training Memo no. 29, 8 Jun 52, sub: Exercise Seek, in Monthly Cmd Rpt, 65th Inf, Jun 52.
[56] Stillwaugh, "Personnel Policies in the Korean Conflict," ch. 4, p. 15.
[57] Monthly Cmd Rpt, 65th Inf, May 52.
[58] Ibid., Mar 52.
[59] Ibid.

only a fraction of the replacements the Army needed.[60] The only solution was to involuntarily reassign personnel from stateside units. This process could not be implemented prior to August.[61]

During the first six months of 1952, the 65th Infantry lost a total of 5,297 soldiers (either casualties or rotations) and gained 3,825. This represented a gain in replacements of almost 100 percent of authorized strength.[62] (*Table*) Selective Service quotas, which did not account for Army policies limiting the assignment of Spanish-speaking Puerto Rican soldiers, played a large part in creating this turbulent environment. Puerto Ricans who did not speak fluent English were eligible for assignment only to the Far East Command or the Caribbean Command. Even this slim range of options was largely eliminated by April 1952. The influx of combat veterans returning from Korea, added to the large number of recent basic-training graduates, resulted in significant overages within Caribbean Command. By April 1952, the command had 16,971 enlisted men on hand against 6,290 authorized spaces.[63] This virtually guaranteed Spanish-speaking Puerto Rican soldiers an overseas assignment upon completion of basic training. As the 65th Infantry neared its authorized strength, the division started diverting incoming Puerto Rican replacements to other units.

TABLE—3D INFANTRY DIVISION REGIMENTAL TURNOVER
JANUARY–JUNE 1952

Regiment	Casualties	Rotation	Total Losses	Replacements
7th Infantry	1,230	4,140	5,370	2,496
15th Infantry	774	4,311	5,085	1,790
65th Infantry	1,334	3,963	5,297	3,825

Personnel Problems in Eighth Army

The huge turnover in personnel during the first six months of 1952, with seasoned combat veterans leaving in droves and often being replaced by untested or inexperienced personnel, threatened to degrade the

---

[60] Selective Service called up 90,163 men in the first two months of 1952. In sharp contrast, only 53,858 were called up over the subsequent four months. *Annual Report of the Director of Selective Service for the Fiscal Year 1952* (Washington, D.C.: Government Printing Office, 1953), p. 91. The reduction reflects President Truman's unexpected reversal of his August 1951 decision to add 68,000 authorizations to the Army. Stillwaugh, "Personnel Policies in the Korean Conflict," ch. 4, pp. 4–5.

[61] Ibid., ch. 4, p. 16.

[62] Figures based on Monthly Cmd Rpts for all three regiments for the period Jan–Jun 52, Historians files.

[63] Cmd Rpt no. 2, U.S. Army Forces Antilles, 10 Dec 52, p. 26.

effectiveness of American ground forces throughout Korea. By the spring of 1952, Eighth Army was rotating some sixteen- to twenty-eight thousand men per month. This was the equivalent of one to one-and-a-half infantry divisions and an increase over the fifteen- to twenty thousand rotated monthly over the previous year.[64] "There was no rotation for a Chinese or North Korean except in a wooden box or without a leg," General Clark wrote after the war. "But rotation for us in Korea meant that we no sooner got a team working effectively than key men were finished with their part of the war and were sent home, to be replaced by recruits from the United States."[65]

The Army's Chief of Staff, General Collins, expressed his concern over the effects of the current rotation policy on Eighth Army. "It has been, frankly, a mystery to me," he told Clark, "how the Eighth Army has been able to retain its combat efficiency in light of the fact that we simply cannot furnish non-commissioned officers and young officers from the States who have the experience comparable to the men whom they replace."[66] The fact that the Eighth Army's infantry regiments were able to continue the fight without suffering a catastrophic collapse ensured that the policy, however flawed, remained in effect.

By the autumn of 1952, even General Van Fleet was sufficiently concerned with the problems created by individual rotation that he drew attention to the issue. Given his long-standing preference for using firepower to offset enemy numerical superiority, Van Fleet attached particular importance to maintaining a high level of combat readiness within his artillery units. He complained in the October command report that "the artillery had lost the ability to shoot quickly and accurately and blamed this on the rotation program that had stripped the artillery units of its veteran gunners."[67]

In defense of the Army's decision to implement individual rotation, there was no viable alternative. Given the inconclusive nature of the ongoing truce talks, which were dragging on with no foreseeable end, the Army was forced to choose between rotating individuals, rotating entire units, or adopting a policy of no rotation identical to that of the Chinese and both Korean armies. The last course of action, given that American soldiers were not fighting for their homeland, would have quickly led to significant and perhaps even insurmountable morale problems among U.S. fighting men. Rotating entire units would have placed a tremendous burden on the logistical system, given

---

[64] Hermes, *Truce Tent and Fighting Front*, pp. 186–87, 199.

[65] Mark W. Clark, *From the Danube to the Yalu* (Blue Ridge Summit, Pa.: Tab Books, 1988), p. 192. General Clark is in error with regard to the Chinese, who rotated their combat units in Korea annually.

[66] Ltr, Collins to Gen Mark W. Clark, 20 Aug 52, Van Fleet Papers.

[67] Hermes, *Truce Tent and Fighting Front*, p. 351.

General Collins (left) chats with General Clark (center) and Colonel Cordero-Davila at the 1st Commonwealth Division airstrip.

that it is far easier to transport individual soldiers than entire units with all of their equipment from the United States to Korea and then back. While rotating entire units might have improved unit cohesion, every time a new division entered the line it would still contain a large percentage of recently inducted enlisted men who had not seen action in Korea.

Even though the policy of individual rotation was the least of several evils, it proved especially disruptive to the 65th Infantry when compared to other regiments. The language barrier between continental officers and Puerto Rican enlisted men was made worse by the dwindling numbers of experienced bilingual NCOs. South Koreans filled the ranks of numerous American combat units in 1952 but were usually distributed on the basis of two or three per rifle squad.[68] Because South Korean augmentees did not

---

[68] In the wake of a second influx of KATUSA personnel in early 1952, some units in the 3d Division organized Korean rifle platoons led by South Korean NCOs and American officers. Interv, Mark J. Reardon with Col (Ret) James S. Boatner, 2 Mar 07, Historians files, CMH.

benefit from the U.S. Army's rotation plan, they were motivated to learn enough English to communicate with American noncommissioned and commissioned leaders. The same held true for Puerto Rican replacements diverted from the 65th to other units.[69] Thus, at any given time, a continental platoon leader in an infantry regiment other than the 65th had to deal with a relatively small number of soldiers who could not speak English.

For whatever reason, neither the 3d Division nor the 65th's regimental commander, who was bilingual, implemented a policy mandating English tutoring for Spanish-speaking Puerto Ricans. Undoubtedly, it would have proved difficult to teach 90 percent of the regiment to speak English while in a combat zone, although most new replacements had received some language instruction during basic training.[70] Because the majority of junior enlisted men spoke only Spanish, it did not make sense to assign English-speaking sergeants to the 65th Infantry. The pool of Spanish-speaking NCOs within the entire Army, however, was extremely small. At this point in the war, most had already served in Korea and were under no obligation to return. Requests for more Puerto Rican lieutenants went unanswered.[71]

The 3d Division chain of command, left with no other recourse, sought to solve the 65th's leadership problems by appointing Spanish-speaking junior enlisted soldiers as NCOs. The consequences of this policy, and the impact of the manpower turnover that affected the regiment as well as the entire Eighth Army, would be put to the test once the 65th returned to action.

---

[69] Culp, *Training and Future Utilization*, p. 5.

[70] The 19-week training curriculum included 71 hours of language instruction. On 20 September 1952, this program was increased to 20 weeks of training and 110 hours of formal language instruction. Cmd Rpt no. 2, U.S. Army Forces Antilles, 10 Dec 52.

[71] Monthly Cmd Rpt, 3d Inf Div, Mar 52.

Chapter 9

DEFEAT AT OUTPOST KELLY
JULY–SEPTEMBER 1952

On 3 July 1952, as armistice talks continued, the 3d Infantry Division returned to Line Jamestown, relieving the South Korean 1st Division northwest of Yonch'on. The 65th Infantry replaced the South Korean 11th Regiment in the northeastern half of the division sector while the 7th Infantry took over for the South Korean 15th Regiment in the southwestern part. The relief took place over a 24-hour period as platoons and companies of the 65th Infantry successively moved into the positions occupied by the South Koreans. Communist forces north of the Yokkok, a tributary of the Imjin River that flowed laterally across the front of the 65th's newly assigned sector, acknowledged the arrival of the 65th with a burst of machine-gun, artillery, and mortar fire at 2230. This was followed thirty minutes later by an unsuccessful Chinese probe against a Company F outpost. Just after midnight, an enemy squad attacked a listening post in front of Company K but was driven off after a brief fight.

Despite the probes and the enemy shelling, the 65th assumed control of its sector without great difficulty. On 5 July, the remainder of the 3d Division joined the 65th on the front lines. Facing it was the Chinese *344th Regiment, 115th Division, 39th Army*, deployed east of Imjin, as well as the *353d* and *354th Regiments, 118th Division, 40th Army*, deployed west of the river. Five to seven artillery battalions and an armored regiment supported the Chinese infantry units.[1]

Over the next few days, the Communists sent a number of raiding parties to probe the 65th Infantry while keeping up an almost constant barrage of artillery and mortar fire. The regiment countered with equally aggressive patrols. Early in the morning of 6 July 1952, a Company E patrol ambushed a group of enemy soldiers, killing or wounding three in the

---
[1] Monthly Cmd Rpt, 3d Inf Div, Jul 52. Unless otherwise noted, all Cmd Rpts are in Entry 429, Rcds of the AGO, RG 407, NACP.

opening moments of the fight. Supplied with a generous amount of automatic weapons in comparison to the U.S. troops, the Chinese soon gained the upper hand, killing three Americans and wounding another five, including the platoon leader, 1st Lt. Donald A. Sidler, before both sides broke off the engagement.

The 65th's sector then lapsed into relative calm for the next several days as the Chinese switched their attention to the 7th Infantry. Elements of the 7th Infantry manning Outposts Big Nori and Little Nori as well as Outpost Kelly were clustered together near a prominent bend in the Imjin eight miles west of Yonch'on and came under attack in quick succession. The enemy fired more than four hundred artillery rounds in a two-hour attack against the Nori outposts alone.[2] Despite numerous casualties on both sides, the 7th Infantry held firm.

On 17 July 1952, the Chinese shifted their emphasis once more to the 65th Infantry's sector by probing Outpost King and several neighboring positions on the south side of the Yokkok. The regiment repulsed all three assaults at the cost of only one wounded soldier. The good fortune of the 65th changed three days later when a combat patrol from Company A investigated a stream crossing near the union of the Yokkok and Imjin. Mindful of enemy flares that lit up the night sky, the patrol advanced slowly and cautiously toward the crossing, led by the company commander, 1st Lt. Fred W. Wood. A veteran officer, Wood had served with airborne units during World War II and had volunteered for duty in Korea. Over the nine months that he led the 1st Platoon of Company A, the officer established such a brilliant record as an aggressive leader that he had become the company commander.

As the patrol neared the crossing, three Chinese fighting positions guarding the ford unleashed an intense volume of mortar and machine-gun fire. Hard hit by the first volley, Wood and his men nonetheless established a defensive perimeter and returned fire. Wood charged forward with a squad to destroy the nearest machine-gun nest; but as they took out the enemy position, he was mortally wounded. Four more of his soldiers were wounded and a fifth soldier went missing in action. In the end, the patrol succeeded in withdrawing from the stream crossing, but Lieutenant Wood was unaccounted for when his men finally reached friendly lines.[3]

First Lt. John D. Porterfield Jr., who had previously commanded Company A, went searching for the missing officer along with 1st Lt. St. Clair Streett Jr., one of Wood's platoon leaders.[4] Creeping through the

---

[2] Ibid.
[3] Ibid.
[4] Ltr, 1st Lt John D. Porterfield Jr. to David Porterfield, 22 Jul 52, Historians files, CMH.

heavy fog toward the river crossing during the predawn hours, the pair found Wood badly wounded but still alive only a hundred yards from the enemy lines. They attempted to carry him back to friendly lines. "We hadn't gone thirty yards when the bastards opened up on us with a tank," Porterfield later wrote. "The fog had begun to lift. There was [sic] no holes on the [river] bank so we just hit the dirt and prayed that the next round didn't tear us to pieces."[5] Porterfield sent Streett back for help while he comforted Wood. By the time help arrived forty-five minutes later, Wood had died. "He was the finest platoon leader I have ever known," Porterfield would recall, "He loved his men and they loved him."[6] The fallen officer received a posthumous Silver Star for his "intrepid leadership and gallantry under enemy fire."[7] With Wood gone, Porterfield again assumed command of Company A.

Four hours after the patrol had been ambushed, Company C launched a raid against a platoon-size Chinese outpost, killing 15 and wounding another 12 enemy soldiers. Friendly casualties included 3 killed, 26 wounded, and 3 missing in action.[8] Lieutenant Clark was among the wounded. "Due to intense Chinese artillery and mortar fire, [much of] the company was prevented from approaching the objective," he remembered. "Second Platoon, with fixed bayonets, fought for an extended period, killing all enemy on Hill 167 before being ordered to withdraw. Our withdrawal, bringing our dead and wounded over open terrain, was under continuous artillery/mortar fire."[9] Following this engagement, the Chinese shifted their efforts to Outpost Kelly in the 7th Infantry zone for the remainder of the month.

On 20 July, heavy rains ushered in the monsoon season. Over the next eleven days, over eight inches of rain fell in the division sector, causing the Imjin to rise from its normal depth of two to three feet to nearly twenty-eight feet. Communications trenches and weapons bunkers collapsed in some places under the deluge of water. The 3d Division's commander, General Dulaney, reported that 201 bunkers in the unit's forward area had caved in, killing one soldier and injuring another three. Scores of other bunkers became uninhabitable. "Rehabilitation of these fighting positions," Dulaney wrote, "became a high priority task in all front line units."[10]

On 28 July, the Chinese took advantage of the weather to attack and capture Outpost Kelly. The 7th Infantry regained the position three days

---

[5] Ibid.
[6] Ibid.
[7] GO, HQ 3d Inf Div, 30 Nov 52, sub: Award of Silver Star Medal to 1st Lieutenant Fred W. Wood, in Monthly Cmd Rpt, 3d Inf Div, Nov 52.
[8] Monthly Cmd Rpt, 65th Inf, Jul 52.
[9] Interv, author with Clark, 17 Jun 00.
[10] Monthly Cmd Rpt, 3d Inf Div, Jul 52.

later with a battalion-size counterattack. Although the disputed hilltop remained in friendly hands, enemy fire continued to pound it regularly.[11]

Several key personnel in the 65th Infantry became casualties during the month of July. They included the commander of the 2d Battalion, Major Stoeckley, who was wounded in action and evacuated. His successor, Lt. Col. Carlos Betances-Ramirez, became the only Hispanic to command a battalion in the 65th during the Korean War. A graduate of the University of Puerto Rico, 42-year-old Betances-Ramirez had served with the Puerto Rican National Guard's 295th Infantry Regiment in Panama and Hawaii during World War II. He was one of only seven Puerto Rican National Guard officers who had received Regular Army commissions after the war.[12] A 1948 graduate of the Advanced Infantry Officers Course at Fort Benning, Georgia, he went on to serve with the 5th Division at Fort Jackson, South Carolina, and then at the Army's Ground General School at Fort Riley, Kansas. While at Fort Riley, Betances-Ramirez became a major and then a lieutenant colonel. After completing the General Staff Course at Fort Leavenworth, Kansas, in May 1952, he was assigned to the 40th Infantry Division in Korea but asked to serve instead with the 65th Infantry. Seeing him as a natural fit for the 65th, the Department of the Army approved his request. Betances-Ramirez reported to Korea in May 1952 and joined the regiment the following month.

When Betances-Ramirez arrived, the regiment was doing fairly well keeping its manpower up while the 3d Division as a whole was not. "The situation is critical," General Dulaney reported, "because not only were rotation losses greater than the previous reporting period, but the forecast for August [1952] is even greater with an estimated 2,200 to be rotated."[13] As a result, he ordered his chief personnel officer to begin transferring soldiers from the 65th to offset shortages in other regiments. Dulaney also noted, "Although the number of Puerto Rican replacements received . . . placed the [65th] regiment in an over-strength situation, the division is [still] desirous of obtaining such personnel."

Dulaney went on to record, however, that the newest increment of Puerto Ricans the division had received were generally non–English speaking and included very few noncommissioned officers. He requested that a greater percentage of English-speaking Puerto Rican soldiers be sent to the division in the future along with additional NCOs and at least nine Puerto Rican lieutenants.[14]

---

[11] Monthly Cmd Rpt, 3d Inf Div, Aug 52.

[12] Lt Col Carlos Betances-Ramirez, "An Autobiography," n.d., Unpubl Monograph, Historians files.

[13] Monthly Cmd Rpt, 3d Inf Div, Jun 52.

[14] Ibid.

Chaplain 1st Lt. Harvey F. Kochner of the 15th Infantry blesses a flag held by Colonel Betances-Ramirez and M.Sgt. Angel J. Rivera, 23 August 1952.

The 65th continued to defend the northeastern portion of the division's sector along Line Jamestown during the first two weeks of August. For the second month in a row, heavy rains hampered the Americans, causing extensive damage to trenches and fighting positions in addition to washing out bridges. The enemy kept all patrols and raiding parties from the 65th away from their line with heavy volumes of machine-gun and small-arms fire. The Chinese also delivered a growing amount of artillery and mortar fire on the regiment's main line of resistance as well as into its rear areas, disrupting the 65th's supply routes nearly every day. Intelligence reports estimated that the enemy had deployed eight artillery battalions against the 3d Division, which represented a denser concentration of field pieces on their front than ever before. On several occasions, the Chinese augmented their artillery barrages with cannon fire from tanks and self-propelled guns.[15]

On 11 August 1952, the regiment began Operation CAPTIVATE, a divisionwide effort to lure the enemy into sending out more patrols so the Americans could capture more Chinese prisoners. The 65th suspended all

---

[15] Monthly Cmd Rpts, 65th Inf, Aug 52, and 3d Inf Div, Aug 52.

Pvt. Gilberto Torres-Rosario stands guard near the entrance of the 65th Infantry command post.

movement within its sector and initiated a program of atypical firing patterns for the artillery and unusual vehicular movements with the intent of prompting the Chinese to investigate. Seven platoon-size patrols from the 65th, sent into no-man's-land during the hours of darkness, were positioned to intercept incoming enemy reconnaissance units. The Chinese, however, refused to take the bait and the operation ended inconclusively two days later. On 19 August 1952, the 65th handed its sector over to the 7th Infantry and then reverted to corps reserve near Tongduch'on-ni. From there, the 3d Battalion went to the Kimpo peninsula west of Seoul to guard a large facility holding Communist prisoners. The 1st Battalion relieved the 3d Battalion on guard duty at the end of the month.

During the month, the 65th Infantry received many letters from Puerto Rican soldiers serving with other units in Korea requesting transfers to the regiment. "The most frequently expressed reason for this transfer is language difficulties," wrote Cordero-Davila, confirming that many Hispanic soldiers coming to Korea at this stage in the war knew little English:

> The inability to express [himself] easily creates in the Puerto Rican soldier hardship in his performance of duty. In a Spanish-speaking unit the Puerto Rican soldier sheds this handicap and enjoys a feeling of equality in competing with his fellow soldiers. Also, he performs his duties with more confidence since there is no question of misinterpretation and misunderstanding.[16]

Colonel Cordero-Davila apparently did not try to improve the English-speaking skills of his Puerto Rican soldiers as other Army units had with their South Korean augmentees. Nor did Cordero-Davila make use of his unique ties to the National Guard and civil government in Puerto Rico by suggesting that a greater percentage of English-speaking soldiers be sent or that recruits receive some English-language instruction before deploying to

---

[16] Ibid.

Korea. Either Cordero-Davila felt that such measures and requests would be futile in the main, given the lack of time and resources available to him, or else he believed that he could manage well enough in the current situation to get the job done.

The Struggle for Outpost Kelly

September 1952 opened with the 3d Division still defending Line Jamestown northwest of Yonch'on. The division's missions included maintaining contact with the Chinese through daily patrols, capturing prisoners of war for interrogation, and continuing to improve and develop Line Jamestown.[17] General Dulaney assigned the 7th Infantry to defend the northeastern segment of the division's sector and the 15th Infantry to defend the southwestern half. The 65th Infantry stood in I Corps reserve until 10 September, when it moved forward to relieve the 15th Infantry.

The regiment occupied a 3 ½–mile-long stretch of the division's line with Colonel Gendron's 3d Battalion to the northeast and Colonel Betances-Ramirez's 2d Battalion reinforced by the division's 3d Reconnaissance Company to the southwest. Major Davies' 1st Battalion stood in reserve. Capt. Harold D. Burke's heavy mortar company was located to the rear of the 3d Battalion, while Capt. Gustav Grevillius' tank company, the regimental headquarters, and Company D (Heavy Weapons) of the 1st Battalion took positions behind the 2d Battalion. The 1st Commonwealth Division stood on the left flank of the regiment while the 7th Infantry manned the line to its right.[18]

Enemy forces facing the 3d Division included the Chinese *115th and 116th Divisions, 39th Army*.[19] Opposite the 65th Infantry was the *2d Battalion, 348th Infantry Regiment*, which faced Colonel Gendron's 3d Battalion on the right, and the *3d Battalion, 348th Infantry Regiment*, which faced Colonel Betances-Ramirez's 2d Battalion on the left.[20]

At the beginning of the autumn of 1952, Communist forces became increasingly aggressive as they fought for various points of high ground overlooking the Eighth Army's main line of resistance. The enemy was intent on improving his position before the onset of winter so he could bring extra pressure on UN negotiators. To secure the desired terrain, the Communists had to push Eighth Army off the outpost line it currently occupied. Combat centered around five key terrain features: Bunker Hill (Hill 122) in the 1st Marine Division sector near Panmunjom, Outpost Kelly in

---

[17] Monthly Cmd Rpt, 3d Inf Div, Sep 52.
[18] Monthly Cmd Rpt, 65th Inf, Sep 52.
[19] Unit Rpt no. 698, in Monthly Cmd Rpt, 65th Inf, Sep 52.
[20] Monthly Cmd Rpt, 3d Inf Div, Sep 52.

the 3d Division sector, Old Baldy (Hill 275) in the 2d Division sector west of Ch'orwon, and Capitol Hill and Finger Ridge in the South Korean II Corps sector in east-central Korea.

The job of defending those assorted heights was particularly dangerous because they were up to a mile forward of the United Nations' main line of resistance.[21] While doctrine permitted commanders to withdraw from these positions when they were no longer tenable, ongoing truce talks bestowed increasing political importance on even the smallest elevations. This meant that while unit commanders nominally had the authority to withdraw from an outpost that was in danger of being overrun or destroyed, they were required to launch a counterattack at the first opportunity to regain lost ground.[22] Not everyone agreed with such practices, despite the political importance assigned to these terrain features. A report from the neighboring 1st Commonwealth Division noted, "There was a strong tendency to feel that the retention of an [American] outpost is a matter of honour and [to] insist that it shall be defended to the last man and the last round, regardless of its tactical significance."[23]

The 65th Infantry had the task of defending Outpost Kelly, situated a mile or so west of the Imjin where a bend in its course formed a large cul-de-sac behind the allied front line. The outpost consisted of four automatic-weapons bunkers situated for all-around defense and a circular trench that ringed the crest of the hill.[24] There were also several sleeping bunkers and a command bunker located within the defensive perimeter. The 3d Division had preregistered artillery fire around Kelly and kept a large stockpile of ammunition and rations there in case the Chinese cut the supply trail that ran from the front line to the outpost.[25] Two platoons from Company C, 1st Battalion, manned Outpost Kelly; an understrength platoon from the same company manned nearby Outpost Tessie; and single rifle squads occupied Outposts Nick and Betty. All four positions stood along a northeast-southwest ridgeline running roughly parallel to the west bank of the Imjin. Three adjacent outposts, nicknamed Big Nori, Little Nori, and the Bubble, were located two-thirds of a mile to the northeast on a separate hill mass overlooking a bend in the Imjin. The 3d Battalion maintained a squad from

---

[21] According to Army doctrine, the outpost line is sited 800–2,000 yards beyond the main line of resistance. See Department of the Army, FM 7–40: *The Infantry Regiment* (Washington, D.C.: Department of the Army, 1950), p. 257.

[22] Ltr, Lt Col Betances-Ramirez to Col Lopez-Duprey, 4 Nov 52, Historians files.

[23] Jeffrey Grey, *The Commonwealth Armies and the Korean War: An Alliance Study* (Manchester, England: Manchester University Press, 1988), p. 144.

[24] Ann. 2 (Intelligence) to Opns Order no. 16, 192200I Sep 52, in Monthly Cmd Rpt, 65th Inf, Sep 52.

[25] Ltr, Col (Ret) Duquesne A. Wolf to author, 7 Jul 00, sub: Outpost Kelly, Historians files.

Defeat at Outpost Kelly

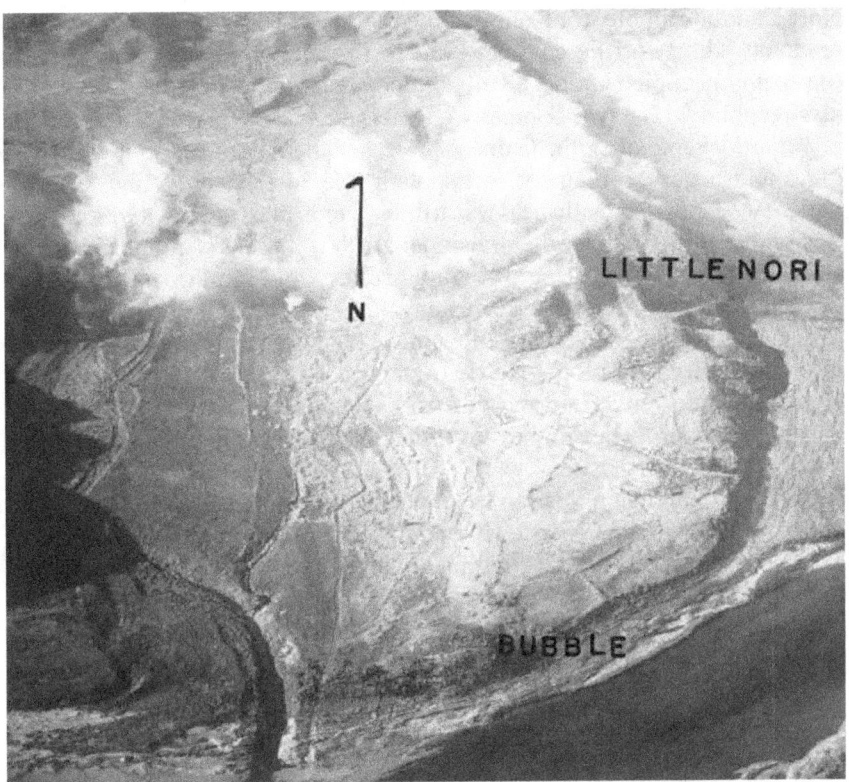

Aerial view of the Bubble, Little Nori, and Big Nori (immediately north of Little Nori). Outposts Tessie and Nick are on the far left, partially shrouded by white smoke. Outpost Kelly (not pictured) is just to the west (left) of Tessie and Nick. The Imjin River runs diagonally across the lower right corner before curving upward.

Company I on Big Nori (Hill 117), two squads from the same unit on Little Nori, and a rifle squad from Company K on the Bubble.[26] On 15 September, Colonel Cordero-Davila ordered the 3d Battalion to strengthen the outpost line by sending two additional rifle squads to reinforce the Bubble. The reinforcements would occupy the position only during the hours of darkness.[27]

The 65th developed several plans to recover the outposts if one or more of them fell to the Chinese. If the enemy occupied Big Nori, Little

---

[26] Troop Disposition, 17 Sep 52, in Monthly Cmd Rpt, 65th Inf, Sep 52.
[27] Ibid.

Nori, and the Bubble, for example, the regiment would immediately counterattack with two rifle companies to restore the positions.[28] Likewise, if the enemy occupied Outpost Kelly but not Tessie and Nick, the 65th would also respond with a two-company counterattack.[29]

In mid-September, the Chinese increased the volume of their daily barrages and began probing for soft spots in the 3d Division's line. General Dulaney responded with heavier artillery and air strikes. On 13 and 14 September, for example, the divisional artillery fired 254 rounds in retaliation for the Chinese firing of eighty artillery and mortar rounds against the 65th Infantry. Four F–51 Mustang fighter-bombers also flew retaliatory air strikes against suspected Chinese positions.[30] Despite the increase in enemy activity, Colonel Cordero-Davila continued to assume that the Chinese would remain on the defensive for the foreseeable future.[31] The enemy, however, believed they had detected a vulnerable spot in the 65th's defensive line: Outpost Kelly.

The Communist operation to seize the outpost began on 17 September around 2250 when a Chinese rifle company from the *2d Battalion, 348th Regiment*, probed Kelly. At that time, Kelly contained two reinforced platoons from Company C, commanded by 1st Lt. Robert E. L. Stevens.[32] Although the National Guard officer had been trained as an air defense artillery officer, he had ended up commanding an infantry company on one of the most highly contested pieces of terrain at that stage of the war.[33]

Forty minutes after the attack began, the defenders reported that the situation was "bad" and called for reinforcements.[34] Defensive artillery fire and an almost constant stream of illumination flares allowed Lieutenant Stevens and his men to hold on until the Chinese finally withdrew at 0100, leaving behind four dead and a dozen wounded.[35] Friendly casualties were two wounded. The enemy probed Kelly twice more that evening with no greater success.[36]

During the predawn hours of 18 September, Company B, commanded by 1st Lt. William F. Nelson, relieved Company C. The 26-year-old company commander had been an enlisted man in World War II and

---

[28] Attack Plan Barbara, 101700 Sep 52, in Monthly Cmd Rpt, 65th Inf, Sep 52.
[29] Attack Plan Donna, 102206 Sep 52, in Monthly Cmd Rpt, 65th Inf, Sep 52.
[30] Unit Rpt no. 702, in Monthly Cmd Rpt, 65th Inf, Sep 52.
[31] Unit Rpt no. 706, in Monthly Cmd Rpt, 65th Inf, Sep 52.
[32] Company C had 241 officers and men assigned, well in excess of the 206 personnel it was authorized. Actual Strength, 17 Sep 52, in Monthly Cmd Rpt, 3d Inf Div, Sep 52.
[33] *Official National Guard Register (Army) for 1951*, p. 1010.
[34] 2d Bn Staff Jnl, Entries 59–62, 17 Sep 52, in Monthly Cmd Rpt, 65th Inf, Sep 52.
[35] 2d Bn Staff Jnl, Entries 1–7, 18 Sep 52; Regimental Intel Jnl, Entry 401, 18 Sep 52; Monthly Cmd Rpt, 65th Inf, Sep 52.
[36] Daily Chronology, in Monthly Cmd Rpt, 65th Inf, Sep 52.

had attended West Point after the war, graduating in 1950.[37] Under his direction, two platoons from Company B manned Kelly while another platoon (about forty men) occupied Tessie. A squad of ten men detached from Company B occupied Outpost Nick.[38] For this mission, Nelson's company operated under the tactical control of Betances-Ramirez's 2d Battalion.

Although Lieutenant Nelson had arrived in Korea in 1951, he had little experience commanding troops in combat. Perhaps for that reason, the 65th's chief intelligence officer, Maj. George D. Putnam, had suggested that Cordero-Davila assign a different rifle company to the defense of Outpost Kelly. The colonel broached the subject with Nelson's commanding officer, Major Davies, but Davies opposed a last-minute move because he felt it would lower morale and set a bad precedent. Company B thus retained the mission to man the outpost.[39]

Before Lieutenant Stevens passed control of Kelly over to Lieutenant Nelson, he briefed the Company B commander and his platoon leaders on the enemy situation and warned them that the Chinese were likely to attack again. He told Nelson to be especially alert at dusk. He wanted everyone to remain at their posts throughout the night and all subordinate leaders to closely supervise their men so no one became complacent. Not long after the briefing, however, some of Nelson's troops began drifting back to the bunkers rather than stay in the cold and exposed trenches. Nelson apparently did not object, a fact noted by a member of the regimental intelligence section attached to Company B.

As it had all day, sporadic Chinese artillery and mortar fire fell on Outpost Kelly. At 2033, Nelson requested that the artillery unit supporting him prepare its howitzers to fire variable-time (air burst) high-explosive shells around his position in the event of an enemy attack.[40] Less than an hour later, two reinforced companies from the Chinese *2d Battalion, 348th Infantry Regiment*, assaulted Kelly from the southwest, northwest, and northeast. (*See Map 11.*)

The attack could hardly have been better timed, for Lieutenant Nelson was at that moment briefing his platoon leaders, artillery liaison officer, and forward observers in the command bunker. The group heard small-arms fire; but before the officers could react, the headquarters' wooden door flew open and several hand grenades thumped onto the floor. A platoon leader who was close enough to the door to get partway through before the grenades went off was blown outside by the force of the explosions.

---

[37] *Register of Graduates and Former Cadets, 1802–1980*, p. 538.
[38] Regimental Intel Jnl, Entries 541–42, 20 Sep 52, in Monthly Cmd Rpt, 65th Inf, Sep 52.
[39] Ltr, Wolf to author, 7 July 00; Interv, author with Clark, 17 Jun 00.
[40] 2d Bn Staff Jnl, Entry 54, 18 Sep 52, in Monthly Cmd Rpt, 65th Inf, Sep 52.

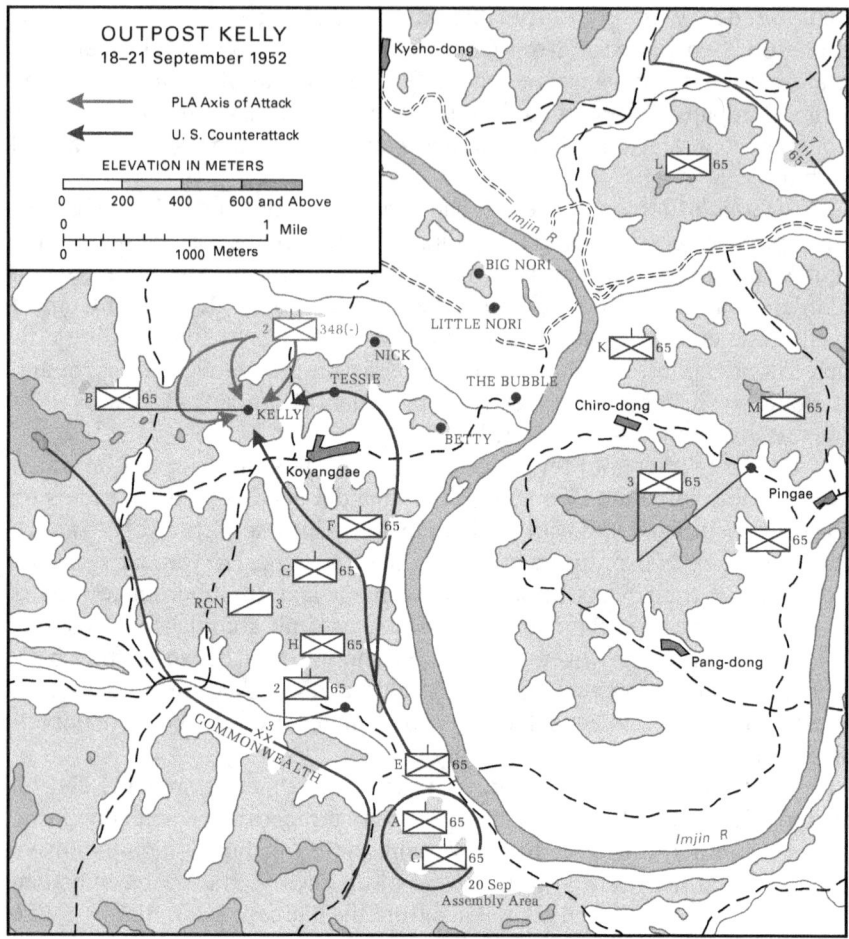

MAP 11

He tumbled to the ground at the feet of three Chinese soldiers armed with submachine guns who were preparing to enter the shattered bunker. Wounded in the leg but still nimble enough to scramble away before the surprised Chinese soldiers could react, the lieutenant climbed over a trench and descended the hill. Outpost Kelly, he knew, was almost certain to fall unless he or someone else could get help right away.[41]

At the time of the attack, the forward observer attached to Company B had been talking with the supporting field artillery battalion's fire direction

---

[41] Ltr, Wolf to author, 7 Jul 00.

center. When the Chinese flung open the bunker door to throw their hand grenades, he shouted a brief warning over the radio. After that, all contact with Nelson's unit ceased. "So it was known immediately that the outpost was under attack but nothing else," wrote 1st Lt. Duquesne "Duke" Wolf, the regiment's assistant intelligence officer:

> Cordero was alerted and he immediately called Division Headquarters to relay the situation to them. He was reluctant to commence artillery fires on and around Kelly for fear of killing his own troops. He was also reluctant to commit the regimental reserve in a counterattack to retake the outpost lest they be subjected to friendly fires as well as enemy fires.[42]

As Cordero-Davila wavered, the Chinese swept across the hill, taking one machine-gun position on the northwest corner of the outpost from the rear and killing its crew. The Chinese then advanced along the trenches, clearing out the defenders before they could respond effectively to the attack from within their own perimeter. By 2219, the Chinese were in complete control of Outpost Kelly.[43]

While the attack on Kelly was taking place, a reinforced Chinese platoon assaulted a nearby outpost held by the 3d Reconnaissance Company. The enemy troops penetrated the outer wire but could go no further due to the intensity of the American fire. The attackers withdrew at 2300 after suffering ten killed and twenty-five wounded.[44] Just as that firefight was tapering off, the rifle platoon from Company B that was occupying Tessie and the squad that was guarding Nick abandoned their outposts—without receiving orders to do so—to link up with a Company E combat patrol moving along the valley between the outpost line and the regiment's main positions. Although the Chinese had largely ignored the two small outposts that night, the units guarding them had clearly decided that the enemy planned to overrun them at any moment. That turned out not to be true, and another patrol from Company E soon reoccupied both positions. On the morning of 19 September, the soldiers of Company B returned to their positions on Tessie and Nick.[45]

That same morning, Chinese soldiers forced several of the captured men from Nelson's company to dig new positions for them around Outpost Kelly within sight of the 65th Infantry's main line and Outpost Tessie. Afterward, they marched the captives north toward the primitive prisoner

---

[42] Ibid.

[43] Regimental Intel Jnl, Entries 446 and 453, 18 Sep 52, in Monthly Cmd Rpt, 65th Inf, Sep 52.

[44] Ibid.

[45] Regimental Intel Jnl, Entries 541–42, 20 Sep 52, in Monthly Cmd Rpt, 65th Inf, Sep 52.

of war camps that would become their new homes.⁴⁶ The presence of these helpless American soldiers on Outpost Kelly contributed further to Cordero-Davila's indecision. "Again there was a reluctance on the part of the Regiment and Division to begin shelling the enemy for fear of killing our own troops," recalled Wolf, "and also a reluctance to launch a counterattack to retake Outpost Kelly."⁴⁷

Colonel Betances-Ramirez, observing the scene through his binoculars, also chose a cautious response because of the American captives on the hill. He looked on in frustration as "two Chinese officers walked arrogantly among the wounded lying everywhere and a small group of POWs being assembled by a couple of Chinese soldiers. The rest of the company had been destroyed. I stopped a friendly artillery concentration that was to be fired to save our wounded and POWs still on the hill."⁴⁸ The presence of friendly wounded and captured troops around Kelly did not prevent Betances-Ramirez from directing a nearby tank to open fire on the two Chinese officers, forcing them to scramble for cover. Members of Company B who had not been captured or killed continued to filter back to U.S. lines throughout the morning.⁴⁹

During the Chinese attack on Outpost Kelly, Nelson's unit had suffered 82 casualties—more than 40 percent of its deployed strength—including 4 killed, 20 wounded, and 58 missing.⁵⁰ Some of the missing in action showed up over the next two days. Those that did not had either become prisoners of the Chinese or had been killed in action but not recovered by friendly forces. The survivors of Company B claimed to have killed 52 Chinese soldiers and wounded another 114.⁵¹ In light of how quickly the outpost fell, however, these suspiciously precise figures appear somewhat inflated.

Counterattack and Defeat

The loss of Outpost Kelly brought General Dulaney, the 3d Infantry Division commander, and Lt. Gen. Paul W. Kendall, the new I Corps commander, to the regimental command post on the morning of 19 September. The generals returned later that afternoon, accompanied by the Eighth

---

⁴⁶ Regimental Intel Jnl, Entries 477, 482–83, 19 Sep 52, in Monthly Cmd Rpt, 65th Inf, Sep 52.

⁴⁷ Ltr, Wolf to author, 7 Jul 00.

⁴⁸ Ltr, Col Carlos Betances-Ramirez to author, 4 Jul 00, Historians files.

⁴⁹ Regimental Intel Jnl, Entries 477, 482, and 483, 19 Sep 52, in Monthly Cmd Rpt, 65th Inf, Sep 52.

⁵⁰ Regimental Intel Jnl, Entry 501, 19 Sep 52, in Monthly Cmd Rpt, 65th Inf, Sep 52.

⁵¹ Unit Rpt no. 707, in Monthly Cmd Rpt, 65th Inf, Sep 52.

Army commander, General Van Fleet.[52] As a result of the high-level interest in retaking Kelly, Colonel Cordero-Davila ordered his staff to prepare a plan for a counterattack to retake the outpost. During the late evening of 19 September, almost twenty-four hours after Nelson's company had been overrun, Cordero-Davila finally ordered the 1st Battalion to retake the lost outpost.[53] By then, the intelligence section estimated, a reinforced Chinese rifle company equipped with light machine guns and four 60-mm. mortars had dug in at Kelly.[54] While Major Davies was getting his troops ready, Cordero-Davila directed Colonel Betances-Ramirez to probe the hill with a platoon from Company E to determine the strength of enemy forces at Kelly. The remainder of the company was to be prepared to follow up rapidly if the probe revealed that the Chinese had abandoned the outpost or held it only lightly.[55]

Believing that a single platoon would prove inadequate for the task, Betances-Ramirez ordered two platoons from Company E to carry out the mission. At 0520 on 20 September, the men from Company E set out to investigate Kelly. One rifle platoon, designated the A element, jumped off from Outpost Tessie. A second platoon, the B element, departed from the main line of resistance.[56]

Less than an hour later, the commander of Company E and the leader of the B element, 1st Lt. Harrold L. Gensemer, got into a brief firefight near the base of the hill and then stormed into the trenches of Outpost Kelly at the head of his platoon.[57] The unit's approach had been masked by heavy fog, allowing it to get in close before the Chinese could react effectively. The absence of the customary American artillery preparation prior to the assault added to the element of surprise. However, the A element did not arrive in time to support its sister platoon. It was still slowly working its way along a narrow trail when the Chinese responded to Gensemer's unexpected appearance by sweeping the hillside with heavy artillery, mortar, and automatic weapons. Soon, casualties began to mount in both platoons from Company E.

Unable to maintain his foothold, Gensemer ordered his men to withdraw. At 0800, dragging their wounded along, both platoons returned to their original starting points.[58] An artillery forward observer accompanying one of the platoons reported that the Chinese had at least one hundred

---

[52] Entries dtd 191045, 191625 Sep 52, Opns Jnl, in Monthly Cmd Rpt, 65th Inf, Sep 52.
[53] Section II, Narr of Opns, in Monthly Cmd Rpt, 65th Inf, Sep 52.
[54] Ann. 2 (Intelligence) to Opns Order no. 16.
[55] Monthly Cmd Rpt, 65th Inf, Sep 52.
[56] 2d Bn Staff Jnl, Entry dtd 0520, 20 Sep 52, in Monthly Cmd Rpt, 65th Inf, Sep 52.
[57] Regimental Opns Jnl, Entry dtd 0618, 20 Sep 52, in Monthly Cmd Rpt, 65th Inf, Sep 52.
[58] 2d Bn Staff Jnl, Entry dtd 0800, 20 Sep 52.

Soldiers from the 65th Infantry carry a wounded comrade back to friendly lines during the fighting at Outpost Kelly.

men manning the outpost.[59] He called for an air strike, but the mission was canceled when other observers reported that friendly wounded were lying exposed on the hillside.[60]

Nine hours later, Company E launched a second effort against the outpost with all three rifle platoons and its heavy weapons platoon. Air strikes and direct fire from the regimental tank company supported the assault. The latter unit drew intense return fire from the enemy that resulted in one tank being disabled by a mortar shell.[61] By 1830, the bulk of the attacking force was pinned down by a torrent of Chinese automatic weapons; but one platoon pressed forward to the outpost's communications trench. Thirty-five minutes later, the southern peak of Kelly was reported in friendly hands.[62]

---

[59] Regimental Intel Jnl, Entries 560 and 561, in Monthly Cmd Rpt, 65th Inf, Sep 52.
[60] 2d Bn Staff Jnl, Entry dtd 0930, 21 Sep 52, in Monthly Cmd Rpt, 65th Inf, Sep 52.
[61] Regimental Opns Jnl, Entry dtd 1620, 20 Sep 52, in Monthly Cmd Rpt, 65th Inf, Sep 52.
[62] Regimental Intel Jnl, Entry 589, in Monthly Cmd Rpt, 65th Inf, Sep 52.

By 2000, however, heavy enemy fire forced the platoon to relinquish its gains.[63] Lieutenant Gensemer ordered his men to pull back. His company had 1 killed, 10 wounded, and 16 missing.[64]

As Company E withdrew, the 1st Battalion was making its final preparations to attack Outpost Kelly. At 2015, Company A, commanded by Lieutenant Streett, passed through the 2d Battalion along the main line of resistance and headed for Kelly.[65] Lieutenant Streett, who back in July had made a heroic effort to save his company commander, Lieutenant Wood, during the action near Ch'okko-ri, was a 1949 West Point graduate and had served with the 511th Airborne Infantry at Fort Campbell prior to coming to Korea.[66] When Streett's last platoon cleared the main line of resistance at 2115, Company C, commanded by Lieutenant Stevens, fell in behind Company A.[67] One platoon from Company B was positioned on Tessie and Nick to provide additional support to the assault.

At 2105 on 20 September, almost two days after the outpost fell, the two companies from the 1st Battalion began their assault to recapture Kelly.[68] Company A was hit by Chinese mortar and artillery fire as it advanced toward the hill. Lieutenant Streett noticed that many of his soldiers had fallen out of the main attack formation and were straggling behind. He also noticed that airburst artillery rounds fired by the Chinese were sowing panic among some of his men. Streett decided to fall back and reorganize.[69] Incoming fire directed against Nick and Tessie also forced the platoon from Company B to withdraw.[70]

While Company A regrouped, two understrength platoons from Company C got to within a few hundred feet of Outpost Kelly. At 0100, Major Davies ordered the remainder of Company B to move forward to the main line of resistance and await further orders. As the unit began advancing, it was hit by mortar fire that killed 4, wounded 16, and scattered all but 26 men.[71] Soon afterward, Davies directed the remnants of Company B to return to the battalion assembly area with their casualties.[72] After hastily

---

[63] 2d Bn Staff Jnl, Entry dtd 2000, 20 Sep 52, in Monthly Cmd Rpt, 65th Inf, Sep 52.
[64] 2d Bn Staff Jnl, 20 Sep 52.
[65] Regimental Intel Jnl, Entry 592, in Monthly Cmd Rpt, 65th Inf, Sep 52.
[66] *Register of Graduates and Former Cadets, 1802–1980*, p. 517.
[67] Regimental Intel Jnl, Entry 594, in Monthly Cmd Rpt, 65th Inf, Sep 52.
[68] 2d Bn Staff Jnl, Entry dtd 2110, 20 Sep 52, in Monthly Cmd Rpt, 65th Inf, Sep 52.
[69] 2d Bn Staff Jnl, Entry dtd 2320, 20 Sep 52.
[70] Regimental Intel Jnl, Entries 596–97, in Monthly Cmd Rpt, 65th Inf, Sep 52.
[71] 1st Bn Staff Jnl, Entry 2, 202400 to 212400 Sep 52; 2d Bn Staff Jnl, Entry dtd 0310, 21 Sep 52; both in Monthly Cmd Rpt, 65th Inf, Sep 52.
[72] 1st Bn Staff Jnl, Entry 4, 202400 to 212400 Sep 52, in Monthly Cmd Rpt, 65th Inf, Sep 52.

A howitzer of the 39th Field Artillery Battalion fires in support of the 65th Infantry's counterattack to regain Outpost Kelly.

reorganizing one of its platoons, Company B succeeded in reoccupying Nick and Tessie before daylight.[73]

After U.S. artillery batteries spent the night shelling Outpost Kelly, Companies A and C renewed their assault at 0440 on 21 September.[74] The defenders responded with intense artillery, mortar, and small-arms fire. Company C reached a communications trench at the base of the outpost, where it engaged the Chinese in a grenade battle for thirty minutes before the enemy was forced to retreat.[75] Emboldened by success, the lead platoon of Company C continued its advance, reaching the southern crest of Outpost Kelly at 1130. Heavy mortar fire forced it to return to the communications trench.[76] Mounting losses, which hampered the ability of both company commanders to sustain the assault, prompted Major Davies to

---

[73] Regimental Intel Jnl, Entries 609 and 610, in Monthly Cmd Rpt, 65th Inf, Sep 52.

[74] 2d Bn Staff Jnl, Entry dtd 0440, 21 Sep 52, in Monthly Cmd Rpt, 65th Inf, Sep 52.

[75] Regimental Intel Jnl, Entries 632–34, 21 Sep 52, in Monthly Cmd Rpt, 65th Inf, Sep 52.

[76] Regimental Intel Jnl, Entry 642, 21 Sep 52, in Monthly Cmd Rpt, 65th Inf, Sep 52.

order a complete withdrawal.⁷⁷ The 1st Battalion was back in its preattack positions by late afternoon. The failed attempt to regain the outpost had cost the unit forty-four casualties.⁷⁸

Colonel Cordero-Davila was not yet prepared to concede defeat. Early on the morning of 22 September, Companies A, C, and D relieved Companies K, L, and M on the right wing of the regimental sector. The bulk of the 3d Battalion then moved to an assembly area behind the main line of resistance and prepared to assault the hill. Company I remained in place for a further twenty-four hours before it was relieved by Company B.⁷⁹ Organizing the mission was a new battalion commander, Lt. Col. Lloyd E. Wills, who had replaced Colonel Gendron two days earlier.

Colonel Wills

Wills had enlisted in the Army prior to World War II and had volunteered for the paratroopers after the attack on Pearl Harbor. He jumped into Normandy on D-Day as a master sergeant with the 101st Airborne Division. In recognition of his superior duty performance, Wills received a battlefield commission in late August 1944. Four months later, he was reassigned from regimental staff to become the chief operations officer for the 3d Battalion, 506th Parachute Infantry Regiment. He served in that position throughout the siege of Bastogne until the end of the war.

Following World War II, 39-year-old Wills remained in the Army, attending the Infantry Advanced Officer's Course and the Command and General Staff College between various assignments that included command of three infantry companies.⁸⁰ Given his impressive combat record

---

⁷⁷ Regimental Intel Jnl, Entry 650, 21 Sep 52.

⁷⁸ The regiment recorded seventy-one battle casualties; however, many of them were late entries from Company E. The four Company B soldiers killed by mortar fire are listed by name. Unit Rpt no. 709, in Monthly Cmd Rpt, 65th Inf, Sep 52.

⁷⁹ 3d Bn Staff Jnl, Entries 3–7, 22 Sep 52, and 4, 23 Sep 52, all in Monthly Cmd Rpt, 65th Inf, Sep 52.

⁸⁰ *Official Army Register; Volume I, United States Army Active and Retired Lists, 1 January 1953* (Washington, D.C.: Government Printing Office, 1953), p. 812; DA Form

and postwar accomplishments, it would appear that Wills went to the 65th to make up for the regiment's lack of experienced senior leaders.

As the 3d Battalion drew up plans to recapture Kelly, the problems encountered by the 65th in retaking the outpost had attracted the attention of the corps and division commanders. The first in a succession of visitors, General Dulaney had arrived at the regimental command post on the afternoon of 22 September. The following morning, he appeared again, accompanied by General Kendall. The corps commander informed Cordero-Davila that any plan to recapture Outpost Kelly had to include provision for the immediate supply of barbed wire, entrenching tools, and other fortification materials to ensure adequate defense against counterattack. He also wanted Cordero-Davila to make sure that each man on that hill understood what to do and where to go. Proper execution, Kendall emphasized, would ensure an adequate defense against enemy counterattacks.[81]

Kendall's pointed talk with Cordero-Davila suggested that the I Corps commander felt that the 65th Infantry's leader had not taken enough personal interest in the effort to ensure its success. Kendall's visit may have also encouraged Cordero-Davila to seek extra resources from General Dulaney. Shortly after Kendall departed, indeed, a tank company from the 64th Heavy Tank Battalion arrived to provide direct fire support to the regiment. The 65th also received an additional 4.2-inch mortar platoon from the 15th Infantry.

Having prepared for over thirty-six hours, the 3d Battalion finally launched its assault on Outpost Kelly early on the morning of 24 September. The assault was observed by a number of senior visitors, including General Dulaney and Brig. Gen. Charles L. Dasher, the 3d Division assistant commander.[82] A thirty-minute artillery concentration, supported by direct fire from the regiment's own tank company and from howitzers of the 58th Field Artillery Battalion, preceded the attack. Capt. William C. English's Company K and 1st Lt. Frederick Bogell's Company L moved forward abreast while Company I, under 1st Lt. Ben W. Alpuerto, remained in reserve. Accompanied by two platoons of M46 tanks, the leading companies crossed the line of departure at 0555.[83]

66, Ofcr Qualification Rcd, n.d., sub: Wills, Lloyd Earl—032060, Military Rcds Br, NPRC.

[81] Regimental Opns Jnl, Entries 221500 Sep 52 and 231000 Sep 52, both in Monthly Cmd Rpt, 65th Inf, Sep 52.

[82] Dasher later moved forward to Company F's observation post to observe the assault. Regimental Opns Jnl, Entry dtd 240550 Sep 52, in Monthly Command Rpt, 65th Inf, Sep 52.

[83] Regimental Intel Jnl, Entry 788, in Monthly Cmd Rpt, 65th Inf, Sep 52; 64th Tank Bn, Monthly Cmd Rpt, Sep 52.

Defeat at Outpost Kelly

As Company K approached Outpost Kelly from the east, the Chinese pinned down its leading platoons with small-arms, machine-gun, artillery, and mortar fire. With casualties mounting, confusion broke out within the unit. At 0700, Captain English asked for permission to pull back and reorganize but got a negative reply. Shortly thereafter, at 0720, the battalion lost radio contact with the unit.[84]

Lieutenant Bogell's men meanwhile succeeded in reaching high ground overlooking the outpost, but the Chinese defenders pinned them down. Moments later, an enemy mine blew a track off one of the supporting tanks. Another M46 bogged down trying to recover the disabled vehicle. Efforts to retrieve both M46s proved successful, although Chinese mortar fire killed one man and wounded seven.[85]

Unable to contact Company K, Colonel Cordero-Davila directed Colonel Wills to commit his battalion reserve. Wills ordered Alpuerto's Company I to move forward to assume Company K's mission.[86] As Lieutenant Alpuerto maneuvered his force toward Kelly, enemy artillery zeroed in on his company, fracturing it with several direct hits. The men of Company I began to scatter and to drift back to the regiment's main line. Losing contact with Lieutenant Alpuerto after the enemy artillery strike, Colonel Wills dispatched his battalion operations officer, Capt. Paul O. Engle, to assist Company I. Wills then began to gather up and reorganize stragglers on the battlefield to restore the momentum of the attack.[87]

In the meantime, two squads of Company L clung precariously to a trench on the south slope of Outpost Kelly, pinned down by Chinese artillery, mortar, and automatic-weapons fire. Their commander, Lieutenant Bogell, repeatedly sought permission to withdraw; but Cordero-Davila ordered him to hold at all costs.[88] The only troops available to reinforce Bogell at this point were two reorganized squads from Company I. While Cordero-Davila prepared to commit them, Colonel Wills telephoned General Dasher to inform him of the situation. Having seen extensive combat in World War II, Wills disagreed with his less-experienced regimental commander's decision to send two platoons to seize an objective that three companies had failed to secure. Persuaded by Wills' argument, Dasher bypassed the regimental chain of command and authorized Wills to cease the attack and to continue the reorganization of his unit.[89]

---

[84] 3d Bn Staff Jnl, Entries 12–13, 24 Sep 52, in Monthly Cmd Rpt, 65th Inf, Sep 52.
[85] Monthly Cmd Rpt, 64th Tank Bn, Sep 52.
[86] 3d Bn Staff Jnl, Entry 16, 24 Sep 52, in Monthly Cmd Rpt, 65th Inf, Sep 52.
[87] 3d Bn Staff Jnl, Entry 18, 24 Sep 52; Hermes, *Truce Tent and Fighting Front*, p. 302.
[88] 3d Bn Staff Jnl, Entry 22, 24 Sep 52.
[89] Ibid., Entry 27, 24 Sep 52.

Exhausted men of the 65th Infantry take time out before returning to the battle for Outpost Kelly.

At 1130, what was left of the force on the slope below the crest of Outpost Kelly began to withdraw.[90] "The disintegration of companies 'K' and 'I' was not gradual or orderly," a command report would later note. The executive officer of the 3d Division artillery, Col. Thomas J. Counihan, added that he had personally witnessed "men in full flight . . . without helmets, weapons, or even shirts."[91] In the meantime, General Dulaney himself encountered thirty to fifty stragglers in a similar state of undress moving along what was known as the new road, a recently constructed trail to the northeast of the 65th Infantry's main line.[92] The 3d Battalion returned to its original positions by 1745 on 24 September. It had suffered 141 battle casualties during the attack.[93] At 1500 the following day, the 3d Division suspended all operations by the regiment against Kelly.[94]

---

[90] Opns Narr, in Monthly Cmd Rpt, 65th Inf, Sep 52.
[91] Reorganization of the 3d Inf Div, HQ, 3d Inf Div, 8 Nov 52, in Monthly Cmd Rpt, 3d Inf Div, Nov 52.
[92] Ibid.
[93] Unit Rpt no. 712, in Monthly Cmd Rpt, 65th Inf, Sep 52.
[94] Monthly Cmd Rpt, 65th Inf, Sep 52.

Defeat at Outpost Kelly

Analyzing the Failure

Compounding the disaster at Kelly, the Chinese took Big Nori on 25 September, first probing the position and then attacking with two infantry squads.[95] A platoon from the Greek Battalion, having relieved the 1st Battalion, 65th Infantry, recaptured Big Nori on 27 September; but the outpost fell back into enemy hands later that day after a friendly air strike mistakenly dropped several 1,000-pound bombs on the Greeks, killing one officer and four enlisted men. The dazed and depleted Greek Battalion was forced to withdraw when the Chinese counterattacked in the wake of the bombing. Kelly and Big Nori were the only positions the 3d Division lost during September 1952.[96]

If the battle for Outpost Kelly looked like an uncoordinated affair, it was hard fought nonetheless. The 3d Division expended more than 10,000 rounds of artillery supporting the attack on 24 September.[97] Meanwhile, the 65th Infantry's mortars fired more than 15,000 rounds and the tanks almost 2,400. The infantry went through 400,000 machine-gun and small-arms rounds along with some 8,400 hand grenades.[98] On top of that, Air Force and Navy aircraft flew 113 close air support missions, some 447 sorties, in support of the 65th Infantry between 19 and 30 September. On 19 September alone, Navy F–4U Corsairs and F–9F Panthers, aided by Air Force F–51 Mustangs and F–80 Shooting Stars, flew 63 sorties. At one point, the aircraft dropped a cluster of napalm canisters that engulfed the entire hill in flames and destroyed several Chinese bunkers.[99]

The 65th Infantry suffered 413 battle casualties during September: 352 at Outpost Kelly, including 45 killed and 97 missing.[100] Among the losses were no fewer than 15 officers.[101] This was the highest number of battle losses the 65th had suffered since its arrival in Korea. The regiment's struggle during the period was rewarded with a single Silver Star, won by 2d Lt. Vidal Rodriguez-Amaro.[102]

---

[95] Unit Rpt no. 713, in Monthly Cmd Rpt, 65th Inf, Sep 52.
[96] Monthly Cmd Rpt, 3d Inf Div, Sep 52.
[97] Unit Rpt no. 712.
[98] Monthly Cmd Rpt, 65th Inf, Sep 52.
[99] Monthly Cmd Rpt, 3d Inf Div, Sep 52.
[100] Unit Rpts 689–718, in Monthly Cmd Rpt, 65th Inf, Sep 52. This figure is slightly higher than the number of casualties in the monthly command report summary.
[101] Monthly Cmd Rpt, 65th Inf, Sep 52.
[102] GO no. 373, HQ 3d Inf Div, 21 Dec 52, sub: Award of the Silver Star Medal, 2nd Lieutenant Vidal Rodriguez-Amaro, in Monthly Cmd Rpt, 3d Inf Div, Dec 52. An unknown number of soldiers were later recognized for their valor during the Outpost Kelly battle. See GO no. 190, HQ 3d Division, 16 Jun 53, sub: Award of the Silver Star, 1st Lieutenant Edward P. Behne, Historians files, CMH. Lieutenant Behne's award cites

Despite the high number of casualties, Cordero-Davila rated the morale of his troops as excellent in a report to division at the end of September.[103] Although that may or may not have been true, the battle at Outpost Kelly had unquestionably been a shock to those who had witnessed or participated in the fight. The commander of Company G, Capt. George D. Jackson, later recalled one scene with particular horror:

> Through a brutal trick of psychological warfare, the Chinese allowed mortally wounded Puerto Ricans to leave the outpost within full view of an entire battalion. . . . The sight . . . will forever be indelibly pictured in my mind. One man lost his legs and managed to propel himself [sitting] on a steel helmet. In this position he proceeded slowly and feebly to push himself down the hill with his hands until he finally died.[104]

In his monthly command report, Cordero-Davila attempted to deflect criticism by attributing the failure at Kelly to the problems with the rotation policy rather than to poor training or to substandard leadership.[105] He noted that from January to September 1952 the regiment had rotated eight thousand seven hundred men, more than twice its authorized strength.[106] As a result of this turnover, it had lost many of its combat-experienced personnel at the company and platoon levels and unit cohesion had also suffered.

Cordero-Davila specifically cited a critical shortage of NCOs as a major reason for the setback. Almost fifteen hundred experienced NCOs in the upper three grades (sergeant E–5 to sergeant first class E–7), he said, had departed the regiment in the first nine months of the year. In return, only 435 sergeants had arrived to replace the losses; by September 1952, a number of these men had become casualties. As a result, company commanders were forced to assign inexperienced privates as squad leaders and platoon sergeants, positions normally reserved for staff sergeants and sergeants first class. In many cases, the inexperience and lack of leadership at the squad and platoon levels became only too apparent when the company commanders and platoon leaders were killed or disabled on the battlefield.

Cordero-Davila insisted that the lack of experienced platoon sergeants and corporals had seriously affected the combat efficiency of the regiment. He nonetheless contended that the deficiency was counterbalanced by the regiment's high esprit de corps, "which is motivated by the pride the Puerto

---

his actions as a platoon leader in Company E during the counterattack on 20 September 1952.

[103] Monthly Cmd Rpt, 65th Inf, Sep 52.

[104] Statement, Maj George D. Jackson, 9 Feb 60, sub: Manpower in the 65th Infantry, p. 2, Historians files.

[105] Monthly Cmd Rpt, 65th Inf, Sep 52.

[106] Ibid.

Rican soldiers feel for this unit."[107] To remedy the shortage of skilled manpower, he recommended that the 65th receive a monthly quota of four hundred sergeants with a fair proportion of them from the upper three grades. He also requested that Eighth Army transfer Puerto Rican sergeants from other units to the 65th Infantry "insomuch as no continental NCOs are being assigned to this organization."[108]

The critical shortage of NCOs, however, was hardly unique to the 65th Infantry. The 64th Tank Battalion command report for September 1952 observed:

> The Army-wide ceiling on enlisted promotions has resulted in this organization being short a considerable number of its authorized noncommissioned officer grades. As of the close of the period, the battalion had thirty-four percent of its master sergeant (E–7), forty percent of its Sergeants First Class (E–6), fifty percent of its sergeants (E–5), and seventy percent of its authorized number of corporals (E–4).[109]

An Army Field Forces team surveying conditions in Korea reinforced that observation by noting "a critical shortage of noncommissioned officers of squad leader and platoon sergeant caliber in infantry units."[110] The report went on to note that the Army had failed to provide enough noncommissioned officers to the theater and that many noncommissioned officers who had already served in the war zone were being diverted elsewhere unless they volunteered for combat duty. Finally, many older noncommissioned officers lacked the physical fitness necessary for service with infantry units in Korea. The team added that a lack of qualified officers aggravated the shortage of NCOs.[111]

At the beginning of September, the 65th Infantry had 136 officers on hand versus the 153 it was authorized.[112] The bulk of this shortfall, a total of fifteen positions, was clustered in the rifle companies and platoons.[113] Strangely enough, Cordero-Davila never mentioned the shortage of officers as a factor contributing to the failure of the regiment. Perhaps as with many other Eighth Army regimental commanders, he had learned to accept the problem as a matter beyond repair.

---

[107] Ibid.

[108] Ibid.

[109] 64th Tank Bn, Monthly Cmd Rpt, Sep 52, refers to a complete halt in Army-wide enlisted promotions during 1952 due to budget constraints.

[110] Army Field Forces Combat Obsvr Team no. 7, FEC, Oct–Nov 52, Rcds of U.S. Army Operational, Tactical and Support Organizations (World War II and Thereafter), RG 338, NACP.

[111] Ibid.

[112] Actual Strength as of 1800 on 1 Sep 52 in Monthly Cmd Rpt, 3d Inf Div, Sep 52.

[113] Ibid.

Although Cordero-Davila had not mentioned the language barrier as being a serious problem, it was becoming increasingly difficult for English-speaking officers to communicate with their primarily Spanish-speaking subordinates.[114] Language had not been a major issue in 1950 and early 1951 because most of the officers who served with the regiment during its deployment to Korea were conversant in Spanish. Moreover, many of the NCOs and enlisted men assigned to the regiment during that period were World War II veterans who spoke relatively good English. By the spring of 1952, however, it was clear that the situation had changed. Few of the 65th's replacement officers spoke Spanish, and only a handful of the newly arrived sergeants and enlisted men could communicate in English.

Personnel turbulence, soaring casualty rates, uneven training, and an inability to communicate effectively may have contributed to the 65th's failure to regain Outpost Kelly. It is also clear that Colonel Cordero-Davila's lack of combat experience, manifested most significantly by his inability to coordinate ground maneuver with supporting fires, played a significant role in the fiasco. Colonel Wills' appeal to General Dasher over the head of his regimental commander is ample proof that at least one of Cordero-Davila's battalion commanders lacked confidence in his superior's abilities. Dasher's decision to overrule Cordero-Davila indicates that some within the 3d Infantry Division headquarters had their doubts as well.

A divisional report after the battle noted, "There was much to indicate that Colonel Cordero was not a disciplinarian."[115] General Kendall, the I Corps commander, had also formed a poor initial impression. Describing the regimental commander's behavior during the battle for Outpost Kelly, he wrote: "Cordero became . . . [so] nervous that . . . [by] the end of the action he was utterly incapable of commanding his regiment. His speech was incoherent and his judgment was utterly futile." Kendall added that Cordero-Davila was "incapable of properly commanding a regiment of infantry in combat" and recommended his relief from command.[116]

General Van Fleet acted quickly on Kendall's request, sending a letter to General Clark, head of the Far East Command, voicing his own concerns about Cordero-Davila. "My review of the recent fighting involving the 65th Infantry and my visits to the unit," he said, "convince me beyond doubt that the 65th Infantry Regiment has retrogressed [*sic*] in combat fitness under Colonel Cordero-Davila's leadership and that he does not have the leader-

---

[114] Hermes, *Truce Tent and Fighting Front*, p. 303.
[115] Ltr, CG, 3d Inf Div, to CG, IX Corps, 8 Nov 52, in Monthly Cmd Rpt, 3d Inf Div, Nov 52.
[116] Ltr, Kendall to Van Fleet, 30 Sep 52, Van Fleet Papers.

ship or professional capacity to reestablish acceptable standards."[117] Van Fleet recommended the relief of both Cordero-Davila and Dulaney soon afterward. Clark concurred.

On 8 October 1952, Maj. Gen. George W. Smythe replaced General Dulaney as the 3d Division commander. The 53-year-old Smythe was a 1920 West Point graduate who had served with the 33d Infantry in the Panama Canal Zone in 1932 and during World War II had commanded the 47th Infantry, 9th Division, in North Africa, Sicily, and Europe. He ended that war as assistant commander of the 80th Division. Prior to taking over the 3d Division, Smythe had spent the previous six months commanding the 24th Division in Japan.[118]

In the second major change for the 65th Infantry, Colonel Cordero-Davila stepped down as regimental commander on 11 October.[119] "I am very proud of having commanded such a group of loyal, brave, and aggressive fighters," Cordero-Davila would later remark during an interview with *Stars and Stripes*. "It is with regret that I leave them. I shall pray that God will protect and guide them in their future actions."[120] He returned to Puerto Rico as a hero and resumed his position as the executive director of the Puerto Rican Housing Authority.[121]

In a letter to the former I Corps commander, Lt. Gen. John W. O'Daniel, General Van Fleet observed that the 65th Infantry at Outpost Kelly "simply didn't have the stuff." While he felt that Cordero-Davila had failed as a combat commander, Van Fleet also spread the blame to Cordero-Davila's superior, General Dulaney. "It became necessary to relieve the 3d Division with the 1st South Korean Division," wrote Van Fleet, "which actually has proved to be a better unit. The 3d got steadily worse under Dulaney and a number of his subordinates, who didn't seem to have the drive to keep it sharp. Their bayonets got awfully rusty after your departure. The Division is now under George Smythe and is making a fast comeback."[122]

"I am sorry to hear about the 65th, but I was not surprised since I was never too sure of its former commanding officer," O'Daniel responded:

---

[117] Msg, 301405Z Sep 52, Van Fleet to Clark, Eighth U.S. Army, Entry 429, Rcds of the AGO, RG 407, NACP.

[118] "Major General George Winfered Smythe, USA," Department of Defense (DoD) Ofc of Public Information Bio Memo, n.d., Historians files.

[119] GO no. 40, HQ 65th Inf, 11 Oct 52, Rcds of U.S. Army Operational, Tactical and Support Organizations (World War II and Thereafter), RG 338, NACP.

[120] "Puerto Rican CO Lauds Islands' Fighting Forces," *Pacific Stars and Stripes*, 5 Nov 52, copy in Historians files.

[121] "General de División Juan Cesar Cordero Davila (1958–1965)," in Jose Angel Norat, *Guardia Nacional de Puerto Rico: Historia y Tradiciones* (San Juan: Guardia Nacional de Puerto Rico, 1987), pp. 476–79.

[122] Ltr, Van Fleet to O'Daniel, 20 Oct 52, Van Fleet Papers.

The rest of the division, however, I imagined has been doing its stuff in a passable manner, although that isn't as good as one expects of the 3d. Bob Dulaney, I thought when I left there, was fighting his problems rather than solving them and I told him so. With his background, he certainly should have done a better job than he did. I am afraid he developed a swelled head and was somewhat bull-headed. That may account for his missing some of the things that he should have seen and done.[123]

Despite the departures of Dulaney and Cordero-Davila, many problems remained with the 65th and some of its toughest days still lay in the future.

---

[123] Ibid.

Chapter 10

COLLAPSE AT JACKSON HEIGHTS
OCTOBER 1952

On 1 October 1952, the 3d Division passed from the operational control of I Corps to IX Corps, the latter commanded by Lt. Gen. Reuben E. Jenkins. The month opened with the 3d Division in reserve near Yongp'yong, sixteen miles south of Ch'orwon. Under the leadership of General Smythe, the 3d Division embarked on a 21-day intensive training cycle aimed at welding units into "confident, hard hitting teams, capable of successfully accomplishing any assigned missions."[1] The first five days were devoted to administration, resupply, and inspections. The following two weeks were devoted to tactical training.

According to the division's master schedule, sixty hours of training were to occur each week. The effort would begin at the squad and section levels and culminate with a field problem focusing on the battalion combat team in the attack. The exercise would emphasize combined-arms tactics that incorporated the use of both infantry and tank weapons.[2]

In the end, some of the battalion field problems had to be canceled because the 3d Division received orders to relieve the South Korean 9th Division earlier than planned. The combined-arms training that did occur proved to be of marginal use because both the 3d Division Artillery and its 64th Heavy Tank Battalion were serving elsewhere under the operational control of I Corps. Furthermore, the lack of regulation firing ranges at the division's training camp limited efforts to improve marksmanship.[3]

When the 65th Infantry went back into action, it did so with a new commander, Col. Chester B. De Gavre.[4] The 45-year-old De Gavre, who

---

[1] Monthly Cmd Rpt, 3d Inf Div, Oct 52. Unless otherwise noted, all Cmd Rpts are in Entry 429, Rcds of the AGO, RG 407, NACP.
[2] Ibid.
[3] Recommendations Narr, in Monthly Cmd Rpt, 3d Inf Div, Oct 52.
[4] GO no. 40, 11 Oct 52, 65th Inf, General Orders, Rcds of U.S. Army Operational, Tactical, and Support Organizations (World War II and Thereafter), RG 338, NACP.

took over from Colonel Cordero-Davila on 11 October, was a 1933 West Point graduate who had attended the Infantry School, the Command and General Staff College, and the Armed Forces Staff College. He had served with the 65th Infantry as the regimental headquarters company commander between 1937 and 1939.

De Gavre, who learned Spanish while he was with the regiment, left Puerto Rico in 1939 to become one of the first U.S. Army officers to take parachute training. He then joined the staff of the Airborne Command at Fort Bragg under Maj. Gen. William C. Lee. During World War II, he had served as the chief of staff of the 1st Allied Airborne Task Force, participating in the Italian campaign and Operation Dragoon landings in southern France. Prior to taking over the 65th Infantry, he had briefly served as the X Corps chief personnel officer.[5]

De Gavre had lobbied for command of the regiment upon learning of Cordero-Davila's impending departure. His previous assignment with the regiment had left a very good impression:

> It was highly respected and fathers and sons and grandfathers had been in the regiment. And so in that respect it was a very prestigious position and place to be and I enjoyed it. The old non-coms were terrific people. They were professional all the way and their hearts were in the right place. They wanted to do a good job. They were eager to have their children and grandchildren become good soldiers and it was a good organization, I thought.[6]

When De Gavre arrived at the regiment, he realized things had changed dramatically. "When I got there, there were none of the Puerto Ricans that spoke English except a few of the old NCOs and, very fortunately, a few of the officers I had served with in Puerto Rico years ago," he later told historian Clay Blair. "My adjutant . . . was a very good friend of mine named Silvestre E. Ortiz, who was a lieutenant in my headquarters company when I was [previously stationed] down there." As for the enlisted soldiers themselves, "The recruits didn't speak any English," he remarked. "They didn't do anything, know anything or care about much." The bulk of the officers were "American," meaning continental. There were only "a very few Puerto Ricans, some very good ones and some poor ones."[7]

---

[5] *Register of Graduates and Former Cadets, 1802–1980*, p. 389; "Brigadier General Chester Braddock De Gavre," Department of Defense Office of Public Information Bio Memo, 14 Aug 58, Historians files, CMH.

[6] Interv, Clay Blair with Chester B. De Gavre, n.d., Clay and Joan Blair Collection, MHI.

[7] Ibid.

The views of Captain Jackson, the Company G commander and a veteran of Outpost Kelly, seemed to confirm De Gavre's first impression. In his opinion, many of the enlisted soldiers in the 65th were poorly motivated, lacking strong NCO leadership and behaving accordingly. Jackson recalled:

> After 'Kelly Hill' command of these young soldiers became extremely difficult. Their nervousness was evidenced by firing in the darkness at nothing and throwing hand grenades at every sound in front of the main defensive line. Problems were encountered in maintaining out-guards (listening posts) and patrols—especially in the platoons which had no officer leader.[8]

Although a number of new replacements arrived in October, the strength of the 65th Infantry dropped from 3,926 at the beginning of the month to 3,774 by its end. Acknowledging the shortage of NCOs, Eighth Army sent to the regiment 2 master sergeants (E–7), 6 sergeants first class (E–6), and 16 sergeants (E–5).[9] While De Gavre welcomed the additional NCOs, many of the newcomers lacked combat experience and the leadership abilities of some had yet to be tested. Meanwhile, a shortage of officers continued to plague the 65th. Of the 153 officers authorized, the unit had only 125 on hand, a net shortage of 28. This reduced the availability of company grade officers to supervise and conduct unit training.[10]

On 13 October 1952, two days after assuming command, Colonel De Gavre ordered everyone in the unit to get a haircut and shave. The troops were also prohibited from wearing mustaches "until such a time as they gave proof of their manhood."[11] "I gave some fast and hard thought to this and the decision was hard," he told Blair:

> The first thing I decided to do was to shape this outfit up and bring it back to Jesus, so to speak. They all had long hair, they all had mustaches and beards and I said "This has got to end right now. This regiment is going to shave clean by Monday morning." Well, that didn't set well at all.[12]

The order provoked a strong response from the officers and men. "I objected," Colonel Betances-Ramirez, the 2d Battalion commander,

---

[8] Statement, Maj George D. Jackson, 16 Feb 60, sub: The Battle for Jackson Heights, Historians files.

[9] Unit Rpt no. 739, in Monthly Cmd Rpt, 65th Inf, Oct 52.

[10] Monthly Cmd Rpt, 65th Inf, Oct 52.

[11] Memo, Lt Col Carlos Betances-Ramirez, 12 Sep 98, sub: Analysis and Comments of the 3d Division's Staff Study dated 8 Nov 52, Historians files; Regimental Personnel Jnl, Entry 131400 Oct 52, in Monthly Cmd Rpt, 65th Inf, Oct 52.

[12] Interv, Blair with De Gavre, n.d.

recalled. "Placing in doubt a soldier's manhood was, in my opinion, the ultimate insult."[13] Betances-Ramirez was not alone in his objection. "The chaplains came to me and said that I was going to be murdered within 24 hours if I persisted in this order," De Gavre told Clay Blair.[14] Nonetheless, he issued the order. "It got done and I wasn't murdered."[15]

To many in the regiment, the order suggested that the new commander lacked cultural sensitivity. Yet, Colonel De Gavre had previously served with the regiment for two years and had taken the measure of the men and their NCOs. There was little question in General Smythe's mind that discipline in the 65th had seriously lapsed under Colonel Cordero-Davila.

In addition to the shave order, De Gavre issued directives to improve the conduct and appearance of his soldiers. A memorandum published shortly after he took command offered insights into his command philosophy. "The following practices," he wrote, "are considered unsuitable for military personnel and will be discontinued immediately."[16] The list included "haphazard" lacing of boots; carving on the stocks of weapons; wrapping towels, rags, or other material around rifles and carbines; and wearing towels, jacket hoods, and caps under steel helmets.[17]

"We started to shape it up in every way that you can imagine," De Gavre later told Blair, "saluting, haircuts, [shining] boots . . . [the regiment also] stopped the vandalizing and throwing away their weapons." His remark referred to reports of soldiers who were on patrol discarding rifles after encountering the enemy so they would not be burdened when they ran to the rear. "You can't believe the things that went on," De Gavre said, "but I did everything possible to shape it up."[18]

By demanding that his men improve their personal appearance and the condition of their equipment, De Gavre hoped to persuade Smythe that the 65th Infantry was capable of adhering to the same standards of military courtesy and discipline exhibited by the 7th and 15th Infantries. He also realized that the chain of command would not tolerate the 65th maintaining a separate identity as long as the regiment continued to perform poorly in combat. Additionally, by easing concerns within the division, De Gavre

---

[13] Ltr, Lt Col Carlos Betances-Ramirez, 12 Sep 98, sub: Analysis and Comments of the Third Division's Staff Study dated 8 Nov 52, p. 9, Historians files.

[14] Interv, Blair with De Gavre, n.d.

[15] Ibid.

[16] Memo, Regimental Personnel Jnl, 19 Oct 52, sub: Personnel Conduct and Appearance, in Monthly Cmd Rpt, 65th Inf, Oct 52.

[17] Ibid.

[18] Interv, Blair with De Gavre, n.d.

hoped to minimize interference as he went about rehabilitating the regiment's reputation.

On 1 October 1952, the 65th Infantry embarked on an intensive training program at Changmol, ten miles southeast of Ch'orwon, to correct its many shortcomings. The regiment spent the first five days reconditioning equipment, resupplying units, and holding inspections. On 6 October, the 65th embarked on what was to have been a comprehensive training cycle; but restrictions on high-angle firing announced by the 3d Division that very day prevented any live-fire mortar practice from occurring for the next three days.[19] Then, on 9 October, the 65th had to share the firing ranges with the Belgian Battalion, which was conducting 81-mm. mortar and 75-mm. recoilless-rifle firing in the area. A division ordnance inspection the following day created yet another disruption.[20] To make matters worse, the regiment received word that, as a result of theaterwide shortages caused by recent heavy fighting, it would receive no ammunition that it could use for training.[21]

Understandably, the 65th's battalion and company commanders complained that without ammunition their unit training "lacked realism."[22] Some also lamented that the quality of training suffered immensely because company commanders and platoon leaders lacked the time to prepare their lessons properly.[23]

Perhaps as a result of these complaints, company commanders received additional assistance from the regimental staff during the second week of training. "This was most productive," Captain Jackson remembered, "as we were able to concentrate on weaknesses that had become apparent at 'Kelly Hill.'"[24] Jackson's unit, Company G, for example, focused on countering enemy assault tactics by learning how to detect and destroy Chinese forces at the maximum possible distance. Jackson also instituted night-attack competitions in which one of his platoons would defend a position while another tried to take it. He hoped these exercises would instill aggressiveness in his soldiers while also revealing weaknesses in how they responded to attacks. In particular, he stressed that a properly defended outpost required listening posts stationed along every avenue of approach.[25]

---

[19] 2d Bn Staff Jnl, Entry dtd 1130, 7 Oct 52, in Monthly Cmd Rpt, 65th Inf, Oct 52.
[20] 2d Bn Staff Jnl, Entry no. 2, 8 Oct 52, in Monthly Cmd Rpt, 65th Inf, Oct 52.
[21] Unit Rpt no. 728, in Monthly Cmd Rpt, 65th Inf, Oct 52.
[22] Unit Rpts nos. 731–35, in Monthly Cmd Rpt, 65th Inf, Oct 52.
[23] Statement, Maj George D. Jackson, 9 Feb 60, sub: Manpower in the 65th Inf Regt, p. 3, Historians files, CMH.
[24] Ibid.
[25] Ibid., pp. 3–4.

Despite the lack of ammunition for training, the 65th pressed on with company and battalion field exercises on 16 and 17 October while operating under division control. Ammunition finally became available on the last day of the training cycle, prompting the regiment to extend its program through 20 October in order to conduct live-fire exercises.[26]

In light of the swampy and unhealthy conditions at the training camp, the restrictions on live-fire exercises, the various inspections imposed by division headquarters, and the lack of small-arms ammunition for most of the period, it is not surprising that the 65th got less than optimum results from the October training cycle. Although some units, such as Captain Jackson's Company G, used the period productively, the regiment as a whole still had much work to do before it regained its former confidence and combat proficiency.

Taking stock of the situation, Captain Jackson concluded that many of the sergeants in the 65th Infantry were still unprepared to carry out their duties during intense combat: "We needed more time to select and [instruct] untrained personnel for supervisory duties of NCOs. For example, we selected one of the recruits to be a squad leader based upon his outstanding work ethic, especially for digging emplacements." That young squad leader would go insane as a result of the stress of constant incoming artillery fire during G Company's next major engagement.[27]

The 3d Division's reserve period coincided with a series of small-scale Communist attacks aimed at seizing key terrain in Eighth Army's western and central sectors. On 5 October, the Chinese attacked the South Korean 9th Division on White Horse Mountain, five miles northwest of Ch'orwon. The 9th Division soldiers repulsed the attack as they did two subsequent assaults. Enemy troops also launched a major attack against the French Battalion on Hill 281, just southwest of White Horse Mountain, to draw off reinforcements that might otherwise have been sent to aid the South Koreans. After seven days of fighting, the Chinese failed to take either White Horse Mountain or its satellite, Hill 281, although they did seize an outpost on Hill 391, seven miles northeast of White Horse Mountain near the boundary between the 9th Division and U.S. 7th Division. Hill 391 constituted the southern portion of a larger hill mass known as Iron Horse Mountain (Hill 388). Both the peak of Iron Horse Mountain, almost three miles to the north of Jackson Heights, and Camel Back Mountain (Hill 488), one-and-three-quarters miles to the northeast, dominated the allied outpost.[28]

When the South Koreans retreated, they left behind 2d Lt. Eugene R. Barno, a forward observer with the 7th Division's 49th Field Artillery Battalion

---

[26] Unit Rpts nos. 736–39, in Monthly Cmd Rpt, 65th Inf, Oct 52.

[27] Interv, author with George D. Jackson, 3 Jun 00, Historians files, CMH.

[28] Statement, Maj George D. Jackson, 9 Feb 60, sub: Terrain Analysis, Jackson Heights, p. 1, Historians files.

Aerial view of Jackson Heights (Hill 391) as seen from the south. Friendly defensive positions are visible in the lower center of the photograph.

collocated with the South Koreans on Jackson Heights, and his reconnaissance sergeant. The commanding general of the 7th Division ordered the 17th Infantry to immediately launch a company-size counterattack to rescue the stranded Americans. Maj. Earl C. Acuff's 1st Battalion, 17th Infantry, received the mission. The regimental operations officer, Capt. Harold G. Moore Jr., informed Acuff that Company G from the 2d Battalion would be attached to his unit.[29]

---

[29] 1st Lt Robert E. Whedon, "Recapture of a ROKA Outpost, 12–13 October 1952," Mil Hist Detachment, 8086th Army Unit, Army Forces Far East, Historical Reference Collection, CMH.

As Acuff's men prepared for the counterattack, Lieutenant Barno transmitted a message to the 49th Field Artillery Battalion's fire-direction center asking them to plaster the hill with high-explosive shells timed to explode twenty to forty yards in the air. He hoped the shelling would discourage enemy efforts to locate surviving members of the South Korean garrison but spare the lives of friendly soldiers trying to avoid capture by hiding in a bunker. The ploy was partially successful. Barno later recalled:

> About this time, a Chinese patrol of four men came to the bunker [where he was hiding]. One of them squatted down and tried to look in. . . . I raised my carbine and pulled the trigger. It didn't go off. The four scrambled to the top of the bunker, talking excitedly. They dropped a grenade at my feet. It went off and I wasn't hit. A second, and I think a third, were dropped at my feet and I still wasn't hit. . . . I threw the only grenade I had about ten feet from me. The blast hit my left eye and shrapnel hit my left hand. I could hear groaning on top of the bunker. A few moments later, a VT [variable time] round came in directly over the bunker. No more groans. Silence.[30]

At 0315 on 13 October, the 17th Infantry's Company G, led by several South Korean guides, began making its way toward Hill 391. When the company reached a point approximately seven hundred fifty yards south of its objective, the unit commander, 1st Lt. Thomas H. Maddox, deployed his recoilless rifles and mortars in a support position near a friendly outpost known as the Sandbag Castle. Maddox's infantry platoons were able to reach the base of the hill before they were spotted. A firefight broke out as the Chinese stubbornly contested Maddox's attack. By late morning, however, the Americans had fought their way almost to the crest. The attackers located Barno, slightly wounded but alive, a short while later. His reconnaissance sergeant had already succeeded in making his way to South Korean lines. As the Americans consolidated their positions, increasing Chinese artillery fire forced Maddox to call for a smoke screen to conceal his men from enemy observation. The shelling tapered off slightly, but enemy artillery rounds continued to land nearby despite the lack of visibility.

When Maddox's troops ran low on ammunition, the 7th Division used several liaison aircraft to drop supplies to the unit. Reinforced during the afternoon by a platoon of Company E, Maddox held Hill 391 against a Chinese counterattack. At dusk, the 7th Company of the South Korean 51st Infantry exchanged places with the Americans. Maddox's unit had lost one man killed and twenty-three wounded. Hill 388, immediately north of Hill 391, remained in enemy hands.[31]

---

[30] Gene Barno, "My Army Experiences, 1951–1953," Mar 95, Historians files.
[31] Whedon, "Recapture of a ROKA Outpost," p. 44.

The attacks on the Eighth Army line north of Ch'orwon prompted Van Fleet to authorize Operation SHOWDOWN, which began on 14 October 1952. His goal was to seize a series of enemy-held hills and ridges in the Iron Triangle from which the Communists were raiding allied outposts. Van Fleet gave the mission to the U.S. 7th Division and to elements of the South Korean 2d Division. After eleven days of fierce fighting, the allies gained most of their objectives but at a heavier cost than expected. When the operation ended on 25 October, the Chinese were already making preparations to regain the territory they had lost.

Defense and Loss of Jackson Heights

The IX Corps headquarters ordered the 3d Division to relieve the South Korean 9th Division in the sector between Ch'orwon and Kumhwa on the night of 24–25 October. General Smythe deployed the 7th Infantry and the Belgian Battalion to defend the western half of the divisional front. The 65th Infantry and the 3d Reconnaissance Company took responsibility for the eastern wing. The 2d Battalion, 15th Infantry, acted as the division reserve, while the remainder of the 15th Infantry and the Greek Battalion became the IX Corps reserve.[32]

Opposite the 7th Infantry was the *341st Regiment* of the Chinese *44th Division* deployed on the front line and the *340th* and *342d Regiments* standing in reserve. The Chinese *87th Regiment* of the *29th Division* faced the 65th Infantry. Although the enemy units had suffered considerable losses during the previous month, their overall quality was thought to be good.[33]

American intelligence estimated that the Chinese had deployed sixteen battalions of artillery against the 3d Division. They were capable of delivering heavy and effective fire up to seven-and-a-half miles to the rear of the division's main line and "very heavy effective concentrations on short notice" against the line itself.[34] Overall, the Communists had continued to develop their defensive positions "with vast improvements . . . across the line of contact."[35] These included layered strong points and interconnected trenches, vehicle obstacles, and new minefields along likely avenues of approach to counter American tanks. The latter was significantly important because the terrain in that sector was fairly open when compared to the rest of Korea.

When the 65th moved into position at the front on 24 October, relieving the South Korean 51st Infantry, it took responsibility for a section of

---

[32] Monthly Cmd Rpt, 3d Inf Div, Oct 52.
[33] Ibid.
[34] Ibid.
[35] Ibid.

the line that began seven miles north of Ch'orwon and ended a few miles northwest of Kumhwa.[36] Colonel De Gavre placed two battalions forward and one battalion to the rear. Colonel Willis' 3d Battalion defended the western half of the regimental sector. Company I stood on the left, Company K in the center, and Company L on the right. Company M, the heavy-weapons unit, was located in a reserve position about one-half mile behind Company L. Capt. Theodore L. Alvarez sited his regimental headquarters company four miles behind the 3d Battalion. With it were Captain Grevillius' regimental tank company and Captain Burke's regimental heavy mortar company.[37]

Betances-Ramirez's 2d Battalion and the 3d Reconnaissance Company held the eastern flank of the regimental sector with Lieutenant Gensemer's Company E on the left and Capt. Willis D. Cronkhite Jr.'s Company F on the right. Capt. Francis L. Champoux's Company H, the battalion heavy-weapons unit, stood in reserve behind Company F.[38] Captain Jackson's Company G occupied a forward outpost on high ground approximately one mile north of Company F's position on the main line of resistance. Maj. Albert C. Davies' 1st Battalion, the regimental reserve, occupied a position one-and-a-half miles to the rear of the 2d Battalion.

Company G assumed control of Hill 391 (soon dubbed Jackson Heights after the name of its company commander) late in the night of 24–25 October, taking over from the 7th Company of the South Korean 2d Battalion, 51st Regiment.[39] Within Company G, 2d Lt. Lowell M. Davis commanded the 1st Platoon, 2d Lt. Angel L. Carrion-Maldonado led the 2d Platoon, and 2d Lt. Henry A. Brown was in charge of the 3d Platoon. First Lt. Manuel Rodriguez-Rodriguez had the weapons platoon.[40] Captain Jackson regarded Davis and Rodriguez-Rodriguez as solid performers in battle. Lieutenant Carrion-Maldonado was an unknown, having joined the company only a few days earlier. Brown was hampered by an injury and unable to contribute much, but he did not want to sit around in the rear while his unit was on the outpost.[41]

---

[36] Opns and Intel Staff Jnl, 230001 to 242400 Oct 52, in Monthly Cmd Rpt, 65th Inf, Oct 52.

[37] Map Overlay for Unit Rpt no. 724, 231800–241800 Oct 52, in Monthly Cmd Rpt, 65th Inf, Oct 52.

[38] Champoux had served as a rifle company commander in the 101st Airborne Division's 327th Glider Infantry Regiment during World War II. He transferred from the 187th Regimental Combat Team (Airborne) to the 65th Infantry.

[39] *Pacific Stars and Stripes* originated and popularized the term Jackson Hill. Today, Jackson Heights is located just north of the Military Demarcation Line. See Hermes, *Truce Tent and Fighting Front*, p. 307.

[40] Interv, author with George D. Jackson, 30 Jul 01, Historians files.

[41] Ibid.

As Jackson settled his unit into the position, he reflected on the situation. "The outpost," mused Jackson, "was located in the midst of Chinese territory. There was scarcely a spot in it that was not covered by constant enemy observation. Though I never pinpointed the enemy's observation on the west, it was effective."[42] Two principal avenues of approach, one from the north and the other from the southwest, were the most likely routes the Chinese would use when attacking the outpost.

Jackson Heights was at least two thousand yards in front of the main line, which placed it beyond the range of most of the heavy weapons organic to an infantry battalion. "Our 81-mm. mortars," recorded the Company G commander, "could

Captain Cronkhite

barely reach the rear of the outpost with HE [high explosive] from their firing positions behind the main line. The 4.2-inch mortars of regiment [located even farther to the rear] were of little assistance also. It was pretty well resolved before I took off for the relief that the fire support for this outpost would be my own organic [infantry] weapons and the artillery."[43]

As the South Koreans withdrew, they left behind approximately six hundred rounds of 60-mm. mortar ammunition. They also left a communications trench, several well-maintained bunkers that would be used for the command posts of each infantry platoon, the company command post, and a separate bunker for the attached 58th Field Artillery Battalion forward observer. The remaining fortifications, however, were in unsatisfactory condition, with the 2d Platoon's positions in the worst shape. In addition to the handful of fighting bunkers, there were some caves in the 3d Platoon area that could be employed as makeshift defensive positions that offered some measure of protection against incoming fire.[44]

---

[42] Ibid.

[43] Statement, Maj George D. Jackson, 9 Feb 60, sub: The Battle for Jackson Heights, p. 1, Historians files.

[44] App. B, Narr of Opns, n.d., sub: Informal Discussion Between Colonel De Gavre, Lt. Col. Root, and Captain Jackson concerning the sequence of vents [sic] on Jackson Heights . . ., in Monthly Cmd Rpt, 65th Inf, Oct 52.

Captain Jackson observed that even though much was needed in the way of building materials, "the resupply situation was [so precarious] . . . that all we were able to get was rations, water, grenades and flares. Resupply of the outpost was extremely hazardous."[45] The barbed wire and mines that existing maps showed as surrounding the position did not exist, and they were not projected to arrive anytime soon.[46]

At 1100 on 25 October, the Chinese began to shell Jackson Heights from Camel Back Mountain with 76-mm. guns, seriously wounding three soldiers with the first three rounds.[47] The Chinese guns, which had been shelling the allied position for the past several weeks, were capable of hitting virtually anywhere on the hilltop with their opening shots. The shelling continued throughout the day, with the Chinese firing some two hundred fifty artillery and mortar rounds that wounded six more Americans.[48] Company G could do little more than hunker down and take the punishment.

The fire continued through the night. Company G responded with a steady stream of illumination flares to keep the Communists from approaching on foot. Chinese patrols nonetheless probed the unit's positions at 0320 but withdrew after a five-minute firefight. Two more of Jackson's men fell during the brief skirmish.[49] Ten minutes later, listening posts detected several Chinese platoons approaching Jackson Heights on both flanks. (*Map 12*) Supporting artillery engaged the force on the western flank while Jackson's own 60-mm. mortar section fired to the east. The protective barrage soon forced the enemy to retreat.[50] Later that morning, a burst of sniper fire took down one more American.[51]

"The next morning," wrote Jackson, "we found out the extent and effect of the enemy's observation. While preparing fortifications, the enemy clobbered us with much artillery, which resulted in several casualties. I then determined that we would work on fortifications at dawn and dusk, have [a] 100% alert at night, and try to rest during the day with squad security only."[52] Chinese activity for most of 26 October was confined to intermittent artillery and mortar fire with the exception of an hour-long barrage in the late afternoon that mortally wounded one soldier. At 2125, Company G listening posts reported sounds of digging to their

---
[45] Ibid.
[46] Statement, Jackson, 9 Feb 60, p. 2.
[47] 2d Bn Opns Jnl, Entry 8 dtd 1350, 25 Oct 52, Unit Rpt for Oct 52, in Monthly Cmd Rpt, 65th Inf, Oct 52.
[48] 2d Bn Opns Jnl, Entry 13 dtd 1850, 25 Oct 52, in Monthly Cmd Rpt, 65th Inf, Oct 52.
[49] Ibid., entry dtd 0320, 26 Oct 52.
[50] Informal Discussion, De Gavre, Root, and Jackson.
[51] 2d Bn Staff Jnl, Entry 18 dtd 0600, 26 Oct 52, in Monthly Cmd Rpt, 65th Inf, Oct 52.
[52] Statement, Jackson, 16 Feb 60, p. 2.

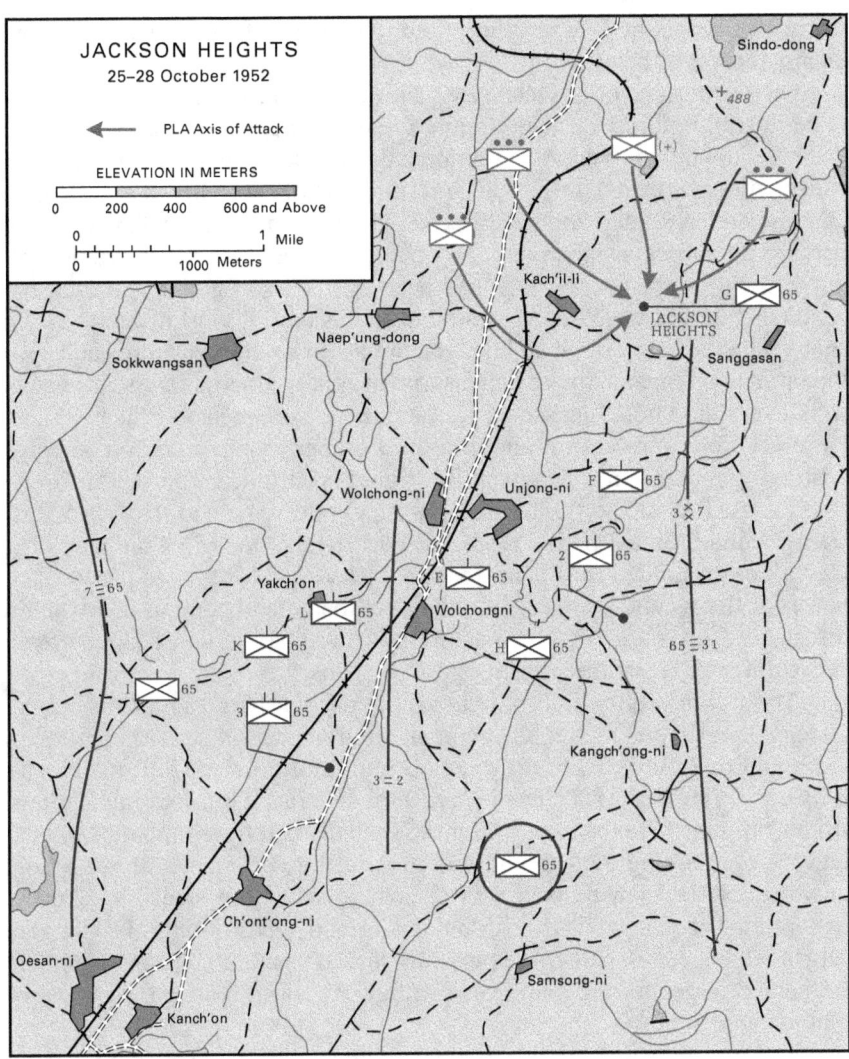

MAP 12

front. The defenders responded with small-arms and mortar fire, which temporarily forced the enemy to abandon his efforts. A few minutes later, a listening post on the company's southwest flank reported the approach of Chinese soldiers and then engaged them with grenades.[53] Throughout

---

[53] The 2d Battalion Staff Journal puts the time at 2150. See Entry 32 for 26 Oct 52; Informal Discussion, De Gavre, Root, and Jackson.

the rest of the night, U.S. artillery fired in support of Company G to keep enemy patrols at bay.

On the morning of 27 October, a Chinese platoon attacked the Company G perimeter, igniting a fifteen-minute firefight. The Americans detected an enemy company moving up to reinforce the attack and engaged it with grenades, mortar fire, and artillery. The resulting explosions killed at least two Chinese and wounded another fifteen.[54] The Communists retaliated with a barrage much heavier than any they had delivered over the previous two days. Locating the enemy guns had been difficult so far, Captain Jackson recalled, "but was absolutely impossible on this day."[55] Most of Company G sought shelter in the sandbag bunkers, but at least two men from each platoon remained outside to prevent a surprise attack. "Incoming rounds came from every direction," Jackson said, "and there were plenty of them."[56]

At 0935, a mortar round hit the company's ammunition supply, destroying much of it. Lieutenant Rodriguez-Rodriguez reported that only about a quarter of the 60-mm. mortar stockpile remained. By 1245, the enemy bombardment had wounded at least twelve men in Company G.[57] Casualties continued to mount, forcing Jackson at 1700 to request assistance for the wounded, whose growing numbers had begun to overwhelm his medics. He received a response from the 2d Battalion headquarters: "Be calm, aid [is] on the way."[58]

About the same time, Lieutenant Rodriguez-Rodriguez informed Jackson that several men in the company mortar section had become casualties and that only two of his three 60-mm. mortars were still working.[59] Between 1730 and 1800, enemy artillery severed wire communications from Company G to the rear. A Chinese shell also hit the command bunker, leaving only a single NCO and one man in the communications section unwounded. Jackson himself was elsewhere when the shell hit. Shortly thereafter, Lieutenant Carrion-Maldonado also went down. His platoon sergeant had been wounded the previous day, so Captain Jackson appointed the senior sergeant in the company, M.Sgt. Belisario Noriega, as the new platoon leader.[60]

At 1800, the enemy intensified shelling and Jackson ordered his men into fighting positions, believing that a ground attack was imminent. His

---

[54] 2d Bn Staff Jnl, Unit Rpt for Oct, Entry 5, 27 Oct 52, in Monthly Cmd Rpt, 65th Inf, Oct 52.

[55] Statement, Jackson, 9 Feb 60, p. 2.

[56] Ibid.

[57] 2d Bn Staff Jnl, Entries 18–21, 27 Oct 52, in Monthly Cmd Rpt, 65th Inf, Oct 52.

[58] Informal Discussion, De Gavre, Root, and Jackson.

[59] Statement, Jackson, 9 Feb 60, p. 3.

[60] Ibid.; Interv, author with Jackson, 30 Jul 01.

intuition proved correct, for the Chinese soon launched a reinforced company-size attack from the north. Company G fought back with small-arms and automatic-weapons fire, inflicting numerous losses upon the attackers and forcing them to withdraw.

Late that night, Company G detected Communist troops moving to the east and west of its position in large numbers. Up to this point, the American use of listening posts to provide early warning, followed by liberal doses of artillery and mortar fire, had sufficed to keep the enemy in check. Jackson expected to use the same method; but when he called for fire against the Chinese, he was told that his company had been allocated only one hundred rounds of illumination and high explosive for the night. "This was the time, you will remember, of the big ammunition shortage in Korea," recalled Jackson in frustration, "economy was the rule of the day."[61]

Between 2035 and 2100, the Chinese hit Jackson Heights with a tremendous artillery and mortar barrage, immediately followed by a two-company ground attack.[62] Company G responded with small-arms fire and its one functioning 60-mm. mortar. An enemy shell hit the ammunition depot a second time, however, sowing confusion among the defenders.

With casualties mounting, according to Jackson, "the morale situation became critical. . . . Several platoon leaders asked about withdrawing. Knowing that the Puerto Rican cares much for the evacuation of the wounded, I gave the excuse that we could not withdraw and leave all our wounded to the Chinese."[63] Jackson called for maximum defensive fires around the outpost, observing afterward, "When this fire did come, it was extremely effective and killed many [of the] Chinese who were backing up the assault elements."[64]

At 2130, as Captain Jackson was discussing the situation with Sergeant Noriega, his communications sergeant told him that Company G had received orders from the battalion commander to withdraw. Jackson attempted to verify the order by radio but was unable. "I could not get the Puerto Rican operator at battalion to put the battalion commander on the radio," wrote Jackson afterward. "Whether he didn't understand me or want to understand, I will never know. I therefore ordered the withdrawal."[65]

The 2d Battalion's daily staff journal shows that Colonel Betances-Ramirez ordered Company G to withdraw from Jackson Heights and that this decision had not been prompted by a request that originated with

---

[61] Statement, Jackson, 9 Feb 60, p. 3.
[62] 2d Bn Staff Jnl, Entry 37, 27 Oct 52, in Monthly Cmd Rpt, 65th Inf, Oct 52.
[63] Statement, Jackson, 9 Feb 60, p. 3.
[64] Ibid.
[65] Ibid.

Company G.⁶⁶ Betances-Ramirez's decision appears to have been based solely on the colonel's own appraisal of the worsening tactical situation.

Jackson instructed his platoon leaders to withdraw simultaneously down separate routes along the hill's eastern and western slopes. As he descended the hill with the 3d Platoon, following a trail running along the southwest finger of Jackson Heights, his group encountered some Chinese soldiers. Following a heavy firefight, the platoon broke contact and ran down the west side of Jackson Heights. In the meantime, the remnants of the 1st and 2d Platoons safely retreated down the east side.[67] In all, Company G endured a loss of three killed and twenty-three wounded on Jackson Heights that day.[68] Among the dead was Lieutenant Rodriguez-Rodriguez. By 0100 on 28 October, almost all of the surviving members of Company G had succeeded in rejoining the rest of the 2d Battalion.[69]

Company G's tenacious stand demonstrated that the men of the 65th Infantry, whether new replacements or veteran soldiers, were able fighters when properly led. For several days, the defenders of the outpost had endured repeated and massive artillery barrages, withdrawing only when a numerically superior force of Chinese infantry threatened to overrun their position. Sergeant Noriega, who played a key part in the defense of Jackson Heights, exemplified that spirit and received the Distinguished Service Cross for the "extraordinary heroism" he exhibited during the fight.[70]

Breakdown on Jackson Heights

At 0100 on 28 October, Colonel De Gavre ordered the 2d Battalion to retake the southern portion of Jackson Heights. Since the unit occupied a sector along the regiment's main line and could not afford to commit more than one infantry company without compromising its position, De Gavre gave Betances-Ramirez temporary control of Company A from the 1st Battalion to augment the attacking force.[71] He also instructed the 1st Battalion to be prepared to send Company C forward under 2d Battalion control if that became necessary.

Spearheading the attack would be Captain Cronkhite's Company F, supported by Lieutenant Porterfield's Company A from the 1st Battalion.

---

[66] 2d Bn Staff Jnl, Entry 44, 28 Oct 52, in Monthly Cmd Rpt, 65th Inf, Oct 52.

[67] Informal Discussion, De Gavre, Root, and Jackson.

[68] 2d Bn Staff Jnl, Entry 43, 27 Oct 52, in Monthly Cmd Rpt, 65th Inf, Oct 52.

[69] One man entered friendly lines several hours later. Ibid., Entry 3 for 28 Oct 52.

[70] GO no. 698, HQ EUSAK, 27 Jul 53, sub: Award of Distinguished Service Cross to Master Sergeant Belisario Noriega, Rcds of U.S. Army Operational, Tactical, and Support Organizations (World War II and Thereafter), RG 338, NACP.

[71] App. C, Opns Narr, 10 Dec 52, in Monthly Cmd Rpt, 65th Inf, Oct 52.

A West Point graduate, 30-year-old Cronkhite had been in Korea only four months.[72] Porterfield, on the other hand, had already earned enough rotation points to return to the United States. He volunteered, however, for what another officer called "one more shot of glory."[73] Accompanying Cronkhite's command group would be 1st Lt. Gerald A. Wilcomb, a forward observer from the 58th Field Artillery Battalion.[74] Colonel Betances-Ramirez told Cronkhite:

> He was sending my company, F Company, out to retake the hill. . . . I would be followed by A Company that would pass through me and retake a little bit more territory. When A Company passed through me, F Company would withdraw and come back to the line. . . . I did not pack to stay. I packed to go out, kick some butt and come back home.[75]

Captain Cronkhite was unaware that De Gavre later told Betances-Ramirez to keep Company F on Jackson Heights and return Company A to the control of 1st Battalion.[76] It is unclear whether this order came down after Cronkhite received his instructions or if the captain or his battalion commander misunderstood the original directive. Whatever the cause, there was uncertainty among the attacking companies right from the start regarding who would remain on Jackson Heights and who would return after they took the objective. The confusion was not limited to the infantry company commanders. Cronkhite's artillery observer, Lieutenant Wilcomb, and his counterpart with Company A, 2d Lt. Jonas W. Glassgow, differed in their notions about what would occur after the recapture of Jackson Heights.[77]

The 2d Battalion began its attack thirty minutes behind schedule, at 0615 on 28 October, because the 3d Reconnaissance Company was late in replacing Company F on the main defensive line.[78] Companies A and F then set out for Jackson Heights with Cronkhite's unit in the lead. One of his platoons was still manning a small outpost forward of the main line, so Cronkhite had to make a quick stop to collect the unit. "We picked that platoon up on the way out to make the attack—not the best way to do a military operation," he remarked. "You normally pick a company that is not on the line, because you want them rested and organized if possible."[79]

---

[72] *Register of Graduates and Former Cadets, 1802–1980*, p. 495.

[73] Col Gerald A. Wilcomb, "Korean War Memoirs," 9 Jan 97, p. 7, Unpubl Monograph, Historians files.

[74] Interv, Willis D. Cronkhite III with Willis D. Cronkhite Jr., 17 Oct 96, Historians files.

[75] Interv, Cronkhite with Cronkhite, 17 Oct 96.

[76] App. C, Opns Narr, 10 Dec 52.

[77] Bn Opns Jnl, Entry dtd 1145, 28 Oct 52, in Monthly Cmd Rpt, 58th FA Bn, Oct 52.

[78] 2d Bn Opns Jnl, Entries 13–14, 28 Oct 52, in Monthly Cmd Rpt, 65th Inf, Oct 52.

[79] Interv, Cronkhite with Cronkhite, 17 Oct 96.

Once the platoon had rejoined the company, the attack force continued moving toward its objective. Colonel De Gavre arrived at the 2d Battalion observation post in time to watch the assault kick off.

Based on the light defensive fire that came at the Americans from the top of the hill, the enemy presence on Jackson Heights seemed to amount to a reinforced platoon.[80] This may have been because the Chinese had withdrawn most of their troops to a safer location after seeing the exposed nature of the outpost. Whatever the reason, Cronkhite's unit reached the base of Jackson Heights at 0710 in good order and then began to ascend the slope.[81] The Chinese soldiers on top, while few in number, put up a spirited defense. The Company F commander remembered:

> One enemy soldier was foolish enough to stand up on top of the hill . . . with a bunch of sticks of dynamite tied on to some prima cord. He would twirl them around his head and throw them down at us. They blew up on the way down. It kind of shook us up a little bit. There were also machine gunners shooting . . . at us, things like that.[82]

Company F's weapons platoon responded with a steady stream of bullets from two .30-caliber and four .50-caliber machine guns.

Under the cover of that supporting fire, Company F swept up the southern face of Jackson Heights and drove the Chinese off the summit. Captain Cronkhite reported the objective secured at 0955.[83] However, Cronkhite was shocked at the terrain his men had just taken: "There were no assembly areas . . . it was just a . . . 60 degree slope, no place was flat on top, it was just a razorback ridge . . . and there was another enemy-held hill at the top of the ridge."[84] Satisfied that the mission to retake Jackson Heights had been accomplished, Colonel De Gavre departed for regimental headquarters.[85]

As Company F ascended the hill, Company A followed a short distance behind. Enemy artillery fire soon began to fall among Porterfield's troops, however, and only two of his infantry platoons pushed on to join Company F at the top of the hill. A third remained pinned down at the base of Jackson Heights. Even so, by noon it appeared that the attack had been a success. Friendly casualties so far had also been relatively light. Twenty enemy soldiers were dead and thirty-seven more reported wounded during the engagement.[86]

---

[80] App. C, Opns Narr, 10 Dec 52.
[81] 2d Bn Opns Jnl, Entry 15, 28 Oct 52, in Monthly Cmd Rpt, 65th Inf, Oct 52.
[82] Interv, Cronkhite with Cronkhite, 17 Oct 96.
[83] 2d Bn Staff Jnl, Entry 32, 28 Oct 52, in Monthly Cmd Rpt, 65th Inf, Oct 52.
[84] Interv, Cronkhite with Cronkhite, 17 Oct 96.
[85] App. C, Opns Narr, 10 Dec 52.
[86] 2d Bn Staff Jnl, Entry 35, 28 Oct 52, in Monthly Cmd Rpt, 65th Inf, Oct 52.

Conditions on Jackson Heights soon began to deteriorate, however. First, Company A became intermingled with Company F, presenting Chinese gunners with a lucrative target. "I hadn't spoken to Porterfield after getting the attack order," observed Cronkhite. "I knew he was a pro, and if I took the hill, he'd be right behind me, pass through and attack the next objective. . . . We had not coordinated the plan of attack because I was told he would pass through me and two company commanders don't need to coordinate for that [type of] operation."[87]

A seemingly endless stream of Chinese artillery and mortar rounds slammed into the newly recaptured position. With wounded Americans trickling back down the hill, Lieutenant Wilcomb watched as Company F began to disintegrate. "Three or four of the troops," he remembered, "received small flecks of shrapnel in the face and started leaving the hill. Some unwounded troops started helping them down which sort of gave them a legal ticket off the hill. One soldier, the only one carrying a carbine, looked at me, gave me the magazine out of his carbine, and took off after the others."[88] Casualties mounted, and "every wounded man seemed to be getting more and more help getting back."[89]

With the momentum of the attack rapidly falling off, Lieutenant Porterfield called a meeting to decide what to do next. Cronkhite recalled that in light of the heavy Chinese mortar and automatic-weapons fire no one favored advancing any deeper into enemy territory. If both companies remained on Jackson Heights, however, the shelling would continue to inflict heavy casualties among the closely packed troops. As the most experienced commander present, Porterfield decided that Company F would hold the position and Company A would withdraw.[90] The time was about 1200.

The decision presented Lieutenant Porterfield with a significant problem. After taking losses to enemy artillery for almost two hours, the Company A commander was unsure whether he could quickly evacuate all his wounded. According to Cronkhite, who clung to the belief that his unit would also be leaving shortly, Porterfield accepted his offer to use Company F troops to help carry Company A's wounded back to the battalion aid station.[91] "It was [standing operating procedure] in that sort of situation," remarked Cronkhite, "to send six men out with the litter to go

---

[87] Interv, Cronkhite with Cronkhite, 17 Oct 96.
[88] Ibid.
[89] Ibid.
[90] Wilcomb, "Korean War Memoirs," p. 8.
[91] This statement is at odds with that of [then] Lieutenant Wilcomb, who remembers that Porterfield ordered Company F to remain on the position while Company A returned to the main defensive line. Interv, Cronkhite with Cronkhite, 17 Oct 96.

back, because four men just couldn't do it. We needed spares to give somebody a break. And so six men per casualty and we were getting a number of casualties. . . . So a lot of my troops went back to the [main] line because I ordered them to go."[92]

Moments after Porterfield made the decision for his company to withdraw, a Chinese 76-mm. round scored a direct hit on the assembled group, killing Porterfield; 2d Lt. William E. White, one of his platoon leaders; and Lieutenant Glassgow, the artillery forward observer attached to Company A. "The Chinamen had a lucky round, a lucky mortar [*sic*] round that landed in his lap. He [Porterfield] died instantly," recalled Cronkhite.[93] Cronkhite also lost one officer wounded, 1st Lt. Malcolm A. Gibbs, who had gone to see what the meeting was about. A piece of shrapnel hit Gibbs in the neck between his helmet and body armor, wounding him severely. The blast also stunned Lieutenant Wilcomb, who had just left the meeting when the round exploded.[94]

Porterfield's death had an immediate impact on his men. "I noticed troops now going down the hill in small groups and some singly," Wilcomb remembered. "I could see some strung out in the valley below heading south."[95] Second Lt. Donald E. Lauzon, one of the surviving platoon leaders from Company A, later wrote a letter to a friend stating: "The boys as a whole were great until they lost their officers, then they bugged out."[96] Lauzon had both eardrums blown out by a shell that landed less than a yard away.

About this time, Cronkhite reestablished radio communications with the battalion. The Company F commander informed Betances-Ramirez that Porterfield had been killed and that their troops were no longer in a position to hold Jackson Heights due to the exposed terrain and the intense enemy fire. Betances-Ramirez directed Cronkhite and his men to remain in place while sending Company A back to friendly lines. Cronkhite dutifully acknowledged the order, turning away to discover that the only Americans remaining on the summit were one infantry squad and several Company F officers, among them Lieutenant Wilcomb.[97] "All of Company A was gone," he remembered. "How many of them bugged out when their com-

---

[92] Ibid.
[93] Ibid.
[94] Wilcomb, "Korean War Memoirs," p. 8.
[95] Ibid.
[96] Ltr, Lt D. E. Lauzon to Lt Philip Efland, 4 Nov 52, encl to Rcd of Court-Martial 359333, United States vs. Juan Guzman, 23 Nov 53, Washington National Records Center (WNRC), Suitland, Md.
[97] Wilcomb, "Korean War Memoirs," p. 8; 65th Inf Personnel Section, Ofcr's Roster, 65th Inf, 22 Oct 52, Historians files.

pany commander got killed, how many of them had carried litters back, I'll never know."⁹⁸ The soldiers from Company F, many of whom had already departed while helping wounded comrades to the rear, also began leaving in greater numbers as word of Porterfield's death spread to their unit.

At 1705, Cronkhite radioed the 2d Battalion command post that only ten men remained on Jackson Heights. He requested permission to withdraw his meager force. Shortly thereafter, all communication with Company F ceased. Ten minutes later, 2d Lt. Edward P. Behne, a Company H platoon leader, reported that several dozen Company F soldiers were assembled on Hill 270, an outpost located a few hundred yards southwest of Jackson Heights.⁹⁹ He ordered the men to go back up the hill to rejoin their companies. Some were willing to comply, but most refused.¹⁰⁰

Colonel Betances-Ramirez made his way to Hill 270 to talk to the group. Addressing the men in Spanish, he told them "about [the importance of] being members of the 65th Infantry and [that] it was the pride of Puerto Rico. . . . I tried to bolster their patriotism and point out the offense they were committing and if found guilty what the punishment would be. I . . . ordered them to move to Jackson Heights."¹⁰¹

Only six men agreed to return to the summit. Betances-Ramirez then asked Lieutenant Behne to search nearby bunkers in an effort to locate other members of Company F. Behne located more troops, including a number who had been asleep, and gathered them outside so they could hear the battalion commander speak. When Betances-Ramirez addressed them a second time and determined that most still would not obey his commands, he took down the names of the six soldiers who indicated a willingness to go as well as thirty-eight names of those who did not want to return to Jackson Heights.

The regimental commander appeared at the 2d Battalion command post shortly after Betances-Ramirez went out to talk to the men. De Gavre overheard a battalion radio operator reporting that Company F was returning to the main line of resistance. The message was checked and found to be Company A returning to the MLR. De Gavre asked Betances-Ramirez why Company A had not returned sooner. The battalion commander stated

---

⁹⁸ Interv, Cronkhite with Cronkhite, 17 Oct 96.

⁹⁹ 65th Infantry Certificate dtd 3 Nov 52, Historians files, contains the names of six soldiers from Company F who agreed to go back up Jackson Heights as well as thirty-eight soldiers who refused to return. The other men seen by Behne were probably replacements who were not allowed forward of the main line of resistance for their first ten days in the unit and soldiers with a high number of rotation points who were permitted to remain behind when Company F moved out.

¹⁰⁰ Ibid.

¹⁰¹ Board of Review Findings, Court-Martial Case 360555, Ofc of the Judge Advocate General, Washington, D.C., 20 Aug 53, WRNC.

that it was because the men of Company F had withdrawn from the hill and it was necessary to keep Company A up there. Betances-Ramirez admitted to De Gavre that the confusion may have resulted from "a misunderstanding since he previously informed Commanding Officer, Company F, that it was his intention that upon taking the hill Company F would be relieved and Company A would stay."[102]

Although a large part of Company F was unwilling to return to Jackson Heights, the regiment still planned to move barbed wire, sandbags, timber, and other building materials up the hill in order to repair the position's bunkers and to improve its defenses. At 1700, a party of Korean Service Corps laborers carrying fortification materials and ammunition left the MLR bound for Jackson Heights.[103]

About that time, Captain Cronkhite ordered his remaining infantry squad on Jackson Heights to carry the badly wounded Lieutenant Gibbs to the rear and then come back.[104] When the Company F officers descended the hill a short while later, looking for signs of the infantry squad, they found the officer's body resting on a litter with no one else around. "He was dead," Cronkhite lamented. "The men had just abandoned the body and . . . didn't bother to come back and rejoin us."[105] Cronkhite and his platoon leaders, with no troops left to command, decided to return to 2d Battalion headquarters. "Betances-Ramirez had apparently already ordered me back by that time," recalled Cronkhite, "but I found that out [only] later."[106]

Cronkhite and his lieutenants made their way back to friendly lines with the Chinese shooting at them the entire way. En route they met Korean laborers coming up the hill carrying rations, ammunition, barbed wire, and fortification material. "Never did find out who was in charge of the Koreans but I didn't want a bunch of them to get killed," Cronkhite remembered. "I just shooed them on back."[107]

That evening, De Gavre conferred with the assistant division commander, General Dasher. In light of the uncertain situation, De Gavre said, the regiment should reinforce the main line of resistance and cease further attempts to retake Jackson Heights for the night. Dasher approved both recommendations.[108] De Gavre also instructed the 2d Battalion commander to reinforce Hill 270 and the section of front line closest to Jackson Heights

---

[102] App. C, Opns Narr, 10 Dec 52.
[103] Ibid.
[104] Wilcomb states that the remaining officers on Jackson Heights carried Gibbs down. Wilcomb, "Korean War Memoirs."
[105] Interv, Cronkhite with Cronkhite, 17 Oct 96.
[106] Ibid.
[107] Ibid.; App. C, Opns Narr, 10 Dec 52.
[108] Ibid.

in case the enemy decided to counterattack. To stiffen those defenses, De Gavre gave Betances-Ramirez operational control of Company B from the 1st Battalion. Meanwhile, the rest of the 1st Battalion would get ready to assault Jackson Heights the following morning.[109]

Having returned to friendly lines with his surviving officers, Captain Cronkhite reported to Betances-Ramirez that only the dead were left on Jackson Heights. Afterward, during a meeting with the regimental commander, De Gavre told him, "Cronkhite, I can't decide whether to give you a medal or kick you in the ass. I think you did everything you possibly could to make the operation a success, but it was not a success, it was screwed up."[110]

Cronkhite accompanied his commander to a meeting with General Smythe and members of his staff at the 3d Division headquarters. "I wasn't really interested in what they were saying," remembered Cronkhite, who at this point had not slept for two days. "But I did hear them say that the division commander did tell the regimental commander that he'd have to relieve somebody, they couldn't stand for a screw-up like this without somebody paying for it. Apparently they picked the battalion commander."[111]

General Smythe subsequently relieved Colonel Betances-Ramirez for his "inability to control or influence this whole action."[112] Captain Jackson, however, considered Betances-Ramirez a superb commander "who understood the needs of his men and fought for them."[113] Maj. Harry M. Elam, the 2d Battalion executive officer, replaced Betances-Ramirez as the interim commander. A reserve officer, Elam was a 1943 graduate of Officer Candidate School and a veteran of World War II.[114]

Meanwhile, Major Davies' 1st Battalion launched a counterattack to recapture Jackson Heights. At 0225 on 29 October, Lieutenant Stevens' Company C departed its rear assembly area and headed for the main line of resistance. A heavy fog rolled in, obscuring Jackson Heights and prompting Stevens to request a round of artillery on the objective so he could maintain his orientation.[115] His request went unheeded. Fortunately for Stevens, guides from the 3d Reconnaissance Company showed up and

---

[109] App. C, Opns Narr, 10 Dec 52; 2d Bn Staff Jnl, Entry 41, 28 Oct 52, and Regimental Intel and Opns Jnl, 28 Oct 52, all in Monthly Cmd Rpt, 65th Inf, Oct 52.

[110] Interv, Cronkhite with Cronkhite, 17 Oct 96.

[111] Ibid.; App. C, Opns Narr, 10 Dec 52.

[112] Ltr, Lt Col Carlos Betances-Ramirez, 12 Sep 98, sub: Analysis and Comments of the 3d Division's Staff Study dated 8 Nov 52, p. 6, Historians files.

[113] Interv, author with Jackson, 30 Jul 01.

[114] Elam did not take command until 0800 on 31 Oct 52. See 2d Bn Opns Jnl, Entry 2, 31 Oct 52, in Monthly Cmd Rpt, 65th Inf, Oct 52; *U.S. Army Register: Volume II, Retired Lists, 1 January 1967* (Washington, D.C.: Government Printing Office, 1967), p. 200.

[115] 1st Bn Staff Jnl, Entry 7, 29 Oct 52, in Monthly Cmd Rpt, 65th Inf, Oct 52.

led the lieutenant and his company to the line of departure, which they crossed shortly after 0500. Around 0625, the company reached the base of Jackson Heights, where it made a short stop to reorganize. Forty minutes later, the two leading infantry platoons, trailed by the third infantry platoon and weapons platoon, advanced up the hill without taking enemy fire. The Chinese, as it turned out, had abandoned the outpost. Company C secured the objective at 0720.[116]

Major Davies immediately dispatched a party of South Korean laborers carrying supplies and fortification materials to Jackson Heights. Shortly thereafter, however, one of Lieutenant Stevens' platoon leaders noticed:

> My first squad was missing. . . . I couldn't find it so I started back and that is when I first saw the men leaving. I stopped the first group and asked them where they were going. One man said "we can't stay on this hill." When I asked why, he mumbled something in Spanish and I couldn't understand him. I went straight to the C.O. and told him about what was happening.[117]

At 1050, Major Davies informed De Gavre that fifty-eight men from Company C had wandered back to the main line of resistance and refused to return to Jackson Heights. By 1325, an even larger number of stragglers had congregated near the 2d Battalion command post.[118] That afternoon, Major Davies ordered Lieutenant Stevens and all of his remaining men to return to friendly lines. In addition to all of the platoon leaders, only 2 men from the 1st Platoon, 4 apiece from the 2d and 3d, and 13 men from the weapons platoon had remained on the hill.[119] Afterward, Major Elam directed a platoon leader from Company B to send one squad to Jackson Heights along with thirty Korean laborers to recover the bodies of the Americans who had fallen on the hill.[120]

After investigating the incident, Colonel De Gavre confirmed that Company C had retaken Jackson Heights without firing a shot: "There were, however, bodies of both friendly and enemy dead on the position. [The soldiers'] unauthorized withdrawal is believed to have been solely from fear of what might happen to them."[121] Moving up the fog-shrouded slope of Jackson Heights, many from Company C had chanced upon the bodies of

---

[116] 1st Bn Opns Jnl, Entry 10, 28 Oct 52, in Monthly Cmd Rpt, 65th Inf, Oct 52.

[117] Court-Martial Case 360550, 3d Inf Div, 14 Dec 52, WNRC.

[118] Regimental Intel and Opns Jnl, Entries Between 0225 and 1325, 29 Oct 52, in Monthly Cmd Rpt, 65th Inf, Oct 52.

[119] Memo, HQ 65th Inf, n.d., sub: Company C, 65th Infantry Regiment, Roster by Platoon and Location of EM [Enlisted Men] on 29 Oct 52, Historians files.

[120] 2d Bn Staff Jnl, Entry 10, 29 Oct 52, in Monthly Cmd Rpt, 65th Inf, Oct 52.

[121] Monthly Cmd Rpt, 65th Inf, Oct 52.

enemy soldiers and comrades from Companies A, F, and G. In many cases, the dead had been mutilated by both American and Chinese artillery fire. Unnerved by the gruesome sights, the enlisted men had begun drifting back without orders to the main line, eventually reducing the American presence on Jackson Heights to Lieutenant Stevens, his platoon leaders, and fewer than thirty men.

On the night of 29 October, General Smythe pulled the regiment off the front line. The failure of the unit to retake Jackson Heights, he explained, "was not due to enemy action, but rather to the disintegration in discipline and esprit de corps. As a result, the 65th Infantry was relieved of responsibility for its sector."[122] The 15th Infantry took its place.[123]

Assessing the Failure

On 30 October 1952, Smythe sent the greater part of the 65th Infantry to Sach'ong-ni, a village in the 3d Division rear area, where it began a new course of individual and small-unit training. Some elements of the 65th, including the 3d Battalion and a portion of the 1st Battalion, as well as elements of the regimental tank company and the heavy mortar company, remained behind for a time to assist the 15th Infantry. The following day, Major Elam officially assumed command of the 2d Battalion.[124]

During the last week of October, when the 65th had served at the front near Jackson Heights, it had suffered 121 losses, including 97 battle and 24 nonbattle casualties.[125] Lieutenant Porterfield received a posthumous promotion to captain and a Bronze Star for valor.[126] Lieutenant Gibbs received a posthumous Silver Star.[127] As a result of the failure on Jackson Heights, the 65th sent 1 officer and 122 enlisted men (14 from Company A, 76 from Company C, and 32 from Company F) to the division stockade for refusing to attack the enemy as ordered and for misbehaving before the enemy.[128]

---

[122] Monthly Cmd Rpt, 3d Inf Div, Nov 52.

[123] Regimental Intel and Opns Jnl, 290001 Oct to 292400 Oct 52, in Monthly Cmd Rpt, 65th Inf, Oct 52.

[124] 2d Bn Staff Jnl, Entry no. 1, 31 Oct 52, in Monthly Cmd Rpt, 65th Inf, Oct 52.

[125] Unit Rpt nos. 743–48, in Monthly Cmd Rpt, 65th Inf, Oct 52.

[126] GO no. 11, 3d Inf Div, 7 Jan 53, sub: Award of Bronze Star Medal to 1st Lieutenant John D. Porterfield, in Monthly Cmd Rpt, 3d Inf Div, Jan 53; Certificate, The Adjutant Generals Office, 15 Jan 53, sub: Posthumous Promotion of John D. Porterfield, Historians files.

[127] GO no. 14, 3d Inf Div, 11 Jan 53, sub: Award of Silver Star Medal to 2nd Lieutenant Malcolm A. Gibbs, in Monthly Cmd Rpt, 3d Inf Div, Jan 53.

[128] Unit Rpt nos. 747–49, in Monthly Cmd Rpt, 65th Inf, Oct 52.

The 65th Infantry's discipline troubles continued after the loss of Jackson Heights. On 2 November, the 15th Infantry ordered the 2d Platoon of Company L, 3d Battalion, to mount a combat patrol in front of the main defensive line the following night. Attached to the platoon were a mortar squad, an engineer antimine detachment, a medical detachment, and a mortar forward observer with a radio operator. The platoon leader in charge was 2d Lt. John R. Wasson, a 24-year-old West Point graduate who had completed his officer training with the 82d Airborne Division's 325th Airborne Infantry before joining the 65th.[129] When he was tapped for the mission, however, Wasson had been in the field for only ten days and had led only two patrols, both of which had gotten misoriented.[130]

On the night of 3 November, Wasson's patrol of forty-seven men departed the 15th Infantry's main line. By the time the patrol reached the outpost line, two men had already fallen out. Proceeding onward, the force reached a Company I listening post, where guards challenged it. This caused about a dozen men to throw down their weapons and equipment in panic and to flee back toward the main line, two hundred yards to the rear. Lieutenant Wasson went back, rounded up the men, and pointed out that it had been a friendly listening post that had challenged them.[131]

The patrol continued on its way until it reached a large ditch some three hundred yards from the Imjin. At this point, some of the soldiers declined to go farther. With time and more persuasion from Lieutenant Wasson, they did move forward another two hundred yards before stopping again. Wasson pulled the entire platoon back to the closest terrain feature that afforded cover, a large ditch, and radioed the company commander to inform him of the difficulties he was having.

Following that break, he ordered the men forward once more. The bulk of the platoon complied; but five men, including individuals from the mortar, communications, and medical detachments, remained in the ditch with the patrol's sole 60-mm. mortar. Wasson was only one hundred yards from the river when two more squads turned to the rear. By the time the lieutenant had crossed the Imjin, only one other officer, Lieutenant Wasson's radio operator, and three men from the engineer detachment were still with him. The rest of the 2d Platoon refused to cross over. Wasson and his tiny group proceeded to the patrol's objective, having traveled a total distance of over three miles. The rest of the 2d Platoon, in the meantime, waited for

---

[129] *Register of Graduates and Former Cadets, 1802–1980*, p. 539.
[130] Court-Martial Case 360543, 7 Dec 52, WNRC.
[131] Ibid.

approximately one hour, first near the river and then at the ditch, before leaving for the rear. Upon returning himself, Wasson reported the results of his patrol and then preferred charges against twenty-two of the thirty-nine soldiers in his platoon.[132] The charges included desertion with intent to avoid hazardous duty and willful disobedience of a superior officer. As a result of the incident, the 15th Infantry returned the entire 3d Battalion to the 65th Infantry.

---

[132] Ibid.

Chapter 11

COURTS-MARTIAL, RECONSTITSUTION, AND REDEMPTION NOVEMBER 1952–JULY 1953

Eleven days after the incident involving the patrol led by Lieutenant Wasson, Lt. Col. John Baker, the 3d Division's staff judge advocate, with the concurrence of General Smythe, the division commander, referred the initial set of court-martial charges against 1st Lt. Juan E. Guzman of Company A, 65th Infantry. The first member of the regiment tried for the mass combat refusal, Guzman was also the only officer brought up on charges.

The 33-year-old Guzman was a Puerto Rico National Guard officer whose military record had been good prior to the incident at Jackson Heights. A graduate of the Agricultural and Mechanical College in Mayaguez, Puerto Rico, he had enlisted in the National Guard in 1939, subsequently serving in the Panama Canal Department, the Hawaiian Islands, the continental United States, and Puerto Rico during World War II.[1] Between 1946 and 1950, Guzman had been a member of the Inactive Reserve, where he had received a commission in 1948.

Prior to arriving in Korea, Guzman had been a weapons instructor with the 296th Infantry Regiment at the Recruit Training Center, Camp Tortuguero, Puerto Rico, for nearly two years. "His efficiency reports reflect that, as an instructor in weapons and other non-combat duties he was an excellent officer," wrote Maj. Gen. Eugene M. Caffey, the judge advocate general of the Army who later reviewed Guzman's case.

---

[1] Transmittal of Rcd of Trial Involving Sentence to Dismissal in the Case of 1st Lt Juan E. Guzman, 9 Feb 54, Court-Martial Case 359333, 23 Nov 52, WNRC.

According to Caffey, Guzman was "mentally, morally, and physically well qualified and possessing energy, resourcefulness and the ability to achieve results."[2] Guzman had arrived in Korea on 18 October and had been assigned to Company A two days later. On 23 October, Lieutenant Porterfield, the company commander, had appointed him the company executive officer. Guzman had therefore been in Korea for only ten days when he found himself as the second-in-command of the company and the acting 1st Platoon leader. Jackson Heights had been his first combat experience.

The trial of Lieutenant Guzman began on 23 November 1952. He faced charges that he had willfully failed to obey the order of a superior officer and had willfully failed to engage the enemy. The maximum sentence for both was the death penalty. The Puerto Rican officer pleaded guilty to the first charge and not guilty to the second.[3]

At the court-martial, Guzman defended himself by arguing that his platoon had lacked sufficient weapons, ammunition, and radios to secure Jackson Heights, having been notified of the assault by Lieutenant Porterfield only minutes before Company A moved out. According to Guzman, Porterfield had also failed to provide him with a clear concept of the platoon's mission. Porterfield had simply ordered Guzman to follow the unit in front of him. Finally, the Puerto Rican officer contended that his platoon had attempted to follow orders but heavy mortar fire had pinned them down. He had then gotten orders to remain in place until the bombardment ceased.[4]

In the end, Guzman was found guilty of the charge of willfully failing to obey the order of a superior officer and not guilty of willfully failing to engage the enemy. The court sentenced him to dismissal from the service, with total forfeiture of all pay and allowances, and confinement for five years at hard labor. Hugh M. Milton II, the assistant secretary of the Army, upheld the court's decision.[5]

Had Guzman been unfairly singled out for court-martial? Lt. Col. Carlos Betances-Ramirez, the former 2d Battalion commander who had known Guzman in Puerto Rico, thinks not. According to Betances-Ramirez, Lieutenant Guzman was fluent in English and "most definitely" understood

---

[2] Ibid.

[3] Ibid. Because of privacy issues and the fact that the court-martial records are not available to the public, only the case numbers of the enlisted soldiers have been cited. Lieutenant Guzman is the exception because he was an officer and the results of his court-martial are public record. See DA, General Court-Martial Order no. 31, 3 Mar 54, MHI.

[4] Ibid.

[5] Court-Martial Case 359333, 23 Nov 52; DA, General Court-Martial Order no. 31, 3 Mar 54, MHI.

the orders he had received from Porterfield and Elam prior to and during the attack. "He was asked if he understood the order and he acknowledged having understood them," recalled Betances-Ramirez, who upon the lieutenant's return had placed Guzman under arrest after disarming him. "In my opinion . . . he just panicked after seeing and hearing what was going on at the outpost as he got closer and closer. The enemy mortar fires, small arms fire, exploding grenades, and the walking wounded and litter cases coming down. . . . I suspect he simply got scared."[6] According to the former battalion commander, Guzman's repeated refusals to obey a direct order from his superiors required the action taken against him and the sentence that followed.[7]

Almost immediately after the battle ended, the 3d Division's staff judge advocate began reviewing the statements of everyone at Jackson Heights in order to identify which individuals had refused to fight. For those whose names Betances-Ramirez had written down, the decision to refer charges was fairly clear. In other individual cases, several fellow soldiers had to be interviewed before a similar decision could be made. By the end of November, the division staff judge advocate reported that sufficient evidence existed to bring court-martial charges against eighty-eight enlisted soldiers from the 65th Infantry.[8] The charges ranged from desertion to avoiding hazardous duty to willfully disobeying the lawful orders of a superior officer and misbehavior before the enemy.[9]

The courts-martial for the regiment's enlisted soldiers began on 7 December, when 10 men went on trial: 7 from Company L, 2 from the regimental Medical Company, and 1 from Company M. All of them had refused to follow Lieutenant Wasson during the combat patrol on 3 November. Charged with desertion to avoid hazardous duty and willful disobedience of a superior officer, most pleaded not guilty to all charges.[10] The arguments of the men varied. Some declared that Lieutenant Wasson, who had a reputation for getting lost, had gone past the objective and gotten lost once again. Others maintained that he moved so quickly the men were unable to keep up and had lost track of him when he turned north along the river prior to crossing it. The Company M mortarmen claimed that

---

[6] Ltr, Betances-Ramirez to author, 24 Jul 00, Historians files, CMH.

[7] Ibid.

[8] Daily Staff Jnl of the Staff Judge Advocate, 27 Nov 52, in Monthly Cmd Rpt, 3d Inf Div, Nov 52. Charges were later brought against one more Company F soldier. See entry in Daily Staff Jnl for Staff Judge Advocate on 7 Dec 52 in Monthly Cmd Rpt, 3d Inf Div, Dec 52. Unless otherwise noted, all Cmd Rpts are in Entry 429, Rcds of the AGO, RG 407, NACP.

[9] Recapitulation of General Court-Martial Activities, in Monthly Cmd Rpt, 3d Inf Div, Dec 52.

[10] Court-Martial Case 360543, 7 Dec 52, WNRC.

Wasson ordered them to deploy the mortar in the ditch. Having received no further orders, they said, they stayed there when the remainder of the platoon departed.

Witnesses for the prosecution, who included Lieutenant Wasson as well as three members of the engineer detachment and the platoon's radio operator, countered that the soldiers had received a series of clear orders and chose to disobey. Their testimony proved to be compelling; the accused, a group that included the infantry squad leaders and the mortar and weapons squad leaders, were all found guilty. Most received bad conduct or dishonorable discharges and one to two years' confinement at hard labor.[11]

Three more courts-martial for Wasson's men followed. The first, which involved eight soldiers, took place on 11 December. All of the men were found guilty of at least one charge and were sentenced to dishonorable discharges, forfeiture of all pay and allowances, and one year in confinement at hard labor.[12] Two days later, seven men from Company L were found guilty during the second trial. The third, involving four more soldiers from Wasson's platoon, convened on 15 December. Since they were the first group of men that day who had refused to complete the patrol, Wasson considered these men instigators of the mass disobedience that followed. All were found guilty and sentenced to sixteen to eighteen years' confinement at hard labor. General Smythe later reduced their length of confinement to terms of nine to ten years.[13]

As the trials for Wasson's men were ending, the courts-martial for the men accused of abandoning Jackson Heights were just getting started. On 10 December, five soldiers from Company C were tried for desertion and willfully disobeying a lawful order from a superior officer. All were convicted and sentenced to dishonorable discharge, total forfeiture of all pay and allowances, and thirteen years' confinement at hard labor.[14] On 11 December, the 3d Division staff judge advocate filed charges against another fourteen enlisted men of Company C for misbehavior before the enemy at Jackson Heights.[15] The ensuing trials resulted in guilty verdicts for all the men accompanied by varying degrees of punishment. Among the harsher penalties, four men from Company C were sentenced to dishonorable discharges, total forfeiture of pay and allowances, and two to eight years' confinement.[16] Another four men from Company C

---

[11] Monthly Cmd Rpt, 3d Inf Div, Dec 52.
[12] Court-Martial Case 360559, 11 Dec 52, WNRC.
[13] Court-Martial Case 360545, 15 Dec 52, WNRC.
[14] Staff Judge Advocate Daily Jnl, 10 Dec 52, in Monthly Cmd Rpt, 3d Inf Div, Dec 52.
[15] Staff Judge Advocate Daily Jnl, 11 Dec 52.
[16] Ibid., 14 Dec 52.

received dishonorable discharges and eleven months' confinement at hard labor.[17]

More trials followed in rapid succession. By the end of December 1952, an additional forty-one soldiers had been tried and found guilty.[18] Their defense was not helped by testimony that often included lapses in memory, hesitation in answering the questions posed by the prosecution, and other accused comrades who willingly identified those who had accompanied them down the hill without orders. The sentences again varied. A few received bad-conduct discharges, some dishonorable discharges, and still others were not discharged at all. A number forfeited all their pay and allowances, but a few did not. All were sentenced to confinement at hard labor, although some had received as little as six months while others had received two to five years.[19]

On 1 January 1953, four Company C soldiers were acquitted by a court-martial for misbehavior before the enemy at Jackson Heights. On the same day, charges against another three men of Company C and five men of Company F were "returned to the Commanding Officer, 65th Infantry Regiment without action" and "dismissed for lack of sufficient evidence."[20]

The bulk of the enlisted soldiers involved in the trials were either privates or privates first class. Only two were corporals. The majority were twenty-two to twenty-three years old, with the youngest being nineteen and the oldest thirty-one. The vast majority were draftees. Most had nine or ten years of education, but a significant proportion had twelve years. Several had completed one or two years of college. Even so, all but one tested inferior (Class IV) or very inferior (Class V) on the Army General Classification Test (AGCT). Language difficulties, coupled with cultural differences within the secondary education system, had resulted in the low test scores.

The motivation of the average draftee, when compared to the long-serving regular soldiers of the regiment's initial enlisted contingent, is different enough to warrant further examination. Before entering the military, many Puerto Rican draftees had never left their home island, even to visit the continental United States. About half had records of service prior to abandoning Jackson Heights that were described as excellent, while the remainder held ratings of good or satisfactory. Only one had previously been court-martialed. Finally, most had served only about a year in the Army, four months of which they spent in basic training and six months in

---

[17] Ibid., 12 Dec 52.
[18] Ibid., 16–26 Dec 52.
[19] Ibid., 16–22 Dec 52.
[20] Staff Judge Advocate Daily Jnl, 1 Jan 53, in Monthly Cmd Rpt, 3d Inf Div, Jan 53.

reserve.[21] With the language barrier hampering the establishment of strong bonds between the unit's officers and men, it is not surprising that these young draftees chose to save themselves rather than risk injury or death on a remote Korean hilltop.

On 26 January 1953, the last man tried in connection with Jackson Heights, an enlisted soldier from Company F charged with misbehavior before the enemy, was acquitted.[22] In all, 103 enlisted members of the regiment had been charged for offenses committed at Jackson Heights on 28 and 29 October or during the patrol on 3 November. Of these, five had been acquitted and eight had charges against them dismissed. Ninety-one soldiers, including one officer, received sentences with varying degrees of severity. Without question, the fiasco on Jackson Heights and its aftermath had been the 65th Infantry's darkest hour in Korea. It remained to be seen whether the regiment could regain its honor or would return home under a dark cloud.

The 65th was not the only unit to experience a mass combat refusal in Korea. On 16 July 1952, Col. George C. Mergens' 23d Infantry, 2d Infantry Division, began to relieve another regiment holding an important hill mass known as Old Baldy (Hill 275). In the midst of the operation, the Chinese launched a coordinated assault that pushed two American companies off the high ground. At 1130 on 19 July, Colonel Mergens assembled a composite force, consisting of Companies A, B, I, L, and M (-) under his regimental executive officer, to retake the hill. Unfortunately, Mergens neglected to inform his executive officer of his new responsibilities until forty-five minutes before the composite force was scheduled to move out. Predictably, the assault achieved minimal results in exchange for heavy casualties.[23]

Three more days of piecemeal efforts in pouring rain succeeded only in grinding up the 23d Infantry's 1st and 3d Battalions. During this process, the regiment suffered 54 killed and 310 wounded.[24] The strength of the regiment's infantry companies was so diminished that recently arrived replacements were hastily formed into platoons and committed to battle. On the morning of 22 July, the regimental executive officer went forward to determine why the latest assault on Old Baldy had not taken place. He found seventy men from Company G and fifteen soldiers from other units sitting at the base of the hill. The men refused to move forward in response to his orders.

---

[21] Memo for record, author, n.d., sub: Statistics for Personnel Tried by General Court-Martial (Nov–Dec 52), Historians files.

[22] Staff Judge Advocate Daily Jnl, 26 Jan 53, in Monthly Cmd Rpt, 3d Inf Div, Jan 53.

[23] Monthly Cmd Rpt, 23d Inf, Jul 52.

[24] Ibid. The sequence of attacks included the provisional battalion on 18 July, Companies I and L on 19 July, Company K on 21 July, and Company G on 22 July. The last named faltered soon after it began.

When Colonel Mergens learned of this development, he ordered the regimental executive officer "to shoot as many men as necessary to get the others to go back to the hill." The executive officer divided the soldiers into small groups and delivered a speech to each group. None of the men responded to his entreaties. They were eventually arrested and transported to the rear.[25]

The 23d Infantry had experienced an almost complete breakdown of unit cohesion as a result of its regimental commander's mishandling of the tactical situation. The problems within the 23d were solved by replacing an ineffective leader. In the case of the 65th Infantry, Companies A and F had abandoned Jackson Heights after a company commander was killed, leaving the surviving officers and a few of their fellow soldiers to their fate. The following day, Company C of the 65th did the same without suffering a single casualty to hostile fire. After examining the events at Jackson Heights, the Eighth Army's senior leadership determined that the 65th's problems had much deeper roots.

On 13 November, the very day charges were referred against Lieutenant Guzman, General Van Fleet wrote Army Chief of Staff General J. Lawton Collins requesting that the 65th Infantry be relieved of its combat mission in Korea. The Eighth Army commander's letter was based on a study by Maj. John S. D. Eisenhower, son of the president-elect of the United States, which he had obtained from the commanding general of the 3d Division.

In his postwar memoirs, Major Eisenhower, then serving as the 15th Infantry's chief operations officer, described his role as the lead investigator into the failures of the 65th Infantry. While briefing the major on his mission, the commander of the 3d Division, General Smythe, told Eisenhower: "John, that regiment can't fight the way it's set up. I want it thrown out of the division or integrated with Puerto Ricans and Continentals like they are in every other division. Now write a study and make it logical."[26]

Eisenhower prefaced his report by noting that Smythe considered the 65th Infantry "totally unfit for combat."[27] Eisenhower's study of the 65th's "dereliction" in Korea noted "a general apathy toward modern combat" in the regiment, which he blamed on the ethnic background of its Puerto Rican personnel, adding that "a similar situation existed with this Regiment in France in World War II."[28] He devoted less than half a page to the 65th's

---

[25] Ibid.

[26] John S. D. Eisenhower, *Strictly Personal* (New York: Doubleday & Co. Inc., 1974), p. 148.

[27] Ltr, Maj Gen George W. Smythe to CG, IX U.S. Corps, 8 Nov 52, sub: Reorganization of the 3d Inf Div, in Monthly Cmd Rpt, 3d Inf Div, Nov 52.

[28] Ltr, HQ Eighth Army, 14 Nov 52, sub: Preparation of Letter Concerning Disposition of 65th Infantry Regiment, Security Class Gen Corresp 1952, Rcds of U.S. Army Operational, Tactical, and Support Organizations (World War II and Thereafter), RG 338, NACP.

satisfactory record in 1950 and 1951 and more than five pages to 1952, concentrating on its failures at Outpost Kelly and Jackson Heights.

Eisenhower also highlighted the regiment's poor administrative record (its accountability of military property was worse than the division's other 2 regiments) and the fact that the 65th had the highest number of self-inflicted wounds (35 as opposed to 29 for the other 2 regiments combined) and missing in action (141 compared to 20 for the other 2 regiments) in the division. He dismissed the fact that the 65th had the lowest court-martial rates (69 as opposed to an average of 205 for the 7th and 15th during 1951–1952) by attributing it to "an indulgent attitude" on the part of former regimental commanders. "It is obvious," Major Eisenhower concluded, "that in view of the repeated disintegration of companies under fire, the 65th Infantry can no longer be entrusted with a sector of the United Nations battlefront until radical improvements are made."[29]

The study commissioned by General Smythe and written by Major Eisenhower contains several important misinterpretations. There was, for example, no evidence to support the conclusion that the regiment had suffered from apathy in combat during World War II. The 65th Infantry's exposure to combat during that conflict had been extremely limited. The Eisenhower study also glossed over the regiment's successes in 1950 and 1951, the communication barriers between English-speaking officers and Spanish-speaking enlisted soldiers, and the absence of qualified bilingual NCOs.

Expanding on Eisenhower's conclusions, General Smythe wrote a letter to the IX Corps commander, Lt. Gen. Reuben Jenkins, stating that while "the 65th Infantry with its original complement of NCOs performed in a credible manner," the regiment had declined rapidly in the first half of 1952 as less capable officers and NCOs joined the unit. The limited action the 65th saw in early 1952 obscured that weakness for a time, but the surge in fighting that autumn laid bare the sorry state of the regiment. As a result, he said, "during September, October, and November it has disintegrated in discipline and esprit de corps to the point where it is no longer a battle worthy unit."[30]

After blaming the regiment's failures on "the language barrier" and "the complete lack of NCOs," Smythe recommended to General Jenkins three possible courses of action. The Eighth Army should either assign another combat-trained regiment to the 3d Division, add a combat-trained regimental combat team to the division while the 65th underwent intensive training for at least four months (preferably under Eighth Army supervision), or give the 3d Division authority to reconstitute the 65th Infantry

---

[29] Ibid.
[30] Ibid.

with 60 percent continental personnel while distributing the remaining Puerto Ricans throughout the Eighth Army.[31]

After reviewing Eisenhower's study and Smythe's letter, the IX Corps commander informed Van Fleet that the 65th "could not be made into a battle-worthy unit with less than six months of training and then only after it has been assigned a large complement of experienced Regular Army noncommissioned officers."[32] He also added that an all–Puerto Rican regiment could no longer be justified. Agreeing with the first of Smythe's recommendations, Jenkins requested that the Army transfer the 30th Infantry from the continental United States to Korea for duty with the 3d Division.[33]

On 14 November 1952, General Van Fleet officially requested that the Department of the Army inactivate the 65th Infantry. "The increasing difficulty of realizing the full combat potential of the 65th Infantry Regiment has become a matter of great concern to me," he informed General Collins. "The problem associated with the rotation of personnel has affected all units, but in this regiment it has been further complicated by linguistic difficulties and the lack of qualified Puerto Rican NCO replacements."[34]

Van Fleet admitted that the regiment had given an "excellent" account of itself in the early fighting in Korea. This was because "it had a high percentage of career soldiers and its noncommissioned officer personnel were, for the most part, bilingual. This situation no longer exists."[35] An obvious solution to correct the lack of qualified Puerto Rican NCOs, Van Fleet continued, "would be to integrate continental NCOs in the regiment." When this had been done in the past, however, it had proved successful only when the NCOs spoke Spanish.[36] A recent survey, indeed, had shown that of thirteen hundred Puerto Rican replacements, only three hundred spoke any English.[37]

Van Fleet went on to note that the character of combat operations in Korea accentuated the difficulties imposed by the language barrier:

> Action in this theater is characterized by wide frontages necessitating considerable decentralization of command, numerous patrol and small unit actions, and most combat activity [is] initiated during the hours of darkness. . . . It is a matter of life or death when reactions to orders

---

[31] Ibid.
[32] Ltr, CG, IX Corps, to CG, Eighth Army, 10 Nov 52, Van Fleet Papers, GML.
[33] Ibid.
[34] Memo, CG, EUSAK, to DA, 14 Nov 52, sub: Replacement of the 65th Infantry Regiment, Rcds of U.S. Army Operational, Tactical, and Support Organizations (World War II and Thereafter), RG 338, NACP.
[35] Ibid.
[36] Ibid.
[37] Ibid.

must [be] instantaneous to maintain the integrity of an outpost, escape an ambush, or repel a mass attack during the night.[38]

The general added that the deterioration of the regiment had not been perceptible "as it had not been tested for a considerable period of time," asserting that the 65th had not engaged in "any actions of unusual severity" until the battle for Outpost Kelly.[39]

In Van Fleet's opinion, the full extent of the 65th's problems had been exposed when its soldiers had been driven from Jackson Heights by a "decidedly inferior force." Even though approximately twenty-five thousand rounds of artillery had been fired in support of the U.S. counterattack, the men of the 65th had displayed a "marked apathy" in attempting to retake the hill. "This action was not the result of a lack of leadership on the part of the small unit leaders," he reported. "On the contrary, as a result of attempting to demonstrate the proper offensive spirit in the attack, many of the company officers of the battalion [exposed themselves unnecessarily and] were killed."[40] Van Fleet also noted:

Repeated attempts to regroup and rally elements of the regiment were fruitless . . . the regiment was relieved and put in reserve to undergo training for approximately twenty-two days. It was again put in the line and again relieved after demonstrating by unsatisfactory performance of patrol missions that it was unsuited for combat. Charges have been preferred against approximately 129 [sic] men for failure to comply with orders.[41]

Van Fleet then presented General Collins with two options to solve the problems with the 65th Infantry. The first involved inactivating the regiment as a Puerto Rican formation, spreading the troops throughout Eighth Army, and then reconstituting the unit with mostly continental personnel. He opposed this course, however, because spreading Spanish-speaking troops throughout the Eighth Army would not in itself solve the language problem and "the political implications of inactivating a 'racial' regiment might not be desirable."[42]

Instead, Van Fleet suggested shipping the regiment back to Puerto Rico as a training unit, noting, "The 296th National Guard Regiment . . . could be returned to an inactive status, thereby making space available . . . for the activation of another RA [Regular Army] regiment."[43] Although Van Fleet reported no firm decision had been made as to which regiment would be used to round out the 3d Division, he clearly had one in mind, writing

---

[38] Memo, CG, EUSAK, to DA, 14 Nov 52.
[39] Ibid.
[40] Ibid.
[41] Ibid.
[42] Memo, CG, EUSAK, to DA, 14 Nov 52.
[43] Ibid.

that consideration should be given to the return of the 30th Infantry to the division.⁴⁴ He concluded his letter to Collins by requesting that expeditious action be taken to relieve the 65th Infantry "with an infantry regiment of continental personnel."⁴⁵

A Time of Uncertainty

As General Van Fleet's proposal made its way through channels, the 65th Infantry spent most of December training while serving as IX Corps reserve. "In order to build awareness of small unit capabilities and confidence in organic weapons," reported Colonel De Gavre, "the training has been entirely at squad level." He detailed how each squad had been organized into two fire teams, each with a light machine gun, and instructed in the basic principles of fire and maneuver. In an attempt to make the tactical scheme popular with the soldiers of the regiment, the headquarters staff gave it the Spanish name *El Anzuelo* (Fishhook) and posted small mimeographed posters with the word throughout the regimental area. The use of a Spanish rather than an English word to explain a basic tactical principle showed just how few English speakers there were among the enlisted men of the 65th but may have also reflected an effort on the part of De Gavre to rebuild the regiment's esprit de corps by honoring its unique cultural roots.⁴⁶

A shortage of sergeants in the regiment hampered the training program as it had for the previous twelve months. "While training is progressing satisfactorily the serious and most pressing need is for non-commissioned officers throughout the regiment, in all key units and at all levels," reported a frustrated De Gavre. "Supply, administration, maintenance, nearly all key jobs are being occupied by young inexperienced soldiers. This is particularly true in the rifle companies." The regimental commander then highlighted the rifle squads, the heart of any infantry outfit, as the weakest part of the unit: "In the rifle platoons we find corporals and privates first class as platoon sergeants with little or no experience beyond that of the men in the platoon. In addition, most of these men have but a passing knowledge of English and cannot transfer the platoon leader's instructions and orders to their comrades."⁴⁷

Meanwhile, General Smythe had also realized that he could not rely on external sources to alleviate the chronic shortage of sergeants. He therefore directed his staff to create a noncommissioned officer academy

---
⁴⁴ Ibid.
⁴⁵ Ibid.
⁴⁶ Monthly Cmd Rpt, 65th Inf, Dec 52.
⁴⁷ Ibid.

designed to prepare junior enlisted soldiers for NCO duties. The neighboring 25th Division agreed to provide some instructors and equipment on the condition that it could also use the school. While Smythe agreed to the partnership, he believed that each division should develop its own curriculum. As a result, the 3d Division's training program focused on teaching leadership skills from the perspective of an infantry small-unit leader in combat. To facilitate this goal, the divisional engineer battalion constructed a mockup of a section of the main line of resistance, complete with trenches, individual and automatic-weapons bunkers, and defensive wire installations, to serve as a training aid for the NCO academy.[48]

On 6 December 1952, the IX Corps commander, General Jenkins, and the 3d Division commander, General Smythe, visited the 65th's command post. They asked De Gavre if the regiment would be capable of going back on the line and, if so, when. The colonel responded that the unit would be ready within two weeks.

Taking him at his word, Smythe moved the regiment back into the line on 22 December. The 65th Infantry assumed responsibility for a sector north of Ch'orwon recently defended by the 15th Infantry, which moved into corps reserve. The departing regiment reported that enemy activity had been "light," with the Chinese making no attempt to capture additional ground. Indeed, when the 65th sent reconnaissance and ambush patrols up to two miles forward of the outpost line, they failed to make contact with anything more than small groups of Communist soldiers.[49]

On 28 December, the South Korean 2d Division relieved the 65th Infantry. Although De Gavre's regiment had been at the front for less than a week, he believed it had displayed some improvement. "The past month the regiment has gathered itself together," the colonel wrote in his monthly report, "and shown signs of better spirit and improved efficiency."[50]

December also brought an infusion of new leadership to the 65th. Lt. Col. Edward E. Cruise replaced Major Davies, who had led the 1st Battalion for seven months. Lt. Col. William E. Cox replaced newly promoted Colonel Elam, who had commanded the 2d Battalion for two months. Colonel Cruise, a 1929 West Point graduate, was a 47-year-old veteran of World War II who had been assigned to the Military Assistance Advisory Group to Formosa from 1951 to 1952.[51] Cox, considerably younger at thirty-four

---

[48] Monthly Cmd Rpt, 3d Inf Div, Dec 52.
[49] Monthly Cmd Rpt, 65th Inf, Dec 52.
[50] Ibid.
[51] *Register of Graduates and Former Cadets, 1802–1980*, p. 368; *Official Army Register, 1 January 1953*, p. 166.

COURTS-MARTIAL, RECONSTITUTION, AND REDEMPTION

A 60-mm. mortar firing position sited in a trench line near Outpost Harry

years of age, had also served in World War II.[52] During the month, another 13 officers and 161 enlisted men rotated through the 65th. Two more officers and five enlisted men transferred to other units.[53]

The beginning of January 1953 found the 65th Infantry, along with the rest of the 3d Division, beginning a nine-week training program. As the exercises began, Colonel De Gavre told his company and battalion commanders that they should achieve four major goals. The first was to improve combat aggressiveness by means of daily bayonet practice and an emphasis on offensive operations during unit exercises. The second objective was to identify potential NCOs within the regiment by encouraging untried privates to act as squad leaders during training. Individuals with promise would go to the newly established NCO academy. De Gavre's third objective was to improve rifle marksmanship by ensuring that each man had zeroed his weapon on a known-distance firing range and had

---
[52] *Official Army Register, 1 January 1953*, p. 159.
[53] Ibid.

honed his shooting skills by practicing with silhouette targets. Finally, De Gavre stressed small-unit attack problems that required laying down an accurate and sustained base of fire in support of a fast and hard-hitting maneuver element.[54]

Overall, the program called for a minimum of fifty-eight hours a week for combat elements, one-third of which would concentrate on night training. A total of eighteen hours per week would go to battalion field problems, which would occupy most of the second, third, and fourth weeks. Those field problems were typically attack exercises that involved artillery and a platoon of mortars. Support elements, such as the medical and service companies, would conduct a minimum of twenty hours of training per week in addition to continuing their missions to provide support for the combat units. All soldiers were to receive instruction in map reading, compass reading, field sanitation, first aid, and crew-served weapons employment.[55]

The South Korean Infantry Demonstration Team attached to IX Corps, which assisted the 65th Infantry, performed a series of squad and platoon attacks that stressed the close integration of fire and maneuver. It also staged a mock ambush demonstration on 4 January that the entire regiment witnessed. "The regiment [was] impressed with the demonstration," reported De Gavre, "and the benefit derived is noted in the way the infantry squads of the regiment emulate the principles demonstrated [by the South Koreans] in their small unit attack problems conducted later."[56] It was perhaps ironic that South Korean troops, whom U.S. commanders had held in low regard earlier in the war, were now called upon instead of an American unit to train the regiment in small-unit tactics.

In addition to tactical exercises, each battalion undertook a special construction project to make up for a shortage of training aids. The 1st Battalion developed a popup human silhouette target, which the entire regiment used extensively during squad attack problems. The 2d Battalion constructed a model reinforced squad defensive position consisting of two prefabricated machine-gun bunkers, several firing positions, a communications trench, and a metal foxhole cover that could protect soldiers during artillery and mortar attacks. The 3d Battalion improvised a 150-foot bridge across the swiftly flowing Hantan River without engineer assistance.[57] By the end of January 1953, De Gavre had achieved most of his goals despite a spell of extremely cold weather, the ongoing shortage of NCOs, and the paucity of training aids.

---

[54] Monthly Cmd Rpt, 65th Inf, Jan 53.
[55] Ibid.; Monthly Cmd Rpt, 3d Inf Div, Dec 52.
[56] Monthly Cmd Rpt, 65th Inf, Jan 53.
[57] Ibid.

The nine-week training program was cut short on 27 January 1953, when the 3d Infantry Division relieved the 25th Infantry Division near the Iron Triangle. The 65th Infantry, augmented by the Belgian Battalion and one platoon of the 7th Infantry's heavy mortar company, relieved the Turkish Brigade and a battalion of the U.S. 14th Infantry. The 65th assumed responsibility for the right flank of the division's sector, which straddled the Hantan valley northwest of Kumhwa. The unit dug in on a series of low hills that were about a mile south of two higher ridges, Hill 1062 (more commonly known as Papa-san) and Hill 717, both held by the Chinese. The enemy's positions afforded him not only superior observation, De Gavre reported, but also four excellent routes of attack into the regiment's sector.[58] Because the 65th had inherited an eight-mile front from the Turks, it was necessary to place all three battalions on line with each deploying all three of its rifle companies forward. The reserve consisted of the Belgian Battalion, which occupied positions along Line Wyoming two thousand yards to the south.

Following standard practice, the regiment dispatched one or two ambush patrols per company each day. None made contact with the enemy.[59] Even so, De Gavre reported to General Smythe, "the unit's combat efficiency and morale increased materially during the month of January."[60] He attributed the improvement to the long and hard days of training and to the positive and aggressive leadership exhibited by most of the unit commanders.

Even so, the regiment remained desperately short of NCOs at the close of January, prompting De Gavre to recommend once more to Smythe that a "maximum effort" should begin to increase the number of sergeants in the unit. He reported that "in preparation of defensive positions, including digging, constructing bunkers, policing and installing wire, the absence of effective NCOs was the greatest handicap."[61]

The 65th suffered only two battle casualties during January 1953.[62] There were also 255 nonbattle losses, mostly weather-related injuries caused by freezing temperatures during the day and even worse conditions at night. The unit sent 8 officers and 180 enlisted men stateside while it transferred 1 officer and another 10 enlisted men to other units. Inbound replacements numbered 21 officers and 298 enlisted personnel. The leadership of the 65th described unit morale as excellent, an appraisal that squared with a dramatic dip in the number of disciplinary problems.

---

[58] Monthly Cmd Rpt, 65th Inf, Feb 53.
[59] Ibid.; Monthly Cmd Rpt, 3d Inf Div, Jan 53.
[60] Monthly Cmd Rpt, 65th Inf, Jan 53.
[61] Ibid.
[62] Ibid.

The 65th Infantry stayed in defensive positions along the front for most of February 1953. Since enemy activity remained "light," the troops kept busy with engineering projects. Many of the bunkers the regiment had inherited from the 25th Division were improperly sited, had poor fields of fire, or were incapable of withstanding artillery or mortar fire. To remedy these problems, construction teams assisted by Company D, 10th Combat Engineer Battalion, completed sixteen new fighting bunkers and reconstructed another six. Despite the frozen ground, which proved a great obstacle to digging, the construction or improvement of fifteen hundred yards of communications trenches enhanced movement along the main line during daylight hours. The regiment also laid down new minefields while clearing "safe lanes" through existing minefields for the use of patrols. Troops installed fourteen hundred ten yards of concertina wire and five hundred ninety yards of other types of obstacles under the cover of darkness and in the face of occasional enemy sniper and mortar fire.[63]

De Gavre observed his troops carefully to find areas where they could improve. While inspecting the front lines, for example, the colonel observed that his men were not making the best use of their machine guns. He found that they often chose poor locations for their weapons and neglected to position their guns where they could lay down effective grazing fire during hours of darkness. As a result, De Gavre set aside additional time during training to teach machine gunners how to employ the weapons properly.[64]

During the month, the 65th carried out 211 ambush patrols and 25 reconnaissance patrols. Only two made contact with the enemy. During the night patrols, the men regularly used their newly issued infrared night vision devices even though the devices proved temperamental in the field and difficult to maintain. The enemy, for his part, probed the regiment twice, a platoon-size effort the first time and a company-size attack the second. As a result of these encounters, the 65th sustained five killed and thirty-five wounded but inflicted eighty casualties on the Chinese.[65]

During the 65th Infantry's stay on the front line, General Maxwell D. Taylor replaced General Van Fleet as the Eighth Army commander. A 1922 West Point graduate, 52-year-old Taylor had served as the assistant division commander of the 82d Airborne Division and as the commanding general of the 101st Airborne Division during World War II. Prior to arriving in Korea, he had served as the Department of the Army's assistant chief of staff for operations.[66]

---

[63] Ibid., Feb 53.
[64] Monthly Cmd Rpt, 65th Inf, Apr 53.
[65] Monthly Cmd Rpt, 65th Inf, Feb 53.
[66] *Register of Graduates and Former Cadets, 1802–1980*, p. 337.

Taylor made an immediate and positive impression on his new command. Visiting each unit, he repeatedly stressed the importance of planning and rehearsing patrols, providing units in reserve with a complete eight-week training program before they went back on the line, moving artillery battalions frequently to maintain their mobility, and better concealing defensive positions sited atop bare hills.[67]

At the point when Taylor took charge, Eighth Army totaled seven hundred seventy thousand men. This figure included one hundred forty thousand American combat troops organized into seven divisions as well as a large number of U.S. combat support and service support units. (*See Map 13.*) The South Koreans contributed twelve infantry divisions representing approximately one hundred twenty thousand combat troops. The remaining elements of the United Nations Command included units varying in size from the Commonwealth Division of twenty-four thousand to separate battalions and companies from nations such as Belgium and Ethiopia. Arrayed against them was a combined North Korean and Chinese force of more than 1 million men, at least three-quarters of whom were Chinese.[68]

Rebuilding the Regiment

Late in February 1953, General Smythe received formal notice that the Department of the Army had decided to reconstitute the 65th Infantry as a fully integrated regiment with non–Puerto Rican personnel assigned in the same proportion as in other U.S. regiments. During the night of 27–28 February, as a result, the 7th Infantry and the Belgian Battalion took the unit's place at the front so the 65th could go into division reserve and begin the reconstitution process.[69] The IX Corps placed the 25th Infantry Division's 14th Infantry under the operational control of the 3d Infantry Division while the 65th was being reconstituted.[70]

The effort to rebuild the 65th had four phases. During the first phase, which began in early March, the regiment received 264 NCOs from the 2d, 25th, 40th, and 45th Infantry Divisions and the 5th Regimental Combat Team.[71] In the second phase, 8–12 March, 874 enlisted soldiers transferred in from the 2d, 7th, 25th, 40th, and 45th Divisions and the 5th RCT. During the third phase, which began on 15 March, almost 2,100 Puerto Rican

---

[67] Hermes, *Truce Tent and Fighting Front*, p. 391.
[68] Ibid., pp. 367–68.
[69] Monthly Cmd Rpts, 65th Inf, Feb 53, and 3d Inf Div, Feb 53.
[70] Monthly Cmd Rpt, 3d Inf Div, Mar 53.
[71] Memo, U.S. Eighth Army, 10 Mar 53, sub: Reconstitution of 65th Infantry Regiment, Adjutant General Section, Gen Corresp, Rcds of U.S. Army Operational, Tactical, and Support Organizations, RG 338, NACP.

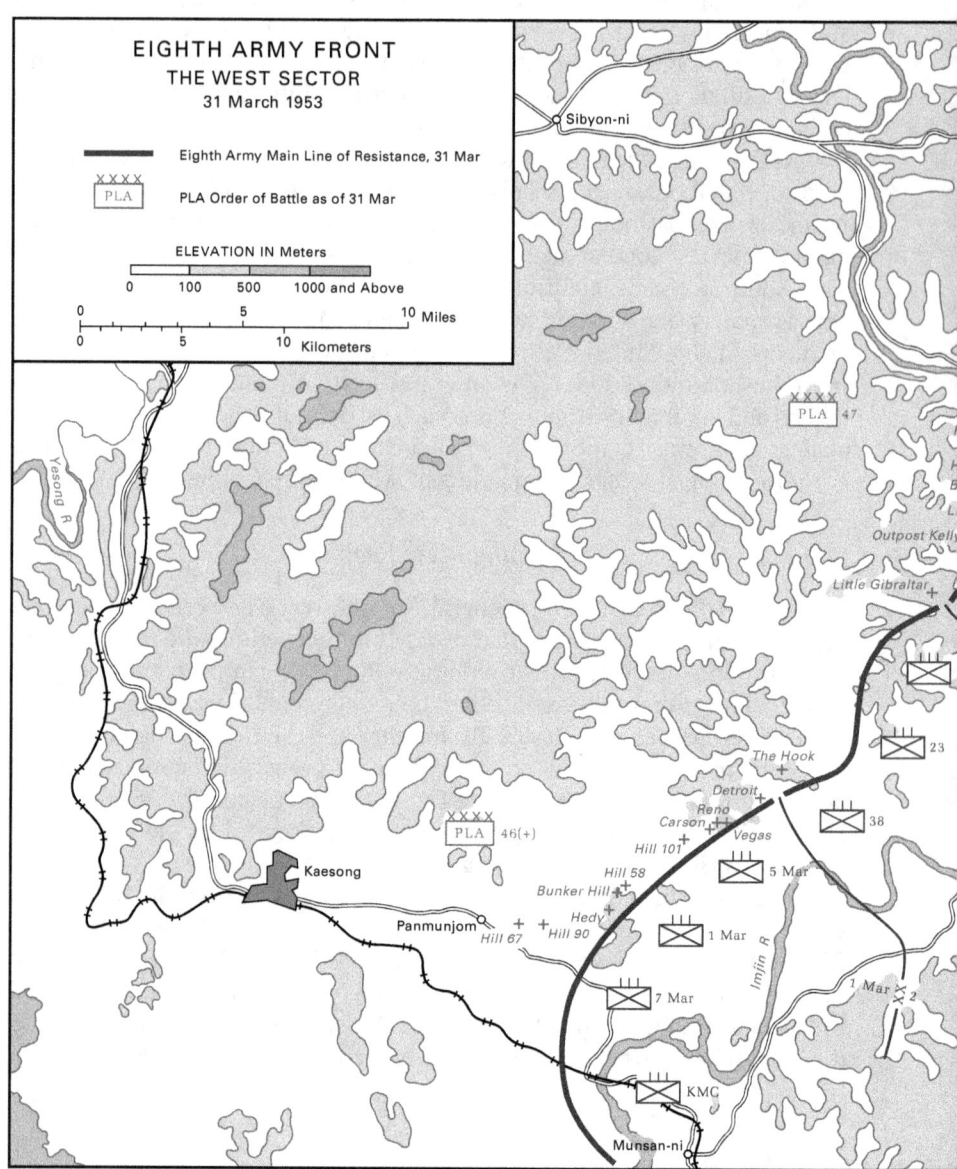

MAP 13

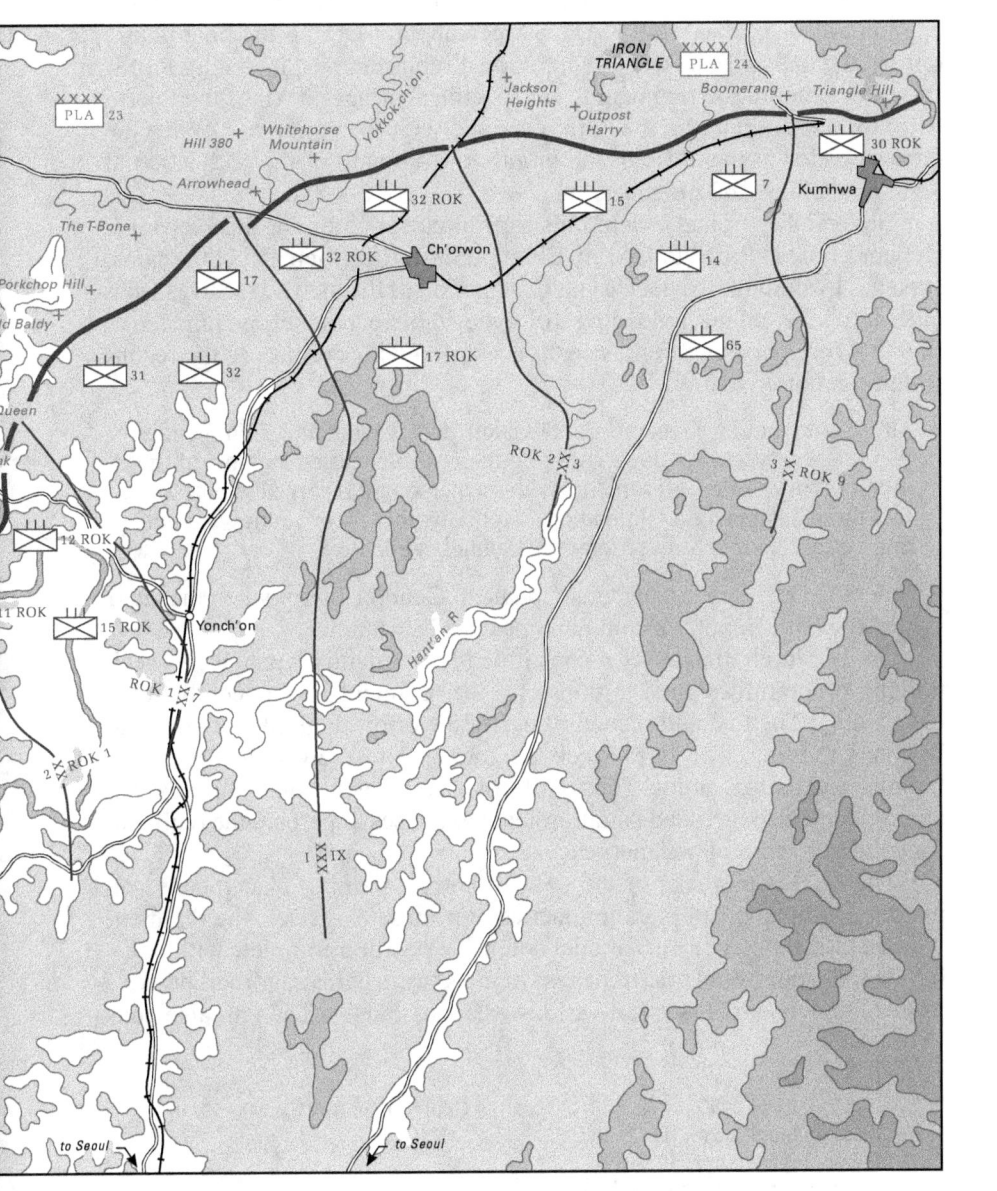

soldiers moved from the 65th Infantry to the 1st Cavalry Division and to the 2d, 7th, 24th, 25th, 40th, and 45th Divisions.[72] Three days later, the regiment also received 250 KATUSA personnel.[73] During the final phase, toward the end of March, 1,041 individual replacements, including 8 officers, were sent to the regiment to fill specific shortages.[74] All of the Puerto Rican officers serving in the 65th remained with the regiment.[75] When the process ended at the close of the month, the strength of the 65th stood at 3,567, including 160 officers.[76]

General Taylor had ordered his staff to closely monitor the exchange. He sent a note to the Eighth Army Chief of Staff, Brig. Gen. Paul D. Adams, stating, "I would like to get De Gavre's opinion of the men he receives from other units. I want no 'unloading' [of undesirable personnel] on him."[77] An Eighth Army personnel representative charged with overseeing the reconstitution reported to Taylor:

> The Commanding General, 3d Division and Regimental Commander feel that everyone involved is giving their wholehearted support to the project. They were well satisfied with the personnel received to date and feel there has been no "unloading." Actually, they believe they are getting better than a cross-section of personnel available.[78]

Colonel De Gavre gave a personal update to General Taylor when the latter visited the 65th Infantry's command post on 28 March.[79]

On 31 March, the newly reconstituted 65th Infantry began a six-week training program designed to transform the regiment into a "combat efficient team." The first and second weeks of the effort focused on individual weapons training. The third week was devoted to crew-served weapons training and squad tactics. The fourth involved mostly squad and platoon tactics, but it also included battalion-level exercises to prepare the regiment for combat in case of an emergency.

The final two weeks of the 65th Infantry's training plan focused on platoon, company, and battalion tactics. For these exercises, the regiment built an infiltration course; a model defensive position complete with fighting and sleeping bunkers, trenches, tunnels, minefields, and barbed-wire fences; a bayonet course; and various weapons ranges. The unit also con-

---

[72] Ibid.
[73] G–1 Jnl, Entry 3, 13–14 Mar 53, in Monthly Cmd Rpt, 3d Inf Div, Mar 53.
[74] Ibid., multiple entries, 15–31 Mar 53.
[75] Memo, Eighth Army, 10 Mar 53.
[76] Monthly Cmd Rpt, 65th Inf, Mar 53.
[77] Memo, 3 Mar 53, CG, Eighth Army to CofS, Eighth Army, encl to Memo, Eighth Army, 10 Mar 53.
[78] Memo, Eighth Army, 10 Mar 53.
[79] G–1 Jnl, dtd 281130 Mar 53, in Monthly Cmd Rpt, 3d Inf Div, Mar 53.

Sleeping bunker used by UN soldiers. These were normally located behind the main line of resistance.

structed volleyball courts and softball fields for physical training and athletic recreation.[80]

During the first four weeks of training in April, the regiment began to show renewed signs of confidence and pride. During the month, eight officers and sixty-four enlisted men departed and eight new officers and some three hundred fifty enlisted men arrived. The unit organized its first formal parade on 12 April, where General Smythe awarded two Silver Stars and two Bronze Stars to three members of the regiment. Eight days later, elements of the 2d Battalion staged a demonstration, "The Squad in the Attack," for General Jenkins who afterward complimented the men on their performance.[81] On 27 April, the battalion staged a second demonstration, "The Platoon in the Attack," for the new assistant division commander, Brig. Gen. Wilbur E. Dunkelberg.[82]

April also brought a significant change in the war. The election of Dwight D. Eisenhower, who succeeded Harry S. Truman as president of the United

---

[80] Monthly Cmd Rpt, 65th Inf, Mar 53.
[81] Ibid., Apr 53.
[82] Ibid.

States in January, coupled with the death of Soviet leader Joseph V. Stalin in March, created a political environment favorable to ending the Korean conflict. On 26 April, as a result, UN and Communist emissaries returned to Panmunjom after a six-month hiatus. Communist negotiators made a key concession, expressing their willingness to allow prisoners of war to decide whether to return to their homelands. This opened the door to further negotiations. As a sign of mutual good faith, both sides agreed to an immediate exchange of the sick and wounded, Operation LITTLE SWITCH, which resulted in the repatriation of 684 UN and 6,670 Communist personnel. The two sides then sat down to the laborious task of hammering out a peace accord.[83]

While that was taking place, the 3d Infantry Division gained a new commander: on 10 May, Maj. Gen. Eugene W. Ridings replaced General Smythe.[84] A 1923 West Point graduate, 53-year-old Ridings had previously served as the assistant division commander of the 23d Americal Division in the South Pacific during World War II, where he won two Silver Stars. Prior to taking command of the 3d Division, General Ridings had served as the deputy chief of staff for Army Field Forces Far East.[85]

Vindication and Homecoming

On 12 May, at the end of the 65th Infantry's six-week training cycle, the 3d Division alerted the regiment that it would relieve the 15th Infantry and elements of the 5th Regimental Combat Team in the sector between Ch'orwon and Kumhwa, the area the 65th had occupied at the end of 1952.[86] Over the next three days, the 2d and 3d Battalions took up their forward positions while the 1st Battalion stood behind them in reserve.

Facing the 65th were elements of the Chinese *216th Regiment, 72d Division*, and *221st Regiment, 74th Division*, both part of the *24th Army*. Fourteen battalions of artillery supported the two Chinese regiments. American intelligence believed that the morale and discipline of the enemy was high and that his combat efficiency was "good."[87]

The Chinese decided to test the 65th as soon as it had taken up position on the front line. Shortly after midnight on 16 May, U.S. observers detected an enemy battalion moving toward Outpost Harry. Located about two-and-a-half miles southeast of Jackson Heights, Harry was manned by elements of the 15th Infantry reinforced with Company G of the 65th Infantry. The American defenders called in artillery, breaking up the Communist attack

---

[83] Hermes, *Truce Tent and Fighting Front*, pp. 414–19.
[84] Monthly Cmd Rpt, 3d Inf Div, May 53.
[85] *Register of Graduates and Former Cadets, 1802–1980*, p. 341.
[86] Monthly Cmd Rpt, 65th Inf, May 53.
[87] Monthly Cmd Rpt, 3d Inf Div, May 53.

The west portion of Outpost Harry as seen from the American main line of resistance farther to the south

before it came within small-arms range of Harry. The enemy soon replied in kind, however, using the cover of an artillery barrage to launch a three-pronged thrust against the outpost. The fighting lasted until 0330, at which time the Chinese again withdrew. The Americans claimed fifty-two enemy soldiers killed and seventy-five wounded.[88]

After the probe against Harry, the enemy remained fairly quiet for the rest of the month. During the same period, the 65th carried out thirty-eight ambush patrols that yielded one contact, a raid that resulted in contact, and four combat patrols that led to one firefight, all of which resulted in an estimated twenty-one Chinese soldiers killed and fourteen wounded.

Having taken moderate casualties in May (57 battle and 208 nonbattle deaths or injuries) and with new soldiers continuing to join the regiment, the 65th gained in net strength during the month. Over that period, the regiment rotated 14 officers and 39 enlisted men back to the United States and transferred another 2 officers and 29 enlisted men to other Eighth Army units. In return, it received 35 officers and 362 enlisted replacements. On 1 June, the strength of the regiment stood at 4,148 men. This included 169 officers, well above the unit's authorization of 152.[89]

---

[88] Ibid., Monthly Cmd Rpt, 65th Inf, May 53.
[89] Ibid.

The beginning of June 1953 found the 65th still on the front line—the old trace of Line Missouri—with the 2d Battalion on the left, the 3d Battalion on the right, and the 1st Battalion reconstructing Line Wyoming in the rear. After being relieved by the 15th Infantry on 5 June, the regiment shifted its position a kilometer to the northeast, putting the 3d and 1st Battalions on the forward line. The 2d Battalion went into reserve along a southern branch of the line known as Missouri Switch.

Perhaps incited by the movement of the 65th, the Chinese sent a force to probe the regiment. At 0300 on 10 June, a company of Chinese infantry supported by artillery and mortars attacked Company B of the 1st Battalion. Penetrating the U.S. defensive perimeter, the enemy entered the trenches occupied by the center platoon where they engaged the Americans in hand-to-hand combat. The battle lasted for some forty-five minutes until friendly forces counterattacked and expelled the Communists. Sporadic fighting continued until 0430, when the enemy finally broke contact.

Company B had 1 soldier killed and 14 wounded in the action, while the Chinese left behind 30 dead. Patrols later recovered Chinese uniform winter caps, submachine-gun magazines, and propaganda leaflets and found evidence that the enemy had removed many more of his casualties from the battlefield. Company F, supported by a section of tanks, retaliated for the Chinese attack by raiding the enemy that afternoon, inflicting an estimated 103 casualties, including 53 confirmed killed, and losing 3 killed and 33 wounded in the process.[90]

The pair of clashes on 10 June sparked a flurry of fighting in the 3d Division's sector. Over the next five days, the Chinese made several more attempts to seize Outpost Harry. These efforts varied in size from company-size probes to full-scale regimental attacks, always supported by dense concentrations of artillery and mortars backed by tanks functioning as artillery. The 15th Infantry defended the outpost tenaciously while the 65th Infantry's 3d Battalion provided supporting fire, engaging the Communists with heavy machine guns and mortars. The enemy managed to penetrate the 15th's positions on several occasions, but well-coordinated counterattacks and intense artillery concentrations hurled them back each time. The surge of fighting resulted in steep casualty figures for both sides. By 18 June, the 3d Division had sustained 275 killed, 1,199 wounded, and 40 missing in action, almost all at Outpost Harry. The division estimated that Communist casualties were in excess of 4,200.[91]

As the fighting continued, the 65th Infantry's 2d Battalion launched a series of company-size raids against the Chinese in an attempt to divert

---

[90] Monthly Cmd Rpt, 65th Inf, Jun 53.
[91] Monthly Cmd Rpt, 3d Inf Div, Jun 53.

American soldier equipped for raiding and patrolling operations in Korea during early 1953. Carrying an M1 Garand rifle, he is also wearing an armored vest to protect his upper torso from bullets and fragmentation.

enemy reinforcements from the battle for Harry. The regiment inflicted an estimated 90 casualties on the enemy, including 65 killed. In return, the 2d Battalion suffered 104 casualties, including 10 killed, 90 wounded, and 4 missing in action. Chinese artillery, mortar, and rocket concentrations caused the bulk of the losses, often forcing the Americans to break contact to avoid even greater casualties.[92] General Ridings called the 65th's effort "highly successful in that the enemy was denied the use of one of his best routes of approach into the friendly position."[93]

One officer of the regiment, 1st Lt. Richard E. Cavazos, received the Distinguished Service Cross for his role in the battle for Outpost Harry. On 14 June, Cavazos led his company in a raid on the entrenched Chinese, inflicting heavy casualties on the enemy and personally evacuating five wounded men to the safety of friendly lines. Not until he was assured that all of his men had returned from the raid would he allow treatment for his own wounds.[94]

All told, the 65th participated in five major actions during June 1953, including three company raids in addition to the struggle for Outpost Harry. The regiment displayed no hesitation during offensive operations even though the Chinese showered the attacking Americans with huge concentrations of artillery and mortar fire. When fighting on the defensive, the 65th held its ground stubbornly and counterattacked at the soonest opportunity. The regiment sustained 196 battle and 147 nonbattle casualties during the month, including 26 killed, 165 wounded, and 5 missing in action.[95] The regiment's performance during the fighting at Outpost Harry, which was as intense as fighting at Jackson Heights or Outpost Kelly, validated the Army's decision to reconstitute the unit as a fully integrated regiment and represented a major step in the 65th Infantry's redemption in the eyes of the division, corps, and army leadership.

At the beginning of July 1953, the regiment continued to man the front line near the base of the Iron Triangle, with the 1st Battalion on the left, the 2d in the center, and the 3d (with the 3d Reconnaissance Company) on the right. The unit's mission—to defend and improve its positions while patrolling its area of responsibility—remained unchanged. As before, the 65th occasionally raided the Chinese to gather intelligence and to keep the offensive spirit of the regiment in good shape. On 6 July, for example,

---

[92] Monthly Cmd Rpt, 65th Inf, Jun 53.
[93] Ibid.
[94] GO no. 832, HQ EUSAK, 10 Sep 53, sub: Award of Distinguished Service Cross to 1st Lt Richard E. Cavazos, Rcds of U.S. Army Operational, Tactical, and Support Organizations (World War II and Thereafter), RG 338, NACP. He remained in the Army and later rose to the rank of four-star general.
[95] Monthly Cmd Rpt, 65th Inf, Jun 53.

Company K conducted a well-executed raid that inflicted fifty enemy casualties while incurring thirty-three.[96]

As the armistice talks at Panmunjom reached their final stage, the Communists made one last bid to claim more territory and to teach the South Korean Army a lesson. On 13 July, elements of six Chinese armies attacked five South Korean divisions defending the sector near Kumsong, which lay near the seam of the U.S. IX Corps zone and the South Korean II Corps zone. The outnumbered South Koreans fought stubbornly but had no choice but to yield ground to the enemy.

During the first three days of the offensive, the Chinese succeeded in penetrating the line held by the South Korean Capital Division in the American IX Corps sector and also in the portion of the South Korean II Corps area defended by the 3d and 6th South Korean Divisions. Since these units were located on the flanks of a salient jutting into Communist territory, the South Korean 5th and 8th Divisions were threatened with encirclement. To prevent this from occurring, General Taylor ordered the South Korean II Corps and the Capital Division to fall back some eight miles until they reached the Kumsong River. This would aid allied efforts to hold off the Chinese by straightening out the current defensive line.[97] Unfortunately, the South Koreans retreated farther south than Taylor originally planned, allowing the enemy to cross the river.

On 13 and 14 July, the American 2d Division relieved the 3d Division, with the 38th Infantry taking over from the 65th, so the 3d Division could move eastward to help the South Koreans. At the same time, the American 187th Airborne Regimental Combat Team relieved portions of the South Korean 9th Division, permitting IX Corps to shift additional troops eastward to reinforce the threatened left flank of the Capital Division.[98]

Between 14 and 15 July, the bulk of the 3d Division took up a blocking position behind the South Korean Capital Division, which was guarding the right wing of the IX Corps sector a few miles east of Kumhwa. When the Capital Division received Taylor's orders to pull back, it withdrew south through a defensive line held by the 7th and 65th Infantries. The Chinese did not attempt to pursue the Capital Division as it passed through American lines.

Over the next several days, South Korean counterattacks regained some but not all of the ground lost to the Chinese. The front stabilized again on 19 July, and the conferees at Panmunjom began deciding the final terms of the armistice. On 26 July 1953, after receiving word that a truce would

---

[96] Monthly Cmd Rpt, 65th Inf, Jul 53.
[97] Hermes, *Truce Tent and Fighting Front*, p. 475.
[98] Ibid.

be signed the following day, Eighth Army began making plans to redeploy the 3d Infantry Division southward out of what would soon become the demilitarized zone separating the two Koreas.[99]

In the final days of the war, the 65th Infantry gained a new commander. Colonel De Gavre, who had overseen the difficult but ultimately successful process of rebuilding the regiment after Jackson Heights, moved on to become the senior adviser to the South Korean 12th Division. His replacement, 42-year-old Col. Claude M. Howard, was a 1934 West Point graduate who served as a battalion commander with the 88th Division in Italy, where he had earned a Silver Star, a Bronze Star, and a Purple Heart.[100]

The 65th Infantry's final combat operation took place on 27 July, when 2d Lt. George W. Baird led a reconnaissance patrol from Company B north of the U.S. line. Upon spotting a group of fifteen Chinese soldiers, Baird called for artillery fire which quickly dispersed the enemy.[101] The patrol returned without further incident. On 27 July 1953 at 1000, Communist and UN negotiators signed a truce and notified all commanders that a cease-fire would go into effect at 2200. At 1500, the Chinese unleashed a storm of steel that inflicted numerous casualties throughout the 65th's sector. Then, at 2145, the barrage ceased as suddenly as it had begun. Fifteen minutes later, an eerie silence fell across the entire front. The Korean War had ended.

The men of the 65th Infantry spent the remainder of the month policing their assigned sectors and moving all ammunition and equipment farther south. By 1800 on 31 July, the regiment could certify to division headquarters that all of its men were out of the demilitarized zone.[102] Taking stock of the last month of the war, the 65th Infantry had suffered 171 battle and 95 nonbattle casualties. Many of the combat losses were the result of the surprise enemy barrage that heralded the end of the conflict.[103]

The 65th Infantry remained in Korea through the autumn of 1954, providing border security and acting as a reserve unit in case hostilities recommenced. The regiment, as well as the 3d Division and the Eighth Army, retained its edge through individual and small-unit training, battalion and regiment alerts, division staff exercises, and frequent formal and

---

[99] Monthly Cmd Rpts, 65th Inf, Jul 53, and 3d Inf Div, Jul 53.

[100] *United States Military Academy Register of Graduates and Former Cadets* (West Point, N.Y.: Association of Graduates, 2002), pp. 4–181; John P. Delaney, *The Blue Devils in Italy: The Story of the 88th Division* (Washington, D.C.: Infantry Journal Press, 1947), p. 340; *History of the 349th Infantry Regiment, 88th Infantry Division* (Kensington, Md.: 88th Division Association, 1973), p. 5.

[101] Monthly Cmd Rpt, 65th Inf, Jul 53.

[102] Ibid.

[103] Ibid.

unannounced command inspections. Soldiers took classes on how to cope with chemical, biological, and radiological hazards, as well as how to prevent cold-weather injuries and disease. Dozens of men graduated from the division's NCO academy each month, bringing an end to the shortage of noncommissioned officers that had haunted the 65th for so long.[104]

As the UN commanders gained confidence that the Chinese and the North Koreans did not plan to resume hostilities, at least in the near term, the U.S. Army began to redeploy some of its forces from Korea. After being relieved of its assignment to the 3d Division on 3 November, the 65th Infantry returned to Puerto Rico later that month. Exuberant crowds greeted the regiment when it disembarked at San Juan. At that point, the unit had been away from the island for over four years. On 2 December, the U.S. Army assigned the regiment to the 23d Division; but for all practical purposes, the 65th had ended its days of service with the Regular Army. On 10 April 1956, the Army relieved the 65th Infantry from its assignment to the 23d Division and then inactivated the regiment at Camp Losey, Puerto Rico. Although no longer a part of the active Regular Army, the 65th Infantry was destined to live on as a military unit long after Korea. Juan C. Cordero-Davila, the popular island politician and housing authority administrator who had commanded the 65th as a colonel in 1952, had risen to the rank of brigadier general despite the incident at Jackson Heights. Yielding to pressure from Cordero-Davila, the Department of the Army allotted the 65th Infantry to the 92d Infantry Brigade of the Puerto Rico National Guard on 6 February 1959, after withdrawing the regiment from the Regular Army.[105]

The 65th Infantry represented the most visible, though not the only, contribution that Puerto Ricans made in fighting the Korean War. Approximately sixty-one thousand Puerto Ricans served in the U.S. Army during the conflict. Of these, forty-eight thousand joined in Puerto Rico and the remainder came from the continental United States. Over the course of the war, some seven hundred fifty Puerto Ricans died in battle and some twenty-four hundred were wounded.[106]

Why did Puerto Ricans fight in Korea? When that question was asked during a unit reunion forty-six years after the end of the conflict, the men in a group of 65th Infantry veterans agreed: "We fought because we were soldiers of the United States and of the regiment. It was our duty."[107]

---

[104] Monthly Cmd Rpts, 3d Inf Div, Aug–Sep 53.

[105] Rpt, DA, 30 Jun 94, sub: Lineage and Honors, 65th Infantry (The Borinqueneers), Historians files.

[106] "Participation of Puerto Ricans in the Armed Services with Emphasis on World War I, World War II, and the Korean War," Headquarters, Antilles Command, 1965, sec. 2, p. 1, CMH.

[107] Min, Lajas Veterans Association Mtg, Lajas, P.R., 30 Jul 00, Historians files.

Conclusion

The story of the 65th Infantry regiment during the Korean War is one of pride, courage, heartbreak, and redemption. In many ways, the 65th Infantry's experiences reflect the strengths and weaknesses of the American Army of that era and indeed of the entire nation. Initially better equipped, trained, and manned for combat than most of its sister infantry formations, the 65th perhaps fell prey to the social ethos and military manpower policies of a nation that had not yet come to terms with its new preeminent role in world affairs. Like the rest of the allied forces on the Korean peninsula, the Puerto Rican unit found itself mired in a bitter war of attrition in which military technology could not always compensate for the rugged terrain, harsh climate, and a relentless, determined enemy willing to spend the lives of its own soldiers to achieve political and military objectives. As always under such conditions, morale and leadership at all levels were key elements of success on the battlefield. If the 65th did not always triumph in combat, its performance was no different—in many ways it was better—than American infantry units fighting in similar conditions throughout the twentieth century.

For the historical record, it is clear that the 65th Infantry went through three distinct phases during the Korean War—four if the "integration" period is considered. During the first phase, from the regiment's arrival in Korea in September 1950 until the following May, it performed well, reflecting its ethnic, geographic, and linguistic cohesion; superior training; and high personnel fill. In general, its continental officers spoke Spanish and its enlisted ranks understood English so internal communications were not a problem. More important, all of its soldiers were long-term volunteers who knew one another well and its high performance reflected the teamwork vital for military success. Finally, all sources agree that the leadership within the regiment, especially that of its commander, was decisive in knitting together all elements and making it an effective combat force. As a result, the performance of the 65th during the early days of the Korean War was outstanding. The regiment stood out as one of the major assets of its new parent unit, the U.S. Army's elite 3d Infantry Division.

The second phase began during the late spring of 1951 and lasted for another year. During this period, most members of the original force, both cadre and troops, departed, either through attrition or through the completion of a one-year combat tour. In their place arrived cohorts of Puerto Rican National Guardsmen whose level of experience and training was inferior to that of the regulars they replaced. On the other hand, many were also long-term volunteers, their integration into the regiment was gradual, and much of the unit cohesion exhibited earlier was preserved. More problematic was the February 1952 arrival of a Puerto Rican National Guard commanding officer, Col. Juan C. Cordero-Davila, who had little battlefield experience or formal military education. The appointment may have made political sense at the time, but the new commander's eventual failure to train and lead what was slowly becoming an entirely different unit because of personnel turnover would prove devastating and result in his relief within eight months in command. During this period, only the presence of several able battalion and company commanders and noncommissioned officers held the unit together.

Roughly between May and September 1952, the National Guard soldiers were replaced by a third wave, or rotation, of enlisted soldiers, generally draftees or new volunteers with basic military training and experience and little if any comprehension of English. Similarly, few of the newly arrived leaders in the regiment possessed a working knowledge of Spanish or the Latino culture. Gone was even the memory of the cohesion and camaraderie that had characterized the earlier groups along with their hard-earned combat experience and general military savvy. The collective weaknesses of the regiment had remained cloaked by the static nature of the war, which featured few of the difficult tactical maneuvers executed during the first year of the conflict. Yet, most of the unit's problems that emerged during this period could be traced to poor leadership both within the 65th Infantry and within the 3d Infantry Division itself. But leadership and experience problems within the regiment were no different from those that beset other Army combat units, reflecting larger national manpower policies as well as the nature of the conflict itself, which had become a stalemated, set-piece war of attrition that seemed to have no logical end in sight.

Before taking a closer look at the fighting experienced by the 65th during these more trying phases, a word needs to be said about the language problem upon which an official investigation later laid blame for the unit's alleged marginal performance. Such communications problems are certainly not unique to the 65th and have in fact been faced by military forces since time immemorial. Moreover, the existence of this "problem" could hardly have been a revelation to the unit's chain of command, having existed since the regiment's inception many decades before.

Given the U.S. Army's tactical command and control system at the time—one that served it well throughout the entire century—the individual responsible for addressing such difficulties was clearly the division commander supported by his theater superiors. For an infantry division commander, his most important subordinates were his three combat regimental commanders; likewise, his most important units were his three combat regiments and their nine infantry battalions. Together, leaders and men, they represented the absolute core of his fighting strength. For other forces and functions—planning, logistics, intelligence, fire support, engineers, communications, etc.—he had a large management staff that was in turn supervised by a chief of staff and at least one assistant division commander, both senior officers. The division commander himself would have been expected to visit his regimental commanders on an almost daily basis whenever possible.

In the case of the 65th Infantry, the 3d Division commander ought to have noticed the existence of any serious language communication problems and taken steps to correct them as quickly as possible. Arranging for basic or refresher Spanish-language classes for his continental cadre and similar English-language classes for his Hispanic soldiers ought to have been simple tasks supported by the immense resources of the theater command. If such action was not taken—it appears that such was the case despite the extensive training time available to the unit in the spring of 1952—then the regiment's higher level chain of command must be faulted. In the same way, if Colonel Cordero-Davila's training regimen erred on the side of inspections and "spit and polish" drills akin to peacetime operations, then it was the responsibility of the division commander to intervene and mentor his much-less-experienced-but-motivated subordinate. Perhaps the 3d Division commander at that time, Maj. Gen. Robert L. Dulaney, never took ownership of this somewhat unusual unit whose ethnic composition made it an anomaly in the U.S. Army of the time.

The appointment of Colonel Cordero-Davila to command the regiment was based primarily on political rather than military considerations. Cordero-Davila was the only National Guard officer sent from the United States to command a regular infantry regiment in Korea. Although National Guard regimental commanders with the 40th and 45th Infantry Divisions deployed with their regiments to Korea, they were replaced by Regular Army officers after rotating home. Cordero-Davila had limited combat experience and had attended an abbreviated version of the Army's yearlong Command and General Staff College. Instead, he owed his assignment to his close ties with Puerto Rico's political elite, which might also have made his superiors hesitant to address shortcomings in his command.

As noted above, during the first half of 1952 and the first months of Cordero-Davila's tenure, personnel turbulence within officer and enlisted ranks of the regiment worsened, causing it to lose much of its hard-won combat efficiency. For this reason, the regiment was taken out of line for four months of refresher training; however, the results were not entirely successful. In addition to the many regimental command inspections and administrative requirements during this period, supply problems and tactical developments also caused problems. Periodic ammunition shortages within Eighth Army limited the regiment's ability to conduct live-fire exercises and realistic combined-arms training, while major components of the 65th were sometimes detached for emergency frontline duties. More important, after Cordero-Davila's experienced battalion commanders rotated home, he delegated tactical training to his individual company commanders. Not surprisingly, if a company commander was good, his unit trained well; if the opposite was true, the unit's combat effectiveness suffered. The result was an unevenly applied training program, with some elements of the 65th benefiting more than others.

Despite personnel turbulence and training problems during the first half of 1952, the failure of the regiment at Outpost Kelly in September was not inevitable. Had 1st Lt. William F. Nelson insisted that his men remain on full alert, Company B might have held its position. Indeed, his relaxed attitude reflected the guidance of the regimental commander, who believed that the Chinese would remain in a defensive posture despite warnings to the contrary from division headquarters. At the very least, the sudden increase in the number and aggressiveness of enemy patrols, as well as the frequency and intensity of Chinese artillery and mortar barrages, ought to have put the colonel on guard. Perhaps overconfident in the strength of his defenses and lacking combat experience himself, Cordero-Davila chose to downplay indications of impending Chinese offensive action.[1]

Company B's complacent attitude toward local security, coupled with the number of soldiers declared missing in action after the loss of Outpost Kelly, suggests that the unit was literally caught sleeping when the enemy attacked. Capt. George D. Jackson, the Company G commander, later testified that "Company B had been surprised (patrols found dead men in their sleeping bags), and overcome rapidly by the attacking Chinese."[2] Given some warning, Company B should have been capable of defeating an attack by two reinforced Chinese companies. Instead, the Chinese surprised and killed many Company B troops before the unit could react, forcing the bulk of the unit's unwounded survivors to flee.

Cordero-Davila's failure to order a swift counterattack once the outpost had fallen into enemy hands is inexplicable. Almost twenty-four hours

---

[1] Warren Franklyn, "Puerto Ricans Vow Changing Hill's Name," *Pacific Stars and Stripes*, 28 September 1952, copy in Historians files, CMH.

[2] Statement, Maj George D. Jackson, n.d., sub: Manpower in the 65th Infantry, p. 3.

Conclusion

elapsed before he issued an order to retake Kelly. Although the colonel was concerned that a counterattack supported by artillery would endanger American soldiers still held captive on the hill, he might have succeeded in recovering both them and the outpost had the regiment moved before the enemy had time to consolidate his gains. Even after the Chinese had marched the Company B prisoners to their rear and many of the American wounded made their way back to friendly lines, the regimental commander remained paralyzed with indecision.

In the end, too much time elapsed before Cordero-Davila acted. According to the assistant regimental intelligence officer, Cordero-Davila attacked only at the insistence of the I Corps commander, Lt. Gen. Paul W. Kendall.[3] If this is true, the 3d Division commander, General Dulaney, also bears some responsibility for the delayed response that left the enemy with ample time to prepare an effective defense. Finally, Cordero-Davila's belated counterattack took place in a piecemeal fashion, with platoons and companies acting in isolation, in contrast to the coordinated, large-scale concept outlined by the formal plan. Lacking sufficient direct and indirect combat power to affect the enemy defensive fires, the penny packets of attacking American infantrymen found it impossible to close with the enemy. The fact that the Americans attacked only from one direction at a time also made it relatively easy for the Chinese to repel their assaults.

The episode also underlined the lack of combined-arms capability necessary for success. Although the 65th called in artillery and air strikes against the Chinese defending Kelly, the supporting fire was poorly coordinated with the infantry assaults. Too much time elapsed between the end of the friendly artillery and air strikes and the beginning of the counterattacks, allowing the enemy to recover and man his defenses. In addition, counterbattery fire did not have any significant impact on Chinese artillery.

Finally, Colonel Cordero-Davila and his battalion commanders failed to inspire their men by accompanying the assault elements. Captain Jackson later recounted:

> During the counterattack on Kelly Hill by the 3d Battalion he [Cordero-Davila] was in my CP (which afforded a very good view of the Kelly battle). When we reported to him that members of the 3d Battalion were moving to the rear, he said that he had a report from the battalion commander that they were still attacking.[4]

An experienced commander would have looked for himself if there were any doubts.

---

[3] Ltr, author to Wolf, 7 Jul 00, Historians files.
[4] Ltr, Jackson to author, 2 Jun 01, Historians files.

The abandonment of Outposts Tessie and Nick on the night of 19 September and the loss of Big Nori on 25 September also reflected on the 65th Infantry and raised serious doubts within the 3d Division and I Corps about Cordero-Davila's ability to lead the regiment in combat. General Dulaney's decision to relieve Cordero-Davila and replace him with Col. Chester B. De Gavre was correct. As De Gavre had previously served with the regiment, Dulaney thought him better equipped than most commanders to turn the 65th around. But some of De Gavre's leadership decisions are also questionable. Requiring his troops to shave all their facial hair including moustaches, a traditional symbol of Puerto Rican masculinity, when added to rumors of other unmerited disciplinary actions, could hardly improve unit morale.

Whatever De Gavre's good intentions, he lacked the time to accomplish much else before the 65th received orders to defend Jackson Heights. During the fighting, Captain Jackson's Company G held the position against significant odds until ordered to withdraw. First Lt. John D. Porterfield Jr.'s Company A and Capt. Willis D. Cronkhite Jr.'s Company F retook it in a well-executed assault. Most of Companies A and F, however, refused to remain on the ridge in the face of artillery fire that killed or wounded Company A's officers. The regiment's last chance to redeem itself collapsed when the bulk of Company C abandoned Jackson Heights the following morning, this time without being prompted by enemy opposition. Their behavior, however unfortunate, was not that unusual in wartime under harsh combat conditions. Nevertheless, as a result of the latter event, the Army's theater leaders took harsh measures, approving mass courts-martial of those involved, with one officer and fifty-one enlisted men receiving stiff sentences for desertion, misbehavior before the enemy, and willfully disobeying a lawful order from a superior officer. Additionally, thirty-nine other soldiers were convicted of similar offenses when they refused to follow another officer in November.

By mid-January 1953, mostly as the result of letters written by the Puerto Rican soldiers to their friends and families back home, newspapers in the United States and Puerto Rico began to feature stories describing the courts-martial of the men of the 65th Infantry.[5] On 27 January, the *New York Times* ran an article noting that the governor of Puerto Rico and the Puerto Rican press had asked the Army for an official inquiry into the events at Jackson Heights and the courts-martial of the Puerto Rican soldiers.

---

[5] Lindsey Parrot, "88 U.S. Soldiers Convicted of Quitting Battle in Korea," *New York Times*, 25 January 1953; "Korea Trial Involves 92 men," *New York Times*, 26 January 1953; copies of both in Historians files.

CONCLUSION

On 3 February 1953, General Collins, the Army Chief of Staff, during one of his appearances before the House Armed Services Committee, was asked about the 65th Infantry and the courts-martial following its defeat at Jackson Heights. Collins described the 65th has having been "a very well trained" and "very ably led unit" when it first arrived in Korea, "where it distinguished itself in action." He blamed the subsequent failure of the regiment on the rotation policy, the inability of the men to speak English, and the lack of battlefield experience of its officers. "The Puerto Ricans have proven in action in earlier fighting in Korea that they are gallant people and that they will fight just as well as anyone else if they are properly trained and properly led."[6]

As a result of the publicity, the U.S. Congress, the government of Puerto Rico, and the press all demanded an investigation of the incident. A more thorough investigation took place, leading the secretary of the Army to pardon those convicted. As did the original appointment of Cordero-Davila to command the regiment, the decision to commute the sentences of those convicted would seem to have been a political one.

The 65th's uneven performance in combat during the latter half of 1952 had also put its very existence in jeopardy. In 1950 and 1951, a powerful combination of division, corps, army, and theater commanders believed in the regiment. By the autumn of 1952, the opposite had become true, and the chain of command was working to get rid of the regiment.

A letter from General Van Fleet to Maj. Gen. Thomas J. Cross, a former 3d Division commander and longtime veteran of the division, provides some insight into the hard-line approach commanders had adopted toward the 65th Infantry in the wake of Jackson Heights. "Your old division is coming along exceptionally fine under George Smythe with the exception of the 65th," wrote Van Fleet. "That will never be corrected until we can restore to the division its old regiment now at Fort Benning."[7]

Even so, not everyone within the Army chain of command felt poorly disposed toward the 65th Infantry. Despite problems on Jackson Heights, the regiment still had enough supporters to convince the Army to rebuild the 65th as an integrated regiment rather than disband the unit and send it home in shame. Unlike the all-black 24th Infantry and all-white 34th Infantry, both of which the Army inactivated during the Korean War after senior commanders perceived them as being unreliable in combat, the 65th Infantry was not removed from the Army's rolls. The 65th vindicated the Army's decision to retain it when it defended Outpost Harry in early 1953,

---

[6] U.S. Congress, House of Representatives, Committee on Armed Services, *Operation Smack* (H. Res. 121), 83d Cong., 1st Sess., 3 Feb 53, p. 43, copy in Historians files.

[7] Ltr, Van Fleet to Maj Gen Thomas J. Cross, 31 Dec 52, Van Fleet Papers, GML.

finishing the war on a high note and allowing the regiment's colors to return to Puerto Rico with pride.

The 65th Infantry in Korea—its glory, decline, failure, and redemption—is the unique story of a one-of-a-kind regiment. Its Puerto Rican composition set it apart from other Eighth Army units in Korea and led to unique challenges, specifically of language, that no other regiments had to face in equal measure. The Army's official explanation for the regiment's failures in 1952—that the Spanish-speaking enlisted men could not communicate with their officers—masked other factors that played a role in the defeats at Outpost Kelly and Jackson Heights. Chief among them, the rotation policy never provided enough experienced NCOs so the regiment could be properly led. The lack of seasoned leaders also hurt the 65th's training program during those periods when it went into reserve. Above all, the failure of the unit's parent division and corps commanders to remedy the problems needs to be highlighted.

The 65th Infantry, a historically Puerto Rican regiment, ended up being the last segregated unit to fight in Korea. Its service and sacrifices reveal not only broad truths about that war but also specific insights that may help future soldiers and scholars understand why a particular unit will succeed or fail on the battlefield.

BIBLIOGRAPHICAL NOTE

Primary Sources

The sources for this account, with the exception of the first chapter, were monthly command reports, operations orders, intelligence estimates, combat interviews, and maps compiled or composed before, during, or just after the combat operations in this book. The documents come not only from the 65th Infantry but also from adjacent and sister regiments; attached formations such as the 58th Field Artillery and the 64th Heavy Tank Battalions; and higher headquarters such as I Corps, IX Corps, X Corps, and Eighth Army. Although changes in the Army regulations governing the preparation and submission of monthly command reports at the regiment and division levels lowered the detail available in operational summaries from February 1953 onward, Far East Command sources generally filled the gap.

The bulk of these documents are located in Entry 429, Records of the Adjutant General's Office, 1917, Record Group (RG) 407, at the National Archives and Records Administration II in College Park, Maryland. This record group includes not only material generated during combat in Korea but also command reports from organizations that supported the 65th, including the 296th Infantry, the Military District of Puerto Rico, U.S. Army Forces Antilles, and the U.S. Army Caribbean Command. Other useful material, primarily dealing with Eighth Army, is in the Records of U.S. Army Operational, Tactical, and Support Organizations (World War II and Thereafter), RG 338, also at College Park. Many of the photographs collected for this book are in the Records of the Office of the Chief Signal Officer, RG 111, maintained by the Still Pictures Branch at College Park.

The National Archives' National Personnel Records Center in St. Louis, Missouri, provided a great deal of invaluable material, particularly company morning reports and details from the individual personnel files of the regiment's officers and men. Trial records for the soldiers who were court-martialed came from the U.S. Army Court of Criminal Appeals in Arlington, Virginia.

Very informative materials covering the fighting in April 1951 are located in the Papers of the Office of the Chief of the Imperial General

Staff (War Office [WO] 216), National Archives of Great Britain, Kew, London. Of particular interest is "Impression of the British Commonwealth Part in CCF Offensive on 22–26 April 1951 as Seen by Lieutenant General Sir HCH Robertson KBE DSO Who Was in The Area" (WO 216/325).

Oral History Interviews and Manuscript Sources

The U.S. Army Center of Military History's specialized archive houses a number of unpublished Korean War manuscripts and a complete collection of the combat interviews compiled by Eighth Army's military history detachment. The most useful of these included the first draft of Maj. Elva M. Stillwaugh, "Personnel Polices in the Korean Conflict" (1953); Maj. Henry A. Jeffers and Cpl. Charles L. Reinhart, "Assignment and Reassignment in Korea: July 1951–July 1953" (1954); and 1st Lt. Edward H. Ross, "The Puerto Rican Induction Program and the Use of Puerto Rican Troops" (Antilles Historical Department, 1948).

While Eighth Army combat interviews do not deal specifically with the 65th, they provide detailed coverage of other 3d Division units as well as events in which the 65th was involved. Some of the interviews deal with specific operations such as COMMANDO and DOUGHNUT rather than with a specific unit. In addition to narratives prepared by historians, these interviews often contain photographs, maps and overlays, transcripts of verbatim testimony by participants, and extracts from operational documents.

For information on the regiment prior to World War II, the Center of Military History's collections of War Department Annual Reports, General Orders, Bulletins, and the *Army and Navy Journal* were especially valuable. So was the Center's collection of Army Field Artillery School interviews with artillery officers who had recently returned from Korea.

The U.S. Army Military History Institute at Carlisle Barracks, Pennsylvania, houses the Matthew B. Ridgway Papers. This collection spans the period 1907–1993, with the bulk of the material concentrated between 1942 and 1955. The Ridgway Papers include a detailed finding aid, official correspondence, personal correspondence, oral history transcripts, and photographs. Of equal worth is the Joan and Clay Blair Jr. interview collection, Combat Leadership in Korea. Compiled by Mr. Blair while he was conducting research for *The Forgotten War: America in Korea, 1950–1953* (New York: Times Books, 1987), the collection is limited in scope because it deals primarily with the first year of the conflict.

The Military History Institute also maintains a collection of veterans surveys that proved helpful in compiling background material for this book. Although the ability of old soldiers to recall clearly and to portray their experiences five decades after an event limits the overall usefulness of these materials, some veterans attached to their surveys additional items such as personal memoirs. Closer to the events, these can sometimes be of particular value.

The research library of the Virginia Military Institute's George C. Marshall Foundation in Lexington, Virginia, hosts an 85-cubic-foot document collection donated by the family of General James A. Van Fleet. One of its seven subgroups is devoted entirely to his service as commanding general of Eighth Army in Korea. The Van Fleet Papers also include a large number of photographs, making this one of the largest collections in the Marshall archives.

Secondary Sources

Several published works on the Korean War proved useful. Roy E. Appleman, *South to the Naktong, North to the Yalu, June–November 1950*, U.S. Army in the Korean War (Washington, D.C.: Office of the Chief of Military History, 1961), provides an extremely clear view, albeit from a United Nations perspective, of the events that took place during the first year of the conflict. Billy C. Mossman's follow-on volume, *Ebb and Flow, November 1950–July 1951*, U.S. Army in the Korean War (Washington, D.C.: U.S. Army Center of Military History, 1990), begins with the Chinese entry into the war and concludes with the initiation of armistice talks. While Mossman's timeline makes sense from a strategic perspective, it does not analyze how U.S. forces in Korea were affected by significant changes in Communist battlefield tactics. The third volume of the U.S. Army's Korean War series, Walter G. Hermes' *Truce Tent and Fighting Front* (Washington, D.C.: Office of the Chief of Military History, 1966), covers the 65th Infantry's failure to retake Outpost Kelly in September 1952 but is less detailed when discussing Jackson Heights and the unit's integration in March 1953.

Lynn Montross and Capt. Nicholas A. Canzona, *U.S. Marine Operations in Korea, 1950–1953*, 5 vols. (Washington, D.C.: Historical Branch, Headquarters, U.S. Marine Corps, 1957), vol. 3, *The Chosin Reservoir Campaign*, was written soon after the end of the war. Because of its early date, many of the sources were still classified and thus unavailable to the authors. Even so, the book provides a detailed glimpse into U.S. Marine Corps operations during November and December 1950.

The official historical sources this book employs are not confined to those of the U.S. Army and Marine Corps. South Korea's *The History of the United Nations Forces in the Korean War* (Seoul, Korea: Ministry of National Defense, 1977) discusses not only South Korean activities but also details the experiences of other UN contingents. The second of two volumes in General Anthony H. Farrar-Hockley's British history of the war, *The British Part in the Korean War* (London: Her Majesty's Stationary Office, 1995), provides valuable insight into the Gloucestershire Battalion's plight. Farrar-Hockley, who served as the battalion's adjutant, also recorded those events in a personal memoir, *The Edge of the Sword* (London: The Companion Book Club, 1955), which he wrote shortly after he returned home from two years in captivity.

There are only a few commercially published English-language sources on the 65th Infantry in Korea. Of those, the most well-known work, William W. Harris' *Puerto Rico's Fighting 65th U.S. Infantry: From San Juan to Chorwon* (San Rafael, Calif.: Presidio Press, 1980), proved to contain passages more dramatic than factual.

Abbreviations

AAA	Anti-Aircraft Artillery
AFA	Armored Field Artillery
AGCT	Army General Classification Test
AGO	Adjutant General's Office
BCT	battalion combat team
CG	commanding general
CMH	U.S. Army Center of Military History
CSA	chief of staff of the Army
DA	Department of the Army
DoD	Department of Defense
DPMO	Defense Prisoner of War/Missing Personnel Office
EUSAK	Eighth U.S. Army in Korea
FA	Field Artillery
FEC	Far East Command
FM	field manual
GHQ	General Headquarters
GML	George C. Marshall Library
GO	general orders
HE	high explosive
HQ	headquarters
KATUSA	Korean Augmentation to the United States Army
MHI	U.S. Army Military History Institute
MLR	main line of resistance
NACP	National Archives II, College Park (Md.)
NCO	noncommissioned officer
NPRC	National Personnel Records Center
PLA	People's Liberation Army (China)
PORTREX	Puerto Rico Exercise
PRNG	Puerto Rican National Guard
RCT	regimental combat team
RG	record group
ROK	Republic of Korea (South Korea)
RTC	Replacement Training Command
TNA	The National Archives (Great Britain)

UN	United Nations
UNC	United Nations Command
VHF	very high frequency
VMI	Virginia Military Institute
WD	War Department
WNRC	Washington National Records Center

Map Symbols

Military Units

Function

Armor	▭
Armored Cavalry	▨
Cavalry	◿
Field Artillery	⊡
Infantry	⊠

Size

Platoon	•••
Battery, Company, or Cavalry Troop	I
Battalion or Cavalry Squadron	II
Regiment	III
Brigade	x
Division	x x
Corps	x x x
Army	x x x x
Army Group	x x x x x

Examples

Company A, 65th Infantry

2d Battalion, 65th Infantry

5th Marine regiment

British 29th Independent Brigade Group

Headquarters, 1st Cavalry Division

North Korean *I Corps*

Chinese *40th Army*

Index

Acuff, Maj. Earl C., 243–44
Allen, Lt. Col. Edward G., 36, 38, 48, 53, 72, 87, 90, 96–97, 124, 145
Almond, Maj. Gen. Edward M.
  advance into northeastern Korea and, 41–68
  evacuation from Hungnam to Pusan, 68–76
  military background, 41
  Operation ROUNDUP, 95–97
  opinion of Puerto Rican soldiers, 47, 50
  Pusan Perimeter role, 28–29
Alpuerto, 1st Lt. Ben W., 228, 229
Alvarez, Capt. Theodore L., 246
Ammon, Capt. George F., 20
Ammunition shortages, 16, 20, 48–49, 55, 132–33, 171, 200–202, 241–42, 250–51, 298
Armistice talks, 291–92. *See also* Panmunjom, Korea.
Armstrong, Capt. George E., 53, 55, 70
Assistant Secretary of the Army. *See* Milton, Hugh M. II.
Austin, Lt. Col. John D., 182, 183, 187
Azurin, Col. Mariano C., 105–06

Baird, 2d Lt. George W., 292
Baker, Lt. Col. John, 265
Barno, 2d Lt. Eugene R., 242–44
Bathurst, Brig. Gen. Robert M., 189
Behne, 2d Lt. Edward P., 231n102, 257
Belgian Battalion. *See* Index of Units.
Betances-Ramirez, Lt. Col. Carlos, 212
  and courts-martial of troops, 266–67
  and Jackson Heights operations, 246–59

  objection to orders about troops' appearance, 239–40
  opinion of Guzman, 266–67
  and Outpost Kelly operations, 215, 222, 223
  replacement by Elam, 259
Big Nori, 216, 217–18, 231
Blair, Clay, 238–40
Boatner, Brig. Gen. Hayden L., 159
Bogell, 1st Lt. Frederick, 228, 229
Bolte, Maj. Gen. Charles L., 18–19
Borinqueneers. *See* Index of Units, U.S. Army, 65th Infantry.
Bowen, Brig. Gen. Frank S., 108
Boyle, Capt. Charles E.
  Chinese spring offensive, 124–25
  comments on General Ridgway's visit, 88
  Operation ROUNDUP and, 96
  views on Gibson, 153
Bradley, Brig. Gen. J. Sladen, 127
British Army. *See* Index of Units.
Brodie, Brig. Thomas, 122, 127–28, 130–33
Brooke, Maj. Gen. John R., 1
Brown, 2d Lt. Henry A., 246
Bubble, the, 216, 217–18. *See also* Big Nori.
Bunker Hill, 215
Burgos, 1st Lt. Eladio, 20
Burke, Capt. Harold D., 215, 246
Burns, Capt. Carl M., 197

Caffey, Maj. Gen. Eugene M., 265–66
Capitol Hill, 216
Carne, Lt. Col. Joseph P., 130, 133
Carrion-Maldonado, 2d Lt. Angel L., 246, 250
Carsely, 1st Lt. Albert E., 39, 57–59
Cartegena, Sgt. Modesto, 117

Casualties
  65th Infantry, 40, 49, 75, 76, 86, 91, 99, 144, 160, 161, 170, 173, 179, 183, 184, 185, 187, 191, 205, 212, 222, 226–27, 230, 231–32, 250–51, 255–56, 261, 279, 280, 287, 288, 290–91, 292
  and combat effectiveness, 21, 30, 173, 187–88, 229
  enemy, 40, 54, 59, 67, 81, 97n63, 144, 150, 158–59, 164, 168, 181, 183, 184, 185, 191, 222, 280, 288, 290
  friendly, 16, 32, 45, 49, 61n61, 76, 95, 147, 158–59, 172, 176n54, 183, 185, 194–95, 199–200, 211, 218, 254
Cavazos, 1st Lt. Richard E., 290
Centeno, Cpl. Gonzalez S., 91–92
Chamberlain, 1st Lt. Smith B., 147–48
Champoux, Capt. Francis L., 246
Changjin Reservoir, 41–68, 76
Changmol, Korea, 241–42
Changyong, Korea, 32–38
Chief of staff, Army. *See* Collins, General J. Lawton.
Childs, Lt. Col. George W., 12, 30–31, 64–66, 67–68. *See also* Task Forces, CHILDS.
Chinese Army. *See also* Index of Units.
  3d Division advance to Seoul and the Imjin and, 91–109
  assault on Line Utah, 117–18
  assessment of tactics in autumn 1951, 169
  attacks against X Corps in northeastern Korea, 45–61, 66–67, 70, 72
  attacks of October 1952, 242
  distribution of Christmas cards and signs, 184
  final attacks before the armistice, 291–92
  Gloucestershire Regiment and, 127–34
  improvement in defenses, 199
  Iron Triangle, 279, 290–91
  Jackson Heights, 248–61
  Line Jamestown, 180–82
  Line Utah attacks, 121–22

Operations
  CLEANUP, 169–73
  COURAGEOUS, 104–08
  DAUNTLESS, 112
  DOUGHNUT, 155–59
  KILLER, 98–99
  PILEDRIVER, 145–53
  RUGGED, 112
  WOLFHOUND, THUNDERBOLT, and EXPLOITATION, 80–91
Outpost Harry, 286–90
Outpost Kelly, 215–30, 299
response to U.S. raiding parties in January 1952, 187
small-unit patrols and raids against, 183–84
spring offensive, 122–27
withdrawal from Uijongbu, 108
Chip'yong-ni, Korea, 95–97, 98
Chol, Lt. Col. Suk Jong, 52
Ch'orwon Valley, 139–62
Clark, General Mark W.
  and combat readiness of 3d Infantry Division, 19–20
  on Cordero-Davila, 234–35
  replacement of Ridgway, 199
  and rotation policy, 120, 206
Clark, 1st Lt. Walter B., 191–93, 194n26, 195, 198
Collins, General J. Lawton, 116, 274–75
  Cordero-Davila's transfer to Korea and, 189–90
  courts-martial investigation, 301
  Major Eisenhower's study of the 65th, 271
  rotation policy and, 161, 206, 273
Colon-Mateo, Sgt. Victor G., 84
Conley, Col. Edgar T., 152
Cordero, M.Sgt. Juan, 84
Cordero-Davila, Brig. Gen. Juan C.
  analysis of Outpost Kelly defeat, 232–33
  athletic program, 202
  casualties during first month in command, 191
  and communications training, 196
  discipline improvements, 195–96
  Exercise KAISER I, 203
  indecision of, 222

INDEX

inexperience of, 297
leadership issues, 297–300
military background, 188–89
operations in the Bubble, 217
Outpost Kelly, 219, 221, 222, 223, 228, 229, 232, 234–35, 298–99
political nature of appointment, 297
replacement by De Gavre, 235, 238, 300
replacement of Lindsey, 188, 190
rotation issue comments, 204
training program, 202–04, 297
transfer to Korea, 189–90
unit reviews and command inspections and, 196–97, 202
Coulter, Maj. Gen. John B., 31, 73, 82
Counihan, Col. Thomas J., 230
Courts-martial
acquittals, 269
Army inquiry into, 300–301
of enlisted soldiers, 267–70, 271, 300
of Guzman, 265–67
media articles about, 300
ranks of enlisted troops involved, 269
total number of enlisted soldiers charged, 270
Cox, Lt. Col. William E., 276–77
Crahay, Lt. Col. Albert, 125
Craig, Lt. Col. Clayton C., 191, 204
Cronkhite, Capt. Willis D. Jr., 246, 252–59, 300
Cross, Brig. Gen. Thomas J.
command philosophy, 178
Line Jamestown defense, 179–82
military background, 177–78
plans for cease-fire period, 183–84
replacement by Dulaney, 198
and replacement of Lindsey, 190
replacement of Soule, 177
return of 8th Cavalry to parent division, 184–85
Van Fleet's letter to, 301
Cruise, Lt. Col. Edward E., 276
Culp, Col. William W., 119–20

Dammer, Lt. Col. Herman W.
advance into northeastern Korea and, 47–48, 49, 53, 66–67, 69

and attack on Hills 449 and 262, 87
continental background of, 20
and evacuation from Hungnam to Pusan, 74
Operation RIPPER, 103
Operation ROUNDUP, 96–97
Operation WOLFHOUND, 80–81
replacement by Johnson, 123
Daniels, Capt. John T., 168
Dasher, Brig. Gen. Charles L.
and bypassing of Cordero-Davila's orders, 229, 234
Jackson Heights operations, 258–59
Outpost Kelly operations, 228, 229
Davies, Maj. Albert C., 198, 223
Jackson Heights operations, 246, 259–61
Outpost Kelly operations, 215, 219, 225–27
replacement by Cruise, 276
Davis, 2d Lt. Lowell M., 246, 260
Davison, Maj. Lorenzo P., 2–3
De Gavre, Col. Chester B.
and concerns about the 65th's abilities, 240–41
cultural sensitivity and, 240
efforts to improve conduct and appearance of troops, 239–41
initial views of the 65th, 238
Jackson Heights operations and, 252, 253, 254, 257–61
military background, 237–38
and need for more NCOs, 279
reconstitution of the 65th, 284
replacement by Howard, 292
replacement of Cordero-Davila, 235, 238, 300
and training, 275, 277–79
Dean, Maj. Gen. William F., 16, 27
Department of the East, 4
Department of Puerto Rico
absorption by the Department of the East, 4
establishment of, 1
insular police force and, 1–2
Mounted Battalion of the Puerto Rico Regiment, 3
Puerto Rico Regiment, U.S. Volunteers, 3–4
Draftees, 195, 204, 269–70, 296

313

Dulaney, Maj. Gen. Robert L., 211, 212
　issues with the leadership of the
　　65th, 297, 300
　military background, 198
　Outpost Kelly and, 215, 218,
　　222–23, 228, 230, 299
　replacement of Cross, 198–99
　replacement by Smythe, 235–36
Dunkelberg, Brig. Gen. Wilbur E., 285
Durkee, 1st Lt. Richard W., 107

Eisenhower, Dwight D., 285–86
Eisenhower, Maj. John S. D., 271–73
El Imparcial, 22
El Mundo, 22
Elam, Col. Harry M., 259–61, 276
Engineer support, 57, 66, 67, 131–32,
　149, 167–69
Engle, Capt. Paul O., 229
English, Capt. William C., 228, 229
Exercise KAISER I, 203
Exercise SEEK, 204

Faith, Lt. Col. Don C. *See also* Task
　Forces, FAITH.
Far East Command, 18, 22, 27–28, 41
　Clark's replacement of Ridgway, 199
　and loss of Gloster Battalion,
　　133–34
　Ridgway's replacement of
　　MacArthur, 115–16, 119
　rotation policy, 121, 161–62
　status quo policy of 1952, 199
Figueroa, Maj. Maximiliano, 20
Finger Ridge, 216
Frederick, Capt. Floyd, 20
French Battalion, 242
Friedman, Capt. William A., 23–24, 36

Garcia, Sgt. Alfonso, 91–92
Garcia, WO2 Sady, 21
Gavin, Col. John A., 21, 29, 36
Gendron, Lt. Col. Thomas J.
　military background, 197–98
　and Outpost Kelly, 215
　replacement of Kederich, 193,
　　194n26, 197
　replacement by Wills, 227
Gensemer, 1st Lt. Harrold L., 223–25,
　246

Gibbs, 1st Lt. Malcolm A., 256, 258, 261
Gibson, Col. Erwin O., 161n67
　and combat experience of new of-
　　ficers, 174
　Line Jamestown defense, 180–81
　military background, 152–53
　Operation CLEANUP, 167, 168–69
　replacement of Harris, 152
　replacement by Lindsey, 181
Glassgow, 2d Lt. Jonas W., 253, 256
Gleason, Lt. Col. William T., 182, 183,
　192, 197
"Glosters." *See* Index of Units, British
　Army, 1st Battalion, Gloucester-
　shire Regiment.
Governor of Puerto Rico. *See* Muñoz
　Marin, Luis.
Greek Battalion. *See* Index of Units.
Green, Sgt. Augustine O. Jr., 166–67
Grevillius, Capt. Gustav, 215, 246
Griffin, Capt. Carl H., 22–23, 24–25
Growdon, Lt. Col. John S., 104,
　106–07. *See also* Task Forces,
　GROWDON.
Gudgel, Capt. Edward F. Jr., 48
Guffain, Capt. Tomas H., 48
Guthrie, Col. John S., 52
Guzman, Lt. Juan E., 265–67, 271

Hagaru-ri, Korea, 61–68
Hamch'ang, Korea, 39–40
Hamhung, Korea, 62, 64
Han River
　3d Division movement toward, 97–98
　movement of UNC troops to south
　　bank, 78
　Operation RIPPER, 99–104
　Operation THUNDERBOLT, 82–86, 95
Hantan River, 145–53
Harris, Maj. John, 156, 164–65, 173,
　174–77, 182
Harris, Col. William W., 22, 30, 47, 134
　and 65th Infantry soldiers' abilities,
　　11–12, 50, 75–76
　and advance into northeastern
　　Korea, 46–68
　assignment of South Koreans to
　　65th Infantry, 34–36
　celebration of 65th's 52d anniver-
　　sary, 144

Chinese spring offensive, 124
and deployment of personnel overage to Korea, 21
and evacuation to Pusan, 68–76
on hunting down North Koreans, 36
and Line Utah objective, 117–18
military background, 11
and mission to liberate Seoul,
92–94
mistakes made in arriving at Wonsan,
49–50
No Name Line defense, 136–37
Operation KILLER, 100–104
and rescue of Glosters, 130–33
Ridgway's visit, 88–89
shipboard meetings on way to
Korea, 26–27
training of troops on new mortars,
25–26
transfer to Tokyo, 152
and Twin Peaks battle withdrawal,
148
Hawkins, Lt. Col. Wilson M., 131. *See
also* Task Forces, HAWKINS.
Henry, Maj. Gen. Guy V., 1–2
Hernandez-Guzman, Pvt. Badel, 174–75
Higgins, 1st Lt. Walter N., 53
Hills, numbered. *See also* Bunker Hill;
Jackson Heights; Old Baldy;
Twin Peaks.
117. *See* Big Nori.
275. *See* Old Baldy.
281, 176, 242
292, 176
391. *See* Jackson Heights.
409, 34
477, 174–76
487, 166–73
608, 158
682, 153–62
717, 153–62
Hoge, Lt. Gen. William M., 165
Howard, Col. Claude M., 292
Hungnam, Korea, 52, 68–76
Huston, Lt. Col. Milburn N., 19
Huth, Maj. Henry, 128, 131–32, 133

Imjin River, 98–109, 111–12, 114, 117,
121, 123, 125, 180, 194, 209,
210, 211, 216, 262

Integration
of Puerto Rican troops into 3d Divi-
sion, 120, 177
and reconstituting the 65th,
281–86
Interwar period, 6–7
Iron Triangle
August–December 1951, 163–85
Eighth Army's advance toward,
145–53
geographical boundaries, 111, 153
January 1953, 279
June 1953, 290–91
Operation DAUNTLESS, 111, 114
Operation SHOWDOWN, 245

Jackson, Capt. George D. *See also*
Jackson Heights.
comments on defeat at Outpost
Kelly, 232
and intensive training, 241, 242
Jackson Heights, 246–59, 298, 299,
300
views of enlisted soldiers, 239, 242
Jackson Heights, 247, 248, 252. *See
also* Big Nori; Bunker Hill;
Hills, numbered; Old Baldy;
Twin Peaks.
assessing failure at, 261–63
Betances-Ramirez's order to withdraw, 251–52
breakdown on, 252–61
and courts-martial, 265–75
defense and loss of, 245–52
early operations, 242–44
failure to obey orders and unauthorized withdrawal, 257–58,
260–61
punishment of officers and enlisted
men, 261
Jenkins, Lt. Gen. Reuben E., 237,
272–73, 276, 285
Johnson, Lt. Col. Lawrence A.
2d Battalion command, 123,
147–50, 170
military background, 123
Operation CLEANUP, 170
replacement of Dammer, 123
replacement by Young, 179
Twin Peaks battle, 147–50

Kaesong, Korea, 159
Kaltenborn, H. V., 165
Kang, Brig. Gen. Moon Bong, 132
KATUSA. *See* Korean Augmentation to the United States Army.
Kederich, Lt. Col. Charles H., 187, 193, 197
Keiser, Maj. Gen. Lawrence B., 32–34, 36
Kendall, Lt. Gen. Paul W., 222–23, 228, 299, 234
Kim Il-Sung, 15. *See also* North Korea.
Korea, 15–16, 46, 56. *See also* North Korea; South Korea; specific locations and battle sites.
Korean Augmentation to the United States Army (KATUSA), 27–28, 34–36, 207–08
Korean Service Corps, 258
Kot'o-ri, Korea, 64, 66–67
Kumch'on, Korea, 39–40

Language issues
   appointment of Spanish-speaking NCOs, 208, 273
   communication difficulties, 234, 260, 272, 275, 296, 302
   continental officers' Spanish proficiency, 192, 193, 295, 296, 297
   and desertion of troops, 269–70
   English as official language, 12, 193
   failures to teach English, 202–03, 208, 214–15, 297
   language training, 90n36, 208
   and morale, 94, 214
   Puerto Ricans' English proficiency, 22, 193–94, 208, 238, 266–67, 295
   replacement officers and, 234
   request for English-speaking NCOs, 212
   rotation of bilingual NCOs, 207–08
   and South Koreans, 207–08
   summary, 296–97
Lauzon, 2d Lt. Donald E., 256
Lavergne, 1st Lt. Paul, 83, 85–86
Levy, Lt. Col. Julius W., 153–54
Lindsey, Col. Julian B.
   military background, 181–82
   raid against Chinese forces, 184
   replacement by Cordero-Davila, 188, 190, 191
   replacement of Gibson, 181
   views on rotation policy, 188
Lines
   Charlie, 72
   Delta, 135
   Fox, 72, 73
   Jamestown
      1st Battalion move to, 197
      defense of, 179–85, 215
      Exercise SEEK, 204
      geographical boundaries, 174
      improvement of 65th's positions on, 191
      Operation COMMANDO, 174–77
   Kansas
      establishment of, 111
      extent of, 121
      fortification of, 143
      Operation PILEDRIVER and, 143, 145–53
      Operation RUGGED and, 112, 114
      Van Fleet's order to defend, 139
      withdrawal to, 127
   Mike, 72
   Missouri, 288–90
   No Name, 135–36, 139, 141
   Peter, 72
   Utah
      Chinese attacks, 121–22
      defense of, 117–18
      misfire incidents, 117
   Wyoming, 143, 145–53, 163, 279
Little Nori, 216, 217–18. *See also* Big Nori.
Lockerman, 1st Lt. Julian F., 84–85, 86
Lostumbo, Capt. Dominick J., 20

MacArthur, General Douglas
   on 65th Infantry, 40
   letter to speaker of the House, 115
   operations north of 38th Parallel, 41–76
   replacement by Ridgway, 115–16
   North Korean invasion of South Korea, 17–18
   and Ridgway's request to move to 38th Parallel, 109

and rotation policy, 121
and Truman, 46, 109, 115–16
MacLean, Col. Allan D., 59
Maddox, 1st Lt. Thomas H., 244
Magner, Capt. George J., 70, 84
Majon-dong, Korea, 64–67
Mao Zedong, 122
Martin, Joseph W., 115
Martinez, Sgt. Angel G., 10
Martinez, Capt. Jose M., 20
McDonnell, Capt. Patrick J., 20
McKinley, William, 1
Mead, Brig. Gen. Armistead D.
    evaluation of 3d Division performance, 77–78, 99
    Gloucestershire Regiment rescue, 131–32
    replacement by Newman, 177
    Task Forces Dog and Childs, 64–68
Mergens, Col. George C., 270–71
Milburn, Brig. Gen. Bryan L., 152
Milburn, Lt. Gen. Frank W., 78, 97, 139–40, 144
    and Chinese spring offensive, 122
    Gloucestershire Regiment rescue, 130
    Operations
        Courageous, 108
        Doughnut, 156
        Goose, 152
        Ripper, 103
        Wolfhound, 80–82
    replacement by O'Daniel, 165
Milton, Hugh M. II, 266
Moore, Col. Dennis M., 52
Moore, Capt. Harold G. Jr., 243
Moore, Col. William T., 187–88
Muña, Capt. Antonio, 48, 66–67
Muñoz Marin, Luis, 18–19, 23, 24. See also Puerto Rico.
Myers, Capt. Arthur W., 27, 93–94, 96, 124–25. See also Task Forces, Myers.

Negron, M.Sgt. Juan E., 136
Nelson, 1st Lt. William F., 218–23, 298
New York Times, 300
Newman, Col. Oliver P., 86, 119, 177
Nieves-Laguer, Cpl. Fabian, 117
NKPA. See North Korean Army.

Noriega, M.Sgt. Belisario, 250, 251, 252
North Korea, 42, 43, 56, 179
North Korean Army. *See also* Index of Units; North Korea; South Korean Army.
    X Corps advance into northeastern Korea and, 45, 48–59
    growing strength in 1950, 53–54
    improvement in defenses, 199
    invasion of South Korea, 16
    Line Utah attacks, 121–22
    Operation Courageous, 104–08
    Operation Dauntless, 112
    Operation Roundup, 95–97
North Korean People's Army (*NKPA*). See North Korean Army.

O'Daniel, Lt. Gen. John W. "Iron Mike"
    military background, 165–66
    Operation Annihilation, 165
    Operation Cleanup, 168
    Outpost Kelly defeat, 235–37
    and replacement of Lindsey, 190
    replacement of Milburn, 165
Ojeda, Lt. Col. Dionisio S., 104–06, 124
Old Baldy (Hill 275), 216
O'Neil, Lt. Col. Thomas A., 69, 145, 156
Operations
    Annihilation, 164–65
    Cleanup I and II, 166–73
    Commando, 174–77
    Courageous, 104, 106–08
    Dauntless, 111–12, 114, 115
    Doughnut, 155–59
    Exploitation, 82–91
    Goose, 152
    Killer, 98–99
    Little Switch, 286
    Piledriver, 143, 145–53
    Ripper, 99–104
    Roundup, 95–97
    Rugged, 111, 112, 114
    Showdown, 245
    Snare, 191
    Thunderbolt, 82–86, 95
    Wolfhound, 80–81

O'Reilly, Capt. Vincent J., 72
Ortiz, Lt. Silvestre E. 238
Outposts
    Betty, 216
    Harry, 286–90, 301–02
    Kelly
        air support, 231
        analysis of the disaster, 231–36, 298–99
        bunkers and ammunition supplies at, 216
        casualties, 227, 230, 231
        Chinese capture, 211–12
        counterattack and defeat, 222–30
        initial struggle over, 215–22
        personnel issues, 232–34
        political importance of, 216
    Nick, 216, 219, 221, 225, 226
    Tessie, 216, 221, 225, 226

Pacific Stars and Stripes, 194–95
Panama Canal Zone, 8
Panmunjom, Korea
    final armistice terms, 291–92
    peace talks, 178–79, 182
    return to peace talks, 286
    signing of the truce, 292
Parra, 1st Lt. Pedro J., 5
Partridge, Lt. Col. John H., 66–67
Péng Déhuái, 122
People's Liberation Army. See Chinese Army.
Philippine Army. See Index of Units.
Porterfield, 1st Lt. John D. Jr., 210–11
    death of, 256–57
    Jackson Heights operations, 252–56, 266, 300
    posthumous promotion and Bronze Star, 261
PORTREX. See Puerto Rican Exercise.
Postwar period, 10–13
Prescott, Capt. Daniel C., 124–25
President, Philippine Republic. See Quirino, Elpidio R.
President, U.S. See Eisenhower, Dwight D.; McKinley, William; Roosevelt, Franklin D.; Truman, Harry S.

Puerto Rican National Guard (PRNG), 23, 155, 189, 204, 212, 214, 296.
    See also U.S. National Guard.
Puerto Rican Exercise (PORTREX), 13, 21, 23, 24
Puerto Rico, 2, 4, 6, 7–8, 10–13, 20–23, 40, 89, 95, 189–90, 257, 293, 301–02
Puerto Rico Department, 7
Pusan, Korea, 68–76, 77–109
Pusan Perimeter, 17–18, 28–29
Putnam, Maj. George D., 219
P'yonggang, Korea, 163–64

Quirino, Elpidio R., 106

Ramirez, 2d Lt. Pablo, 90–91
Ranger companies, 194–95
Red Cross, 94
Regular Army, 1, 4–5, 7, 195, 212, 273, 274–75, 293. *See also* U.S. Army; U.S. National Guard.
Republic of Korea. *See* South Korea.
Republic of Korea (ROK) Army. *See* South Korean Army. *See also* South Korea.
Rhee, Syngman, 15. *See also* South Korea.
Ridgway, Lt. Gen. Matthew B. *See also* Far East Command.
    and attempted rescue of the Glosters, 133
    briefing from Harris, 88
    and Cordero-Davila's transfer to Korea, 189–90
    and deployment of the 3d Infantry Division to Korea, 18
    integration of Puerto Rican troops, 89–90, 119, 177
    Line Jamestown defense, 179
    observation of the 65th's assault on Hills 449 and 262, 87–88
    Operations
        COURAGEOUS, 104–08
        DAUNTLESS, 111–12, 114, 115
        DOUGHNUT, 156
        KILLER, 98–99
        RIPPER, 99–104
        THUNDERBOLT, 82
    replacement by Clark, 199

and request to move to the 38th Parallel, 109
and recommendation for formation of an all–Puerto Rican RCT, 119
thank-you to Harris, 88–89
replacement of MacArthur, 115–16
Van Fleet's plans to move beyond Lines Kansas and Wyoming, 143
Ridings, Maj. Gen. Eugene W., 286, 290
Rivera, Father John, 5
Rodriguez-Amaro, 2d Lt. Vidal, 231
Rodriguez-Rodriguez, 1st Lt. Manuel, 246, 250, 252
ROK Army. *See* South Korean Army.
Roosevelt, Franklin D., 7
Root, Elihu, 3
Rotation policy
 aims of, 120
 changes in June–July 1951, 160–62
 curtailment for the 65th in June 1951, 154
 and defeats at Outpost Kelly and Jackson Heights, 302
 description, 120–21
 effects on the 65th, 161, 173–74, 207
 effects on the Eighth Army in early 1952, 187–88
 frontline soldier priority, 145
 lack of alternatives to, 206–07
 lowering of criteria for, 182n77
 Outpost Kelly operations and, 232–33
 personnel problems in Eighth Army and, 205–08
 points system, 161–62, 183
 postponement of, 121
 and Selective Service's reduction in callups, 205n60

Sanchez-Sanchez, Pvt. Sergio, 10
Segarra, Col. Antulio, 8
Selective Service, 204–05
Seoul, Korea
 I Corps abandonment of, 78
 X Corps recapture of, 41
 Operation KILLER, 98–99
 Operation RIPPER, 99–104
 North Korean capture of, 16
 psychological importance of, 139

struggle for control of, 41, 91–100, 102–03, 122, 134
Serra, 1st Lt. Rafael A., 83–84
Sibert, Brig. Gen. Edwin L., 23, 24
Simmons, Lt. Col. Franklin B. Jr., 160–61, 169, 182
Simonson, Sfc. Tom N., 149
Skelton, 1st Lt. Winfred G. Jr., 191, 193–94, 195
Smith, Col. Aubrey D., 46
Smith, Capt. Claude, 132–33
Smith, Maj. Gen. Oliver P., 29, 53n39, 64
Smythe, Maj. Gen. George W.
 and courts-martial of 65th Infantry troops, 268
 Jackson Heights operations, 245, 259, 261
 Major Eisenhower's study of the 65th, 272–73
 military background, 236
 NCO academy, 275–76
 need for NCOs, 279
 reconstituting the 65th as fully integrated, 281
 replacement by Ridings, 286
 replacement of Dulaney, 236
Sobang Mountains, 153–56, 157–62
Soule, Maj. Gen. Robert H.
 and advance into northeastern Korea, 51–52, 57, 61
 appointment of Mead to evaluate 3d Division, 77–78
 and Chinese spring offensive, 122, 124, 125, 127, 130–31
 criticism of the 65th's combat performance, 86
 evacuation from Hungnam to Pusan and, 73
 Line Utah defense and, 118
 military background, 19
 Operations
  CLEANUP, 167–73
  COMMANDO, 174–77
  DOUGHNUT, 155–59
  EXPLOITATION, 83
  RIPPER, 103
  WOLFHOUND, 81
 orders to establish forward patrol bases, 163

Soule, Maj. Gen. Robert H.—Continued
and personnel readiness of the 65th, 154–55
recommendation for the formation of an all–Puerto Rican RCT, 118–19
regrouping along Line Delta and, 135
replacement by Cross, 177
Ridgway's instructions to use Puerto Rican soldiers throughout 3d Division, 89–90
rotation policy, 160
Task Force MYERS and, 94
Twin Peaks battle withdrawal and, 148
South Korea, 15, 16, 27, 99, 139. *See also* specific locations.
South Korean Army. *See also* Index of Units.
advance into northeastern Korea, 41–68
assignment of Korean troops to 65th Infantry, 27–28, 34–36
Capital Division, 291
Chinese spring offensive, 122–27
evacuation from Hungnam to Pusan, 68–76
Gloucestershire Regiment rescue and, 132
Infantry Demonstration Team, 278
Operations
      COURAGEOUS, 104–08
      KILLER, 98–99
      RIPPER, 102–03
      ROUNDUP, 95–97
reorganization of, 16
Soyang River, 111, 140–45
Speaker of the House of the U.S. Congress. *See* Martin, Joseph W. *See also* U.S. Congress.
SS *Carleton Victory*, 74
SS *Hunter Victory*, 74
St. Clair, Lt. Col. Howard B.
advance into northeastern Korea, 48, 53, 55, 64
attack toward the Han, 97
attack on Hills 449 and 262, 87
evacuation from Hungnam to Pusan, 70
Operation RIPPER, 103

Operation ROUNDUP, 96–97
reconnaissance task force, 81–82
replacement by Simmons, 160
Twin Peaks battle, 146–47, 148, 150
St. John, 1st Lt. Joseph W., 20
Staff judge advocate, 3d Division. *See* Baker, Lt. Col. John.
Stalin, Joseph V., 286
Stevens, 1st Lt. Robert E. L., 218, 219, 225, 259–61
Streett, 1st Lt. St. Clair Jr., 210–11, 225

Tarkenton, Col. James C., 112
Task Forces
  CHILDS, 64–66, 67–68
  CUTTHROAT, 166
  DOG, 64–68
  FAITH, 60–61
  GROWDON, 104, 106
  HAWKINS, 107–08, 152, 156
  MACLEAN, 59
  MYERS, 93–94
  SMITH, 16
Taylor, General Maxwell D., 280–81, 284, 291
Thai Battalion. *See* Index of Units.
Torres-Caban, 1st Lt. Jose, 34
Training, 277–79, 280
3d Infantry Division efforts, 27
aboard ship, 25–26
basic, 89n35, 90n36, 160, 188, 195
for cold weather, 25, 75, 293
and combat effectiveness, 16, 18, 31, 73, 86, 88–89, 171, 196, 234, 237, 273, 277–78, 279, 292–93, 295, 298
combined-arms, 13, 237, 298
Cordero-Davila's approach, 196–97, 203, 297
and discipline, 178, 191–92, 194
language, 90n36, 193, 202–03, 208
live-fire, 242, 298
NCO academy, 275–76, 277, 293
NCOs' effect on, 193, 195, 275–76, 302
opportunities in Puerto Rico, 11, 12, 13, 23
and personnel turnover, 179, 204–05, 232, 239, 296

Index

quality of, 241, 242, 278
tactical, 188, 203–04, 278, 284–85
Truman, Harry S., 205n60, 285
   conference with MacArthur in October 1950, 46
   and North Korea's invasion of South Korea, 17, 18
   removal of MacArthur, 115–16
   Ridgway's request to move to 38th Parallel, 109
Turkish Brigade. *See* Index of Units.
Twin Peaks. *See also* Big Nori; Bunker Hill; Hills, numbered; Jackson Heights; Old Baldy.
   battle for, 146–50
   Operation CLEANUP and, 170, 171, 173
   withdrawal across the Hantan River, 149–50

Uijongbu, Korea, 107–08
United Nations Command
   advance into northeastern Korea and, 51, 54–55, 60
   changes in command, 115–16
   Chinese Army attacks against, 46
   evacuation from Hungnam to Pusan and, 73
   main line of resistance, 216
   Operation KILLER and, 98–99
   Operation RIPPER and, 99–104
   Panmunjom peace talks, 178–79, 182
   withdrawal from Line Kansas, 139
   withdrawal to Han River, 78
USNS *Marine Lynx*, 24–27
U.S. Army, 1, 3, 4–5, 6–7, 8, 18, 21, 22, 28, 161, 189–90, 233, 293, 295, 296, 297. *See also* Index of Units; Far East Command; Regular Army; U.S. National Guard.
   doctrine, 216
   policy, 6, 12–13, 89–90, 120–21, 193, 205
   and enlisted promotions, 233
   and replacements, 89–90, 120, 182n77, 204–05
   and rotation, 120–21, 161–62, 206–08, 232, 301, 302

U.S. Congress, 2–3, 4–5, 301
U.S. National Guard, 7, 184–85, 195, 297. *See also* Puerto Rican National Guard; Regular Army; U.S. Army.
U.S. secretary of the Army. *See* Wright, Luke E.
U.S. secretary of War. *See* Root, Elihu.
U.S. War Department, 1, 2, 3, 4, 5–6
USS *Bayfield*, 74
USS *Freeman*, 74
USS *General A. W. Greely*, 27, 28, 29
USS *General Edwin D. Patrick*, 36
USS *Henrico*, 74
USS *Sergeant Howard E. Woodford*, 24–27, 28, 36

Van Fleet, Lt. Gen. James A.
   and attempted rescue of the Glosters, 133–34
   Cordero-Davila's transfer to Korea and, 190
   Eighth Army command, 115–16, 121–22, 127, 133–34
   and language issues in the 65th, 273–74
   letter to Cross about 65th at Jackson Heights, 301
   letter to O'Daniel about defeat at Outpost Kelly, 236–37
   limited warfare views, 199
   Line Jamestown defense and, 179
   Line Utah defense and, 121–22
   and Major Eisenhower's study of the 65th, 271–72
   military background, 116
   Operations
      ANNIHILATION, 165
      DOUGHNUT, 156
      PILEDRIVER, 143, 145–53
      SHOWDOWN, 245
   order to defend Line Kansas, 139
   order to defend No Name Line, 139
   Outpost Kelly operations and, 222–23
   replacement by Taylor, 280
   and replacement of Cordero-Davila, 235–36
   request for inactivation of 65th, 273–75

Van Fleet, Lt. Gen. James A.—Continued
and rotation policy, 161, 188, 206
"Van Fleet day of fire," 200
views on deterioration of the 65th, 273–74
and withdrawal to Line Kansas, 127

Waegwan-Kumch'on region, Korea, 38–40
Walker, Col. Edward A., 188
Walker, Lt. Gen. Walton H., 41, 47, 88
advance into northeastern Korea and, 56–57, 60–61
death of, 80
meeting with Harris, 30
North Korean invasion of South Korea and, 16–17, 28–29
Wasson, 2d Lt. John R., 262–63, 265, 267–68
Weather issues, 54–55, 75, 91, 98, 105, 160, 164, 166–67, 211–12
Weyand, Lt. Col. Fred, 125, 127
White, 2d Lt. William E., 256
White Horse Mountain, 242

Wilcomb, 1st Lt. Gerald A., 253, 255, 256–57, 258n104
Williams, 1st Lt. Robert C., 27
Wills, Lt. Col. Lloyd E.
military background, 227–28
and Outpost Kelly operations, 227–28, 229–30, 234
replacement of Gendron, 227
Wolf, 1st Lt. Duquesne "Duke," 221–22
Wonsan, Korea, 42–43, 45–59
World War I, 5–6, 199
World War II, 6, 7–10, 15, 22, 23, 120, 137, 201–02
Wright, Luke E., 4–5

Yancey, Col. Thomas R., 120, 153–62
Yap, Capt. Conrado D., 124
Yongam-ni, Korea, 38–39
Yonghung, Korea, 52, 62
Young, Lt. Col. George H. Jr., 179, 191
Yunque, Capt. Marcial, 20

Zapata, Pfc. Rafael A., 22
Zayas, M.Sgt. Pedro J., 164

Index of Units

Belgian Battalion
    Chinese spring offensive, 123–27
    Gloucestershire Regiment rescue, 130
    Jackson Heights, 245
    Line Wyoming, 279
    Operation RUGGED, 112

British Army
    1st Battalion, Gloucestershire Regiment ("Glosters"), 127–34, 130, 133
    27th Infantry Brigade, 45–46
    29th Independent Infantry Brigade Group, 122, 127
    29th Infantry Brigade, 78, 82, 112, 122–27, 130, 139

Chinese Army
    2d Battalion, 348th Infantry Regiment, 215–16, 218, 219
    III Army Group, 118, 121–22
    3d Battalion, 348th Infantry Regiment, 215–16
    IX Army Group, 121–22
    12th Army, III Army Group, 121–22, 141
    XII Army Group, 82
    XIII Army Group, 121–22
    15th Army, III Army Group, 121–22, 141
    XIX Army Group, 118, 121–22
    20th Army, IX Army Group, 66, 121–22, 141
    26th Army, 66, 104, 106–07, 112
    27th Army, IX Army Group, 66, 121–22, 141
    29th Division, 15th Army, 124
    34th Division, 12th Army, 124
    38th Army, 60
    39th Army, XIII Army Group, 45, 60, 112, 121–22, 183–84
    40th Army, XIII Army Group, 60, 112, 121–22
    47th Army, 184
    50th Army, 82, 86
    58th Division, 66
    60th Army, III Army Group, 121–22, 141
    60th Division, 66
    63d Army, XIX Army Group, 121–22
    64th Army, XIX Army Group, 121–22
    65th Army, XIX Army Group, 121–22
    66th Army Group, 98
    76th Division, 66
    77th Division, 26th Army, 66, 163
    78th Division, 26th Army, 112, 163
    79th Division, 27th Army, 59
    80th Division, 20th Army, 59
    80th Division, 27th Army, 163
    87th Regiment, 29th Division, 245
    89th Division, 27th Army, 59
    115th Division, 39th Army, 215–16
    116th Division, 39th Army, 215–16
    140th Division, 171
    141st Division, 171, 173
    148th Division, 50th Army, 82
    149th Division, 50th Army, 82, 87, 91–92
    150th Division, 50th Army, 82, 87
    179th Division, 125, 127
    187th Division, 127, 132
    189th Division, 132
    216th Regiment, 72d Division, 24th Army, 286–87
    221st Regiment, 74th Division, 24th Army, 286–87
    228th Regiment, 76th Division, 112

Chinese Army—Continued
   229th Regiment, 76th Division, 112
   232d Regiment, 78th Division, 112
   233d Regiment, 78th Division, 112, 156, 157–59
   234th Regiment, 156, 157–59
   340th Regiment, 245
   341st Regiment, 44th Division, 245
   342d Regiment, 245
   344th Regiment, 115th Division, 39th Army, 209–10
   353d Regiment, 118th Division, 40th Army, 209–10
   354th Regiment, 118th Division, 40th Army, 209–10
   445th Regiment, 91–92
   447th Regiment, 83, 91–92

Greek Battalion, 231, 245

North Korean Army
   I Corps, 104, 106–07, 121–22
   1st Division, 112
   1st Infantry, 8th Division, 96–97
   4th Division, 16
   V Corps, 98–99
   10th Division, 32
   11th Regiment, 5th Division, 48–49
   15th Division, 112
   41st Infantry Division, 53–54
   45th Division, 112
   69th Infantry Brigade, 112
   507th Brigade, 53–54

Philippine Army
   10th Battalion Combat Team
      Chinese spring offensive, 123–27
      Gloucestershire Regiment rescue and, 130
      Line Utah defense, 117–18, 121–22
      Operations
         COURAGEOUS, 104–06
         DAUNTLESS, 114–15
         PILEDRIVER, 150–53, 163
         RUGGED, 112
      regrouping along Line Delta and, 135
      relationship with American units, 105–06

20th Battalion Combat Team, 174–77

South Korean Army
   I Corps, 42, 45, 56n53, 61, 69, 111, 143, 145–53, 163
   1st Division, 132, 235
   II Corps, 291–92
   2d Division, 245, 276
   III Corps, 111–37, 141–45
   6th Division, 122
   9th Division, 177, 179–85, 237, 242, 245, 291
   51st Regiment, 246
   Capital Division, 291–92
   Infantry Demonstration Team, 278

Thai Battalion, 78

Turkish Brigade
   Chinese spring offensive, 123–27
   Iron Triangle operations, 279
   Line Utah defense, 121
   position in May 1951, 139

U.S. Army
   I Corps
      composition of, 78, 80
      Line Jamestown defense and, 182
      line of resistance in January 1951, 78, 80
      need for reinforcements, 78
      Operations
         COURAGEOUS, 104–08
         DAUNTLESS, 111–12, 114, 115
         EXPLOITATION, 82–86
         GOOSE, 152
         KILLER, 98–99
         PILEDRIVER, 143, 145–53
         RIPPER, 100–104
         ROUNDUP, 96–97
         THUNDERBOLT, 82–86, 95
         WOLFHOUND, 80–81
      position in May 1951, 139–40
   1st Battalion, 17th Infantry, 243–44
   1st Battalion, 65th Infantry
      advance into northeastern Korea, 48, 53–56, 61, 64
      attack toward the Han, 97
      attack on Hills 449 and 262, 87

Index of Units

battle for Hill 682, 158
Chinese spring offensive, 124
courts-martial, 268–69, 271
Jackson Heights, 252–56,
   259–61, 300
Line Missouri, 288–90
Line Wyoming patrol base, 164
misfire incidents, 117
No Name Line defense,
   135–37
Operations
   CLEANUP, 166–73
   COMMANDO, 174–77
   DAUNTLESS, 114–15
   EXPLOITATION, 83–86
   RIPPER, 103
   ROUNDUP, 96–97
outpost defense, 216, 221
Outpost Harry, 286–90
Outpost Kelly, 216–23,
   225–28
reconnaissance and, 81–82, 292
regrouping along Line Delta,
   135–36
special construction project,
   278
troop strength on arrival in
   Korea, 29
Twin Peaks battle, 146–47,
   148, 150
1st Cavalry
   Chinese Army attacks
      against, 45, 51
   Line Jamestown defense, 179
   North Korea's invasion of
      South Korea, 16
   Ranger companies, 194
2d Battalion, 25th Infantry, 245
2d Battalion, 65th Infantry
   advance into northeastern
      Korea, 47–48, 49, 53,
      57–59, 66–67, 69
   attack on Hills 449 and 262, 87
   Chinese raid, 93
   Chinese spring offensive,
      123–27
   combat demonstrations, 285
   courts-martial, 270, 271
   failure to obey orders,
      257–58

and Hill 409, 34
Jackson Heights operations,
   246–59
Line Jamestown defense,
   180–82
Line Missouri operations,
   288–90
Line Wyoming patrol base,
   163–64
Operations
   CLEANUP, 166, 170
   COMMANDO, 174–77
   RIPPER, 103
   ROUNDUP, 96–97
   WOLFHOUND, 80–81
Outpost Harry operations,
   286–90
Outpost Kelly operations,
   223–25
raid against Chinese forces,
   184
regrouping along Line Delta
   and, 135
special construction project,
   278
and Task Force MYERS, 93–94
troop strength on arrival in
   Korea, 29
and Twin Peaks battle, 147–50
2d Infantry Division
   and 23d Infantry, 270–71
   Chinese Army attacks and, 51
   North Korea's invasion of
      South Korea and, 17
   Operation CLEANUP, 171
   Ranger companies, 194
   relief of 3d Infantry Division,
      291
3d AAA Battalion, 97, 164
3d Battalion, 33d Infantry, 21, 24, 29
3d Battalion, 65th Infantry
   advance into northeastern
      Korea, 48
   attack on Hills 449 and 262, 87
   battle for Hill 608, 158
   battle for Hill 717, 158
   battle for the Twin Peaks, 173
   Chinese spring offensive,
      123–27
   courts-martial, 267–68

3d Battalion, 65th Infantry—Continued
   defense of Big Nori, Little Nori, and the Bubble, 216–17
   discipline problems after Jackson Heights, 262–63
   evacuation from Hungnam to Pusan, 72
   Jackson Heights operations, 246, 300
   Line Jamestown defense, 180–82
   Line Missouri operations, 288–90
   Operations
      ANNIHILATION, 164–65
      CLEANUP, 166–73
      COMMANDO, 174–76
      DAUNTLESS, 114–15
      DOUGHNUT, 156
      ROUNDUP, 96–97
   Outpost Harry, 286–90
   Outpost Kelly, 227–30
   regrouping along Line Delta, 135
   special construction project, 278

3d Infantry Division. *See also* 65th Infantry.
   advance into northeastern Korea, 47–68
   appointment of Spanish-speaking NCOs, 208
   Clark's report on the combat readiness of, 19–20
   courts-martial of troops, 265–75
   deployment to Korea, 18
   evacuation from Hungnam to Pusan, 68–77
   Exercise SEEK, 204
   integration of Puerto Rican troops into, 119–20
   Iron Triangle operations, 163–85
   Line Jamestown defense, 179–82, 215
   Line Wyoming patrol base, 163–64
   mission to liberate Seoul, 91–98
   move north in January 1951, 78
   NCO academy, 275–76, 293
   Operations
      COMMANDO, 174–77
      DOUGHNUT, 155–59
      EXPLOITATION, 82–86
      PILEDRIVER, 145–53, 163
      RIPPER, 100–104
      WOLFHOUND, 80–81
   Outpost Harry, 288–90
   Outpost Kelly, 215–36
   personnel changes, 197–98
   racial diversity, 19
   raids against Chinese forces, 187
   Ranger companies, 194
   regrouping along Line Delta, 135
   relief by 2d Division, 291
   relief of South Korean 9th Division, 237, 245
   small-unit patrols and raids of December 1951, 183–84
   Task Force HAWKINS, 107–08, 152, 156
   Task Force MYERS, 93–94
   transfer from I Corps to IX Corps, 237
   use of replacements, 89, 119–20, 155, 185, 205
   weekly training schedule, 237

3d Reconnaissance Company
   evacuation from Hungnam to Pusan, 69
   Jackson Heights, 245, 246, 253, 259–60
   regrouping along Line Delta, 135

7th Infantry
   advance into northeastern Korea, 43, 45, 56–57, 59, 61–62
   evacuation from Hungnam to Pusan, 68–76
   Iron Triangle operations, 279
   Jackson Heights, 245

Index of Units

Line Jamestown defense,
    180–81
Operations
    CLEANUP, 166–73
    COMMANDO, 174–77
    PILEDRIVER, 145–53
    SHOWDOWN, 245
Ranger companies, 194
rescue of Barno and, 244
Task Force MACLEAN, 59
troop strength in September 1951, 173
Eighth Army
    65th Infantry contributions to, 29–31
    advance toward Iron Triangle, 145–53
    advance to north of 38th Parallel, 41–68
    ammunition shortages of 1952, 200–202
    assignment of South Koreans to 65th Infantry, 34, 36
    effects of rotation in early 1952, 187–88
    evacuation from Hungnam to Pusan, 68–76
    forward patrol base establishment, 163
    integration of Puerto Rican troops into, 89–90
    Line Jamestown defense, 179–82
    logistical problems, 200
    main line of resistance in May 1952, 199
    movement to No Name Line, 135–36
    and North Korean invasion of South Korea, 16–17, 28–29
    Operations
        KILLER, 98–99
        PILEDRIVER, 143, 145–53
        RIPPER, 99–104
        SHOWDOWN, 245
        SNARE, 191
    personnel problems, 205–08
    position in July 1951, 159–60
    Ranger companies, 194–95
    regrouping after Chinese spring offensive, 134–37
    reorganization of I Corps front, 197
    and replacements, 89, 118, 119, 187–88
    request to move to 38th Parallel, 109
8th Cavalry, 181, 185
IX Corps
    attachment of 65th Infantry to, 31–32
    engagements in the sector, 31–32
    Jackson Heights operations and, 245–63
    Operations
        COURAGEOUS, 104–08
        KILLER, 98–99
        PILEDRIVER, 143, 145–53
        RIPPER, 100–104
        THUNDERBOLT, 82–86, 95
    transfer of 3d Infantry Division to, 237
10th Combat Engineer Battalion, 102, 103, 117, 140, 148–49, 158, 163–64, 166, 280
X Corps
    65th Infantry attached to, 41–76
    advance into northeastern Korea, 42–59
    Chinese attacks against, 45–64
    elements of, 43
    evacuation from Hungnam to Pusan, 68–76
    force strength in October 1950, 42–43
    Operations
        KILLER, 98–99
        PILEDRIVER, 143, 145–53
        RIPPER, 100–104
        ROUNDUP, 95–97
    Pusan Perimeter role, 28–29
    and recapture of Seoul, 41
    Task Force FAITH, 60–61
    and withdrawal of 1st Marine Division from Hagaru-ri, 64–68

15th Infantry, 3d Infantry Division
  Jackson Heights, 245
  Operations
    CLEANUP, 166–73
    COMMANDO, 174–77
    PILEDRIVER, 150–53
  Outpost Harry, 286–90
  Outpost Kelly, 228
  relief by 65th Infantry, 286
  troop strength in September 1951, 173
23d Infantry, 2d Infantry Division, 270–71
24th Infantry
  Chinese Army attacks against, 45–46, 51
  compared with 65th Infantry, 301
  Ranger companies, 194
  Task Force SMITH, 16
25th Infantry
  65th Infantry attachment to, 38–40
  Chinese Army attacks, 51
  Jackson Heights, 245
  Line Utah defense, 118
  North Korea's invasion of South Korea and, 16
  Operation WOLFHOUND, 80–81
  Ranger companies, 194
58th Field Artillery Battalion, 93–94, 97, 228
64th Heavy Tank Battalion
  attack toward the Han, 97
  evacuation from Hungnam to Pusan, 69
  exchange of personnel, 177
  Line Utah defense, 117–18
  Operation CLEANUP, 167–73
  Operation PILEDRIVER, 145–53
  Outpost Kelly, 228, 233, 233n109
  Task Force CUTTHROAT, 166
65th Infantry ("Borinqueneers").
  See also 3d Infantry Division; Eighth Army; IX Corps.
  Army of Occupation role, 10
  assignment of Korean troops to, 27–28, 34–36, 207–08
  attachment to 3d Infantry Division, 18–24, 36
  casualties, 40, 49, 75, 76, 86, 91, 99, 144, 160, 161, 170, 173, 179, 183, 184, 185, 187, 191, 205, 212, 222, 226–27, 230, 231–32, 250–51, 255–56, 261, 279, 280, 287, 288, 290–91, 292
  celebration of 52d anniversary, 144
  changes in early 1952, 191–98
  compared with 24th Infantry, 301
  deployment to Korea, 18–29
  early combat missions, 32–40
  English proficiency of NCOs, 193–94, 193n25
  fighting withdrawal toward Seoul, 134–37
  Franco-Italian border mission, 10
  French Morocco mission, 8–9
  inactivation in April 1953, 293
  intensive training at Changmol, 241–42
  interpreters, 155
  interwar period role, 6–7
  Iron Triangle, 163–85, 279
  Jackson Heights, 245–63
  limited warfare of 1952, 199–205
  Line Utah defense, 117–18, 121–22
  Major Eisenhower's study of, 271–73
  missions after the truce, 292–93
  officer shortages, 20, 233–34
  Operations
    COURAGEOUS, 104–08
    EXPLOITATION, 82–86
    KILLER, 98–99
    RIPPER, 100–104
    ROUNDUP, 95–97
    THUNDERBOLT, 82–86, 95
    WOLFHOUND, 80–81

INDEX OF UNITS

operations of February 1953, 280
Outpost Kelly, 215-36, 298-99
Panama Canal Zone mission, 8
personnel readiness in June 1951, 154-55
phases during the Korean War, 295-96
postwar period, 10-13
racial composition of, 20-21
Raider Platoons, 194
reconstitution, 281-86
redesignation of Puerto Rico Regiment of Infantry as, 6
refitting and reorganizing, 77-78
and replacements, 21-22, 23, 75, 77, 89-90, 114, 145, 155, 160, 162, 164-65, 173-74, 179, 183, 185, 187-88, 191, 193n25, 204, 205, 239, 252, 270, 273
in reserve, 191-208
return to Puerto Rico, 293
rotation issues in early 1952, 202-03, 204-05
rotation policy effects, 161, 173-74, 207

1st Provisional Marine Brigade, 17
61-68
withdrawal from Hagaru-ri, 68-76
evacuation from Hungnam, 68-76
Korea, 42-43, 45
advance into northeastern 56, 57, 59, 122, 215
1st Marine Division, 29, 48, 53n39,
U.S. Marine Corps
4, 5-6
Puerto Rico Regiment of Infantry,
teers, 3-4
Puerto Rico Regiment, U.S. Volun-
of Infantry, 4-5
Puerto Rico Provisional Regiment
Infantry, 2, 3
Puerto Rican Battalion of Volunteer
borne Division, 17, 291
187th Airborne Infantry, 11th Air-
96th Field Artillery Battalion, 48, 49
World War II role, 7-10
173, 233n112, 239, 287
troop strength, 29-30, 77, 284-85
training, 114, 275, 277-79,
Task Force MYERS, 93-94
citizens, 95
support from Puerto Rican
support for X Corps, 41-76